STRATEGIC THINKING

Thank you for choosing a SAGE product!
If you have any comment, observation or feedback,
I would like to personally hear from you.

Please write to me at **contactceo@sagepub.in**

Vivek Mehra, Managing Director and CEO, SAGE India.

Bulk Sales

SAGE India offers special discounts
for purchase of books in bulk.
We also make available special imprints
and excerpts from our books on demand.

For orders and enquiries, write to us at

Marketing Department
SAGE Publications India Pvt Ltd
B1/I-1, Mohan Cooperative Industrial Area
Mathura Road, Post Bag 7
New Delhi 110044, India

E-mail us at **marketing@sagepub.in**

Get to know more about SAGE

Be invited to SAGE events, get on our mailing list.
Write today at **marketing@sagepub.in**

This book is also available as an e-book.

STRATEGIC THINKING

EXPLORATIONS AROUND CONFLICT AND COOPERATION

Biswatosh Saha
Parthasarathi Banerjee
Ram Kumar Kakani

Los Angeles I London I New Delhi
Singapore I Washington DC I Melbourne

Copyright © Biswatosh Saha, Parthasarathi Banerjee, Ram Kumar Kakani, 2011

All rights reserved. No part of this book may be reproduced or utilized in any form or by any means, electronic or mechanical, including photocopying, recording or by any information storage or retrieval system, without permission in writing from the publisher.

First published in 2011 by

SAGE Publications India Pvt Ltd
B1/I-1 Mohan Cooperative Industrial Area
Mathura Road, New Delhi 110 044, India

SAGE Publications Inc
2455 Teller Road
Thousand Oaks, California 91320, USA

SAGE Publications Ltd
1 Oliver's Yard, 55 City Road
London EC1Y 1SP, United Kingdom

SAGE Publications Asia-Pacific Pte Ltd
3 Church Street
#10-04 Samsung Hub
Singapore 049483

Published by Vivek Mehra for SAGE Publications India Pvt Ltd, typeset in 10/12 Minion-Regular by Tantla Composition Services Private Limited, Chandigarh and printed at Sai Print-o-Pack, New Delhi.

Library of Congress Cataloging-in-Publication Data
Saha, Biswatosh.
   Strategic thinking: explorations around conflict and cooperation/Biswatosh Saha, Parthasarathi Banerjee, Ram Kumar Kakani.
         p. cm.
   Includes bibliographical references and index.
   1. Strategic planning. 2. Strategic planning—Case studies. 3. Critical thinking. 4. Creative thinking. 5. Industrial management. I. Banerjee, Parthasarathi. II. Kakani, Ram Kumar. III. Title
HD30.28.S2335   658.4'012—dc23   2011   2011025893

ISBN: 978-81-321-0690-6 (PB)

SAGE Team: Siddhartha Deb, Aniruddha De, Amrita Saha and Deepti Saxena

Contents

List of Tables and Figures   vii

Preface   ix

Chapter 1: Appreciating Strategy and the Strategist   1

Chapter 2: Strategy and Assets   67

Chapter 3: Strategy and Organization   144

Chapter 4: Markets and Regulation   212

Chapter 5: Institutions of Finance   272

Epilogue   335

References   337

Index   342

About the Authors   348

Tables and Figures

TABLES

2.1	Assets in a Sporting Ecosystem	81
2A.1	Metro Railways in Different Cities	140
3A.1	Ownership Structure of Tata Sons	196
3A.2	Cross Holdings after the Tata Sons Rights Issue in 1996	197
3A.3	Group Dealings of Tata Motors (INR in millions)	198
3B.1	Reliance Group and Its Companies: Over the Years	202
3B.2	Mukesh Ambani's Reliance Group in 2008	203
4.1	Market Structures	222
5C.1	Comparative Direct Listing Costs at AIM and NASDAQ	328
5C.2	Annual Costs of Listings at AIM and NASDAQ	329

FIGURES

3A.1	Structure of Tata Groups Listed Firms—2005	199
4.1	Softbank Group Enterprise System	252
5E.1	Super Endowment Funds Asset Allocation Over Time	334

Preface

This book has been an outcome of a struggle; one that we faced in our pragmatic task of teaching strategy in business schools. Amongst several problems, the most glaring was the missing 'individual' in the mainstream account. If the individual had a role, it was that of a heroic entrepreneur or a leader with charisma. Handling the charismatic leader was a great problem, since charisma could hardly be taught. Students would say that the strategy discourse in class and in texts seemed so far off from what was important in work-life. Critique of students who came from business families, with a close shot view of business in family dinner tables, was particularly scathing. Questions of students, their disinterest in what we had to offer, provided a push to search for an alternative rendition. Our search then was for an analytical description of strategic acts that would not reduce the individual to the status of a 'cog in the wheel'. Our account here is then neither one of structural determinism nor that of celebration of individual agency. It is rather an account—rooted in the perspective of an acting strategist—whose actions are always in an institutional field. A search for power in a socialized or institutionalized field within a background of negotiations and conflicts provides the basic framework.

What we finally wrote down is a narrative stitched together out of pieces that we have tried to teach our students in classes, in various institutions and over different periods of time. So students are, in a way, co-creators of what we have to offer here. Contemporary practices provide all credits to the writer, but a more primitive tradition, such as say the ancient Greek or the Indian, would value the dialogue much more. We were lucky to be able to engage in several such dialogues with students and other colleagues over an extended period of time and in the older tradition would like to record our gratitude to them. As we wrote this book, in parts and pieces, several students and former students read it and sent us their views. Many of them wrote from their experiences as well; we have proudly included several such accounts and we feel delighted to have done so. We extend our gratitude to our students who took time off their schedules to put down their thoughts and read through the text.

This book is written for readers who are closer to practice. The practical result of that has been that the text has minimal references. Although we have used extensively large literature from several domains, we have kept referencing to a minimum. We have used real narratives as illustrations to clarify and instantiate our arguments. The text is also written like a dialogue, and reflects our desire to engage in a dialogue with the reader. Reading the text would be the first act in such a dialogue—but we hope it would be a series of interactions after that as well. In that sense, the text may be seen as an incomplete one. Our attempt in the book, moreover, has desisted from developing and offering a grand theory; we rather provide a collage of concept pieces that would help one appreciate several dimensions of the strategic world. The book thus offers a large canvas. In all these multiple senses this text, in its form, departs from several accepted contemporary practices.

The initial manuscript of the book was written quite some time back and then it lay in hibernation. We thank Dr Sugata Ghosh, Vice President, Commissioning (Books and Journals), SAGE Publications India Private Limited for pushing us to complete the manuscript. We owe him and his team at SAGE Publications a deep gratitude for being patient with our rather slow progress, and as a consequence bear the problems of scheduling and planning for a rather uncertain product. We would also thank Siddhartha Deb, Rekha Natarajan and Aniruddha De along with their team, who saw the book through the editorial process. We owe our gratitude to our respective institutions and colleagues in the Indian Institute of Management Calcutta, Kolkata, National Institute of Science Technology and Development Studies (NISTADS), New Delhi, and XLRI School of Management, Jamshedpur, where we work.

We hope the reader, trying to make sense of what is seen around in the world of practice, would find the book useful. If it helps in any way in providing a sense of the business world around, we would be most happy.

1

Appreciating Strategy and the Strategist

> ... *working one's way into a language is working one's way into a conception of the world.*
> —Ludwig von Wittgenstein, *On Certainty*

1.0 INTRODUCTION: OUR APPROACH IN THIS BOOK

This book takes a pragmatic stance—in a way, therefore, it sides with the practitioner. One outcome of such a bias is that the intellectual journey through what follows is rather bumpy—sometimes even disjointed. It is a weaving of concept pieces. Borrowing from the lexicon of arts, it is rather more like a collage than a coherent painting. We, however, take cover under our belief that the world of action—the domain of the pragmatic—is often of such a nature; it defies coherence. It has multiplicities and contradictions—it is ever-evolving and complex. A strategist[1] in action faces this complexity, or is rather immersed in it. We do not offer frameworks that are well tested through experience or careful validation through evidence from the past. Such frameworks are immensely

---
[1] Throughout the book, we assume a *strategist* to be a person skilled in designing and planning action and policy to achieve a major or an overall goal. Please note that the goal need not always be monetary in nature. For an artist specializing in Madhubani paintings, a style of Indian painting practiced in the Mithila region of India and parts of Nepal, it could be promotion and popularization of the art form or genre in contest with other styles. Business possibilities would also depend on such goals being met.

valuable, especially from an academic viewpoint and several books provide quite good accounts. But, our purpose here is slightly different. The practitioner (or a would-be one), although interested in generalized patterns, also possibly looks for a way to generate unique insights that can indicate the possibility of a novelty—of a 'win', through toppling of extant structures. In writing this book, we are seeking a dialogue with that motive.

What is it then that we offer here? What is our approach? We offer a collage of concepts that do not have the authority of a theory. Concepts may be viewed as linguistic delineations or descriptions. It describes an aspect of the real world—either an object or a practice, often in contrast to other practices and in distinction to other objects. Using a language is, thus, also an act of naming. Naming helps in separating one object from another. It helps in cognition of a 'difference'. Naming subsumes or puts together a set of objects within a similar category that is thus 'named', and at the same time creates a distinction with other categories that are named differently—naming places, an object or a practice in relation with other objects or practices or group of objects/practices. Users of a 'name' acquire cognition of such relations that can then be acted upon. Without a 'name', however, an object does not gain a distinction and cannot be represented without being conflated or mixed up with other objects. A unique world of such an object with unique set of relations with other adjacent objects remains unmanifested or unexpressed—both in cognition as well as in practice. A distinct naming can enable the manifestation or articulation of the distinct world with a different set of relations with other objects.

Strategist of a new management school

Let us consider an example. Suppose one wants to open a world class management school in India. What are the options available?

a) Either follow the established Indian Institutes of Management (IIMs) in order to compete with them; or
b) Try to find new ideas/plans with a difference.

Much of the business world would mimic successes or at least attempt it, and institutional theorists would call it isomorphism. If, however, you want to make a departure—that is, do something different—you are faced with

(Case Study 1.1 contd.)

(Case Study 1.1 contd.)

> a difficult problem. What is the difference you would seek and why? Are all management schools in the world organized similarly? In some sense, every organization is different. So, when you look for similarities, you must be clear about the dimensions on which you want to enquire. Should you look into their funding structure—US universities have a large funding from philanthropic contribution from rich families? Why do we not have that in India? In pre-Independence days, there was considerable educational philanthropy—Birlas financed several institutions, middle-class professionals (technologists, lawyers, scientists) financed the Jadavpur University Engineering School. Why do we not find that today? Is the funding structure in US universities connected to specific legal design, such as inheritance tax laws or the elite's relationship with the educational set-up?
>
> Is the academic space in India and the US similar? In the US, one would find professional societies that wield considerable power and influence; India, in contrast, might present a lack of such societies. What would be your academic goal? Would you like to see academics generating knowledge for the public space, and be seen as neutral arbiters in, say, corporate conflicts? Or, would you prefer partisan lobbying role as the main task? The reputation build-up required to do non-partisan work is quite different from reputation built up as a lobbying group. If you look around, you would find institutions designed differently because they had differences in purpose behind their founding or their working. And such purposes are social or systemic; how your own asset (the management school) is connected to several other asset holders determine both your freedom and your constraints. *Would you consider all such business schools as just business schools or would you group them separately and therefore **name** them separately, taking cognition of differences in their institutional structures?* As one ponders through these questions, we hope you realize how a simple question can raise concerns that would lead you deep into what we would call the institutional structures. You enter into deep questions. But all that we raised were practical concerns—all linkages that we were pointing towards exist in practice—in the boardrooms, in legal texts, in practices of institutions such as Oxford or IIM. And the deeper departure you seek in your strategy, the clearer you would realize you cannot achieve it alone—you need coalitions and alliances. Strategies seeking deeper changes would also need more 'time'—maybe a lifetime or several generations even. You get a sense of 'time'. In gradually developing such alliances, you know the world as it is, in 'practice', and possibly you grow a broader mind as well. Practice possibly is hardest to fathom analytically. It is easier to just get familiarized with a practice. Being analytical about the practical often becomes tricky!

Let us get back to the issue of naming, say of a practice. Naming is a social act—for the reader would easily realize that to have any meaning whatsoever, the 'name' must be inter-subjectively shared or shared in social groups. It is in this sense that using a language introduces us to a conception of the world, and we get socialized as thinkers and actors. Language sets a boundary to what we can think of. A new language that 'names' a distinct institution or practice marks it as differentiated from other practices. The new language opens up new kinds of concerns (that earlier could not be articulated!) to be grasped through dialogue and reflection and often through 'action'. It puts a different set of cards on the table. It helps us 'make sense', and make 'sense' of a 'difference', rather than predict or even explain. It is a tool of reflection. In such novel naming lies condensed the history of tussles and conflicts, of social and business cooperation, and possibilities of innovative acts. We provide several narrations as we proceed. A rich civilization possibly needs a rich linguistic repertoire that can delineate nuanced differences and provide an expression to the differences. Our descriptions in the book, say of markets, would provide for several differences that would be provided different names. Instead of simple 'markets', we would have several types of markets, each with distinctive dynamics. Understanding of such distinctive markets can then be useful to a strategist. The naming of such typologies is also socially shared—created not only in the strategy literature but also across several other disciplines—especially in sociology, political science, law and economics, and so on, and we liberally borrow therefrom. Our attempt here would be to weave in such multiple disciplinary discourses.

There is another reason for engaging in a creative play of concepts. A claim to be living in a knowledge society, where the infinitely varied interests and abilities of individuals would find a possibility of unfolding, would need to give up the arrogance of a theory's authority and be more prepared to accept the unfolding of novelties, of surprises. An actor in such a world needs the power of flexible deployment of concepts more than the 'correctness' of a theory. More importantly, most theoretical claims are partisan claims—*universalization* and *essentialization* of such claims leads to a loss of other perspectives and other 'voices'; multiple languages and a collage of concepts offer a possible way out of the quagmire of authoritarian claims of theory. Concepts are partisan as well—in the sense that they frame reality in a particular way—but it is liberating in the sense that the claim to certitude does not accompany a concept. In fact, every act of 'naming' uproots from the phenomenological richness, and becomes partisan. So what academics can hope to do is, at most, to provide concepts as mere tools of thought and nothing more to the actor immersed in action. That is what we attempt in this book. In adopting such an approach, our inspiration has been what has been called broadly the *practice turn in contemporary social science*, which traces its intellectual roots in the Western intellectual tradition to the works of Wittgenstein, with whose words we began the text.[2]

Contest over pricing norm in early years of electricity industry

To get a glimpse of what we are trying to say, the reader may reflect on the word 'demand', say, in the electricity industry.

The first image is possibly of an annual value of total electricity or electrical energy (or the amount in physical units such as megawatt-hours) consumed in a geographic territory. The next level might be that of a temporal profile of such demand. The third level might relate to a question of how granular the temporal unit of reference is—demand by the month, day, hour, minute or second. The reader would possibly be thinking why demand profile by the hour is important. By now the reader's thoughts might have been deflected to a query on the actual institutional details of the specific electricity market: is an auction/spot market operating for delivery by the hour? It is only such an institutional arrangement that will make data of hourly demand profiles useful. Is the timestamp of a unit of demand (that is, at what time of the day or season is a unit of demand generated) important along with the information on the quantum of demand. Each type of data on demand, readers would appreciate, has a different meaning depending on the differences in the *embeddedness* of the information. Each conjures up images of different sorts on the type of actors and institutions. Several practices, such as pricing practice and its norm, would accordingly change as well. Timestamp of demand would make sense only in a context of time-of-day type of metering. Pricing practice itself would depend on the accepted norm in the industry, which in turn would, in most cases, have a history of conflict with other contesting norms over which the current norm triumphed. Our discussion below provides an illustration.

(Case Study 1.2 contd.)

---

[2]Readers interested in understanding the implications of the 'practice turn' in greater detail may refer to Schatzki, Knorr-Cetina and von Savigny (2001).

(Case Study 1.2 contd.)

> As Max Weber said long back:
>
> Money prices are the product of conflicts of interest and of compromises; they thus result from power constellations ... [The] price system [is] a struggle of man against man ... and prices are expressions of the struggle; they are instruments of calculation only as estimated quantifications of relative chances in this struggle of interests. (Max Weber, 1921/1968: 108)
>
> In the early formative years of the electricity industry in the US, electricity was produced by independent stand-alone producers as well as central generating stations (that we consider the de facto norm today) connected to grids. Independent stations had a significant share of total energy generation. Both types were organized into different industry associations that pursued differing interests. Smaller independent stations fed localized demand in smaller catchments, while the central stations mostly fed the demand for (mainly) electric lighting over very large catchments (use of which was concentrated during night hours). The industry during those times had two competing pricing proposals—the Wright system that became the dominant pricing scheme where users paid a variable charge depending on use and a fixed charge based on the maximum power demand made by the user on the grid (something like a capacity payment); and the Barstow system where the capacity payment depended on the time-of-use of the user's peak demand and thus had incentives for enhancing systemic rates of utilization by pricing higher during system peak hours (note that variation in power demand by time-of-day or season leads to lower system utilization of generating equipment since storage of power is largely infeasible and supply at any point of time generally has to match the instantaneous demand). Both pricing schemes were proposed as a solution to the problems of the existing variable cost pricing due to large fixed costs in the industry, which led producers to give arbitrary rebates to users who would guarantee long usage since that helped generators balance the load. The dominant interests of the central generating stations rejected the Barstow system, since it penalized the lighting consumer group whose demand would be during the system peak times, thus voting in favour of what was then called a 'growth dynamic' of revenue maximization through diffusion of the lighting usage rather than system efficiency and profitability maximization of the generators. The possibility of economies of scale were realized technologically through the introduction of large steam turbines much later and at the time of the espousal of the 'growth dynamic', such technological possibilities were far from being realized. The central stations were worried about gas-lighting taking away the lighting consumption,

(Case Study 1.2 contd.)

(Case Study 1.2 contd.)

or the other group of independent electricity producers such as railroads, which had a daytime load (of motor use of electrical energy) and were looking to balance their load by having the lighting demand. Electricity industry had to choose certain norms of pricing (and the metering instrumentation required to implement the pricing), since arbitrary customer-specific variations (or forms of contemporary individuated pricing) had induced a huge social uproar through a consumer protest on grounds of fairness a few years earlier. The central generating station interest won through exerting influence and manipulating the proceedings of the industry associations generating a discourse around the Wright system and effectively burying the more efficient Barstow system. The Wright system was institutionalized through regulation that recognized electricity as a natural monopoly and introduced severe restrictions on non-grid-connected small generators—such as restrictions on wiring across streets. Such small generators then could not do demand pooling in small pockets; instead, the only pool created was of a massive grid with a large spatial spread. Independent small producers were also denied the advantage of efficient system utilization through (among several other moves) the choice of the pricing norm that did not allow capacity payment based on time-of-day of use (that would have penalized peak time users). The advantage of small generators was thus largely neutralized. Central stations subscribing to the 'growth dynamic' and large-scale expansion that such dynamic warranted became the dominant mode of organizing electricity generation. Regulation as a natural monopoly drew in (low risk) growth capital from bankers such as J.P. Morgan, leading to a rapid volume expansion of the central station mode. Profitability, predictably, fell rather sharply. Time-of-day pricing and metering was reinvented almost a century later. But the new interest in time-of-day pricing usually proceeds without awareness of how old an issue it is (Yakubovich, Granovetter and McGuire, 2005: 579–612).

The Wright system made the timestamp of a unit of demand redundant information while the alternative norm that failed to institutionalize itself would have had a value for the information on the timestamp. Particular articulations of demand and the pricing norm then are tied together or, in other words, they support each other. The fact that money prices, in a quantitative sense (the value), represent a struggle between different conflicting interests is fairly well understood. But the fact that the 'pricing rule' itself is politically laden, favouring implicitly certain modes of organizing or transacting is often totally missed. Understanding the *embeddedness* of information and data takes us to an exploration of the *embeddedness* of practices. In teasing out that understanding, the history of the institutionalization and traces of conflicts that such histories bear would shape our understanding.

With the above clarification, let us move ahead. As we build our argument around concepts we present, we would often 'deconstruct' them—peeling it open, searching for tighter definitions, looking for underlying connections, assumptions and delimitations. In this process, we engage with established concepts and we often argue that several concepts laying claim to universality in the academic discipline of strategy today are bounded in their applicability. The context, in which they were honed up, shaped the language and the boundaries of what was being enquired. Yet such boundaries are not easily realized and explicated, as the concept travels beyond the particularities of the context and gets deployed elsewhere rather unthinkingly. Our account takes a stance against such *essentialization*.

> **Several strategy languages!** Would a strategy language honed up through the experience of a manufacturer such as Ford or the petrochemical process plant of Reliance or a fast moving consumer goods (FMCG) company (say Godrej Consumer Products or Indian Tobacco Company [ITC] Limited) help a practitioner in film-making (say Red Chillies Entertainment or Balaji Films) or a would-be film-financier seeking an entry into Bollywood film-financing? Does difference in practices between these industries or in its economics create the need to develop a different language of strategy? Are the assets that a strategist deals with in an FMCG setting or, say, in a petrochemical process plant and in Bollywood film production similar? If they are not, in what conceptual sense do they differ and how does that shape the acts of a strategist? Is the difference related to the risk or uncertainties associated with the key assets in the two cases? While Reliance would have a massive fixed asset whose maximal utilization would drive their organization enabling a realization of economies of scale, assets in film-making, particularly the stars, would enjoy no such scale economies or even economies of maximal utilization. Too frequent exposure of a 'star' actor might lead to devalorization. Take the case of the oft-used reference to the cost advantage of mass manufacturing; does it hold even when the structure of underlying 'capital equipment' used in the production process change, such as to enable similar processing functionalities (or marginal cost economies) at drastically reduced equipment 'scale/size'—a goal that technology designs around small-scale distributed manufacturing are seeking?

We wonder and we propose that an intellectual commitment to 'a particular language' can often constrain action, while a new articulation around different concept pieces, often borrowed from discourses in other cultures or other disciplines, can aid grasping of facets that were not so important earlier. Multiple contexts would require several languages of strategy today. So, the old language should not be rejected and we do not do that; but in disputing them, we try to articulate more clearly the contexts in which they hold. As we move on, we articulate several concrete instances of such multiplicity of 'contexts'.

Critical thinking around concepts, often aided by dialogue, helps in clearer delineation of concepts. That allows differences to be more clearly articulated without conflating or merging them into an undifferentiated whole. That often helps an actor in action better grapple with complexities of the pragmatic world by enabling development of a sensitivity to discern 'differences', which can also then be acted upon.

> **Risk and uncertainty—significance of the difference**
> Let us, as an instance, take the notion of 'risk' and 'uncertainty', which would be invoked in our later discussions. Several accounts often conflate or mix-up the two concepts. An early work, Knight (1921), proposes a distinction between the two. Risk is determinable, in a probabilistic sense, while uncertainty is indeterminate—it is in the nature of 'ignorance' and cannot be insured against. Unlike risk, uncertainty is not objective and does not assume knowledge of alternatives. Risks, thus, are insurable through a mechanism of generation of information and progressive development of classification schemes that would group similar events together and separate out dissimilar events, thus aiding estimation of 'statistical probabilities' and provision of insurance. Risks, defined as above, then can be routinized through development of an enforceable and credible information discovery system and an algorithm (or process) of handling the information. It can then be delegated to a quintessential 'manager'. Readers can think of developing schemas for determining premiums (or price) of certain risks such as, say, fire insurance of buildings in a city. History of fires in certain locations, nature of fire safety measures installed in buildings and several other factors might help in constructing a risk measure/index to which the premium may be linked. In contrast to risk, handling of uncertainties would require the continuous exercise of entrepreneurial business judgement and would not be amenable to routinization. Conceptual clarity of the 'difference' thus helps us 'take notice' of a difference in the world of practice.

So our attempt in the book would be to deploy linguistic analytics—looking carefully into the semantics of concepts that we invoke, often making the reader stop and think. We do not therefore promise a lucid reading—we offer instead a Wittgensteinian 'involved working into a language'. Concepts, then, do not constrain the 'strategic actors' agency through dishing out of structural regularities, yet it aids reflection—providing a tool to actors. Such reflection can generate an insight even ahead of the validation from practice. Such fresh insights can generate action, conjuring up novel moves. And it can be filled with excitement and energy as actors await with bated breath the outcome of a move, as they witness a future evolve or forces that they unshackled take shape. A hint of excitement around action that strategy embraces follows:

> I remember going to Davos some years back and sitting on a global health panel that was discussing ways to save millions of lives. Millions! Think of the thrill of saving just one person's life and then multiply that by millions. Yet this was the most boring panel I've ever been on. So boring even I couldn't bear it. What made that experience especially striking was that I had just come from an event where we were introducing version 13 of some piece of software, and we had people jumping and shouting with excitement. I love getting people excited about software but why can't we generate even more excitement for saving lives.
> —Bill Gates, on his commencement speech at Harvard after receiving Honorary Doctor of Law Degree.[3]

It is this excitement that the book seeks to address. Engagement with concepts hinges around this end and has a very pragmatic purpose. This is the journey to which we invite the reader.

The plan of this chapter is as follows. We begin by an articulation of what strategy seeks (see section 1.1). We then move on to articulate a view of strategy as a search for power that a strategist engages in (see sections 1.2 and 1.3). We argue that a strategist operates within a strategy milieu, populated by other agents. Strategic acts are conceived and executed within this milieu that is power-infused (see section 1.4). The desire in toppling of the applecart of existing governance, we argue, constitutes a key motive of strategic action (see section 1.5). Altered governance provides the possibility of altering the balance of power that a strategist seeks (see section 1.6). We develop, then, the notion of nodes and nodal power holders, describing a few modes through which a node acquires a power of denial (see sections 1.7 and 1.8). Finally, we explore two dimensions of classifying strategy as typologies—based on the milieu and intent of actors, and based on whether a move seeks a

---

[3]http://www.gatesfoundation.org/default.htm (accessed on 14 June 2007).

decreasing returns based rent or an increasing returns based novel profit. (See section 1.9 for discussion on difference between rent and profit in the specific sense we use in this book.) We implicitly argue that the firm as the predominant mode of organizing is on the decline. Firms were structured for efficient utilization of certain kinds of assets that could be held and controlled solely by a firm. Dynamics of such asset utilization face decreasing returns, and we explore that below. New forms of organizing points towards new engagements and design of governance modes in wider networks involving extra-organizational (or extra-firm) actors and other social institutions and nodal power holders in such institutions. Several crucial assets in the contemporary times are held on a shared mode, making extra-firm organizing crucial as a means of establishing governance over such assets. Several of these assets display dynamics of increasing returns. Reaping of increasing returns require an understanding of a new set of acts (see section 1.10). We end the chapter with a roadmap of the plan of the following chapters (see section 1.11), briefly presenting the summary argument as developed in the following four chapters, where we deal with the notion of assets, organizations, markets and regulation and institutions of finance from the perspective of an acting strategist.

1.1 THE DESSERT OF STRATEGY: REGISTRATION OF A WIN

We do not begin our discussion with an attempt to define what strategy[4] is—something like a definition that can describe the area that strategy addresses would evolve by the end of our discussion in this introductory chapter. We begin by arguing that an enquiry into the 'world of strategy' must be persuaded by a taste of its fruit, since a discourse on strategy addresses an actor in 'action' in the domain of the pragmatic. And in the

---

[4]*Merriam-Webster's Dictionary* defines the word 'strategy' as:

a) the science and art of employing the political, economic, psychological, and military forces of a nation or group of nations to afford the maximum support to adopted policies in peace or war;
b) a careful plan or method: a clever stratagem; the art of devising or employing plans or stratagems toward a goal;
c) an adaptation or complex of adaptations (as of behavior, metabolism or structure) that serves or appears to serve an important function in achieving evolutionary success.

pragmatic world, action is propelled by a premonition of the dessert that 'an action' would lead to. Why else would one act? So, what has strategy to offer as its dessert? Simply put, strategy offers the dessert of victory—a *win*. And a win can only be relative; it needs an opponent, a rival. It seeks to maximize the gain or payoff—a payoff that can have several languages and meanings, often in the terrain of beliefs and philosophies. Overcoming an existing belief on a particular mode of production or organization can also drive strategies. Such motives would be important if we are to make sense of, say, the actions of Richard Stallman[5] or Linus Torvalds[6] in setting up the alternative mode of software code writing that has influenced quite dramatically the dominant belief in the software world. Such motives might be bundled often with a financial motive, but it might stand on its own as well, quite apart from any financial consideration. The world of the non-profit mode need not be non-strategic at all. Strategic win has a financial connotation as well. Strategic success leads to wealth, therefore. The multiple languages of a 'win' or multiplicity of dimensions of cognition of a payoff for the actor is very important in the strategy story.[7]

In other words, strategic success leading to a win has a connotation of successful establishment of dominance. It represents a grasping

---

[5]Richard Matthew Stallman is a software freedom activist and software developer. In 1983, he launched a project to create a free Unix-like operating system, and has been the project's lead architect and organizer. He co-founded the League for Programming Freedom. Stallman pioneered the concept of copyleft and is the main author of several copyleft licences including the GNU General Public License, the most widely used free software licence (GNU stands for 'GNU is Not Unix'—it is a recursive acronym common in open source community).

[6]Linus Benedict Torvalds is a Finnish software engineer best known for initiating the development of the Linux kernel. Linux is a clone of the operating system Unix written from scratch with assistance from a loosely-knit team of software developers across the Net. About 2 per cent of the current Linux kernel is written by Torvalds himself. Since Linux has had thousands of contributors, even such a small percentage represents a significant personal contribution to the overall amount of code.

[7]In a knowledge-intensive technology company, where highly skilled people (say biotechnologists) are engaged in generating a flow of knowledge assets, how would you decide which assets should be monetized? Which kind of assets would you prefer to patent, which ones would you copyright, which ones would you publish in academic journals? Would you provide a monetary reward to expert employees for getting a journal publication? What is the difference between a monetized and a non-monetized asset—do they belong to different strategic turfs? What is the implicit exchange that an expert looks forward to when he/she engages in a publication in an academic journal? Is the nature of that exchange the same as a monetized exchange—if not, would monetization then subvert the basic practices around publication in an academic journal?

of power of sorts—that was within reach and yet was so far off for the aspiring strategist. This is the magical turn and entities at the throes of a strategic win often would be suffused with such a magical aura around them—a déjà vu of sorts that would be infectious. This was what Gates (see his quote at p. 10) was hinting at. This joy remains an abiding good which strategy seeks to accomplish. It is this 'desire' to win that catapults a strategist into strategic action, in designing novel forms of influence, of power-broking, of lobbying. Imagination, novelty and a cunning acumen merge together in the melting pot of strategic action.

1.2 WHOSE STRATEGY IS IT ANYWAY!

Our discussion so far did not specify the strategist subject. This we argue is an important question: who owns a particular strategy discourse? Or, whose strategy would one talk about? A significant position we take is in rooting the individual (the acting subject) at the core of conceptions of strategy. Strategy as strategizing or strategic thinking is what we emphasize and explore. Following the actor is thus what we implicitly argue for. Most established traditions in mainstream strategy scholarship would look into the firm as a unit of analysis, located amidst competitors within a wider environment. The quintessential firm then would be the owner of the strategy discourse, or the strategy would be for or of the firm. This restriction, which the academic discipline of strategy seems to have imposed on itself, is being contested today. Networks and several other non-firm institutions are becoming important in the strategy discourse. In our story, as it would unfold, the strategist leader, his/her cohorts, allies, and possible defectors in rival institutions would constitute a more plausible unit of analysis. We would also move quite freely across firms, in networks and in the dark/ grey areas of inter-firm interstices—areas where the strategist moves around in practice.

> The reader might imagine here a current chief executive officer (CEO) of a firm, who is simultaneously in an inter-temporal race for certain other coveted positions as a future assignment, maybe in a regulatory agency or a much larger firm. Is it not pragmatic to enquire if the structure of the outside race, in terms of what counts in that race, influences what initiatives the CEO

> would be inclined to lead in the organization—at least in terms of setting certain constraints that would bind him/her? Reading of such constraints that are often not articulated with explicitness becomes crucial in several instances—such as a major business process reengineering (BPR) implementation scheme, setting an implicit agenda and drawing certain boundaries on the initiative. In a later chapter (see case study 3.2), we explore few such dichotomies around a specific BPR implementation project.

Analysing the firm, therefore, remains just one among several levels at which understanding of strategizing can be rooted. The individual strategist leader or a cohort or network of firms (or other non-firm institutions of a private or public nature!) or powerful individual actors would often be a counterpoint to a strategy discourse with a firm as the unit of analysis. We would explore this aspect in great detail throughout, but it may be useful to point out here that 'firm' as an entity is a specific legal artefact created to apportion liabilities among several transacting entities under the corporate law (*Companies Act, 1956* in India) that was aimed at creating a limit on the personal liability of people holding statutorily defined leadership positions (such as Managing Director, Chairman or President) on account of corporate action. If such a firm is also a 'listed' entity in stock exchanges, then it also creates a set of shareholders who have a financial interest on the firm represented as a single unified entity (as represented in the balance sheet) without necessarily having control in the strictest sense. Firm as the unit of analysis is relevant only to the extent that a strategy discourse addresses such concerns—either in the legal domain of liability or the concerns of shareholders who are exposed to the integrated firm's balance sheet.

1.2.1 The decreasing salience of the firm

We must understand that in choosing a unit of analysis, we draw a boundary and that limits what we can see and enquire on. Firm as unit of analysis then draws boundaries between firms, representing the firm as an undifferentiated block or whole. It thus underemphasizes the strong inter-firm linkages as well as underplays the fractured nature of a firm's quite incoherent internal canvas. Our account would, in contrast, seek to lend voice to both these aspects that we consider to be most important dimensions of contemporary strategy world. In a later chapter on institutions on finance, we will show how the ecosystem of equity analysts, investment banks and asset managers together in the US today has forced an institutional isomorphism of organizing, accounting and reporting on several constitutive asset pieces held by a peer group of firms. The individual assets (whose bundle constitutes the firm) rather than the whole firm are the contemporary relevant units of analysis for the equity analysts who influence valuation of the firm significantly, especially in the US setting. As we go along, we would discuss several dimensions in which the boundary of the firm is no longer stable or sacrosanct. We would also provide several illustrations of what we are referring to, and we hope it would gradually become clearer. Redefining the firm boundary constitutes a major strategic task today. This redefinition, moreover, occurs by retaining the firm as the accounting unit (say, for declaration of financial results). Strategic acts of redefinition of the boundary affects deeply the accounting result recorded with firm as the accounting unit. Yet the act, which the strategist must understand and execute, often does not (or cannot) pay heed to a strong firm boundary.

In the pragmatic world of strategic action, the network which the strategist is able to piggyback on—networks of beliefs, ideologies and technology stances or even of ethnicities—remain vital in a strategy story. Several important strategic wins are registered not inside the firm but in the extra-organization/firm domain in forums such as, say, an industry association. Our description below provides one such instance from business history. Choice of the unit of analysis would often be dictated by the goal sought by the strategic actor or the purpose of enquiry of the strategy analyst. Thus, a strategy discussion must be informed by an awareness of whose strategy is involved, since that is crucial in setting the vantage point.

Contest over pricing norm in early years of electricity industry (contd.)

In the earlier narrative on the conflict between competing Wright and Barstow pricing schema in early 20th-century US electricity industry, the crucial moves that led to the burying of the Barstow system were all made in industry associations. Associations were the arena of conflict and the crucial strategic wins that had deep consequences for the key leaders and the firms they led were registered in the associations and its dealings with other entities, such as regulators.

(Case Study 1.2 contd.)

(Case Study 1.2 contd.)

> In the early years of the electricity industry, the two national trade associations, Association of Edison Illuminating Companies (AEIC), which included central stations, and National Electric Light Association (NELA), a larger body representing several smaller and independent (or isolated) generators (who made up almost half the electricity generation in 1899), metering companies and equipment producers, were the only national forums in which sustained discussion of central station issues and problems took place. As such, they played a crucial role in setting industry trends. Both had been founded in 1885, the NELA mainly composed of sellers of electricity without ties to Thomas Edison, and the AEIC, true to its name, including Edison's friends and collaborators who had branched out to form central station companies in many cities. AEIC was formed a few months after NELA was formed to create a countervailing association. With Edison's departure from the electricity industry in 1892 (a tussle with J.P. Morgan led to the exit of Edison from what came to be known eventually as General Electric), Samuel Insull became the de facto leader of the Edison circle (this group of four main actors and four more subordinates was later called the Insull circle), whose members dominated the AEIC through the 1890s. The Insull circle held over 90 per cent of AEIC committee and officer positions in the 1890s and, in combination with technical experts from the 'Six Cities' firms (central stations of the six largest cities) they led, delivered all the paper presentations at AEIC and shaped all its technical standard setting activities between 1892 and 1897. But their domination did not extend into the entire industry, since the NELA was a larger association that brought together many smaller firms. The main AEIC firms, however, began to join the NELA early in the 1890s, and by 1897 had become a major bloc. In 1898, Samuel Insull was elected president of both associations, and while not as completely dominant in the NELA as in the AEIC, his circle had become by far the most influential. Along with their subordinates and those AEIC firms that had longstanding membership, the Insull circle was in a majority in only 19 of 75 committees operating between 1901 and 1910, but those rare majorities came when the committee was new or when its policy focus was being initially established. After the policy direction was set, the Insull circle left membership only to return again when there were deviations from the AEIC supported policy direction. The institutional diversity existing in early 1890s between AEIC and NELA was deliberately subverted—differences smoothened out to establish monolithic technical standard and management practices across the industry. This crucial institutional contest shaped the

(Case Study 1.2 contd.)

(Case Study 1.2 contd.)

> outcome of the electricity industry and for close to a century committed it to a path of vertically integrated organization (Granovetter and McGuire, 1998: 156–58).

There are a few important implications of taking a stand of refusing to privilege the 'firm' as the sole unit of strategy analysis, just one of which we bring out at this stage. The salience of the network means that the firm can no longer be viewed as a homunculus with a unity of purpose and a coherence of its constitutive elements. Contradictory purposes might and does indeed coexist inside a firm as a temporal coalition, often contesting for power and influence—as different actors (or senior managers) draw inspiration and power from different networks they are keyed on to. Contradictions and compromises are then the order of the day.

> Think of a professional inside a firm (under administration of a CEO), who is strongly governed simultaneously through norms of a wider professional body, such as a technology group!

Managers, therefore, not only react to the agenda flowing from the top management—through the administrative fiat—but also to signals emanating from extra-firm networks. Practices, such as access to unencumbered resources, right to enter into contracts with outsiders, right to collaborate and publish, which exists at fairly junior levels in several contemporary organizations (especially those in creative industries) enabling managers to interface and conduct business with entities beyond the firm boundary, deepen this network dimension. Investment banks, venture funds or academic institutions can be instances where such modes are deep-rooted.

In other words, what we are arguing is that for the purpose of an academic enquiry on strategy, the setting of the boundary is a function of the purpose of enquiry. In other words, it is important to understand whose vantage point an enquiry is adopting implicitly. From the point of view of the acting strategist, boundary of the firm is nothing sacrosanct except for certain limited purposes, such as the legal purpose of liability apportionment or addressing shareholder interests. Otherwise, boundary of the firm is an outcome of a constructivist agenda of the strategist—the boundaries are redefined through changes in practices and are constructed through repetition of certain practices by actors inside and outside the organization/firm. Readers can think of a supplier firm in the automotive industry that is co-located with the assembler in common factory premises and works together with the assembler and several other suppliers in joint development of the product/components. Managers of the supplier firm in frontline roles or in joint design teams might often work in closer supervision of the managers of the assembler than senior managers of his/her own organization (who might provide only broad guidelines and boundary conditions). He/she might also enjoy access to information not accessible to senior managers of the supplier firm. Such access and an opportunity afforded for close observation often leads to job switches across organizations/firms. Thus, the construction of the firm boundary differs—the boundary in practice for the purpose of accounting and finance would depend on the accounting conventions adopted and might differ from the boundary with respect to information flows, business process responsibilities and sharing and ownership of risks of various kinds involved in carrying out a joint activity. Boundary construction and reconstruction itself would be a major act of the strategist leader.

We will explore this theme in greater detail in the chapter on strategy and organizations (Chapter 3); but broadly what we seek to emphasize now is the fact that the strategy story today, even in the domain of business, cannot be narrated with the firm as an independent building block, since boundaries of firms remain porous and deeply infiltrated by powerful extra-firm interests in several cases. Boundaries of a firm can plausibly be built only with a minimal set of injunctions, leaving the rest to infiltration by network processes. Organizational boundaries can then be thought of as lines demarcating the areas where the fiat of the organization leader runs on the minimal injunctions that are imposed.

1.3 STRATEGY AS A SEARCH FOR POWER

Getting back to where we started discussion in this section, we are arguing that strategy deals with power—power as experienced by actors in the field of action. Multiple levers of power, which actors on the field are acutely aware of, constitute the core of a strategy discourse. Power would also remain materialized (or concretized) through consensus on shared practices, which we would later call 'institutions'. It is through this that power becomes effective, and this power in action is what is of concern to us here. Strategy, in seeking an intervention in such a mesh of power, would need to operate on the practices of the actors. Driven by the 'desire' to win, a strategist usually would, given a chance, seek an untrammelled run over a turf, but that is seldom possible. Existing structures of power—the current modes of governance, such as rules, laws, norms, practices and beliefs as they exist—provide a counterpoint to the strategist's desire for establishing an unchallenged run. It provides inertia. This inertia is most important.

We may point out here that most accounts drawing inspiration from neoclassical type of atemporal, non-inertial frameworks fail to account for this most important aspect of social organization, including that of business. In our second chapter, we elaborate on this and use a language of assets rather than resources to highlight this dimension of temporality and inertia in pragmatic matters of business. A strategist, in executing his/her action, has to locate the act within a concrete societal or business ecosystem and has to contend with existing governance modes within which his/her 'current state of affairs' remains embedded. A pragmatic story of strategy must then portray the countervailing forces to a strategist's moves, as well as seek to understand the limits and horizons of possible moves. Much harm is brought to bear when such limits are lost sight of—leading to destruction of assets and institutions. Strategy, therefore, seeks to tweak modes of governance, to act subversive in toppling the cosy applecart of existing governance modes. It is through an overturning of the existing modes of governance that a win is achieved—a win therefore requires other actors in the milieu to tacitly conform to the new mode of governance proposed through the action of the strategist—it requires cooperation (or submission). In the following section we develop a lexical list of rudimentary concept pieces that would provide something like building blocks to weave the numerous stories that would evolve through the book.

1.4 CONCEPT OF A STRATEGY MILIEU

Since we are arguing that strategy is driven by the individual subject's desire to win—to grapple with power—the acting subject must be at the centre of the schema. Such a strategizing subject is placed in a societal setting or a business setting inside a mesh of power that extends across transaction networks, links him/her up with the world of finance, the world of technology and such multiple worlds. A strategist's desire often takes shape within such concrete settings, within a particular context. This context we would call a '**milieu**'.[8] This milieu is populated by several actors. The winning strategist, the rival (opponent), actors who are followers of a middle path as well as actors who are careless/indifferent about the dominant strategic moves, along with actors who have made durable, credible commitments to either the winning strategist or to the opponent (and are in that sense committed allies) would constitute such a strategy milieu. The manifestation of power within the milieu is felt acutely in regular transactions that the strategist engages in—transactions that are institutionalized and would implicitly submit to certain norms or rules that bind the actors. A milieu is something like an arena where the practice of a strategist can exert an influence. This reach is a practical delimiter, within which strategies must be conjured up. The identification of a strategy milieu is linked to the strategist and centres on the ambitions and desires of the strategist—a perception of threat also emanates from a reading of the milieu.

We distinguish a 'milieu' from the broader notion of 'environment' that is usually evoked. Unlike the notion of the 'environment', which is something like an all-encompassing canvas, representing elements that are beyond control and influence (such as an exchange rate movement), a milieu is very local—very particular to the strategist. It is therefore very concrete as well. The contextual details of the local which often gets lost in a description of the environment constitute most important elements in our definition of the milieu. Evoking the context brings out the relational dimension as well—the relations and links between different actors. Unlike the variables of the environment that is public knowledge and is read by all and sundry, reading of the milieu is more local. It is often more private. For instance, a reading of the intent to sell off a key jointly shared family asset by factions of the owning family would be crucial information; the concept of a milieu alerts us to these possibilities. The relations of power between the actors who inhabit the milieu and the reading of the strategy moves of the actors (that remain necessarily incomplete as we argue below) constitute the milieu. A crafty strategist would identify slippages, missing links and opportunities to drive their moves through within this setting. The notion of a 'milieu' thus forces us to think about concrete *embedding* of the strategic actor and search for the relations between them. The reference to the context would also bring out or focus attention on resources that a context remains endowed with.

---

[8]The word 'milieu' means 'surroundings that somebody lives in and is influenced by'. The connotation is of an immersion. It came into usage in English from Old French.

> Readers would be familiar with the fact that watch-making was at one time almost wholly dominated by the Swiss. It was a high-skill labour-intensive craft manufacturing process. Watch-making skill was moreover carefully transferred from masters to apprentices so as to modulate the diffusion of the skill. For investors/entrepreneurs in countries like the US that did not enjoy access to this skill pool, automation was the only way forward. Automation was also accompanied by vertical integration under organization-based control. Several years later, as automation stabilized in watch-making, the Swiss also had to embrace the technology. But Swiss automated production remained limited to certain stages where scale economies were most pronounced and left several other manufacturing stages, as well as the tasks of marketing, branding, designing, to disaggregated entities that functioned without a notable central administrative control. This choice of the structure was influenced by the fact that the watch-making community in Switzerland, given its history and predispositions, was fiercely independent and over time had developed stable practices that enabled them to exercise various forms of social control (or guild/association based) coordination without getting under a central organizational control. The context specificity of the Swiss experience needs to be understood to appreciate the evolution of the industry and its structure. Yet, as readers would appreciate this context, specificity must be very concretely articulated. This materiality of the context is emphasized in our account here.[9]

Our reference to the context then is not just to point towards the innumerable context-specific variations, but more importantly to force attention on the relational dimension of a strategist's embedding and the specificities of resources that can be pragmatically piggybacked on.

1.5 STRATEGIC MOVES AND STRATEGIC ACTS

A strategist in such a setting of a milieu grapples with power relations that are prevalent. An action is precipitated by a desire to change the current state of affairs or current modes of governance. Fundamentally,

---

[9]See Langlois (1996) for an account of the transformation of the Swiss watch industry over time.

it seeks to engage with the balance of power. This we call the 'strategic move'. This intent behind the move cannot be described through full informational accounts by outside agents, neither can it be observed by others with any accuracy. A strategist often would only gradually reveal the 'intent'—so to say, since pragmatic considerations would limit the extent of disclosure possible. For others, therefore, the strategic intent of the actor can only be inferred through behaviourally observable acts of the strategist. A reading of a series of observable strategic acts or a pattern often would provide a cue to possible intent of the actor. But, in deciphering such strategic moves, we have to give up claims to *certitude*—such inferences are at most something approximating an intelligent guess. This non-observability of the strategic intent has important consequences. A similar strategic act, say an act of diversification, might be driven by different intent in different contexts, shaped by the differences in dynamics of governance across the contexts. Whether it represents an attempt by opportunistic managers to build overextended corporate empires to utilize excess cash flows of a firm would depend on the understanding of countervailing forces and the threat that such forces can bring to bear on firm managers. We provide an interesting contrast below:

> While US financial institutions, as significant shareholders, failed to perform the monitoring role around the 1970s till the rise of the threat of takeovers by private equity or hedge funds (and a tender-offer induced hostile takeover market), banks in Japan, through much of the same period, did succeed quite well in playing the role of a credible monitor, while encouraging build-up of large diversified groups as a counter to the threat of much larger and technologically sophisticated global rivals from the Western world. The financial institutions in the two contexts worked under different regulatory constraints and political mandates. We observe then that a similar act of extensive diversification of corporate assets and conglomeration was driven by different intent of actors in the two contexts. The same act constitutes part of two different types of strategic moves.

It is often, therefore, difficult to ascertain the motives or the intent behind a strategic act—it can possibly be only gradually discovered; a rich description of the context also helps. This non-observability of strategic move, in itself, introduces uncertainty in the strategic world.

A strategic move is driven, we argue, by different psychological states of the actor in seeking a relation with other entities in a milieu. This state of the actor is, however, not visible intersubjectively, that is, it can be hidden. The move can be for seeking a relationship of: (*a*) an alliance; (*b*) a confrontation; (*c*) fluidity or liquidity or deliberate (often well thought out) non-commitment; (*d*) nonchalance or indifference (which differs from fluidity above in the sense that it is not a thought out position; rather it arises out of strategic indifference); (*e*) prevarication or an exploratory sensing out; or (*f*) dependence.

A strategic act, in contrast, is readable by others who observe the act and, in that sense, the act represents something like an observable signal. It is defined with respect to what is observed or read in the milieu. It can be of: (*a*) appeasement; (*b*) rewarding; (*c*) discrimination or differentiation; and (*d*) punishment. While appeasement is an unconditional grant of a favour, reward is a favour granted in exchange of demonstration of a desired behaviour. Punishment refers to the threat held out by the strategist in the form of a credible denial (say of resources, or a positive recommendation, or an enforced exit such as a sacking). Punishment or this threat of denial often acts in the background, so to say, not directly influencing acts of the governed, but rather setting bounds or boundary conditions (or often injunctions) on permissible behaviour. They can be then, like 'contingent clauses', evoked under 'abnormal conditions', so to say. They become crucial under conditions of conflict.

> Readers might think of an engagement with a financial firm on a venture capital type of contract that gives the financial firm rights to replace management if certain milestones are not achieved. In contrast, another contract might provide the same financial stream without such specific milestone related clauses, but a general bankruptcy clause that enables the finance provider certain rights of intervention when the firm approaches conditions of bankruptcy alone. It leaves the managers free till such a state is reached. The implicit boundaries that define possible conflict conditions differ between the two instances, and hence the threat structure remains different.

On the other hand, 'differentiation' is the grant of a departure—such as support from a parent corporate to a spinning off of an asset piece or a particular capability into an independent entity which can then chart out a course of its own while retaining a loose linkage with the parent, which continues to benefit from the growth of the spun-off entity. The following illustration is a case in point:

> Microsoft, in 2007–08, spun off the gaming company Bungee Studios—a star asset in gaming software designing space—into an independent outfit, realizing that growth for Bungee would require it to be released from the corporate yoke of Microsoft. (Chapter 2 provides a longer account.) It is an acceptance of a 'difference' that requires a difference in governance.

This fourfold effect of a strategic act can be sensed within the milieu by other actors and, thus, is like a signal that can be sensed intersubjectively. It is through the crafty use of this signal that a strategist gets a grasp over power and a gradually unfolding strategic move, which can possibly lead to a win, unfolds in the milieu. The design of such levers—such as of rewards—has to be specific to the context to send out a credible signal, since the value and the credibility of the signal depends on the context by others who inhabit the milieu and to whose attention the signal is directed. To recount our example of the firm that is deeply infiltrated by numerous extra-firm networks, the salience of promotion in the firm hierarchy, as a reward, might go down, to the extent that rewards and wins sourced through the networks become valuable to the managers' world. A manager, leading a strictly organizational life, would in contrast, value such rewards rather highly. The following quote from an interview of an associate of a second-rung venture capital firm in Silicon Valley provides another illustration of the 'contextual specificity' of the design of a move:

> All venture capitalists with low status want to establish relations with the dominant venture capitalists of Silicon Valley, such as Sequoia Capital, so that they (Sequoia type leading firms) can pass on projects directed to them which they do not have time to analyze. In order to establish this relation, one must first offer them something. I financed Phone.com from its inception. When the time came for the final round of financing before the company's introduction to the stock market, instead of endorsing the finance entirely on my own thus keeping all the plus value, I proposed to the associates of Sequoia Capital to participate in the final round.

The introduction was going to be a great success guaranteeing high profitability. Sequoia could have refused the offer, because they knew by accepting it, they would engage themselves to render me a future service. [*A gift receiver incurs a debt which has to be returned at a future date within the gift culture of Silicon Valley and several other ethnic business networks!*] They accepted and realized an important plus-value. Since then, I work regularly with them; they send me projects and sometimes invite me to syndications of finance they put in place for a company. [*Alliance with a leader in the milieu forged through a move that makes sense only within the Silicon Valley context; such moves might fail to elicit a similar response in other contexts.*] (Excerpt from Ferrary, 2003)

The distinction that we emphasized, between strategic moves driven by intent and the strategic act that is observable, is analytically important. In emphasizing the 'unknowability' of strategic moves, we are underlining elements of surprise, novelty and the essential analytical incompleteness of strategy processes as practiced. This incompleteness also provides a useful point of engagement for novel strategic moves. We therefore seek a departure from several mainstream strategy discourses, which relies too much on disclosed acts and statements of purpose to understand strategies of different entities. Our story is open to possibilities of sly moves, disguised moves or moves to debilitate and incapacitate the rival—moves that can scarcely be openly declared but constitutes important elements of the armoury of a strategy of conflict. What would be obvious to readers by now is that our description of strategy moves invariably has a temporally evolving (or unfolding) nature; it must have a dynamic setting. We will argue later that only under dynamic conditions, a strategy discourse would have a meaning; 'time' thus is of crucial significance and later in the book we will talk about several dimensions of 'time'.

We provide below an illustration of a narrative of conflict through an ex-post reading of temporal pattern of unfolding of events. As in several accounts of conflicts over corporate control in China, especially that between foreign and Chinese partners, this account on the Danone–Wahaha conflict also reveals disguised or sly moves—build-up of position for an anticipated showdown, and such other modes of conflict.

CASE STUDY 1.3 — The battle for Chinese beverage assets

The battle between the French food and beverage giant, Groupe Danone, and its Chinese joint venture partner—the Hangzhou-based Wahaha Group, by far the largest and most powerful Chinese water and beverage company led by its charismatic founder leader Zong Qinghou (one of the wealthiest businessmen of China)—has been keenly watched globally. The corporate battle for control spilled from the boardroom into the press and the courts and escalated to the highest level of political leadership of the two countries. The stand-off was discussed between the Chinese President Hu Jintao and his French counterpart Nicolas Sarkovsky during the latter's visit to China in November 2007. In the dinner hosted by President Jintao, which the Danone chairman Frank Riboud also attended, a reference was made to the tussle. The political intervention led to a thaw—with both parties issuing a joint statement to temporarily suspend lawsuits and arbitrations to create a friendly environment for peace talks.

The difficulties began in 2005 when Danone officials accused Zong, who founded Wahaha in the 1980s, of forming a series of secret companies that mirrored the joint venture and siphoned off millions of dollars. Danone says that these companies began operating sometime in 2003. In 2005, Danone says, illegal Wahaha-related companies began expanding aggressively, manufacturing a growing share of the company's products. In late 2006, after Danone says that it discovered the parallel companies, Zong agreed to sell a majority stake in those companies to Danone, which intended to fold them into the joint venture. But after signing the agreement, Danone says that Zong pulled out of the deal and then began creating more mirror companies, including his own separate sales division, unsatisfied with the Danone deal. Those moves, Danone says, prompted the company to file a lawsuit in California against a group of corporations in the British Virgin Islands that were registered by Zong's wife and daughter, who have run some of the mirror companies and list California as their residence. *(Was this a build-up of strength ahead of a confrontation?)*

A few days later, Zong, who is one of China's wealthiest businessmen, having turned the small school controlled milk company of the 1980s into the beverage giant with sales of more than USD 1.5 billion in 2006, angrily resigned as chairman of Wahaha, saying he and his family had been slandered by Danone. Zong fought back in public. He never denied the existence of the other companies, but sought to legitimize them. In a letter posted on the Internet, Zong said that Danone officials were fully aware of the outside companies, which were partly financed by company employees, and that Danone wanted to acquire them cheaply. In a series of fiery open letters written to the Danone management, Zong criticized the French group, often vowing to undo their evil deeds.

(Case Study 1.3 contd.)

(Case Study 1.3 contd.)

> Danone appointed Emmanuel Faber, head of Danone's Asia operations, as interim chairman of Wahaha. But Danone had no executives in senior management at Wahaha. Zong, even after his resignation, remained a powerful figure at the company, marshalling senior managers, retail partners (who began preferring the non-joint venture products to the ones coming from Wahaha) and labour unions (with the slogan of our Chairman Zong) to come out aggressively against the Danone management. A group of 13 of the most senior managers of Wahaha jointly conducted a press meet with Zong to declare that if Danone did not drop some of its demand—such as the exclusive claim to the use of the brand name—they would all quit and set up another company. Wahaha executives insisted that the right to use the Wahaha name was not completely owned by the joint venture, despite Danone's statements. Wahaha, in response to the legal challenge in the California lawsuit, filed for arbitration hearings in Hangzhou.
>
> Danone began entering the Chinese market from early 1990s by acquiring well-run companies and from 1996 was operating a series of joint ventures with Wahaha. Danone generally preferred to pay a premium for acquisition, retain the existing management and give them a free hand to run the company. It instead built up a portfolio of assets by taking equity stakes in several companies operating in the milk/beverage/fruit drinks/bottled water business space. In the case of Wahaha, it let Zong run the show, knowing fully well that he ran the company with an iron grip, in his characteristic brash style. Such a strategy paid off well. In China, it was much better placed than other rivals such as Nestlé. Rift with Wahaha also got triggered by Danone's acquisition in competing ventures, which Wahaha opposed. Zong's move to build up a series of operating companies—with financial participation of company insiders, family-men and support from several provincial government—might also have been a surreptitious move in response to the Danone expansion.[10]

1.6 INSTITUTIONS AND POWER IN PRACTICE

Since we have located strategies and strategizing in power dynamics within a strategy milieu, our next task would be to develop a language and concept pieces that can help us understand what we have termed as levers of power. The notion of 'institution' provides one such useful

---

[10]Compiled from reports in *New York Times*, various dates.

concept. Douglass North defined institutions broadly as a 'set of rules or norms' that guide intersubjective human behaviour and transactions in the social domain. They can be either formal rules, in several cases with the backing of laws enforced by the state, or it can be internally devised norms that are followed in practice within networks of transacting entities. Rules that have a legal backing—and in that sense are backed by the power of state enforcement—are a special class of rules that can be very strong. Institutions, as rules, are necessarily shared over social spaces. Often, particular institutions and its shared meaning remain delimited only within certain specific, delimited spaces. Our view then supports a multiplicity of institutions, with differentiated rule sets operating in distinct social or business spaces. In fact, enforcement of rules (or institutions), expansion or contracting of the space (or turf) over which particular rule sets apply or can be credibly enforced constitute important issues in a strategy enquiry.

Institutions can also be (more fruitfully) viewed as shaped by practice. Practice is pragmatic—and often is not strictly rule bound. Practice enjoys the freedom of human agency. Practice is also strategic, for practical action is a contest for power. It is not atomic and arbitrary either. Agents would follow a pattern, a history and a belief that would shape their practice. Practice thus has inertia. However, actions in practice can also violate a pattern. Action, following and violating pattern, together constitutes practices. It is through practical regular practices that an institution is founded. Practices, conceptually, is a looser construct than rules (as articulated in Douglass North) that allows for slippages and transformation, providing at the same time a level of certainty that is required for meaningful acts in the intersubjective space. Thus, institutions can be defined in two different senses—as rules/norms to which Douglass North refers and as founded in patterns of practice. These provide a shared structure within which actions are carried out and made sense of. It is through this that power is sensed and acted upon as well. We discuss the dimension of power, but before that we provide a short illustration of the notion of practices.

> The research practices of a doctor in a well-endowed and networked hospital engaging in multi-site large-scale random control trial (RCT) of a drug or a biomedical device implant differs from the research practices of a doctor operating from a single doctor's clinic where research mostly is carried out in

> 'case research' form. Research practice of a scientist in a drug firm eager to patent differs often from the old university style professor scientist who would prefer an early publication of the findings of a key experimental research into the public domain. Biomedical research practices differ across these different sites or organizations and can be seen as different institutions founded through practices that differ significantly. The different practices are, however, not like strict rules—and we are not talking here of just rule-bound behaviour. Research practices of a single clinic doctor stands a possibility of transforming into slightly different set of practices of large-scale RCT-based research. This possibility of a slippage is important in our description of practices.

North argued that such institutions constitute something like a primitive which must exist before economic transactions and exchanges can take shape. It constitutes the essential bedrock on which exchange occurs. Markets can exist only if institutions exist. Markets in North's account do not, therefore, have the allusion to an 'invisible hand' metaphor.[11] In more simple terms, we can think of any game, say of football or cricket. It is only with a tacit acceptance of a set of rules (even a minimal set) that the game can proceed and winner and looser determined. Such set of rules would be the institutional bedrock. So, when an economic agent maximizes possible returns and transacts accordingly, it is a bounded exercise that is undertaken within the ambit of the norms that constitute the market in the first place. When trading in stocks, therefore, the trader would normally take for granted the norms and rules of transactions in the exchange (or the electronic trading network).

For our purpose, institutions of practice also represent the mode of exercise of power within a set of transacting entities—it defines and elimits the roles of each actor and provides boundary conditions (see case study 1.4). Such delimitation is useful and fundamental to the continuance of transactions—it helps in assuaging uncertainties and lends stability to transactions. From the point of view of the acting

---

[11]Those familiar with the work of Walrus would recall the allusion to an auctioneer who would be working silently, creating the competitive market where price-based clearing occurs. The auctioneer is an institution—a primitive that must exist credibly before the Walrasian market can operate. A Walrasian market is a price-clearing market or where price can bring the market to equilibrium. In other words, excess demand and supply is cleared by a price increase or a price decrease.

Trading networks and distribution channels in Japan

Japanese wholesale and retail trading networks, historically, has developed a business practice of offering 'right to return unsold goods' to retailers and often to several other downstream wholesaling points as well. This business practice has evolved for the network to transact on the risk of dead-stock—concentrating such risks at a point in the chain that is optimally placed in terms of access to information and financial resources to manage and specialize in such risks. The retail point and downstream wholesaling is insured against the dead-stock risk through payment of an implicit insurance premium (or a mark-up that transactions with right to return entail compared to those without such rights) to the risk specialist. Downstream retailers with the right to return would overstock and would not run the risk of 'stock-outs', a situation in which the demand or requirement for an item cannot be fulfilled from the current (on hand) inventory. It would help them stock and display a very large number of stock keeping units (SKUs).[12] This is important in the Japanese consumer markets which have, by certain estimates, the highest proliferation of variety—with a continuous introduction of a large number of SKUs, several of which fail and are withdrawn to be replaced by other varieties. In 1987, a small food retailer displayed about 2,000 items in the shop, while a big supermarket held more than 10,000, while the biggest wholesaler distributed more than 100,000 SKUs of food and liquor, of which more than 20,000 were newly introduced in the last six months. The figure in US would be around 1,700 new introductions and 700–800 withdrawals in 1986 in the food and liquor category (data from Miwa, Nishimura and Ramsayer, 2002: 176; see footnote 11).

Right to return generally exists also with some form of resale price maintenance, since the entity providing the right to return seeks some control (in the sense of exercising a restraint) over the retail price as well, particularly to prevent arbitrage. Readers would realize that 'right to return' is a

(Case Study 1.4 contd.)

---

[12]An SKU is a store specific number and would only be valid at the store where it is being sold (it would not be universal). The SKU number is a vital piece of information to every retail network. Combined with the Universal Product Code (UPC) number, the SKU identifies the product within the trader's inventory database. It not only supplies information about the items cost, but also about the number of items in the store, the number on orders in backlog and the number that can be purchased from other stores in the chain (in case of retail chain). Without the SKU number, channel partner would have no idea about the number of items they carry or what they are spending or earning on that product and their profit margin would be impossible to track.

(Case Study 1.4 contd.)

> crucial business practice—an institution—that serves as bedrock for optimal risk allocation of certain types within the network. Banning of the 'right to return' has been a heavily contested issue in bilateral trade negotiations between the US and Japan, since the US has taken a stand that such practices are exclusionary and monopolistic. In the US, till very recently, 'resale price maintenance' or the practice of manufacturer-suggested retail prices were illegal since it was seen as a form of vertical restraint. Would a ban on 'right to return' weaken the network mode of organization of the wholesale distribution system (Miwa, Nishimura and Ramsayer, 2002)?
>
> (See also case study 4.6 for another discussion on Japanese distribution practices.)

strategist, however, institutions also represent the manifestation in practice of the relations of power between the transacting entities. It often represents the current modes of governance to which all transacting entities necessarily submit. A strategist seeking a new relationship would be more interested in the disequilibrium of this status quo of relations, in toppling the existing modes of governance and establishing new modes altogether. Institutions and practices therefore constitute one important point of engagement for a strategist. The strategist often would change institutions, rewriting the rules of the game as a mode of subversion on the way to a win. Old rules then give way to new ones—on which a new consensus must develop. Inter-firm contracts and contractual terms and conditions, for instance, which delimit the role of each partner, often determine the power balance between transacting partners. Renegotiation of contract term then becomes a key to renegotiation of the balance of power. While contractual negotiation is a simple engagement between two firms/actors, an institutional contest is waged over a larger domain where the 'institution' carries a shared meaning.

Understanding of institutions surrounding a strategist, which we are calling 'institutions of practice', becomes important in deciphering the levers of power as well as the relationships in the strategy milieu. Possible reshaping of certain institutions also provides a means to craft a strategy win through. In the case of a contractual renegotiation, the reshaping is achieved between two parties to a transaction and is relatively easier to achieve (see case study 1.5). In other cases, however, such moves involve several actors and the battles are more long-drawn. Greater or more

> **CASE STUDY 1.5** **Transforming a contract term**
>
> An Indian software firm, after developing software intellectual property (IP) assets, licensed it to its much more powerful European licensee partner, but the licensing was on an upfront fee payment basis, such that the risks of the deal was borne by the licensee alone. Since the value of the IP asset was uncertain at the time of the deal and would only become known at a future point in time, the Indian firm, lacking the bargaining power of a great reputation, had agreed to the upfront payment mode. The upfront payment understandably was low. After a few rounds, however, the Indian firm realized that its IP assets were valuable and were winners in races against other software pieces, but because of the licensing terms, its revenue realization out of the IP assets it had created was low. It then decided to engage in licensing on a royalty mode so that it can share in the risks; if the IP becomes a blockbuster, it stands to realize significant revenues. In contrast, if it fails, there would be virtually no revenues. This, however, was resisted by the licensee and only after a few rounds of refusal by the Indian firm to engage in a licensing contract through the upfront payment route did the licensee agree to a change in the contract terms to a royalty mode of payment. The licensing deal on a risk-sharing mode therefore would include other forms of information access so that the Indian firm knows the possible plays that the IP asset is put into and possibly influence some of it as well. This enhanced voice elevates the Indian firm and changes the relationship with the licensee as the transaction is transformed from a mere one-time cash transaction to a more strategic, temporally dynamic engagement. Several accounts of fast technology catch-up by Korean firms in the 1990s and Japanese firms earlier, where they migrated from simple original equipment manufacturers (OEMs) of Western corporations to own-design or collaborative design manufacturing, provide similar narrations of transformation of roles and contract terms between partners.

extensive coordination often needs to be exercised (see case study 1.6). Rival camps, so to say, would often sponsor and adopt contesting institutions. Strategic moves then take the form of institutional rivalries or contests. In several cases such contests seek to influence the stance of regulation and a change in law is sought. A clinching support from the regulator, in favour of a particular institution, can be the culmination of a contest. We will have occasion to render several such accounts of institutional contests, including the jockeying for the vital vote of support from the regulator or the sovereign authority. To be able to describe and comprehend such institutional contests, we need to give up the notion of the firm as the unit of strategy analysis and need to take cognizance of non-firm institutions as sites of strategic action as well.

A strategic mind, we believe, must be trained in a deep reading of institutional nuances that can provide a hint to identify the contours of conflict, networks of possible allies, and so on. Conflicts, in general, leave an institutional mark—a trail that can be followed. Existence of different industry bodies, such as associations, often indicates a diversity of strategic stances, modes of production, and so on. In Indian film-making, for instance, there are several producer associations—in different regional language domains and in Mumbai. Film Makers Combine (FMC), the Association of Motion Pictures and Television Programme Producers, the Film Producers Guild of India and the Indian Motion Picture Producers Association are a few of them. This multiplicity indicates severalty of strategic stances (which we would discuss in a later chapter in a case on Indian film industry!) and interest groups, while the lone presence of Motion Pictures Association of America as the representative body influencing regulation points to a monopolistic dominance of a single stance and a lack of asset severalty[13] in Hollywood. Can you find out how such multiple associations differ? Does the existence, similarly, of a single software industry association in India signify a lack of institutional diversity in the industry? We provide a few narrations of institutional conflicts.

CASE STUDY 1.6 Regulatory wrangling over patent law

US lawmakers began considering a proposed patent law change in 2007 that pitted two of the most innovation-heavy industries—IT and pharmaceutical—against each other. The most common justification of a patent institution is the argument that it provides to the innovator an incentive to engage in

(Case Study 1.6 contd.)

---

[13]Asset severalty is a notion used by few Austrian economists. It denotes the fact of multiplicity of asset types—each of which might be valuable only in particular segments or might be reflecting differences in practices. Understanding severalty of assets requires us to understand the institutional dimension of asset valuation—that is, the fact that asset valuation is shaped crucially by the underlying institutional description of the market of the asset. Institutional differences cause asset severalties.

(Case Study 1.6 contd.)

innovation through an ex-ante guarantee of monopoly rights to the commercial exploitation of the knowledge-piece. Patents are valuable, and hence in most cases, patents generate a lot of litigation, costs of which can be very high indeed. Cisco Systems had a USD 45 million budget for patent litigation in 2007, which could be escalated if actual litigations increased. Each litigated case (on an IP) can cost as much as USD 10 million roughly, by current legal costs. In another oft-quoted case, International Business Machines (IBM) announced a litigation budget for defending infringement cases brought in against software developers (community) working in the open-source mode to ward off litigation-based threat by the proprietary software camp to the open-source space.

The Bills brought to the US Congress sought to make certain changes that would make it more difficult for patent holders to prove wilful infringement to win the triple-damages awards. The proposal also sought to scrap the practice of considering the entire value of a product/service in calculating damages, even if the infringed patent contributed only a small amount to it. The other important proposal was to remove the 'first to invent' clause—moving away from the romantic notion of rewarding the first inventor (which had to depend on data such as laboratory logbooks) to a more pragmatic approach of rewarding the first to file for a patent. In fact, in 2006 alone, there were at least 100 cases arguing that the first to file was not the first to invent (each costing around USD 300,000 apiece, with a positive result in just one case). Another proposal waiting in the wings was to have a post-grant review window inviting a challenge, rather than initiating a costly legal challenge (where the intermediation of the courts and the associated legal fees becomes costlier). The net effect of all these changes is to weaken the protection offered by the patent institution, while making a fast grant possible leading to a reduction of the possible rent-life of a patent.

One factor that prompted the changes was an increasing recognition that the patent system was leading to increased fragmentation of research portfolios, leading to difficulties of enhanced cross-licensing and IP bundling strategies on which firms such as Cisco (or say Qualcomm) depends. The IP stance of Cisco differs from that of the pharmaceutical product firms such as Eli Lilly or Merck, who depend on single patents to earn prolonged rents over extended periods. Information technology (IT) firms, in contrast, have short-product-lifecycle strategies. Cisco, who played a leading role in

(Case Study 1.6 contd.)

(Case Study 1.6 contd.)

> lobbying for moving the legal changes, was opposed to the stance of the pharmaceutical sector that wanted a more secure IP right granted through a regime of high penalties. For the regulator, the US Patent and Trademark Office (USPTO), there were administrative issues that the office was bothered about. In 2006, around 1,000 patent examiners looked at more than 450,000 patent applications—a huge burden by any measure, and the average time that a patent application had to wait in an active area such as computer science was more than six years. It increased the transaction cost of the property right granted to the private patent-holder. This conflict, leading to a differential lobbying stance, identifies a cleavage among knowledge-economy firms in their IP strategy stance.[14]

The recent move of Google in bidding for the Federal Communication Commission (FCC)[15] auction of spectrum (700 MHz band) resources in the US provides an interesting account of engagement with regulatory processes for creating the enabling conditions for the growth of a particular business proposition. Google and several other players, such as mobile handset manufacturers, and multimedia application and m-commerce developers, are worried about the slow pace of growth of data services over the mobile platform. Lack of interoperability, high cost of spectrum as well as lack of common access conditions into the wireless network is preventing a growth of m-commerce, including internet-based m-commerce, on whose growth Google has placed a positive bet. Below is the letter sent by Google to FCC Chairman, ahead of the January 2008 auction. FCC accepted only two of the four conditions put forth by Google; the condition to allow third party access for wholesaling was not included in the auction terms. Would the Google move succeed? The Google letter follows:[16]

---

[14]Compiled from several documents available at the website of 'Coalition for Patent Fairness', at http://www.patentfairness.org/learn/about (accessed on 10 May 2010).

[15]The FCC is an independent United States government agency. The FCC was established by the *Communications Act of 1934* and is charged with regulating interstate and international communications by radio, television, wire, satellite and cable.

[16]http://www.google.com/intl/en/press/pressrel/20070720_wireless.html (accessed on 12 May 2011).

July 20, 2007
Ex Parte via Electronic Filing
The Honorable Kevin J. Martin
Chairman, Federal Communications Commission
445 12th Street, SW, Washington, D.C. 20554

Re: WC Docket No. 06–150; PS Docket No. 06–229; WT Docket No. 96–86

Dear Chairman Martin:
Google shares your bold vision of using the upcoming 700 MHz spectrum auction to encourage much-needed competition in the wireless and broadband markets. I want to personally applaud your leadership and courage in making the public case for new market entry, and the tangible benefits it will offer all American consumers, including greater availability, higher speeds, lower prices.

As you know, Google submitted an ex-parte letter on July 9th explaining that, in order to promote genuine competition, the Commission must include open platforms as part of the applicable licensing requirements for paired commercial blocks in the Upper 700 MHz Band. In particular, our July 9th letter requested that the Commission should extend to all CMRS-type spectrum licensees clearly delineated, explicitly enforceable, and unwavering obligations to provide (1) open applications, (2) open devices, (3) **open wholesale services**, and (4) open network access.

The Commission's draft order for the 22 MHz "C" Block in the Upper 700 MHz Band reportedly allocates this block on a REAG basis subject to combinatorial bidding and includes some reference to "open access" principles. While these all are positive steps, unfortunately the current draft order falls short of including the four tailored and enforceable conditions, with meaningful implementation deadlines, that consumer groups, other companies, and Google have sought. In short, when Americans can use the software and handsets of their choice, over open and competitive networks, they win. It is also my understanding that the Commission's draft order includes a reserve price of $4.6 billion for the "C" Block, apparently to address unsupported claims about any impact from adopting open platforms conditions. We hereby inform you that, should the Commission expressly adopt the four license conditions requested in our July 9th letter—with specific, enforceable, and enduring rules—Google intends to commit a minimum of $4.6 billion to bidding in the upcoming auction.

Sincerely yours,
Eric Schmidt

1.7 STRATEGY AS INFLUENCING THE VOTING OF NODES

Our narration thus far makes it clear that we are placing strategy in the domain of power. It involves a 'voice' to exercise judgement. Models of equilibrium, therefore, do not lend itself to a strategy story. A Walrasian market, the perfectly competitive general equilibrium model, that clears with price signals cannot account for the existence of a strategist. Equilibrium outcomes are anyway reached in such models, and any deviation can be corrected through marginal changes in either quantities or price of a commodity. There are, therefore, no nodes that have a concentration of power to alter or influence outcomes. This is a non-strategic world. Consider, for instance, several small buyers procuring a certain simple commodity—generally they would not enjoy any power. If you introduce an intermediary wholesale procurer, concentration of the buying function can now produce a power; it can create a node since it creates lumpiness in the outcome. This is one reason why institutional sale dynamics are different from retail sale dynamics. The simplest outcome of such a concentration of power would be a price bargain—a greater discount, say. But this is the simplest mode. The powerful procurement intermediary can also barter access to a 'lumpy sales deal' for other privileges that give it access to or influence over other nodes of power; in other words, a 'voice'—it is then tantamount to two or more nodes exchanging privileges or favours—a kind of a barter transaction or, in Silicon Valley terms, a gift exchange in assets that do not have a market. One reason for the formation of public sector companies and creation of restrictions—say of imports—through instruments of the state in India and other late industrializing countries was to concentrate power at a national level in the government bureaucracy, which can then bargain and negotiate for access (of markets or technology) with other nodes—such as global cartels or monopolies in industries where dominance had become entrenched. In a later chapter on markets, we provide several descriptions of cartels (contemporary as well as old ones) that create a particular market through setting up of specific rules of transaction which the members of the cartel abide by.

Strategy, therefore, can be meaningful only to those occupying seats of concentrated power—the 'nodes'—where decisions can affect outcomes. Disequilibrium and discontinuity are the domains of strategy. Voting of the 'node', therefore, is in the domain of strategy. Voting exhibits a tipping point characteristic—it can have non-marginal or discontinuous effects on the outcome. Voting, as a notion, is closer to the political than the economic domain; control is as important—often more important—than the pure economic motive.

> Readers would recall our earlier description of the tussle between contesting pricing standards/practices in the US electricity industry (see section 1.2.1, case study 1.2). The key man, so to say, in the winning group—Sameul Insull, the erstwhile right hand man of Thomas Edison who took over leadership of the group of firms with a 'central station' interest after the exit of Edison, was a powerful social figure, commanding a social clout which businessmen in several other industries did not have. Observers in contemporary accounts (accessed through archives by the research quoted earlier) noted how Insull and his core group members relished such prestige that came through leading large vertically integrated electricity utilities (central stations). Many ascribed his adoption of the 'growth dynamic' to such motives, often jeopardizing the finances of the firms he led. While aggressive adoption of 'growth dynamic' led to a decline in the short-run profit, a more serious problem was his adoption of the balloon depreciation norms (depreciating equipment at the end of useful life) over which there was a major tussle with his main financiers, including the J.P. Morgan group.

Our argument is not that financial considerations are not important or that the efficiency criterion is not followed. From a pragmatic standpoint, the economic logic—in terms of efficiencies—is often ambiguous, especially in a dynamic setting, where anticipation and expectations play a major role. In our discussion around the context of the electricity rate system (see section 1.0, case study 1.2), the realization of economies of scale in large-scale central generation was an ex-post event after the decline of isolated stations. Readers might realize that the business of equipment suppliers—who were the source of such innovations leading to realization of economies of scale—was already skewed against isolated generators by then (whose market share had drastically fallen from almost 50 per cent in 1899). If we take seriously the anticipatory and expectation-driven nature of investments, then an ability to coordinate a bevy of such related chunks of (anticipatory and uncertain) investments in a particular direction leads to a path-dependent development; the purely economic static efficiency type arguments are extremely difficult to concretize in such settings. Voice and the vote of the holder of the voice become crucial then. Our argument is that such uncertainties have been hugely underemphasized in mainstream economics literature. Pragmatic accounts would have to provide far more space to such uncertainties—and hence to judgemental action. The judgement exercised by the power holder or the actor with a voice is not, however, by any stretch of imagination unconstrained. Several countervails remain—institutional restrictions are important—but within that, there are possibilities of slippages. Our notion of 'institutions of practice' is thus aimed at capturing this dimension of judgement under constraints through the duality of 'institutions' and 'slippages'.

> Our earlier description of the tussle between contesting pricing standards/practices in electricity industry highlighted the role of voting (see case study 1.2)—the political dimension of strategic acts. It showed how close networks spanning across firms can take control over shared inter-firm spaces and influence adoption of a chosen set of policies or norms. The institutional mimicking that led to the diffusion of the technical and managerial standard practices in the industry was backed by the coercive power exercised through the key actors who controlled the seats of power that wielded the voice. The coercive power denied voice to the proponents of the alternative/contesting institution. The choices were, moreover, exercised under uncertainty about the technological feasibility of economies of scale that a 'growth dynamic' approach could support.

The discussion around voting has brought out the importance of 'nodes' or nodal power holders. 'Nodes' can be seen as points of access, where visitations would be made to seek support, resources or some other favour that can be denied as well. Nodes can bring in rules/norms or preserve the sanctity of existing norms; they are *institutional gatekeepers*. Study of strategy, thus, must search for the formation, or contrarily, destruction (or decimation) of nodes of power. A move by a strategist often has to engage with such extant nodes to realize the ambitions of institutional subversion. Two broad types of engagement may be thought of—a move to weaken or strengthen certain nodes or contrarily create alternative nodes, or a move to piggyback on and influence the voting mechanism across the relevant nodes in order to drive through an institutional change: adoption of new practices or transformation of existing ones.

In the second type, a strategist must have an interest in understanding the voting mechanism and seek to influence it in favour of a move being attempted. While in the first type, the mechanism of node formation itself would be a critical area of enquiry.

In our hypothetical example above (see p. 37), related to intermediated procurement, what defines the concentration of power at the level of the intermediary—can shrouding or hiding of information create a 'node'? How vulnerable is such a node to moves by rivals to decimate the node? These then become issues that a strategy discourse must seek to understand. Our description of the electricity rate-system war clearly showed the role of manipulating, of taking the rival camp by surprise and such tactics in influencing the 'voting mechanism'. However, the tactic would crucially depend on the nature of the voting mechanism. Such simple manipulative modes might not work if the rival is endowed with considerable power and is a 'keen' participant in the institutional contest. The nature of the voting mechanism is specific to the strategy milieu and is a key insight that a strategist seeks—the description of the nodes, sources of its power, inertia of the nodes, their ability to act as gatekeepers and the possible slippages that the nodes may be prone to. We describe below the proposals (in summary) of the proponents of the 'open-spectrum' group of telecommunication technology and device firms to win the regulator's vote (FCC) in their contest with the already entrenched lobby of interest groups whose business and investments are committed to a regime of 'property based spectrum'. Co-optation, provision of crossover between alternative technology trajectories (to reduce the future sunk cost of a trajectory), organization of publicly verifiable races of delivery on certain defined parameters of technology performance over a sufficiently long horizon so as not to endanger the current valuation of sunk-capital of the dominant technology trajectory, constitutes some of the key features. The nature of this contest and the attempts to influence the voting mechanism is quite different from the one described earlier on the electricity rate-system contest. Appreciating the 'open spectrum' move would require the reader to go through a slightly long technical description of open spectrum telecom technology (see case study 1.7).

Our discussion above has thus pointed out why it is useful to visualize nodes as points of power that wield influence; particularly in a dynamic setting loaded with uncertainties, the acts of the nodal power holders make lumpy commitments in resources and shapes the unfolding future. The strategic role, in that sense, is entrepreneurial as well. The following contest between Blu-ray and High Definition/Density Digital Video Disc

Case Study 1.7: Lobbying by Open Spectrum Group[17]

The 'open-spectrum' based technologies (Wi-Fi being an early instance of it) are based on transmission of communication signals on open or non-proprietary spectrum. In contrast, the current telecom regime (of mobile telephony) is based on transmission over operator-specific spectrum (which the operator is licensed to operate on). Open spectrum communication is based on the premise that computing intensive end-user equipment can dynamically choose the frequency over which to communicate from a free resource pool of frequencies subject to certain shared protocols. So, mobile communication can be organized without anyone—be it a firm or a government agency—exclusively owning the rights to use of spectrum. The ideal open spectrum system would not have any (or very little) end equipment infrastructure; end-user equipment itself would cooperate with each other to achieve transmission. The rapid pace of development of computing power and miniaturization has made design of such intelligent end-user equipment feasible today. In contrast, the property rights based approach is based on an architecture where computing power was concentrated in central switches operated by the network operator, with the end-user equipment being relatively 'dumb'.

In such a system, the receiver treats signals of all frequencies as similar; so, to distinguish between a signal and a noise, the signal has to be transmitted at high-power. If, then, two transmissions are of the same power—but are on different frequencies, traditional wireless systems would encounter 'interference'—and would fail to decode noise from the signal. Since 1912, when the first regulatory structures for telecommunications was created in the US, this problem of interference was solved by restricting the rights to transmit at frequencies on which communication is possible and the distributing of permits to specific communication providers. Over the years, however, the dramatic increase in computation power and two related theoretical developments have changed how we look at wireless communication. The first of this is called the Shannon's information theory, which states that

(Case Study 1.7 contd.)

---

[17] Open Spectrum Group is a coalition of companies, organizations and individuals working to unlock the potential benefits of public availability of radio spectrum. It is united by the goal of realizing the potential social and economic benefits of this underutilized natural resource by promoting innovative public policies.

(Case Study 1.7 contd.)

there is an inverse correlation between the width of the band of frequencies of electromagnetic radiation that encodes information and the signal to noise ratio, that is, the power of the radiation that encodes the desired communication relative to other sources of radiation with a similar frequency when it reaches the receiver. The implication of this theory is that if a communication is sent using a sufficiently wide band of frequencies, the power of its signal need not be more powerful than the power of other sources of radiation. This implication was not practically usable for wireless communications until substantial computation became cheap enough to locate in receivers and transmitters, but it is now the basis of most advanced mobile phone standards, as well as the basic 802.11 standards and other wireless systems. With increase in computation power in the end-user equipment, it implies that a transmission over a large bandwidth can happen at very low power if a code is attached that the end-user equipment can compute and discern to make out the signal from the noise. This is called the 'processing gain'.

From a policy perspective, the most important thing to understand about processing gain is that it increases as bandwidth and computation available to a wireless network increase. For practical purposes, the wider the band, the less power a transmitter–receiver pair needs in order for a receiver to understand the transmitter, but at the cost of more complex computation. Limiting the bandwidth of a signal, then, limits the processing gain a sender–receiver pair can achieve irrespective of how computationally sophisticated the equipment is. As more devices use a band, their low power builds up locally (their effect on unintended receivers rapidly declines as a function of distance from the transmitter), requiring all the proximate devices to increase their processing gain. With infinite bandwidth and costless computation, this would not present an efficient limit. With finite bandwidth and costly computation, increased information flow through a network will result in some social cost, either in terms of the cost of computation embedded in the equipment, or in terms of displaced communications—the communications of others who have less sophisticated equipment and cannot achieve the same processing gain. This means that the cost of computation and the permission to use wide swaths of spectrum are the limits on how many users can use a specified bandwidth processing gain. Which will be the efficient limit will depend on the speed with which processors become faster and cheaper, relative to the extent to which bandwidth is made available for use in open spectrum

(Case Study 1.7 contd.)

(Case Study 1.7 contd.)

mode. Open spectrum also promises to deliver better on certain parameters of network security and cost of displacement of communication; but currently they remain a theoretical potential without the gadgets that can implement it. Should enough investment flow into the open spectrum space, such advantages might be realized.

Bandwidth available for transmission on open spectrum is thus crucial, and without a wide enough bandwidth available, investments in end-user equipment technologies that can bring down the cost of end-user computation would not be forthcoming. That defines the reason for the conflict between the two groups. The Open Spectrum Group, thus, wanted the FCC not to go for a big-bank licensing of all available spectrum and instead work on creating a combination of licensed and free (open) spectrum to evaluate (at a future date) the technology performance of the two contesting groups. Some of their key suggestions were as follows:

1) The institutional design should include two constraints. First, no more frequencies should be designated for the spectrum market experiment than necessary to make it viable. Certainly, this should be no more than the bandwidth set aside for open wireless networks, given that this approach is most effective at allocating narrow bands, whereas open wireless networks rely on wide bands as a baseline requirement. The spectrums in common must be large enough to draw in credible investments in equipment technology development. Second, the property rights should include a recovery reservation, such that, should our understanding of the relative value of the approaches over time develop to favour much broader permission for open wireless networks, the cost of implementing the change will not be prohibitive.

2) The exercise of the option should be sufficiently into the future (like, say, over the next 10 years), so that taking account of current industry valuation practices, the option does not affect current valuation of investments. This is to assuage the fears of the current sunk investment holders, so as to ease their inertia and minimize the potential cost of change in technology trajectory.

3) To allow open spectrum equipment to use 'underlay' and 'interweaving', which are currently prohibited. These systems allow the equipment to utilize and transmit over a licensed frequency when it is

(Case Study 1.7 contd.)

(Case Study 1.7 contd.)

> locally not in use, and vacate it immediately when the licensed user needs it. Since communication patterns vary over time and place, significant amount of licensed frequencies lie unutilized at every point of time. This proposal seeks to allow open spectrum users to utilize the free spectrum resources, without hurting the interests of the licence holder.
>
> The proposals, as the readers would appreciate, are aimed at co-optation of the powerful entrenched groups to create a space for investments to flow into open spectrum projects and seeking a regulator vote which the licensed spectrum group would not be too opposed to. The fact that the contest was taking place in the public domain with involvement of technologists, economists, and lawyers from academia and from industry associations was also important in shaping the mode of influencing the voting mechanism. The regulator's vote was most crucial here, in the sense that it was the final arbiter (summarized from Benkler, 2002).

(HD DVD) format provides another account demonstrating another type of voting by nodal power holders.

 **Blu-ray and HD DVD—contest for dominance**[18]

> Blu-ray format was promoted by Sony and HD DVD format was promoted by Toshiba. Both companies formed industry groups to promote their own standards and the war continued till 2007. The target market for both technologies was consumer entertainment industry and the access to them was governed by nodes such as Hollywood studies who produce contents and retail chains, such as Wal-Mart, Best Buy, and so on. In this race, the size of the peer group of adopters would be crucial, since without adequate Blu-ray

(Case Study 1.8 contd.)

---

[18]Blu-ray is a next-generation optical disc format. The format was developed by Japan's Sony to enable recording, rewriting and playback of high-definition (HD) video, as well as storing large amounts of data. The initial format offered more than five times the storage capacity of traditional DVDs and held up to 25GB on a single-layer disc and 50GB on a dual-layer disc. Toshiba's HD DVD is a currently defunct high-density optical disc format for storing data and HD video.

(Case Study 1.8 contd.)

> users, content producers would not produce good content, and that would discourage consumer adoption. In the face of uncertainty about which technology would win, it is difficult for nodal power holders to take a stand. Incremental profit calculations and return on equity-type evaluations would be of no help.
>
> Triumph of Sony to outwit Toshiba in the format war can be attributed to its successful alliance of Hollywood studios (Columbia Pictures, Walt Disney Pictures, and 20th Century Fox). It was also successful in converting Warner Bros. and Paramount Pictures, initial supporters of HD DVD format, to adopting Blu-ray. The conversion of Warner Bros. to back Blu-ray was one of the major reasons for the success of Blu-ray as it is the largest home video producer.
>
> Another node Sony captured was retail stores like Wal-Mart and Best Buy. Sony, by incorporating Blu-ray technology in Play Station 3 (bundling!), forced retail chains to allocate space to Blu-ray technology. Toshiba did not have a Play Station equivalent to get access rights into Wal-Mart. The perceived dual benefit to consumer was one of the prime reasons these chains were forced to allocate more shelf space to Blu-ray technology, promoting Blu-ray over HD DVD.
>
> In summary, one can say that Sony was able to influence nodes by deftly manoeuvring multiple adoptions or voting in own favour. Remember, given the dynamics of value of the technology depending on pool size of user base, an initial assemblage of network partners who provide a positive vote can turn the market irreversibly in one's own favour. Can you think of the kind of incentives Sony could have provided to the early voting nodes; how would they have shared risks and gains; what would have been the nature of the business agreements? We will deal with this class of contracting problems in Chapter 4.

1.8 NODE FORMATION

We next provide a discussion on the different possible modes of formation of power around nodes.

1.8.1 Lumpy fixed asset

Several assets are lumpy in nature. The simplest example would be fixed assets such as a turbine or a boiler. It is available in specified sizes and capacities/specifications. Increasing production from the asset beyond the capacity would require another lump or chunk of the asset to be installed. Capacity expansion cannot then be marginally incremental—it can be in lumps only.

Control over a lumpy chunk of fixed asset can lead to the formation of a node. Formation of organization (or a firm) can centre round such lumpy assets. If fixed asset in capacity is a key node creator, enhancing the (relative) investment in it (vis-à-vis, say, investment on expert skilled workmen) would generally empower the node even further—enhancing organizational power and control. Several such holders of lumpy fixed asset, such as in a manufacturing set-up, can constitute an oligopoly—where gaming moves by the asset holders would determine prices and production volumes. They can also prevent entry through demonstrating a credible threat of retaliation. Entry deterrence appears to be most important in such settings. Such lumpy asset holders would engage in races in creating capacities or increasing (enhancing) investments in assets (such as plant capacity). In general, firms would seek strategic parity and moves would be copied very fast—or at least attempts would be made to replicate moves to dull its strategic significance. Strategic parity, in terms of capacity or geographic distribution of assets, can bring stability and a soft oligopolistic rivalry can reign for fairly long periods. Contrarily, moves to disrupt strategic parity or the extant power balance can lead to moves to engage in predation—engagement with attrition with the specific purpose of eliminating a rival from the business space, hastening its exit.

Consider an industry with a large, mature (low volume growth) market in country A, and a smaller (but high growth) market in country B, where control over capacity is a key element in rivalry. Consider also that the two markets were separated through regulation and trade and investment flows were limited for a long time—current regulatory stance, however, favours a greater integration. Would a firm in country B target asset (capacity) creation at a pace faster than anticipated growth rates in its domestic market, or grow slower in the domestic market and invest in the foreign low growth market if it faces a cap in total investments? Would this choice be influenced by the stance of the financial backers of the firm—say private equity groups, financial institutions or wealthy family groups; in particular, what would be the stance of the firm if financial backers are willing to underwrite predation losses? Have you observed the behaviour of Chinese firms over the last decade in several commodity industries? Why are they so aggressive? Why are there sudden spurts in capacity that Chinese firms engage in around periods of entry into international markets? You can take container shipping industry as a case and do a background study.

Power derived out of lumpiness may be thought of on two dimensions:

(1) Lumpiness as an outcome of an aggregation at a point in time—a large manufacturing plant as an aggregated fixed capital under the control of an asset holder, for instance. The aggregation might also be of other assets—rather than physical plant and machinery and assets such as land. Power can be exercised by an entity that acts as a gatekeeper and often also as the aggregator of several legal rights or router of several property rights or sometimes also as the provider of important access to markets, sourcing agencies, know-how, and similar assets including access to finance. Readers may think of the role of CISCO (see case study 1.6) as a key aggregator of several IP assets licensed or otherwise sourced from a wide set of owners. To several innovative companies with IP assets, CISCO acted as a key gateway—a kind of a block router connecting the IP asset holder to the market and the product, which also integrated the different component IP assets.

(2) This asset holder also has an interest in the lumpy asset that abides over time—or, in other words, there is a commitment or durability over a temporal horizon around the lumpy asset. While in the earlier case, our interest was in the spatial dimension—that is, lumpiness at a point in time—here our interest is in the temporal dimension of continuity of such a nodal position. It is often useful to articulate the two dimensions separately, since a holder of a lumpy asset (an aggregation in current time) need not necessarily have a durable horizon of asset holding; or, in other words, he/she might only have a fleeting interest in the asset, retaining high liquidity in contrast to a durably committed position.

Readers may think of a large financial investor in a manufacturing firm with large-scale plants controlled by a business family. The partial asset holding (the share held) of the business family (assuming it intends to hold on to the asset over a long time) is quite different from that of the financial investor in the same lumpy asset, who has a fleeting interest or at most a temporally delimited horizon, as in private equity investment. Listing of the firm in

> the secondary equity market provides an easy exit option to the financial investor—a high liquidity. In fact, the possibility of exit or desertion provides a mechanism through which the liquid asset holder brings in a threat on the asset holder with a more durable commitment. Would blessing such liquid asset holders with immense power be good for the long-term interest of the asset? In the later chapter on assets, we would take up this notion of liquidity and durable commitment of an asset holder in greater detail.

Generally, however, a lumpy asset holder would have a sustained temporal interest in the asset. Exercise of deterrence, as we argued above, is a key concern of such an asset holder—mainly to safeguard interests over the temporal dimension. The node prevents formation of new rules of game, new sets of 'standards' or even the utilization of alternate technological paths or paths that combine resources or assets differently. Preservation of current rules of the game—the current institutions or the institutional architecture—is intimately tied to preservation of valuation of the asset over time. This is an institutional dimension of the role of a node, as a sort of institutional gatekeeper. The link between current institutions and the valuation of an asset was discussed earlier—readers may remind themselves of the discussion around the rate-system in the electricity industry, whose design was loaded with the interests of the 'central stations' as opposed to the small independent generating units (see case study 1.2). Lumpy assets thus include investments sunk in research and development (R&D), current technology standards, logistics chains and sourcing contracts or other kinds of contractually enforced restrictions, explicit agreements or covert cartel arrangements and similar others including of course the stock of land and machineries, and so on. A key purpose of deterrence is to thwart the rise of novelty, and to the extent that rise of a novel market or a product often requires a novel set of rules or means of coordination, the motive of deterrence often stands in the way to market-making of a novel product. The acts of deterrence are not just limited to the market or the inter-firm space, but are also crucially exercised within the firm or the organization by limiting and thwarting radical reconfiguration of resources or processes inside the organization. Deterrence is exercised most often inside the organization through curbs on increasing returns that would have been otherwise feasible, and such deterrence is exercised through sticky agglutination of departments and functions, shifting the focus on a discourse of efficiency. We discuss this aspect of organization in Chapter 3 in more detail.

1.8.2 Information encapsulation

Another significant mode of creation of a 'node' is through encapsulation of information. Encapsulation of information creates private rights; privileged holders of such rights can then engage in exchanges, either in markets or in non-market forms that are closer to barters. Encapsulated information is more than simple aggregation. Holders of such information may deal in access to know-how, markets, logistics, finance, stock markets or privileged access to 'ideas/products in making', including market intelligence. Such nodal powers of the encapsulator provide differential access to the totality of information and thus create architecture of asymmetric information access that supports transactions. An encapsulator also simultaneously undertakes transformation in the information content, since analytics on aggregated information reveals several dimensions not previously decipherable. Digitization has increased such possibilities by increasing the amount (both quantity and type) of information that can be captured and moved at very low costs (both in space and time), tearing it off from the site of its generation. This aspect of node formation—or the route to power—is increasingly becoming important in the digitized economy.

Contemporary information industries have an immense power to decimate old seats of power by challenging traditional forms of information shrouding. It also simultaneously makes it possible to design several novel solutions that can create new nodes through new designs of information shrouds. Just as an illustration, think of the source of power of the New York Stock Exchange (NYSE) specialist trader, who occupies the trading floor (or pit) for each stock. All trades in that particular stock is always routed through the specialist—this monopolization of the route of the transaction makes the specialist a kind of hub that is most informed about market sentiments (as revealed through trade orders). Till around 2002, only the specialist knew about the depth of the market at each point in time—the list of non-cleared transactions, which was not published. Asymmetries were thus created through rule design. National Association of Securities Dealers Automated Quotations (NASDAQ), in contrast, published this deep granular information from very early years (in its Level III screen). Why did NASDAQ choose to publish (or broadcast) an information that NYSE thought should be kept private and encapsulated? Our discussion on NASDAQ later brings out several such issues and conflicts. In fact, if we have to understand strategizing of stock, commodities or derivative exchanges, which in contemporary times are mostly private or incorporated entities, then visualizing 'node' formation through rule designs to create information asymmetries becomes vital. Understanding trade networks or trading companies, such as Japanese *sogo-sosha*s, also needs to appreciate such information assets.

1.8.3 Bundling of assets or information streams

Bundling of information assets or other assets together can also create a node—the specific point of bundling becoming a node at which an exercise of power can occur. Asset bundling acts because bundling thwarts an independent market of the different asset pieces to exist or arise; so the bundling point enjoys a discretion, say in providing access or denying it. Consider a piece of chemical processing technology developed in a chemical process plant. Normally, such a technology did not enjoy an independent market—such as a technology licensing market; and control over the technology was bundled with control over the physical plant. Decisions to license such a technology by the firm would depend on the calculus of the effects it would have on the product market through increased entry and hence on the profitability of the plant assets. On the contrary, if a well-functioning technology licensing market is operational with several independent suppliers offering close or similar types of technologies or even provide a credible threat of development of close/competing technologies in near future, the firm might evaluate the prospects of technology licensing independently from the economics of the product market. In such a case, the technology asset is partially unbundled from the physical asset (operating plant) that is valorized through product sales.[19] The case of the rise of Application Specific Integrated Circuits (ASICs) ecosystem provides an illustration (see case study 1.9).

These are, then, a few ways in which a 'node' might be formed. Different modes of node formation may also be in contest with each other. A firm may induce an unbundling to weaken the power of a node formed around a lumpy fixed asset (and an organization around it), and simultaneously create new nodes by novel forms of information shrouding. We will discuss several such instances in the later chapters. We end this chapter by providing a few typologies and moving towards an implicit definition of strategy.

---

[19]The technology licensing market has immensely expanded in recent years, creating possibilities of unbundling of technology assets from physical plant (capacity) assets.

Appreciating Strategy and the Strategist 51

CASE STUDY 1.9 Rise of ASIC ecosystem and power of unbundling

ASICs are integrated circuits (ICs) designed for particular applications by a specific customer—such as a dishwasher manufacturer who may specify certain product-specific electronic functionality required in its unique product to be achieved by the ASIC. In the very early days of integrated circuit industry, custom circuits were designed by assembling standard ICs and other electronic components in a printed circuit board. However, technical considerations, such as reliability of interconnections, miniaturization requirements and economizing pressures, provided strong incentives to move circuit customization to the IC itself. ASIC is a realization of that goal. It was introduced first in late 1960s and has greatly increased in size and complexity since then. The original method of building ASIC was the so-called full-custom method, involving designing each transistor and interconnection on the IC from scratch, a relatively slow and expensive process. It is still used when the need is to design an IC that must perform at the very highest speed attainable with a given production process, and/or must be squeezed into the smallest possible area of silicon. It requires a close interaction between customer and supplier engineers—achieved through several iterative rounds of prototype designing, simulation and testing. Designing driven by customer site-specific information was closely tied to information specific to the producer's production process, fully tying custom designing to the production assets of the chip fabricators. The crucial breakthrough that allowed unbundling was the development of an architecture that reduced the amount of specialized supplier-generated information that a designer in a customer firm must know to be able to design the custom circuit. The remaining supplier-specific information was encoded into software (tool) that could be shared with the customer. Architectures such as 'gate arrays' (other approaches being field programmable logic device and standard cell ASIC) allowed production of standard semi-processed chips using producer's fabrication knowledge that can then be customized by the design team of the customer through designing and then fabricating the interconnection layer(s). While the architecture was developed within a widely shared expert/academic community, the software tool was designed by ASIC vendors, initially only for their own proprietary use—Fairchild being a pioneer. In 1980–81, founders of LSI Logic, a start-up, developed a suite of ASIC design tools and an extensive library of cell design and made it available to customers. Several

(Case Study 1.9 contd.)

(Case Study 1.9 contd.)

> established firms such as Fujitsu—who had robust software for internal use—refused to follow suit.
>
> Thus, Wilf Corrigan, a founder of LSI Logic, reports the following conversation:
>
>> When I talked to Yasufuku [a senior manager] at Fujitsu and told him that our plan was to put the software in the hands of the customers, he said, 'That is a brilliant strategy. If you do that and the software is good, you will win.' 'Why don't you do that?' I asked. 'Our software is so valuable that if we expose it to outsiders they will steal it.' In fact, [Fujitsu] had been unwilling to transfer the software even to their U.S. subsidiary because they were convinced that once they let the genie out of the bottle, they would never get it back in again.
>
> However, LSI Logic's idea was liked by several customers and eventually other ASIC manufacturers and ASIC toolkit vendors were driven to follow the LSI Logic path. It soon generated a vibrant specialist software toolkit industry—led in the late 1990s by firms such as Cadence (selling hundreds of software packages for different user groups)—who produced software that could be used to design chips made by several producers—unlike the initial software shared by LSI Logic and few other producers in the early 1980s that was producer-specific. The design work of the tool producers like Cadence evolved along a different trajectory than that of the supplier-built software, as they sought standardization across producers and had a different optimization logic driving them. The end result was that many ASIC suppliers that previously established marketplace advantage on the basis of both product design skills and production skills were forced to a position of appropriating benefit from production skills only, since an independent market of designing skills was established as a result of the act of unbundling (excerpts from Hippel, 1998: 629–44).

1.9 TYPOLOGY OF STRATEGIES

Our discussion so far, we hope, has made it clear that strategy has several concerns and several languages—or in other words, it has multiplicities. Particularly important is our emphasis on creative crafting of strategy moves—which leaves it relatively open-ended—with several new possibilities. If we accept that stance, can we still organize our thoughts around strategy in something like a meta-framework that can help us juggle different concept pieces? In trying to provide certain typologies, therefore, we hint at some broad possibilities of organizing our thoughts.

1.9.1 Based on milieu and intent

Our account of strategy is based on the actor strategist's desire for power. So, strategies would differ based on the ambitions of the strategist and the relationship that is sought in the milieu. Recall that the milieu was defined as the intermeshed network of power holders with different kinds of relationship with each other—winner, rival, committed allies, indifferent actors as well as holders of a fluid position (of non-commitment). A strategy has to be conjured up in this particular milieu of the strategist. The intent of the strategist is also extremely important, that is, a strategy design cannot be independent of the intent of the actor. An intent seeking a relation of dependence with a set of collaborators would craft a different strategy from one that harbours an ambition of engaging in confrontation, since what the actor seeks as outcome is so different.

A currently weak actor may make several decoy moves, act coy in terms of current signalling and yet build up positions for a future confrontation—which would be signalled only at a later opportune point in time. This, particularity of a strategy articulation, differs from more common approaches to define it as, for instance, 'a long-term plan to tackle uncertainties or to seek a position of vantage'. We argue that such a definition is inadequate and does not take account of the nuances that are vital in practice. Every actor, in our strategy story and possibly in the real world around us, does not desire a grand win—or a leading position in a milieu. Or in other words, positions of vantage are not reached simply because they are not desired—this possibility must not be ruled out. Similarly, a reading of an impending threat that can challenge survival would lead to one kind of a stance—a fleeing to the most protected area—seeking something akin to an umbrella cover in a safe niche. Contrarily, a confident actor/organization desirous of extending the influence and span of control would explore new markets, new technologies and new turfs. The intent of the actor defines the bounds of what is sought and shapes the acts.

1.9.2 Depending on the dynamics of the industry

The specific dynamics of the industry also makes a great difference to what is sought in a strategic move and how a win is achieved. The industry context has been mainly represented as structures of industry—or the levels of concentration of the industry. We will draw a distinction between two different types of industry contexts—a decreasing returns and an increasing returns mode of surplus generation. Consider an energy intensive, 'fixed asset heavy' industry such as cement. The possible image you can conjure up is of stability. Such industries are decreasing return industries—where too much of expansion runs into problems of decreasing returns as yields on the marginal assets employed or resources used goes down sharply beyond a point. Mainstream theories of economics would mostly address such decreasing returns contexts. Such industries generally would be relatively commoditized, generating pressures of price competition.

In contrast, several contemporary industries like software (most obvious example being operating systems) exhibit characteristics of increasing returns—where a winner continues to win and a loser has no hope whatsoever. The upside of the profit possibility therefore explodes, quite unconstrained by the production limitations that would characterize a cement plant (or firm).[20] Moreover, predictability of the outcome (even in a probabilistic sense) goes down substantially—and uncertainties go up. Increasing returns can set in because of several factors, of which just two kinds of factors we point out here. Consider the impact of very high positive network externalities—either from consumption or production side. From the consumption side, the increase in size of the network of users might lock out alternative offers (particularly if switching costs are substantial)—so all marginal consumers virtually would be bound in to the network of the incumbent, leading to a positive network externality. On the production side, a firms' ability to achieve significant degrees of ex-ante coordination of expectation and investment amongst a large set of complimentary producers (all of whose products inter-work in a system!) would lead to a success of the firm in establishing positive network externalities—leading to a runaway win. Others would not have the rich set of complementing products and would fail—again Microsoft Windows would be an example of success achieved through coordination

---

[20]See, for instance, works of Brian Arthur (1994) or Allyn Young (1928) for a systematic and detailed economics based argument on increasing returns of the first and second kind, respectively!

of complementing products. This is the first type of increasing returns, discussed elaborately in works of Brian Arthur.

Increasing return dynamics can be set off through another mode (the second mode is discussed in Allyn Young's work; see footnote 20), which is closer to a reading of the classical economics literature; that is, through increased specialization and economies of scope. Consider a function—such as a particular business process, like, say, pricing—that has traditionally been carried out inside a firm by its managers. Suppose this function moves to a specialist firm who now contracts with the original firm. If pricing is a firm's internal process, then it possibly would be based on costs (in some form), simply because the firm has an asymmetric access to that information. If it moves to an intermediary—such as an auction house or an e-commerce platform—then several other dispersed information assets (such as information of individual utility of a product amongst consumers) would be utilized in the pricing process. Information assets beyond the control of the firm are essential to make the intermediary role meaningful. Such a quasi-independent auction house would also possibly expand in the direction of scope—removing the function from firms in several other industries on to the platform. Its growth mode, in other words, is across multiple value chains—in the direction of scope as it subverts an increasing list of industries and sectors. Multiple value chains thus get linked through the rise of several such intermediaries in something like a complex densely inter-networked mesh. Our discussion earlier of the rise of the software toolkit industry (firms such as Cadence) for ASIC designing (see case study 1.9) brings out similar dynamics which basically occurs along the scope direction, interconnecting several firm internal processes (often across firms in several different industries), driven by an optimization logic that is different from that of the original process owners. The original processes are then subverted and transfigured along with the rise of the specialist. The notion of increasing return in the above description refers to the possibility of an upside gain that is not limited by asset utilization calculus. Instead, it rides on a process of change whose span actually delimits the potential profits that may be reaped.

Two facets of this mode of realization of increasing returns must be emphasized. The first is to note that the act of shifting a function (or an asset) out of the exclusive control of the administrative coordination mechanism of the firm into a wider network (of several firms!) creates a stronger property right around that asset that is quasi-independent of the parent—the new holder of that right realizes an enhanced autonomy or a 'voice'. It is this partial freeing up from the old constraints that induce a search for the expansion in the scope direction, linking up this asset to several other asset pieces in the milieu in unique ways. Control over the asset is thus essentially shared. This sharing is not necessarily in terms of the cash flow rights over the asset, which might not be there. The specialist third party might have exclusive cash flow rights. In our discussion above, Cadence may not share revenues with the semiconductor producers, although such types of arrangements are not uncommon. What is important, however, is the ability of Cadence to coordinate the process of several semiconductor manufacturers, whose adoption of the 'producer independent' tool would necessarily subvert erstwhile firm-specific processes. The existence of a powerful enough third party outside the administrative control or authority of the organization seems important in driving this coordination.

Would a software division (or an internal software team) have been able to achieve such a feat? Under tight control of the corporation, it might enjoy limited freedom to transact in the market or with multiple producers—recall the initial stance of Fujitsu whose experience was different from that of Cadence! The control structure seems to be then very important. It is also interesting that it was a start-up that first shared the toolkit with customers, deviating from the established practice—the eventual success of this mode was not certain then. The software standardization that created and expanded the toolkit space into a multibillion-dollar industry was not certain either; it was a pregnant possibility which the set of firms made possible with their efforts spanning a decade. The change in control structure or the governance around an asset seems then to precede the rise of novel products. Is it anticipatory as well, which strategic foresight can provide? This is a key insight that managers pursuing increasing returns may take note of. Structures of authority, boundaries of property rights and generation of novelty seem intricately tied up.

We are calling this sharing of control over an asset as 'severalties of property rights' or variegated nature of property rights—where several different owners of an asset piece would exist with significant say (or voice) over deployment of the asset, transacting with each other. Property right discourses generally have talked about the cash flow rights around a property. However, control rights around it seem, from our narration above, to be even more important. In our case above, the structure of the business corporation acted as deterrence to increasing return. Release from the interlocked asset structure prevailing within the corporation opens up a potential frontier to increasing returns. No wonder information now would become crucial to expansion into increasing returns institution. Strategist's role in the current age then is often to restructure in such a manner that one's power is hastened and increased within a milieu that provides increasing returns. Corporate structure has been exercising decreasing returns agglutination or interlocking and consequently is a limiter to increasing returns based expansion on the scope direction. The other aspect which follows from the first is to note that the newly autonomous holder of the asset brings in a novelty—the asset newly formed is not the same as that which was lying inside the firm, because it is now linked to other assets in novel (or hitherto unknown in practice!) ways. The nature or the quality of the asset changes. Readers may think of the difference between the software of Fujitsu as an internal tool and that of Cadence as a widely used tool in terms of what each seeks to optimize.

Decreasing and increasing returns contexts change the mode of strategizing or the basic mechanisms of 'how a win is sought', which would have been clear from the discussion above. However, we explicitly bring out a few key differences below.

- Decreasing return contexts provide stability—the returns sought are in most cases not of the jackpot type; it is close to a rent-like return—there are no significant surprises. Strategy, therefore, concentrates on deterrence to prolong the rent-like stream—to sustain a vantage position or a favourable bundling of assets. Competitors seek strategic parity and copy asset architectures or processes—the emphasis is on balance of power. The deterrence exercised over current competitors, as well as future potential entrants, is a counter, or insurance, to a sharp fall in returns. The motive is closer to risk-aversion. Stability is desirable. Increasing returns contexts, in contrast, searches for jackpot-type returns, while the downside can be a total failure. Profit realizations have a speculative nature and surprises are common. Profit positions, therefore, cannot often be anticipated well. The motives are closer to risk-taking. Increasing returns also has potential for runaway success, which creates monopoly positions difficult to counter. Rivals thus concentrate on creating the next wave, so to say, through introduction of and attempted domination in the next generation product. Rivalry has a killer dimension in the current market and keeps a close eye on inter-temporally evolving future market. Product lifecycles are usually short and an envelope of product variations each with short life and desires for global dominance in the current market is generally observed.

- ○ *Rent and profit*: With a short digression, it may be worthwhile to explicate the sense in which this account treats the difference between rent and profit. First, both refer to a financial surplus—in accounting parlance, both would be called profits. In differentiating between rent and profit, we attempt a focus on the difference in dynamics of generation of the surplus. Rent arises out of a scarcity of certain resources or assets, such as, say, a piece of agricultural land. Understanding of rent and its distribution is derived from the mapping of the current state of affairs. Scarcity refers to this current state, and strategy seeks to preserve the current structure in order to preserve the rent implicit in the current state of affairs. Profits, in the specific sense we use it here, refers to the dynamics of change. Surpluses rooted in the acts aimed at manoeuvring of the dynamics of change, such as, say, the gradual appreciation of the value of a novel product, would be referred to as profits. It would involve work on creating new institutions, new forms of contracting, and new relations (or altered relations) of transactions. Its uncertain, temporally evolving, often speculative nature is what is emphasized. Our discussion in the book would often refer to this specific sense of difference between rents and profits.

- While decreasing returns contexts emphasize the firm as a unit of strategizing, since most moves can be conceived at that level, increasing returns need to consider the wider network with much greater salience; moves are played, won or lost in the network. Firm strategizing has to take a more socialized form. The ability to drive collaboration within the ecosystem is vital. Market making is the key, since a novel differentiated product or a process would often require institutional structures to support transactions. When, in contrast, the market is made (and the broad institutional structure is in place!), acts of managers often are more limited in searching for efficiencies in the current market and preserving the current market and its supporting institutions through deterrence. Decreasing returns prevail then.

- Conflict strategies in decreasing returns industries often lead to growth races or capacity races to preserve strategic parity. Power is wielded mainly around ownership of fixed assets or in preservation of the current institutional structure through cooperation with regulators, banks and powerful nodes. Increasing returns moves, however, seek to open up the current institutional structure and shake up the inertia of existing asset holders—innovative contracting, imagination of novelty, and so on, becomes important. These aspects, therefore, command property right like status, often dwarfing the rights exercised by fixed asset holders. A star scientist or an innovative legal counsel in Silicon Valley can get significant ownership control by contributing to participation in the labour process, something which a labour process participant in a fixed asset intensive decreasing returns setting (say cement plant) cannot think of.[21]
- In terms of property rights, increasing returns contexts demand a more complex structure. Severalties of property rights, mechanisms of sharing of rights, contingent contracts and other modes of sharing control predominate. In decreasing returns contexts, the emphasis is on the deterrence exercised through property rights (deterrence to copying through a patent, say!) and a more bundled right is usually preferred. Increasing returns mode would usually seek unbundling at different points.
- Decreasing returns contexts emphasize commoditization, while increasing returns contexts emphasize differentiation or the cultivation of uniqueness, a departure. Commoditization in decreasing returns contexts not only refers to the commoditization of the product, but also of the processes of production—the labour process[22] or the management process (or the business process in contemporary times). Contests in such areas often would take

---

[21]Such practices of granting property right to skill holders also exist in several clusters in India. A tradition called *kashtakkoottu*, practiced in Tirupur, allows an expert worker to partner (minority stake of 10–25 per cent, say) in a new venture with erstwhile employer by contributing his participation in the labour process, that is, without any fund contribution.

[22]A commoditized labour process contributor can only get the ruling time-rate compensation and would not enjoy significant control rights over the labour process, while an expert with a non-commoditized (at least partially) skill would command a category premium over a pure time rate. In case of some stars, such as in films, they become indispensable in the labour process and offer an example of extremely differentiated labour process participation with astronomical compensation.

a growth perspective rather than a profit perspective as quantities commanded would become important (such as oligopolistic capacity races). Such strategies are supported by a growing organization size. Increasing returns stances might forego the growth path and might prefer more profitable lean stances, might be more speculative and embrace risks as several venture capital (VC) funds do—restricting asset portfolios and funds to small sizes. But such stances seek limited control rights or access rights over assets held by several other asset holders in wide networks.

We argue, therefore, for two kinds of typologies of strategies—based on the intent and based on the nature of 'return dynamics'—whether it presents increasing or decreasing returns. We argue for this because the fundamental desire that drives the strategy moves changes as we move across these categories. So, a clearer delineation of the categories of what is sought sharpens the strategy discussion.

1.10 A SUMMING UP: CLARIFYING OUR ARGUMENT

To recollect, we argued that strategy is driven by the desire to seek power and governance over others in a milieu—it seeks dominance. Milieu, we said, is a useful construct to think of strategies, since power is felt and executed in a milieu populated by different actors with whom the acting strategist is in relations of power. Strategies are conjured up and executed in this milieu seeking to redefine the relations of power. This redefinition often takes the form of changes in institutions; tinkering and subversions of institutions are common therefore. While the understanding of the broad environment (that can be transparently observed by all) is important for strategic decisions, a careful reading of the milieu, which is often a private insight of a strategist, is important in driving through a successful move. We emphasized the rich details of the milieu, with respect to the motives of the actors and the institutions of practice. Finally, we linked this emphasis on the milieu with the argument that strategy typologies need to note the difference in motives that propel strategy action. So, a strategy seeking a relation of dependence with the winner needs to be distinguished from one that seeks the absolute leadership of a winning position. Informed by a reading of the milieu, we can have a more nuanced discussion on strategy.

While discussing and clarifying our stance on 'strategy' and 'strategist', we distinguish ourselves from the mainstream texts on strategic management on the level of analysis (or unit of analysis). The focus of the analysis of mainstream texts is usually at the level of 'firm' whereas we argued for a significant role of the individual strategist (the acting subject) at the core of conceptions of strategy. In our story, the strategist leader, his/her cohorts, allies and possible defectors in rival institutions constitute a more plausible unit of analysis. Our discussion would not get restricted with the 'firm' as the quintessential unit of analysis. We would instead move in inter-firm networks, formal or informal groups, and so on. The modern day industry dynamics involves a large number of collaborations, joint ventures, alliances, spin-offs, subsidiarization, business networks, socio-political networks, cartelization, mergers, acquisitions and many more—understanding these would need us to be flexible. Business families controlling groups of firms, as distinct from shareholders of firms, remain an important constituent of contemporary business. Hence, analysing with 'firm' as the unit of analysis remains just one among several levels at which strategizing may be thought of, appreciated and understood.

The second distinction we made was between increasing and decreasing returns contexts and how the strategy discourse changes as we move between the two contexts, leading to a change in how we approach issues of contracting, property rights and governance, and on how risk articulation happens—whether risk aversion or risk taking is the dominant driving motive of the strategist. While strategies in decreasing returns context target a rent stream and a prolonged life of such a stream through acts of deterrence, increasing returns contexts take the strategist to a world where surprise, speculation and jackpot-type profits are important. Decreasing returns emphasize commoditization, while increasing returns emphasize creation of differentiated assets; novelty becomes important. Our typology, we argue, is superior to that offered by Michael Porter in the classification of generic strategies—where he stresses the difference between the cost leadership and differentiation stance. The central driver in the Porter scheme is cost of the product—where a significant level of standardization of processes, equipment and the final product leads to realization of economies of scale[23] and standardization—driving down costs. Non-standard processes or product variety, in turn, induces a rise in costs and such a stance can only be sustained by creating a differentiated consumption space (such as through branding, advertising, and so on), where the offering is not looked at as a standard mass product anymore.

The Porter classification scheme, we argue, is an extension of the Fordist manufacturing philosophy, which has been disputed by several post-Fordist discourses as well as the practice of firms such as Toyota. (See Womack, Jones and Rose [1990] for an account on lean production.) For instance, with increased flexibility of machines, low set-up and equipment changeover times and (or) costs, coupled with flexible management processes it is possible, as shown by Toyota, to introduce huge variety in product specifications, at no extra cost. The Fordist position depended substantially on non-flexible equipment, which is not as much of a binding constraint today. Flexible manufacturing has enabled mass customization, where extreme differentiation in product specification can be managed without significantly altering underlying cost structures. Such costly flexible manufacturing equipment with large capacity would require high throughput, but not product standardization. So the dichotomy between low costs of a standardized product pitted against the higher cost of producing a differentiated product is not a foundational difference; it is mediated by the capital equipment structure which can change.[24]

Moreover, specialization literature (and the increasing returns dynamics linked to it) shows that reduction in costs often can be achieved by developing specialized assets and variegated property rights around such specialized assets, rather than through a concentration on standardization of processes and equipment that at its core is a commoditizing process. Porter formulation, moreover, misses several perspectives and possibilities—such as the economics on information that lies unnoticed in a production system or the problem of transaction cost—elements

---

[23]Economies of scale arise when the cost per unit of good/service falls as capacity of the production (or size of operation) increases. Often, it is the advantage of starting 'big' (say, Reliance Petroleum Refinery in Jamnagar) or becoming 'big' (say, Gujarat Ambuja Cements Limited). Scale economies often become important because large businesses retain a cost advantage that can be passed on as power prices or realized as higher surplus that can finance investments to sustain or enhance a firm's dominance.

[24]Readers interested in the detailed economics of flexible manufacturing can refer to Pine (1993).

that the contemporary economics literature emphasizes to a great degree. In fact, it would be possible to show that a pure commitment to a Porter cost leadership stance (in designing of production and management system) can actually lead to a high-cost production system if information and transaction cost[25] aspects become important. The experience of Toyota (which we discuss in some detail in a later chapter), in particular, has called to question several of the Fordist assumptions and results, disproving the economics of standardization through invoking transaction cost and information elements.

Our categorization, we argue, is more foundational, since it derives out of a difference in the underlying economics and leads to two different types of motives of the strategist. It is also consistent with new insights from economics of information and transaction costs, which is becoming important in several contemporary contexts. We also believe that the fundamental problem facing a strategist today is to get out of the trap of commoditization—not only in products, but also in processes, including several senior management functions nowadays. Our account, in contrast, provides a significant space to concerns of novelty and the generation of differentiated assets as a key strategy concern. A differentiated product, or more importantly a novel product, requires market-making activities. It requires new contract structures, and other institutional support mechanisms that under-grid the specific market. It is only then that it can grow. Such market-making is essentially an inter-firm process and significantly a social process, where a strategist has to take note of several non-firm institutions and act on it. Our engagement with increasing returns is motivated by this concern. Several contemporary experiences, such as in Silicon Valley, have succeeded by making differentiated asset building possible, while in other cultures, such as India—generally thought to be backward—interesting forms of contracting and organization (or governance) prevailed in spaces such as film-making in Bollywood or in multi-intermediated trading channels or in clusters of knit garment producers in Tiruppur. A few instances of such practices we have tried to articulate in the text that follows. Weaving of a strategy

---

[25]We would discuss later, in greater detail, the concept of transaction cost. Briefly, however, it refers to the cost of overcoming the possibilities of opportunism through design of a costly mechanism to monitor rules and preserve the sanctity and boundary of the property rights amongst transacting agents. Several economists argue that transaction costs rather than production costs constitute a more important component of Gross Domestic Product (GDP)—more than half by some estimates.

story with economics of information and transaction costs along with the traditional reading of 'economies of scale' driven economics of fixed assets provides a new possibility that we explore.

1.11 THE ROADMAP AND PLAN OF THE FOLLOWING CHAPTERS

We begin our discussion in the next chapter by articulating the notion of assets. A strategist, we argue, has an abiding interest in assets, particularly its valuation dynamics over time. Assets, we argue, are institutionally valued, that is, the governance relations of an asset piece with other adjacent assets drive its valuation. Asset values thus are relational and stand only as a system, each supporting the other in a mesh of transaction that remains under governance. The interest of the strategist in asset value thus gets tied up with the interest in governance and institutions that tie up the asset piece with surrounding asset pieces. In contemporary times, especially in increasing returns contexts, we argue that a strategist not only remains concerned with own assets, but increasingly takes an interest in other assets and extending governance or extracting partial rights over such assets. We identify several types of assets that differ with respect to different dimensions such as the nature of rights over the asset, how it is shared and the dynamics that is at the root of its valuation. A few asset types we discuss include fixed asset, common pool assets, shared club or network-based assets, modular assets, star assets, differentiated rules or institutions as assets, and so on. In each category we explore how the specificity of the asset type leads a strategist to design governance around the asset accordingly. We explore several dimensions of joint governance of assets and coordination (and its institutional mechanisms) across several asset holders that drive valuation of assets.

In our next chapter on organization, we articulate a notion of organization as a field of contested power that retains a balance between several nodal power holders. We depart from the notion of a coherent organization—or organization as a homunculus—arguing instead in favour of a reading that provides primacy to the fractures and ruptures inside the organizational canvas. Organization structure, we argue, essentially represents such a balance of power. Episodes of restructuring, several of which we describe, can then be viewed as an attempt to seek a new balance of power by negotiating new boundaries and relationships between the multiple organizational nodal power holders. We also argue that organization can be viewed as a particular mode of exercise of governance driven by executive authority, quite distinct from governance through markets based on contracts, based on price-based competition or on relational assets in inter-organizational networks. Executive authority inside the organization in executing a change remains constrained by the balance of power represented by the existing structure of the organization. Restructuring seeks a change therein. Restructuring as a dynamic process of negotiation enables us also to visualize relations with extra-organizational nodal power holders that an agenda of internal restructuring might take support from.

In our chapter on markets and regulation, we argue for an institutional view of markets—showing how the underlying rule structure in a market is crucial to its ability to transact. If markets are rule based as well, then we argue that regulation cannot be seen as a simple constraint on business. We interpret regulation as rules emanating from an executive authority in different socialized institutional spaces, including that of the government (or State Power). An institutionalized view of business looks at a continuum of rules then—from rules that underpin the market to rules emanating from government bodies. Different sites of generation of rules enjoy different jurisdictional ambits and differ with respect to the dynamics that drives rule formation and/or contests over it. We describe two ways of looking at regulation—one as a countervail to the dominance of a business arising from an executive authority and the other as providing differentiated institutional support that enables a novel product/technology to distinguish itself (such as through institutional labelling of genetically modified [GM] food or organic food) without conflation with other adjacent categories of, say, products. In describing markets, we distance ourselves from the mythical demand–supply driven descriptor and argue instead for three different types of markets—a market as shaped by interconnected inter-organizational contracts that transact in differentiated products/assets that are specifiable (where contract crafting and enforcement provides the governance), a Walrasian market of standard products that clears based on prices (where price competition provides the governance) and a thick network market that transacts in highly differentiated and uncertain assets—such as that in film production (one can think of star actors' engagement in a film project)—where governance is based on inter-temporal assets such as trust or reputation. This distinction enables us to have a finer differentiation of the governance under which a transaction occurs and given the primacy of governance in our narration of strategy, the descriptor of different markets links up to a strategist's concerns.

Our final chapter on the institutions of finance argues that a strategy story in the contemporary world cannot be narrated through an understanding of the product market and what a firm seeks therein. Contemporary financial systems (and intermediaries) are characterized by their ability to centralize large swaths of savings that in turn makes them the major source of external funding that a firm relies on to pursue its growth and investment objectives. The deployment of finance comes along with governance that the financier wields on the firm. The firm strategist has to take note of that. Contemporary financial space represents several and highly differentiated governance across its several nooks and corners, primarily through separation of cash flow and control rights attached to the proverbial unit of financial resource. This differentiated governance makes it imperative for the strategist to understand the institutions of finance, since it is no longer a question of just access to financial resources that linkage with the financial milieu provides. Financial milieu instead provides the governance that would drive the organization. Reallocation and restructuring of control rights, unbundled from cash flow rights around finance, constitute the basis of most contemporary financial engineering and new instrument designing. We explore two different dimensions of governance by the financial milieu—one that progressively commoditizes and/or generates pressures for commoditization (or standardization) of assets and the other that supports the generation of differentiated assets on an increasing returns mode.

Discussion across the chapters weave around the linkages among the (*a*) the property rights to an asset that a strategist enjoys including modes of sharing with others, (*b*) nature of the asset, (*c*) governance sought through design of organization and institution and (*d*) governance imposed by the financial milieu. They all constitute an interrelated set of issues that together constitute for the strategic actor the domain of action. Strategic acts, as we argued, in seeking a 'win' or a grasp over power, attempt a preservation or a subversion (and creation of alternative) of governance structures. This interest in governance ties together the interest in assets, organizations and institutionalized markets. Novel assets often require novel organizational forms or new inter-organizational coordinated governance, new types of financial governance, and so on. We illustrate such linkages at several places in the narrative that follows.

2

Strategy and Assets

2.0 INTRODUCTION

Assets are very important in a story of strategy. In fact, to conjure up an image of a strategist without simultaneously thinking about assets that the strategist commands is well nigh impossible. How does a strategist think about assets? One can think of a firm owning a large cement plant that would require limestone as raw material. Would the cement plant own the assets of the limestone mines or just gain some kind of access right to that asset? Can such preferred access rights to limestone assets (in the form of a contract or a paper asset!), in turn, be treated as an asset, when, say, the cement firm goes for a merger and acquisition (M&A) deal? In this chapter we attempt an engagement with that question. One way to look at it is to get back to our argument developed in the last chapter on the formation of 'nodes' for exercise of power—control over assets provides such a lever, for it leaves open several possibilities of denial of access, or access at reasonable charges (or price), or provide different shades of access to other 'nodes' in the milieu who would be holders of several other related assets.

In this chapter, however, we will deal with another set of issues—issues that are not often discussed adequately in the mainstream strategy literature. We argue that a strategist with a control right or a 'voice' over an asset piece has an abiding interest and an obligation as well in raising the value of the asset (especially in a dynamic environment).[1] Failure to preserve and enhance the value of the asset would expose the strategist to attacks from elsewhere, even to a loss of the property right granted. Evidence from the practice of law and regulation (such as on patents) provides ample instances when a prior property right is negated or its boundaries redefined. Similarly, businesses would throw up several instances where a decaying asset undergoes a change in ownership or a change in its governance. An asset perspective, therefore, also searches for the intent of the asset holder—including the temporal dimension—that is, how long does the asset holder hope to hold on to the asset and enjoy it (so to say). Distinction or differences in intent on this temporal dimension, that is, difference in the length of time over which an asset holder wishes to hold on to the asset, would lead to differences in stance with respect to the asset. An ephemeral interest in the current value of an asset would differ substantially from an abiding interest over a longer time horizon (that can even span across several generations) in asset value. Acts that would be sub-optimal from the first perspective might make great sense from the second one or vice versa.

What we seek to emphasize here is the notion of the obligation of the asset holder in preserving/enhancing asset value—in contests with other assets, of course. This contest is most crucial since it is at the root of valorization of certain assets and devalorization of other assets—a dynamics that we continuously witness in the pragmatic life. This dynamics is played out over time—over a temporal horizon. Strategy concerns cannot then be framed in any static framework—such as the neoclassical frame that is both a-temporal and a-inertial. This immediately raises several questions? What would be regarded as assets (see sections 2.1.1, 2.1.2, 2.2.4 and 2.4.1) and how would such assets get valued, especially in relation to other contesting assets (see sections 2.1.3, 2.1.4, 2.2.3 and 2.4.6)? How can strategy influence such a valuation process (see sections 2.1.4, 2.3.1, 2.3.4 and 2.5.7)? How does the valuation of an asset depend on its relationship with other related or complementary (adjacent) assets (see sections 2.1.5, 2.2.3, 2.2.6, 2.3.5 and 2.4.6)? Is valuation of an asset a function of such mesh of relationship with other assets—that is, can an asset stand on its own or does it essentially stand in relation with other assets (see sections 2.1.5, 2.1.6, 2.2.6, 2.5.1, 2.5.7 and 2.5.9)? Or in other words, does the valuation of a related set of assets in an ecosystem depend on the architecture of the relations (see sections 2.1.6, 2.2.1, 2.3.1,

---

[1] A few property right theories take an 'obligation stance', rooting private right (in the sense of design of a social contract) in such obligations of the right holder.

2.3.3, 2.5.1 and 2.6.1)? Can such architecture be understood as a mesh of governance relations amongst several assets or, in other words, is it useful to visualize assets as part of network of assets linked through particular (and specific) relations of transaction and governance with the network (see sections 2.1.6, 2.2.3, 2.3.4, 2.4.2 and 2.5.6)?

How are novel assets generated (see sections 2.2.4, 2.3.2, 2.4.1 and 2.5.8)? What are the different modes of asset generation or governance and which mode would a strategist choose, either to generate a novel asset or establish governance over a related asset (see sections 2.2.5, 2.4.2, 2.5.3, 2.5.7, 2.5.9 and 2.6.2)? Is it best to establish an asset under shared governance as a common pool asset, as a public asset or as a closely guarded proprietary asset (see sections 2.3.2, 2.5.1, 2.5.2, 2.5.6 and 2.6.3)? If a shared mode is preferred, what would be the rules of sharing of control and voice—that is, the specific governance (see sections 2.3.1, 2.4.6, 2.5.3 and 2.5.7)? More importantly, are there several kinds of assets that we have to deal with, each with distinctive traits requiring different types of management intervention (see sections 2.2.1, 2.2.3, 2.4.1, 2.5.1 and 2.6.1)? In the first chapter, we located acts of strategy in the domain of governance and tweaking of extant governance. In focusing our analysis on the relational dimension of assets in this chapter, we attempt to bring in the institutional dimension of asset and its valuation (see sections 2.1.6, 2.2.5, 2.4.3 and 2.5.9).

To the extent this account is useful, it provides a way to linkup strategy as toppling of governance and the abiding interest of an asset holder in enhancing the value of assets owned (see sections 2.1.3, 2.1.4, 2.3.2, 2.5.8 and 2.6.3). If value of an asset lies in the relational dimension, i.e., in its relation with other assets, it opens up possibilities of visualizing strategic acts as subversions of 'institutions of practice'—which provides the anchor for extant governance and relation between linked assets (see sections 2.3.4, 2.3.5 and 2.5.7). Several related asset holders would also constitute the strategic milieu, defining the arena of action of the strategist (see sections 2.2.6, 2.3.5 and 2.5.9). An understanding rooted in an asset view then can weave a story of enhancing of wealth—a major concern of a strategist (see sections 2.2.5, 2.4.1, 2.4.6 and 2.5.6). We discuss these issues and develop certain unique characteristics of a few types of assets that are becoming important in contemporary times. In particular, we stress the fact that exercising governance over own assets is no longer the only agenda of a strategist while leading a firm (see sections 2.1.1, 2.3.3, 2.5.5 and 2.6.2). Governance over assets lying elsewhere, unbundling and stripping of related assets, influencing valuation of assets and its properties or (various) qualities, deforming 'inter-asset-category boundaries'—all are important activities that a contemporary strategist needs to be open to. Such concerns, however, require a language that can distinguish between asset types and provide a framework to describe the valuation of an asset as a function of its relation with other assets. Before we begin, however, we discuss in some detail how our account differs from the 'resource based view' of strategy arguing why an explicit discourse on assets provides added insights not provided by a perspective that bases itself on the notion of resources.

2.1 ASSETS AND STRATEGY

2.1.1 Assets or resources—A clarification

A strategy narrative generally takes a resource perspective, more so within the 'resource based view'; so, the resources available and the resources that a strategy can leverage upon are often discussed. We make a distinction between 'resources' and 'assets'. The notion of a resource implicitly depends on its representation as an input in a production process that would consume it. Iron ore reserves would then be seen as a crucial resource for an integrated steel plant working on the blast furnace route. An asset, in contrast, has attached with it a notion of lasting value—along with the value of an asset comes simultaneously the question of its durability—a period, so to say. While iron ore may be viewed as a resource, a contractual right, such as a lease to an iron ore mine that provides access to the resource, would be an asset. Asset, thus, has a life. It has a birth and a death and a period over which its value may increase (or accumulate) or decrease. The process of the birth of an asset or its death or its changes in valuation over time can then be of interest and our focus of analytics. Clinical insights of practicing doctors, such as a cardiac surgeon, generated through experience of treating patients over a long period of time, generates an asset (skill or a knowledge asset) that has an accumulative character. Production systems also have similar 'process knowledge assets', often materialized in specific idiosyncratic routines or loose frameworks and beliefs shared among the workmen that lead to 'economies of learning by doing'. It is also accumulative in nature—with costs of production falling with cumulative production volumes. Such cost dynamics are important in industries such as semiconductor fabrication. In some cases, however, assets would decay over time—as with most physical assets that decay with use and lose its productive life. One may think of physical plant and machinery.

A discourse on resources, thus, takes an interest in the fleeting current moment—the current market of the resource, so to say. Analysis is essentially static—a description at a point in time. Assets, on the other hand, would force us to take a dynamic view, since our interest would be in a 'period of time'—the movement of the asset over time is of consequence to us. Assets also would need to simultaneously invoke the notion of control over it—over its use, over its disposal, and so on. It thus links up with our concerns with governance. Assets and resources thus provide two perspectives—two different vantage points from which to engage in an enquiry on strategy. The two vantage points generate and raise different sets of questions and concerns.

The resource-based view works on the notion of value of a resource from the strategy perspective rooted in its non-substitutability, inimitability, scarcity or rarity that enhances its rent producing value—making it the source of a sustainable rent-stream that lasts over a period. The notion of a rent and the notion of its period of sustenance are two pillars of this perspective. This concern with a sustainable rent is what drives a deterrence motive as we argued in the first chapter (see section 1.9). Most accounts of resource-based views have not provided any understanding of how rents are derived, except for linking it to scarcity of some sort—to say that it is derived in a market is to remove beyond the frame of analysis the modes of working of the market or its institutional moorings. Strategic action often shapes up the rarity of a resource—its demand often is an outcome of the acts of strategy. Moreover, is rent preservation the sole purpose of strategic action? In practice, creation of new markets, forging new links between unlinked markets and between different assets seem to be occupying the minds and time of leaders of organizations. We show through several instances how an approach to look at assets in relation to each other (or other assets) provides a way of engaging with the institutional specificities of a market. In our example of the mining lease contract, an asset perspective would prompt the reader to look at the clauses and conditions of the grant of the lease, possibilities of effecting changes in some of such conditions and contractual obligations. The asset exists through an act of creation—possibly by a government (or sovereign) entity; its nature, thus, can be changed as well. The asset immediately has to be thought of as linked to several power holders and other assets held by them. Is not valuation of the asset related to such details the reader might get to know upon enquiry? So, compared to the valuation of a resource that occurs in a mythical market, the asset view grapples with valuation in an institutional market, with its specific rules and governance that also defines the linkage and relations with other assets. Thus, the asset view forces governance to the centre stage of analysis. It also allows us to engage with and understand the role of several assets that do not enjoy a market; yet, practical sense tells us that they are most crucial to a firm's success. The asset view that we adopt provides us these twin advantages. In this sense, an asset perspective may provide fruitful insights for strategic action.

2.1.2 Swimming through resources market or to act strategic?

From another perspective, if we have to talk of 'resource', then we have to simultaneously invoke the concept of a 'resource market'. Without a market, resource as a concept category has little meaning. Different properties of a 'resource' are due to the market—the price, different quality characteristics (such as expert Java programmer or black belt Six Sigma expert) are set in the market that spans across several firms. A strategist leading a firm, therefore, has no say or voice over such a resource, except to get access at a price that is set in the market. This cannot be the source of a strategic advantage, say in an organization, particularly if the resource market is in equilibrium. An organization might benefit by hoarding resources that are scarce or by effective bundling with other resources through an organization-internal process. In both cases, note that the organization then subverts the market—either by restricting the mobility of a resource or by lending it qualities (synergies with other resources), through an organization-internal administrative fiat, which the general resource in the market lacks. This enhanced quality of the resource (or its transformation into a particular form or quality or expertise) would not find a market (or in other words, the added specialization gained inside the organization would not have a market value, at least until a separate category of that specialized resource is created in the market after several organizations diffuse in that specialization, but by then the unique advantage of the organization as a holder of the specialization is gone!). Notion of an asset, however, does not need to ponder about an asset market. Several forms of assets that do not have a market—in the sense that a price-clearing market does not exist—can be easily handled within this perspective.

In contrast to resources, assets usually invoke the notion of control along with it; a connotation of voice remains—so, several other variables other than price and quantity can be focused upon. For instance, a resource perspective would look into listing in NASDAQ as seeking access to financial resources (quantity and price are what would come to the reader's mind), while asset perspective would also help us understand it as a move to build reputation assets, allies as assets (such as influential market makers of NASDAQ due to presence of highly influential investment banks such as Goldman Sachs). The listing would also bring in new forms of governance that would transform how the owner–manager of the organization may look at their company and share control with other key stakeholders. We can also focus our attention better on the organization-internal process that bundles resources—is such bundling capability an asset that can be codified in a business process design and possibly be outsourced? Or, would an organization choose modular assets or contrarily prefer integrated and intermeshed modes of interlinkage between multiple firm-internal assets? We would argue later how this may constitute a crucial pillar for redrawing of organizational boundaries.

'Resources' and 'assets' bring in different focuses to what we discuss. A 'resource' perspective emphasizes linked markets of several resources through which signals flow relatively unrestricted. The task of a strategist then is to gain control over (or hoard) scarce, inimitable resources and gain a rent therefrom. Asset view considers markets to be deeply institutional with several nodal power holders often attempting to preserve of the status quo or the current institutional arrangement. Signals flow between markets only to the extent that institutional arrangements allow for such flows. For an overwhelmingly vast category of transactions, the strategist has to contend with the specific institutional rigidities of the market. Dealing with nodal power holders or 'acting strategic' then becomes crucial.

2.1.3 Valuing asset through relational strategy

We proceed by describing a saga of conflict over telecast rights related to Australian rugby—a narrative that brings out several dimensions of how assets get valorized in a network of related assets, how asset holders share control and governance over assets and how actors often seek deep changes in such modes of governance as an integral part of a strategy act. We interweave the narrative with short pointers that highlight certain aspects that shed light on our theoretical discussion regarding assets and its valuation.

Readers may think about the deep changes that television brought to

> **CASE STUDY 2.1** The Australian Rugby League (ARL)—Contest over control and access to assets
>
> Rugby was brought to Australia by the New South Wales Rugby League (NSWRL) in 1908 when NSWRL organized the first club competition in Sydney. Over time, the league became a national league with teams from beyond Sydney joining in the league. In 1995, it was a 20-team competition. Telecast of rugby league matches started in 1961, with different channels taking turns to telecast matches. In 1990, the Australian Broadcasting Corporation (Channel Two) received rights to telecast matches for three years. In March 1994, through a series of agreements between NSWRL, ARL (of which NSWRL is a member) and Channel Nine (controlled by Kerry Packer), granted exclusive telecast rights on both free-to-air and pay-television, to Channel Nine through Optus Vision till 1999. Rugby league, over the years, had become extremely popular and was the most watched television programme in 1994, with Sydney ratings hovering around 46.7 (up from 17.3 in 1982). Sports had a special significance as an event and as a programming asset for television channels. It had a character of 'now-ness'—the excitement over the uncertainty of outcome of a contest gave it a character that was distinct. Unlike soap operas or films, whose consumption could be postponed, sporting events hooked television viewers to the 'live telecast'. Sports appeared to valorize television broadcast as a form of entertainment compared to other entertainment forms such as cinema theatres. It was a key asset then for broadcasting firms.

the sporting assets—such as a league. It redefined the audience beyond those in the stadium and made the telecast rights the major revenue source that outstripped the revenues from gate-collections and on-site stadium-based revenues. Television broadcast infrastructure, apart from the arena of the sport—the stadium—became crucial. A new set of stakeholders started taking interest in the game, gradually transforming it into 'big business', and sharing control over the sporting assets. If the telecast right of a sporting asset is considered as a derivative asset, does this asset—the 'telecast right'—have a market? How are telecast rights awarded? Is it a pure price based auction type system? In most cases, readers would realize that it is not so. The governance mechanism of the league organizer—say the Board of Control for Cricket in India (BCCI)—that awards the contract would be crucial. Several types of barter exchanges may influence such awards—dealmaking seems to be a better descriptor than bidding for such transactions.

2.1.4 Valuing through governance reform

The Australian Rugby League (ARL)—Contest over control and access to assets (contd.)

News Limited, the rival to Channel Nine (and the Kerry Packer controlled media group) was thus shut out of the telecast rights in the rugby league and it hurt its interests in the Australian pay-television channel Foxtel. News Limited had become a sponsor in January 1994 of the Brisbane Broncos—a team in the League. Brisbane Broncos, through another associate company, brought out a proposal for organization of a 'rival league'. *In the new league, an independent management structure different from that in place through the NSWRL was proposed.* (**An attempt at governance reform!**) Deliberations over two months led to a final August 1994 document christened 'Super-league', whose main points are noted below:

1) A company named 'Super-league' owned by News Corp was to be set up, which would establish an elite national competition (including New Zealand) between 12 privately owned teams, 4 of which would be based in Sydney and the rest in other cities.
2) Super League would conduct an internationally televised World Club Series, involving teams from Australia, New Zealand and UK.
3) News was to obtain 15 per cent management fee from Super League, and profit share allocated to clubs it owned among other benefits. News could own upto 4 of the 12 teams. ARL and NSWRL would conduct tests and retain profits from these matches, and would be given a grant to promote the game.
4) Super League would devise revenue from sponsorship, gate takings, merchandizing, free-to-air and pay television rights. The company was projected to make an operational profit of USD 5 million in 1997 that would rise to USD 12 million by 1999.
5) One stated objective was that 'no other competition should exist in competition to Super League. For success of the initiative, cooperation of a few clubs was required and cooperation of players was essential.

NSWRL and ARL, in response to the threat, forced the execution of a Commitment Agreement with the 20 clubs in the League that would prevent clubs

(Case Study 2.1 contd.)

(Case Study 2.1 contd.)

from participating in any competition not approved by ARL/NSWRL. At a meeting of club representatives and ARL in February 1995, Kerry Packer informed that Nine Network had contracted rights until 2000 and legal action would be taken against any club that failed to honour their commitment. Clubs that did not agree to sign the Commitment Agreement were threatened with suspension. By February end, the Agreements were in place with all the clubs.

News Corporation evaluated the options. What they had earlier hoped was a kind of cooperative reform where the new league could work with ARL/NSWRL and seek changes in the governing body; but the strong determination of Kerry Packer to defend the contract rights made a cooperative reform almost impossible. An aggressive stance of organizing the rival league in defiance of ARL/NSWRL would require substantial financial commitment, mounting a legal challenge and setting up, through a series of contracts, a mechanism that would minimize the liabilities of the players, coaches and others who decided to shift to the new Super League.

News Corp. entered into contracts with several coaches as a first step—with a large signing fee. The coaches supported the Super League approach and tried roping in players with salaries in excess of what they currently earned along with some amount of sign-on fees as a reward for the commitment to a risky new initiative. When the legal challenge mounted by News Corp. came up for hearing towards the end of the year, more than 300 players were already contracted with the new Super League.

The core of News Corp. legal challenge was that the Commitment Agreements signed with the clubs by NSWRL were unfair trade practices, since the NSWRL had taken advantage of their power in the 'Rugby League Competitions Market' to include provisions that had the effect of deterring or preventing competition by making it difficult for a competing league to be established. The position of ARL/NSWRL was that the attempt at establishing Super League was an attempt to destroy the existing competition by unlawful means, including a breach of fiduciary[2] and contractual obligations. The

(Case Study 2.1 contd.)

---

[2] A fiduciary is someone who has undertaken to act for and on behalf of another in a particular matter in circumstances which give rise to a relationship of trust and confidence. A fiduciary duty is the highest standard of care at either equity or law. A fiduciary is expected to be extremely loyal to the person to whom he owes the duty (the 'principal'). He must not put his personal interests before the duty, and must not profit from his position as a fiduciary, unless the principal consents. The word itself comes originally from the Latin word *fides*, meaning faith, and *fiducia*, meaning trust.

(Case Study 2.1 contd.)

filing claimed that the relation between ARL/NSWRL and the clubs was that of a fiduciary, and defection by the clubs amounted to breach of trust. Eight rebel clubs (of the 20 in NSWRL) also filed cross-claims arguing that the Commitment Agreements were null and void since they were made to sign it under duress.

In support of their legal position, ARL/NSWRL immediately made certain changes. Optus made commitment of funds that enabled an immediate raise in the salaries of players; Channel Nine secured its interests by requiring ARL/NSWRL to take its consent should any change be made to the format or frequency or other features of the competition. It also got an extension of its exclusive rights to the league for another five years.

News Corp., on the other hand, entered into contracts with clubs to indemnify them of any liability that might arise out of a breach of their contract or the Commitment Agreement with ARL/NSWRL. Clubs, in return, agreed to field the best possible team in Super League and release players from the purpose. Through its extensive multinational television network, News Corp. also made the Super League part of a set of global sporting assets that dovetailed with each other in terms of their schedules and audiences. In 1995, News group entity British Sky Broadcasting (BSkyB) struck a five-year television deal with Rugby Football League in Britain for £87 million that included a provision for creating a European Super League and switching to a summer season. The European Super League was designed to run alongside the winter season in Australia. It also isolated ARL by specifying that Great Britain could play Super League opposition team at the international level with clubs from European and Australian Super League (ASL) meeting in August to contest the World Cup Challenge. The Super League was thus linked to a global set of related sporting assets and its valuation got affected as a result. The set of coordinated asset pieces were valuable for a global television broadcaster.

As holders of the crucial broadcasting asset that can enlarge the market (and, in other words, demand) of each of the different leagues, News Corp. had the ability to negotiate changes in schedules of key leagues (which obviously faced opposition from the traditionalists!), forging the coordination that created a synergized set of sporting assets. Each of the leagues thus became an element in an integrated sporting bonanza that would be telecast across several geographic markets. The change in valuation of each individual sporting asset lay in such reconfiguration achieved through the coordination by News Corp. Would such coordination have materialized without the television interests that drove News Corp.? What would have been

(Case Study 2.1 contd.)

(Case Study 2.1 contd.)

the alternative sources of power of such hypothetical coordinator to drive through the change?

The legal challenge took dramatic turns. The lower court ruled in favour of ARL/NSWRL, substantially damaging the possibility of holding the Super League. However, an appeal to a higher court overturned the decision in favour of News Corp. The Court upheld the claim of restrictive trade practice. The Court also felt that the relation among players, clubs and ARL were not in the nature of a fiduciary relationship, since changes in the 1980s had all led to incorporation of clubs, ARL and NSWRL as companies limited by guarantee. The League had considerable contractual power over the clubs and could pursue an independent interest as well. This tight control was found to reinforce the absence of mutual trust and confidence considered characteristics of fiduciary relationships.

The legal position on 'fiduciary relation' was untenable mostly as a result of changes in form of incorporation of the leagues and clubs as companies and independent legal entities—shifting from the member-based organizations that they were earlier. The changes were effected through the 1980s in the Australian rugby scene, after television rights brought in new sources of funds into the sporting events and a new set of stakeholders took interest in the leagues. Readers may note that in another domain—stock and commodity exchanges—such changes were effected over the last decade reforming exchanges into corporate entities from member-based mutual benefit organizations. As a contrast possibly, you may note that BCCI in India is organized as a mutual benefit organization of the state-level cricket bodies. International Cricket Council (ICC), the international body in cricket, is similarly organized as a mutual benefit organization of the member country boards.

The legal victory enabled News Corp. to go ahead with Super League in 1996. By 1997, however, both ARL and Super League faced considerable losses. Television ratings of rugby leagues, however, increased substantially. In June 1997, ARL announced its resolve to work towards a single competition and a deal was reached between ARL and Super League to form a merged 20-team competition in 1998, consisting of 8 Super League teams, 11 ARL teams and another new Melbourne team. The renamed National Rugby League was to be run as a 50:50 joint venture (JV) between ARL and ASL. The gradual reduction of teams to 16 in 1999 and 14 in 2000 was agreed to. This happened in the backdrop of massive losses in the Australian market experienced by both Optus and Foxtel and the approval of programme sharing arrangements between Optus and Foxtel in 1997.

2.1.5 Asset ecosystem—restructuring value through control

The narrative above brings out several dimensions of an asset-based perspective. The business interests of News Corp. in getting access (telecast rights) to the sporting events required it to engage in deep processes of influencing the governance of several other related asset holders. In fact, the aim of the intervention of floating a rival league was governance reforms of the league so that a more friendly system of allocation of telecast rights could be driven through. The asset of the telecast right also lacked a classic market that could price it competitively. Moreover, several questions as to how long should an exclusive licence to telecast be were also crucial. A long exclusive contract would essentially mean that the loser would be shut out of access to this most important programming asset for a long period. The aim of News Corp. was achieved through an agreement to share programming between the rival channels that was agreed to by the league (ARL).[3] The readers, we hope, would appreciate how deep the requirement is of a strategic actor to take interest in governance of related assets.

Another dimension of assets is the issue of control over assets and the question of duration of commitment over an asset. A crucial question from a reading of the sports-media saga seems to be the question of how an asset holder commands power over a set of related assets—both to hold them together (the television channel and the league would have, for instance, an interest in ensuring the retention of fair play, of continued uncertainties in the outcome of each game and the tournament, and hence might want balanced teams; an interest that might be in conflict with short-term interests of a team that would like to hoard all best players!) and to effect changes in its governance that suits its business interests. The question then seems to be how an asset holder becomes the *key* in an ecosystem of related assets. Is the money value of asset or its size the most important factor? Does the period over which an asset holder is committed or contrarily hostage to a sunk-asset important as well?

---

[3] Readers may also appreciate why in markets such as that of telecom equipment supply (large concentrated deals), winner-takes-all competitive bids are not held. All bidders get some order volume with the winner getting a larger share. Bidding decides the price, but not the quantity. Does the existence of such bidding systems generate incentives to cartelize? Possibly, yes. Yet, one would realize that winner-takes-all kind of bidding is impossible to organize.

We try and describe the different asset holders within the contemporary sporting ecosystem. Table 2.1 summarizes the different asset holders and the nature of their assets.

2.1.6 Structure of property rights and asset value

As is clear from Table 2.1, there is intense interdependence amongst all asset holders in jointly generating the game and the resultant fan-following around the game. It appears then that different asset holders have interest in the game over different horizons. Media is a key gateway (and an aggregating node with nodal power)—as it is through the media that the bulk of the revenue (often 75 per cent) flows to the sporting ecosystem. They exercise a crucial power of denial, and by connecting particular sporting events, in preference to others, might influence the fate of a sporting event. In that sense, for the sports administrators, it is also a crucial ally as they look at expansion of their own sports in contest for viewership and revenues with other sports. But media has a fleeting interest—one that can switch at relatively low costs compared to other asset holders in the ecosystem. Would excessive media control be good for the game or is the existence of the countervailing force of the clubs with a build-up of strong reputation asset a better option? Readers would realize that the structure of a particular sporting ecosystem would depend also on linkages that allow one to influence or deter other asset holders. While the powerful media could reform certain governance practices in the ARL, in India attempts by the Zee media group to take on BCCI by organizing the rival Indian Cricket League (ICL) after failing to get telecast rights to the valuable cricket games in India did not make much headway.

After ICL was launched in 2007, BCCI suspended the players who signed up for the rival league. Pension of former cricketers (seniors) were stopped, younger cricketers (juniors) were ruled out of selection in the national team, ICL was disallowed use of any stadium controlled by the member state cricket boards, BCCI-certified sporting goods producers were disallowed to supply to the teams playing in ICL, and other national boards were also asked to prevent their players from participating in ICL. Although the Monopolies and Restrictive Trade Practices Commission of India initiated a *suo moto* investigation, no formal case was launched against BCCI's practices. BCCI launched its own league and ICL petered off, failing to get sponsors or viewers. It appears then that the formal and informal relations amongst the asset holders determine who would be the key

Table 2.1: Assets in a Sporting Ecosystem

Asset Holder	Nature of Asset Held
Media	Interested in the derivative right (telecast right) to the game. Investment is for short durations shaped by time periods over which telecast rights are awarded; can replace a particular league with other sporting or non-sporting asset.
Sponsors	Interest fleeting; audience size draws sponsors; investment over limited sponsorship tenure.
League/Sporting Body	Long-term interest in the game, often controlled by people outside the sports. Interest often determined by tenure of office holding and the nature of the contest for positions, say in a regionally federated system, regions often would vie for control of the central offices. Former sportsmen often play a role in governance, with varying degrees of effectiveness in guarding the interests of the game. Contemporary trend is to have the leagues and sporting bodies organized as corporate companies rather than member societies, as is the case with the BCCI.
Sports Infrastructure	Often under the control of league or sporting bodies; sunk investment in fixed capital; dispersion and quality of infrastructure determines the pool of players in waiting.
Teams	Sunk investment in reputation and fan following, often with fan clubs and strong regional following—club reputation leads to monetization of the game and is valuable to media as well.
Players	Sunk investment in expertise; long-term interest in the game. In many cases, are organized in strong player organizations that engage in collective bargaining for protecting and influencing player contract with clubs or sporting bodies.
Coaches	Sunk investment in expertise; long-term interest in the game. In games where clubs are strong, coaches play a greater role in forming the team. Perhaps, players (or networks of players) also have coach allegiances.
Betting Organizers	Being legal in several national jurisdictions, betting organizers provide a clearing centre or a market for betting by dispersed speculators. In countries where betting remains illegal, several underground circuits control it.

Source: Authors.

asset holder—as an instance, one may note that BCCI strongly controls all contracts that lead to monetization of the game, while in the case of the English Premier League, clubs control several of those assets (through sponsorship rights) and in other cases, share revenues with the league organizer.

To summarize, therefore, we argue that an asset perspective brings out into focus the aspect of control very directly. In cases where assets do not have clearing markets—which is true of most assets—it provides a clearer articulation of concerns of a strategist. Clearing markets, to recall, refer to deep markets where a large liquidity exists (on demand and supply side), so that demand–supply changes are adjusted or matched through price changes (refer to Chapter 4 for more detailed discussion on several types of markets). We now shift gears with the hope of having convinced the reader about the utility of adopting an asset perspective. We detail below several different types of assets—an underlying theme being how nature of assets and the governance that aids its growth are intricately linked.

2.2.1 The notion of fixed assets

Traditional accounts would give primacy to fixed assets—as the dominant form, in many cases the only form, of asset that a firm or a strategist commands. Organizations were built around lumps of fixed assets. One can think of plant and machinery in a capital-intensive manufacturing process as a lumpy fixed asset. A fixed capital determined the boundary with another lump of fixed capital representing the other organization, or in other words, ownership over two such plants determined the boundaries of two different organizations. Sunk or fixed capital has been assumed to represent an irrevocable commitment—a strategic commitment.[4] The sunken nature of the asset ties the asset holder to the asset piece for a prolonged duration of time—and this represents an irrevocable commitment. This irrevocable commitment gave the holder of the property right over the fixed asset the right to enjoy the residual (that is, the left over after fulfilling all obligations of fixed payments) of the organization. Everything beyond the contractual obligation (say interest costs)

---

[4]At the same time, several varieties of working capital items did not represent an irrevocable commitment (i.e., they were not fixed). The commitment of such working capital remained limited by contract with working capital providers (say, bankers or trade partners or a financing company).

would, thus, belong to the residual right holder. Such fixed capital was the shock absorber of all risks, bundled together, of risks inclusive of uncertainties that the organization failed to measure or prognosticate at the beginning when it was started. In other words, a business firm could not know beforehand several types of risks and uncertainties and there was no market to buy and sell such risks. Therefore all such unknown and unknowable future risks were bundled together as a sum of capital that would remain as the bedrock of an organization. The returns enjoyed by the fixed asset 'owner' could also be seen as compensation for taking up all such unspecified risks. Even though the fixed asset in most cases remained financed by external bank type funds, the ownership over the asset and the risks of operating the asset, including the risk of capacity utilization, lay with the equity owner.

The primacy of fixed assets, however, must be relative to other categories of assets. We bring out two categories of assets over which fixed assets established its primacy. One was the asset of the labour process participant—the skill of the worker, the musician or the actor, or that of the expert surgeons who would perform a knee-replacement or a cardiac procedure. The other category of asset holders was the different kinds of risk bearers—such as the debt provider. Unlike in a traditional trading circuit (say of silk weaving in India), where the debt-holder would take up several risks and enjoy several rights (or influence) over the production process (and in that sense it was not like a pure bank debt contract) such as over choice of raw material or designs and techniques of weaving, the debt contract of a modern corporation would allow the debt-holder (typically a bank) extremely circumscribed rights under, say, conditions of bankruptcy alone. Contemporary business dynamics show, however, certain novel phenomenon—with respect to both these asset categories—so that the absolute primacy of the fixed asset is increasingly under question. We take up each of these two asset categories and discuss in some detail the underlying theories and concepts along with hints of how the relationship with fixed asset holders is currently under flux.

2.2.2 Skill and creativity of labour process participant as an asset

Generally, labour process participants, in the quintessential description, would only get a wage. It can be a current market wage rate or, in some models, a wage schedule indexed to capture increases in productivity of labour in a kind of deferred compensation mode. The skill holder would, however, lack control rights over the deployment of skills—and the traditional wage contract gives the control right to the use of labour power (or skill) of the skilled worker to the owner of the fixed asset in lieu of the wage compensation. The relation of the skill holder to the fixed asset owner is, therefore, bound through a contract, and in uncontracted states of affairs, the right of the owner prevails. The skill holder bears no risks and cannot enjoy any surprise profits that are not contracted for. This arrangement implicitly reduces labour processes of the skill holder to a state of a commodity—or in other words, it must not have uncertainties or properties that cannot be contracted for. It also need not have an individuality—a special property, such as the idiosyncratic skill of a 'star actor'. The resources (human resources here) must be homogeneous and hence replaceable.[5] This construct of homogenization and smoothening coupled with limiting the ambit of the labour process participant to strictly describable contractual states, removes all uncertainties and risks from the labour process, concentrating it on the holder of the fixed asset, who has then unchallenged control rights to ensure a non-deviant participation in the labour or production process.

The classic Fordist manufacturing system was a manifestation of a state of affairs just described. Ford Motor Company, at the turn of the 20th century, built the celebrated mass production system, concentrating all stages of production in a large vertically integrated factory. This increased the fixed asset capitalization substantially—generating a possibility of economies of scale. The significant 'sunk cost' then drove top managers to concentrate on utilization of assets, speeding up the assembly lines, reducing idling times of men and machines so that the potential scale economies is realized in practice through high capacity utilization. Design of management system (such as through Taylor time studies) sought to enforce discipline on the labour process participants. The moving belt of the conveyor of the mass production system provided a tool—work schedules had to be kept in tune with the speed of the belt. The work process was standardized, systematized, commoditized,

---

[5] Please note the similarity of this stance with several mainstream management thoughts that concentrate on how to create a 'system' such that performance would not suffer if the individual is replaced. Implicitly, it means that the individual cannot have a unique property or characteristic which would be highly valuable to the production system.

routinized[6] and substantially deskilled—offering the possibility of exercise of control by senior management through rollout of scientific techniques (of production planning) to ensure what mattered to the economics of production—capacity utilization (of the fixed asset) and increasing the pace of work so that the costs of production could be reduced.

Now one can relate this to the generic strategy classification by Michael Porter, particularly the *cost leadership* strategy, where you seek to reduce the cost of the product to its barest minimum. A Fordist design provides one way to realize such low cost systems. The argument is: high fixed costs as sunk cost; standardization of product; standardization of each process; simplification of work tasks; deskilling of workforce; vertical integration of supply chain to have control over a high-throughput system; effective control over standardized processes; realization of significant economies of scale through intense coordination; and hence, low cost of product. The Ford assembly line did succeed in bringing down substantially the cost of a car, making it almost affordable to the US worker of those days. It also paid workers more, but workers on the line had to give up control over the labour process, which they enjoyed in the craft-based production system. Even with higher wages, worker turnover was notorious in the Ford factories and absenteeism rampant. While the money value of wages was an important issue, what was more important was the issue of control of the work process—an aspect that is not often realized. Although the Fordist workplace design, in its pure form, hardly exists today, its effect in terms of influencing the underlying logic in design of modern systems, particularly in what we called *decreasing returns* contexts, continues.[7]

2.2.3 Differentiated rules and autonomy as asset

What are the pitfalls or risks of this model or the logic? Can design of low-cost systems be consistent with umpteen product varieties, significant customization and vertically fragmented production

---

[6]It was made repetitive and the attempt was to move to the optimal routine; perfected through repeated acts of doing. Learning by doing and economies of accumulated production volumes relates to such sources of perfection of routine through practice. Readers may also find it interesting to read through the memoirs of Henry Ford. It would provide a reading of the dominant thoughts of those times.

[7]Please see section 1.9.2 for details on decreasing returns context.

systems—features that are very un-Fordist in character? In particular, would differentiated products with umpteen variety necessarily be costly and be sold at premium prices, or in other words, can variety come with cheap costs? If you have noted, the logic of scale economies derives from the lumpy 'sunk cost' of fixed assets. Before we discuss some of the other costs that the argument above neglects, it might be important to underline the fact that in the scheme portrayed above, the worker or the skill holder is seen as a resource and not as an asset. The Ford–Taylor concept of organizing a large 'scale-economy' driven organization was fairly dominant in the US; but elsewhere, particularly in Europe and Japan, there remained powerful dissenting voices that shaped up production systems in quite different modes. In Germany, the discourse on *facherbaiter* (skilled worker) remained quite strong as a lingering cultural heritage; so, a deskilling of the workforce was not seen as a feasible or worthwhile option. We provide an illustration of this through a narration on computer numerical control (CNC) technology development in Germany.

CNC technology development in Germany

Imagery of the *facherbaiter*, along with a fairly strong institutional power of the professional skilled worker through the guilds (and the famed German technical schools), led to a very interesting mode of technology absorption with introduction of CNC machines in the early years of automation. While in the US, the CNC technology development sought to replace the worker or substantially deskill them (commoditizing the labour process in a bid to make it amenable to control), in Germany, the development—at least amongst a small minority—took a different route. CNC was seen more as a prosthetic device—one that extended an inherently human capability, the machining skills of the worker—rather than replacing the skill.

Design of the input interface of the human–computer system was structured differently; unlike the programmer as the input provider (in abstract programming languages) in what was called the offline mode, in Germany several innovative interface designing enabled workers to input data into the CNC system on the shop floor through interfaces such as record–playback system in what has been known as the online mode. The interface consisted of a number of sensors that tracked the workers' movement of the machine tool

(Case Study 2.2 contd.)

(Case Study 2.2 contd.)

> as he navigated using his machinist skills to produce the prototype. Existing skills of the worker could now be translated into the new modes that the computer system required to hasten computation. The historically accumulated skills could interact with the new technology; it was an extension rather than a replacement or redundancy of the old skill, therefore. By pushing down machine input into the lowest level, it reduced costs of operation, while the dependence on worker skills led to lesser requirement of control systems.
>
> Online CNC machines initially found a market among Small and Medium Enterprises, who required cheap, flexible automation, while the growth of flexible manufacturing, even among larger firms, led to a few key innovations of the online technology development stream to get assimilated into more mainstream CNC industry. With the rise of flexible manufacturing, US CNC machine industry almost collapsed while German and Japanese producers moved on to dominate the global industry. The intent of the guild—an important node of power in Germany—in preservation, reproduction of the worker skills, and reinventing its relevance along trajectories of technology developments was surely crucial in development of this alternative mode, which eventually benefited mainstream technology development as well.[8] The cultural construct of the *facherbaiter* sensitized German engineers to a discourse of expert workers, quite unlike the push towards deskilling that was the core of the Taylorist[9] articulation in the US. The cultural imagery was supported by institutions that had a 'voice' and, through the technical schools, could produce a stream of innovations that assimilated technology developments rather than reject it.

In Japan also, firms such as Toyota designed production systems that did not accept several implicit assumptions underlying the Fordist model we described. The successful entry of the Japanese into the US that led to severe loss of market share of the dominant US firms in the pillar industries of transport equipment and electronics sounded the warning bell. As years of study by Western scholars, looking for sources of the famed Japanese process efficiency, revealed the organization of the

---

[8] Interested readers may look into the works of Klaus Ruth for more detailed accounts.

[9] Taylorist systems emphasized simplification and break-up of work into small tasks that could be exactly specified and executed with little expertise. Control over the labour process would thus get enhanced. Expertise always leads to a problem of control as governance over an expert becomes difficult.

Japanese production, it became clear that the Japanese model leveraged, in a unique way,[10] several assets that the typical Fordist system would undervalue or not pay any heed to. We offer below a case in point using Toyota's shop floor experience.

Shop floor governance in Toyota Japan

Although several features of the Toyota Production System have been widely studied, what is of importance to us here is the mode of governance of the shop floor at Toyota. Work and interrelation between workers are highly scripted in extremely detailed 'operating procedures' that have to be followed rigidly without any deviation at Toyota. In spite of such rule-bound rigidity, however, Toyota does not become a 'command-control system'. It is able to retain the character of a learning organization.

In fact, many observers characterize it as a community of scientists carrying out several small experiments simultaneously. The design of the operating procedure is the key. Every principle must find an expression in the operating procedure—that is how it has an effect in the domain of action. Workers on the shop floor, often in teams, design the 'operating procedure' jointly with the supervisor through a series of hypotheses that are proposed and validated or refuted through experiments in action. The rigid and detailed 'operating procedure' specification throws up problems of the minutest kind, while its resolution leads to a reframing of the procedure and specifications. This intertemporal change (or flexibility) of the specification (or operating procedure) is done at the lowest level of the organization, that is, closest to the site of action. Workers, therefore, have significant control rights over the design of work rules that allow worker skills and ingenuity to continuously search for novel micro-solutions around micro-information that often stick to the local micro-context of the work/machine.

One implication of this arrangement is that system design can no longer be rationally optimal and standardized across the organization. It is quite common to find different work norms in contiguous assembly lines because each might have faced a different set of problems and devised different countermeasures to tackle it. Without such variations allowed, right of the worker

(case Study 2.3 contd.)

---

[10]Significant movement along the learning curve reducing costs was also achieved through wastage and defect reduction!

(Case Study 2.3 contd.)

> in design of work rules would have made very little sense. Design of the coordinating process that essentially imposes the discipline that is required in large-scale complex manufacturing systems is therefore customized to variations in man–machine context of the site of action. It evolves through numerous points of negotiation throughout the organization. It implies then that the higher levels of the hierarchy do not exercise the power of the fiat in setting work rules, for such work rules are no longer a standard set across the whole organization.
>
> What is the tool of governance that replaces or compensates for this loss? Do the numerous engagements in negotiations throw up information through the negotiating channels? Is this information richer, in some sense, and can this serve a governance purpose? Under what circumstances would you expect the Toyota kind of design of work rules to deliver superior results compared to the standardization paradigm of a Fordist system? While you ponder over it, it might be interesting to go through the basic Toyota philosophy that underlies its system designing practices. The notion of the ideal production system in Toyota embraces the following:
>
>> ... the ability to deliver just-in-time [or on demand] a customer order in the exact specification demanded, in a batch size of one [and hence an infinite proliferation of variants, models and specifications], defect-free, without wastage of material, labor, energy or motion in a safe and [physically and emotionally] fulfilling production environment.
>
> It did not embrace the concept of a standardized product that can be cheap by giving up variations. Preserving consumption variety was seen, in fact, as one mode of serving society. It is interesting to note that the articulation of the Toyota philosophy was made around roughly the same time that the Fordist system was establishing itself in the US automotive industry.

2.2.4 Risk as key to asset

The description of the Toyota system can be looked at from various perspectives. The pushing down of decision-making to the lowest level can be seen as a mode of sharing of risks with participants in the labour process (the skilled worker and the worker teams). Instead of a standard rational work rule design bearing the entire risk, several decision-makers manage an interrelated set of micro-risks. This mode helps under conditions of increased uncertainties—such as when extreme product variations are encountered or the production conditions undergo frequent or unforeseen changes. This risk participation and the 'voice' enjoyed by the skill holders implies that the Toyota mode of engaging with production workers attempts to assetize their expertise through continuous redesign of the 'operating procedures', which is an organizational asset cumulatively built up. Asset control then goes along with risk bearing on the asset, including its valuation and changes therein over time. Expert workers do not enjoy a financial right—such as setting a price to the skill or independently contract for jobs like a film star would do—but he (or she) exercises control over the work process inside the firm in the shop floor. This is akin to retention of individuality, often in small production teams, for the skill-holding worker. The skill is thus assetized.

Let us go back to the description of the Fordist system with which we began. As we noted earlier, the cost calculus of the argument concerned mostly material costs and costs of fixed assets—the plant and machinery. What other costs would be important? Our argument, for instance, did not consider the cost of monitoring. While standardized work practices (or systems) can be designed to deliver optimal results, actual performance of the system would depend on how well the systems would be followed. This takes us into the domain of governance. We cannot assume that rules would be followed as a matter of course or, in other words, there would be no opportunism—possibilities of deviation from rules, even sabotage of rules and processes. Rules (or even property rights), therefore, would need to be enforced and this would introduce what the contemporary economics literature calls *transaction costs*.

2.2.5 Transaction costs

Accounts of several contemporary economists give primacy to transaction costs—it possibly is a more important category of costs shaping economic outcome than even costs of material or of pure production. Conceptually, transaction cost refers to the cost incurred in getting over the problem of opportunism in exchange and transaction between different economic actors. It is like a cost of governance. Such costs may leave an accounting trace, but it may be in the nature of an opportunity cost as well—the cost of options and possibilities foregone, which does not leave an accounting trace. Opportunism, however, must not be seen as a problem with a moral pang! It also represents an innate characteristic of individuals to resist a complete acceptance of governance. Slippages from governance require opportunism.

Opportunism and strategizing both emerge from dissatisfaction with the current modes of governance. While strategy seeks to overturn the current governance, establishing a new order, so to say—and in that sense, it is an act that seeks to grasp power and is quite ambitious—opportunism represents a fleeing (in a rather surreptitious way!) from the ambit of the arms of governance. Both preserve the space of the individual. For the property right holder or a rule setter, opportunism of the other agents is a problem and the property rights holder or a rule setter has to incur significant cost in protecting the rule or the property.

Consider a patent. Every patent holder must expect litigation on the patent, especially if the patent is potentially of high commercial value. Since patent would establish a monopoly claim over a knowledge area, others not enjoying the monopoly would contest such a claim and jostle for redefining the protected area. A few might also engage in infringements. Enjoying the patent right would, therefore, require the holder to invest in litigation, monitoring of potential infringements (carried out surreptitiously!), monitoring of patent claims of adjoining knowledge areas and litigating (or often infringing) rival's claims, and so on. All this together represents the transaction cost of the property right that a patent offers. While the above description talks of costs that would all leave an accounting trace, more important are transaction costs that are in the nature of an opportunity cost. Suppose design and eventual production of a novel product requires multiple patent holders' consent to the use of their patents and they fail to agree to a mutually acceptable sharing mode—either in terms of cash flow or control rights—the investment in the product market may fail to take off. The system bears no cash costs but opportunities are lost or not acted upon. This dimension of transaction cost is more important.

The transaction cost position argues that every transaction is open to problems of opportunism whether carried out inside a firm or organization under the governance of the internal administration (or fiat!) or between different entrepreneurs or organizations in arm's-length mode, either in contract-based mutually dependent position (as in automotive component and sub-assembly supplies) or in anonymous exchange like markets or in more familiar networks where transacting parties engage in repeated transactions or share a dense social space.[11] This opportunism must be overcome in each mode of governance of the transaction. In fact, one way to understand institutions or modes of governance is to try to evaluate the transaction costs under each mode of governance and search for the mode that offers the least transaction cost solution. Innovative contracting to induce mutually dependent specific investments is often an important strategic act that allows cooperation.

Contemporary accounts often differentiate between static and dynamic transaction costs.[12] Static transaction costs refer to opportunism in repeated and stable transactions. It refers to transactions that are stable. Dynamic transaction costs, in contrast, refer to opportunism in coordination with processes of change, such as investments on novel products that would involve several change processes across several agents/firms in an ecosystem. It refers to transactions that are in a state of flux and concerns relations between transacting parties during such periods of flux. Transaction cost theme in the contexts of choices of vertical integration and network modes is taken up in sections 2.3.2 and 2.5.1.

2.2.6 Assets dispersed through the organization

Invoking the possibility of opportunism in the Fordist description now would complicate the simple story. Standardized rules need enforcement. What is its cost of enforcement or the transaction cost? While the Toyota system, through the grant of partial right in rule-making to the skilled worker, allows the local (sticky) information to influence rule formation, a standard rule regime in a Fordist system does not heed such

---

[11] As a thought experiment, just think whether our own opportunism changes as we move between different social contexts—such as our workplace organization or our extended family or the ethnic community network. Have you seen extremely irresponsible people at your workplace take up huge burdens of responsibility (and execute it with élan!) in other community contexts? How would you explain such multifaceted behaviour? It seems we wear several masks—quite contradictory to each other.

[12] The work of Richard Langlois, among several others, emphasizes this aspect. Langlois' work on economic history has attempted a revisionist historiography that has re-examined the efficacy of arguments on scale and scope from a framework of dynamic transaction costs, often disputing the received understanding. The concept is best articulated in Langlois and Robertson (1995).

micro-information. Such micro-information, thus, are not assetized in any way. Is this a significant opportunity cost? Does the Toyota mode lead to potential increasing returns through effective learning and novel transformation of rules of coordination?[13] Would a standard rule enforcement—that implicitly undervalues the creative capability of the skilled worker—be prone to greater subversions and hence encounter higher transaction cost, such as through greater quality problems or higher defect rates or lower ability to react fast to novel demands?[14] The classic Fordist mode and that followed by Toyota represent quite different routes to realization of a low cost production system. This difference is not captured well in the traditional Porter classification of generic strategies.

In light of the above discussion, you might ask several questions. How common is the Toyota kind of shared governance modes? In organizations that you know, how is the performance measurement system (the Key Performance Appraisals [KPAs], for instance) devised? At which points in the organization are such negotiations held? How dispersed and numerous are such negotiation points? What would be the cost (in terms of time and managerial coordination efforts!) of devising such elaborate and variegated systems as an outcome of a multitude of micro-negotiations? How are such micro-negotiations different from more general 'suggestion schemes' inviting proposals of improvement from employees that are widely prevalent? Returning to our theme on assets, the Fordist kind relies on the primacy of fixed assets—which bears all risks and enjoys control rights exclusively—while the Toyota kind of systems try to gain governance over a distributed asset base (of encapsulated and differentiated micro-information) of several asset holders within the organization. So, governance systems are designed on a shared basis to provide access to the dispersed asset base. This shared mode, however, means a loss of exclusivity in rule-setting and a loss of control weakening

---

[13]Please note that the Toyota philosophy does not call 'novel rule propositions' a solution since there is no finality. Each proposition is a countermeasure to a problem faced—its worth, therefore, relates to the problem and is always open to rebuttal, either in the face of a new problem or through a fresh insight. So, new rule designs cannot be ex-ante anticipated and the scope for surprises remain. This 'falsifiability in practice' institutionalized through the rule-writing method is a key to understanding the Toyota system as a 'learning system'.

[14]Automobile manufacturers with a higher capability to quickly change model-mix in terms of the total output stands to have higher capacity utilization—when total demand (quantity) remains stable but inter-category shifts are more frequent and unpredictable.

the organizational 'fiat';[15] how does organizational power then get exercised under this new context of shared governance? We will return to this theme in our chapter on organizations.

2.3.1 Markets of risk and asset and slipping primacy of organizational fixed assets

We argued earlier that the notion of primacy of fixed assets denied control rights to several other kinds of risk bearers and working capital participants. In a traditional trade circuit, traders (such as traders in silk weaving sector) by extension of credit—as a working capital facility—would have obtained control over a distributed set of dispersed producers, sharing several risks and enjoying an influence over several important production variables. Such arrangements would have a wide range of risk–reward sharing modes, say from a situation where the artisan would own the fixed asset (or tools) required for production to situations where he/she would work on fixed assets that would be leased out by the trader.

The 20th-century notion of equity and its sharp distinction from debt, however, differs from such old notions of capital. Equity capital, mostly invested in a fixed asset mode, enjoyed residual control and took up all uncontracted risks. Debt from the bank provided a large volume of financial resources, with limited rights of the lender under bankruptcy. The equity holder, as the bearer of the risk, thus leveraged access to bank debt to enlarge the investment volume. In such a regime of firms with single owners leveraged with bank-based debt investment, organizations/firms remained the unit of risk bearing and it was indeed sensible to narrate a story of strategy based on firms as units. It was also backed by the legal system—such as banking and financial regulation and tort laws of liability (such as product liability) that was built on the firm as the basic unit for liability assignment. Such simple states of affairs, however, do not exist today. Contemporary financial innovation in creating several kinds of intermediate instruments has blurred the sharp difference

---

[15]Several workplace ethnography studies have indicated this concern for control as a central driver of workplace governance designing. Solutions that potentially can provide greater profits can be scuttled because of loss (or perceived loss) of control of key groups (such as middle managers) over the work process. Old literature around automation and several contemporary accounts on Business Process Reengineering (BPR) type of initiatives would bring that out.

between low risk debt and risk bearing equity. Debt and equity remain two end points of a continuum of hybrid instruments. Along with this is the rise of several risk markets which has introduced the possibility of unbundling of risks that earlier lay, with the holders of the equity alone (since no one else was there to share/bear that risk).

Risk market and contracting: Case of Volumetric Production Payment (VPP) contracts

Let us consider the following contract known as VPP, which became popular during the 1990s in the US gas industry when gas producers were facing constraints on access to investment finance. VPPs were a popular way of financing oil and other mineral exploration in the US before the 1930s banking regulations almost made it impossible for banks to hold such instruments. A VPP was an ownership interest in hydrocarbons in place (in the ground) that entitled its owner to a designated share of production for a limited period of time or until a specific amount of hydrocarbons had been delivered. Under the VPP terms, the holder of VPP would pay the gas producer in advance for the entire amount of gas contracted. In return it got access to a predetermined gas volume, free from the risks of actual cost of production. In case of a bankruptcy of the gas producer, the interest of VPP holder would have precedence and would not pass through the bankruptcy process; instead, they would belong to the VPP holder who could operate the field and claim the contracted gas. Thus, reserves of gas were the main recourse available to the holder of VPP in case of default in supply of contracted gas by the producer. VPP, as an instrument, was neither an equity nor a debt instrument, in the sense that it structured the distribution of risks between the holder of VPP and the gas producer in a rather unique way that either a debt or an equity contract achieves. In normal course of business, VPP holders do not carry production cost risks or other operating risks that are borne by the producer. VPP holder has a fixed volumetric access to gas whose money value would fluctuate with spot gas prices and hence is a risky stream of revenue; gas price fluctuation risk thus lies with VPP holder. There were other contract types that were also common and were closer to the debt end of the spectrum. Gas purchase contracts gave the purchaser a right to purchase gas over a period of time at a fixed predetermined price, payments being made with delivery of gas. In case of a default, however, there would be no recourse except litigation or arbitration. Sometimes, gas purchasers inserted clauses that gave it a kind of first

(Case Study 2.4 contd.)

(Case Study 2.4 contd.)

> lien on gas produced so that gas needed to be sold to them before it could be sold to other customers. Prepayment contracts were another kind where the producer received payment for a fixed amount of gas. Buyers' interest was secured through the right to the gas reserves, which in case of bankruptcy could be exercised like that of a secured lender through the bankruptcy process. VPP differed from the prepayment contracts in that it was outside the purview of the bankruptcy process and hence was devoid of bankruptcy risk. VPP just bore the pure gas (fluctuating) spot price risk—making it easy to convert into a synthetic debt security that could be linked to a general risk index such as the London Interbank Offered Rate (LIBOR)—and marketed to a wide set of general investors, without the specific ability or regulatory approval to deal in gas-specific risks. Readers would have realized that under a VPP contract, the gas producer's equity no longer carries the traditionally bundled risks that it would have carried if exploration investment was internally financed or financed through pure bank debt type financing. Different types of risks—such as gas price risk, production risk, credit default risk, and so on—are each distributed uniquely across different agents (details of contracts from 'Enron Gas Services', HBS case No. 294-076, pp. 7–8).

2.3.2 Risk traded transformation of asset

The above instance shows how innovative financial contracting now can unbundle risks that traditional 20th-century notions of equity bore all alone. The existence of a market that trades in risks or risk-products also induces numerous such innovative contracting acts. In the discussion above, the ability of the VPP holders to convert the gas price risk based VPP pools to a general LIBOR-based security depended on the existence of a market for gas price risk, either in the form of a futures market that would trade in commodity gas price risk (standard contracts are traded in a futures exchange) or in the form of over-the-counter (OTC) markets where trading desks of risk specialists can write customized contracts and exchange risks. In fact, without such markets, crafting of a VPP to take away the bankruptcy risk would have made little sense and a classic prepayment contract would have sufficed. On the other hand, writing of contracts such as VPP and several other derivative instruments would not have been possible without changes in the notions of liability of the firm through regulatory changes in banking and financial sector—in fact, what kind of 'underlying' one can write a derivative on is a legal artefact as well. Let us not forget that much of contemporary derivatives market has opened up this possibility. In coming years, such markets will widen and deepen further. No wonder, with such trades becoming possible, it would be difficult to maintain the traditional separation of control between fixed assets and current/working capital type of assets.

The other force that has created pressures against bundling inside the organization has come from the process reorganization logic. Detailed mapping (often in digital forms) of business processes as well as our access to the very detailed transactions within the business organization through information technology based products/services has made such process assets codifiable and tradable across organizations. Readers may think of a cement plant—intensive in fixed investment, whose operations and detailed process control is driven by complex software and control systems built by firms that spun out of internal process automation teams of some leading cement firms. Recall our earlier discussion of the ASIC industry (see case study 1.9) and the rise of the toolkit industry (firms like Cadence) that provided digitization of the fabricator's process that is relevant for the customers to design the chipset. These process assets, digitized, often can stand on their own—quasi-autonomous of the fixed asset to which they need certain access rights at most. In many cases, significant aspects of operational risks (on different parameters of process performance) would be borne by the process assets rather than the fixed asset. Holder of the fixed asset and the holder of such a process asset then would engage in a form of shared ownership and control right. Several fixed asset intensive operations, such as that of a petrochemical refinery, has this deeply outsourced structure (such as refinery operations of Reliance Industries Limited). These unique process assets may be called 'singular' assets and it has its own markets. Tradability of such singular process assets can result in trading in 'irrevocable commitments' of the old style equity holder. These singular assets are no longer organization specific—they would belong to a genre and can be traded and valued in a wider market that would span across several organizations. What was believed to be the 'irrevocable commitment' built around the fixed asset investment by the equity holder (leveraged through bank based debt finance) now has a trading outlet.

2.3.3 Slipping organizational asset-based boundary

Our argument thus, in summary, is that the existence of risk markets and innovative financial contracting practices today make it mandatory to give up our notion of a strict organization/firm boundary. The basic act of bundling of risks in a firm's equity was the bedrock of the firm boundary and liability apportionment. That bedrock is breached today. Once this belief in and the necessity to define organization on the foundation of the fixed capital is blown over, there would be scanty little left to bind together thousands of business transactions that routinely take place within and that thereby define a business organization. We are admitting then the fact that business firm can possibly break down into thousands of splintered transactions or at least in dozens of business assets of different types. This immediately introduces the possibility of asset unbundling, which we already see happening in several instances. Unbundling requires relations (often forging novel relations!) with other assets in the ecosystem. From a strategy perspective, it widens the domain over which a strategist's influence has to run—it moves beyond the firm and must seek to influence and gain different kinds of access rights over assets held in the wider social space, in other organizations, and so on. A new imperative for networking thus emerges.

Years back, a typical M&A transaction dealt with the firm as a whole or at least one business division or a factory or at least a brand as a whole homunculus. Increasingly, transactions involve sub-homunculus level, where assets that earlier remained lumpy and bundled together can be unbundled. With abundance of information, especially on detailed processes, in the modern era, one can break up the sub-level into risk-categories or risk-weighted asset pieces, and trade takes place with peddling such pieces. In fact, one need not 'buy' a whole asset; instead, one might hold a piece for a while, or just gain certain control rights, implicitly admitting there is no 'owner', but multiple transacting parties can remain busy trading and defining and redefining risks that shape the contents and forms of assets. Typical of such breaking up of assets are visible in most of the recent M&As across the globe.

> The reorganization of the Reliance group affiliates over the past few years (2003–10), that is, in the post-Dhirubhai Ambani era, is a case in point (both Mukesh Ambani and Anil Ambani group firms). The break-ups, the frequent restructuring exercises and resultant demergers reorganize assets held in different firms and link them in ever new ways. It creates an opaqueness for the analyst of the firms seen as independent legal entities. Numerous interlinkages breach the boundary of the firm. This non-transparency at the level of the firm is driven precisely by a new transparency that the asset pieces inside the old firm now enjoy with respect to other asset pieces lying in other firms. Governance with the firm as the unit thus gets frustrated.

Often a private equity fund or strategic investor would ask for breaking up of the hitherto organic assets. Broken assets, as for example, in the recent case of ABN Amro (2009–10), are sold in pieces to different buyers. Ironically, there was apparently a strong economic logic of vertical integration and that of the M-form (organizing multiple businesses owned by a firm under separate divisions under a common corporate control), which now under the asset perspective has been challenged. Economic logic had argued that integrated assets would generate more value remaining together as part of one vertically integrated firm than under separate ownership. A dominant logic of organization, especially of a vertical firm, has been that multiple forms of assets—such as geographic marketing assets, brand assets, distinct manufacturing assets, back-office assets and similar others—delivered higher value and productivity when tied together under common ownership and common executive management. Contrarily, one could buy up process assets where a process asset would constitute a chain of linked assets cutting across divisional boundaries from a typical M-form (multidivisional) firm. As we move on, we will come up with a few illustrations on this aspect.

In fact, today it is possible to argue that the simple and robust organization was an accounting belief. In so far as one individual owned an organization and in so far as there was clear delimited rights to property, an organization remained separated from its neighbouring organization. However, almost all organizations have multiple owners today. Moreover, there are stakeholders who while not owning the organization as an equity holder could nonetheless own through, for example, labour process participation—through assetized skills that shared control rights. These skill holders also move around in a shared pool of liquid resources, highly mobile between different firms/organizations. Further, institutional investors and similar funds that often are owners, in turn, are owned by a mobile mode of ownership. In addition, the rise of several risk markets and markets for assets such as business process know-how (now digitized), organizational information, brands, and so on, create the possibility of asset trading of these organization slices. The boundaries of the organization, thus, remain breached in several ways today, requiring a successful strategist to take a network view—look beyond the firm/organization into assets lying elsewhere in wider networks and social spaces. That takes us to several other categories of assets. Contemporary strategy concerns, we argue, requires a rich asset perspective.

2.3.4 Shift of strategy to off-organization control

From the perspective of the organization, one can think that the homunculus corporation has acted as a shield to sub-corporate risks, which did not have autonomous existence except as part of the bundled corporate risk. One can again recall the argument with the VPP contract and the risk swapping operations described in case study 2.4 of this chapter. Without the specific risk markets, all such risks would have to be bundled as a corporate risk; while with specific risk markets, we can have the possibility of unbundling such risks from the corporate risk. The corporation stood upon a compounded risk and that compounded whole has been the fixed capital to the bankers and the accountants and to the debtors. This buffer of organizational boundary could thus define transaction cost and no wonder also the liability (as in tort) of all internal elements of fixed capital. This truncation at the boundary was also a limiter to increasing returns that were otherwise potentially available often to the internal members of fixed capital based business undertakings. Large corporatist denial to potentially lurking increasing returns could be effected through legal forms of ownership and of liability. The organization, as a risk bundler, then had to organize on decreasing returns principles. (Refer to section 1.9.2 for detailed discussion on differences between decreasing and increasing return modes.)

Uniqueness could not be valued highly when it required transactions with other assets held elsewhere (in other organizations) on an unbundled mode. Uniqueness created, in contrast, problems of governance inside the firm. Readers may recall the initial problems faced by LSI Logic, including the resistance to unbundling from the established leaders, when it started sharing software with customer engineers for ASIC designing, much against the then existing industry practice (refer to case study 1.9) Contemporary finance and the possibility of assessing risks of nearly all asset pieces or business processes including 'particular access rights as asset' have opened up two frontiers of increasing returns based institutions. Let us not forget that the homunculus represented limiter and was an effective bundler of risks or transaction costs. Movement away from the limiter would then potentially open up new types of transactions, new markets and sources of novel profits. The move away from firm as the institutional bedrock to the expanse of assets held institutionally is now very distinct. Strategists wishing to engage with this emerging asset space would need an understanding of the underlying institutional reasons for the inability of such increasing returns frontier to take shape earlier. Overcoming such limitations can then give a new lease of life to such assets that lie hugely undervalued. We provide below a short discussion of two types of such possibilities—two types of frontiers.

2.3.5 New opportunities through increasing returns-based assets

The first frontier of institutions based on increasing return appears to lie in the emergence of new markets based on the vast multitudes' unique assets, aided by emergence of new technologies of production, trade and logistics. One may ask why or how production in the trader-intermediated circuits—say in silk or handloom apparel weaving in India—did not need to organize workers in factories, and take a control right over governance of the labour process. In contrast, several small producers could retain control and be risk bearers in the production system. They remained micro-asset holders who could be connected to even global markets by intermediary organizations. The constraint that a vast number of unique assets pose is an exponentially increased cost of information and transaction. Uniqueness of asset does not allow formation of market transacting in a commodity of generalized asset. In the absence of homunculus-type corporate governor and given the fact that uniqueness limits the emergence of commodity-type markets, the networks and the syndicates offer scope to both increasing returns and stability. A strategist would add significant value to unique assets by way of providing network and multiple forms of joint assets and limited liabilities. Earlier we pointed to instances in the Japanese trading system's ability to allow certain layers of the multi-layered distribution system to take up specific risks (see case study 1.4). A network of agents then takes up different risks, unlike a corporate structure that subsumes all risks in a bundled form. We provide an illustration on ITC e-Choupal in case study 2.5.

In the other frontier of increasing returns based institutions, globalization of commodity happens and consequently global reach and global purveying assume importance. Microsoft Windows may be seen as such an example. In this case, quick variation of the nature of commodity, as for example in standards or in versions as well as in functions and quality, provide the competitive edge. Typical examples would include financial or insurance products, software, contents, and broadcasting or media including sports or leisure. Unlike commodity of the older vintages such as grain, antibiotics (which are standard products), cement or steel that remain stable products (in terms of specification or design or properties) for which volume is the key to strategizing, in the increasing returns institution, a commodity has a far shorter life cycle. Strategy for value addition would depend less on the ability to have stability (through institutional gatekeeping) and more on the capability to maintain a

CASE STUDY 2.5 — ITC's digital intermediation and e-Choupal

ITC e-Choupal, the procurement initiative from ITC, used digital intermediation to provide a platform for marketing of commodities with high index of variety proliferation. In India, as an instance, almost 120 different varieties of wheat get produced, quite unlike agricultural production systems in much of North America. The consumption space also remains differentiated in terms of the properties sought in the wheat product (such as wheat flour) across regions and also other dimensions of segmentation of consumer groups. ITC's information intermediated procurement platform allows it to map the supply side variety on to demand side differentiation. Control over information, often running across the supply chain, also enables ITC to offer 'traceability'—which is important in certain European export markets. In such cases, ITC takes up a limited liability, letting producers retain other risks. The information assets—or the procurement points of ITC—also operate as procurement markets and do not enter into contracts with producers. For a long time ITC has also been operating similar procurement platforms in tobacco—where it built up intermediate assets that could map the wide variety of tobacco crops produced in India into a variety of cigarettes, each of which had a standardized smoke property through blending of different varieties of tobacco. Several other e-commerce platforms, such as Alibaba.com, also provide similar instances (excerpts from Banerjee, 2005).

dynamics—in generating a stream of variations, possibly depending on new combinations of complementary component pieces. Uniqueness of assets in this mode of institution could depend crucially on star performers or magnets that can quickly reconfigure a set of assets distributed in a wide network. Unlike the stability of the commodities such as steel that required following of a scripted routine, and a systematized approach, in this increasing returns frontier, dealmaking, innovative contracting and brilliant insights pave the way for the entry of novelty as opposed to predictability. Our discussion in the sports case (see case study 2.1 and related text) provided an instance of this kind of a move orchestrated by the media owner. Without understanding this mode, we would fail to understand the basic driver of very fast growth and rapid accumulation of profits that we witness in several cases in contemporary times.

CASE STUDY 2.6 — Financial Technologies MCX: Managing assets for increasing returns

The Multi Commodity Exchange of India (MCX), promoted by the software firm Financial Technologies, quickly raced to become the leading commodity futures exchange in India after futures trading was allowed and a set of three exchanges were issued licence by the Government of India in 2003. It left National Commodity and Derivative Exchange (NCDEX), its main rival, way behind in terms of total trading volume (more than 70 per cent) on the exchange. A few key moves were crucial to this runaway success. MCX, quite unlike NCDEX, decided to focus first on the metal commodity futures market—especially bullion. In futures exchanges, the credibility of the clearing price or the settlement price is most crucial, so that traders know that manipulation and cornering would not happen. A credible system to arrive at a settlement price is thus a key asset. Since futures exchanges were being revived in India after a long hiatus of several decades, build-up of such credible asset would require time. In the bullion market, however, such price points were available through exchanges such as Commodities Exchange (COMEX)[16] and Indian traders informally followed those exchange prices. MCX quickly entered into exclusive agreements with those exchanges (in return for a royalty and in a few cases equity stake) for use of their settlement price in MCX and simultaneously broke up the large contract sizes (of global exchanges) into a volume that could generate trade volumes in India. Thus a rupee-denominated contract of a small size, which had the institutional credibility of the settlement process in the oldest commodity exchange, was introduced quickly. It also used its established user base of equity trading software (front-end software used by brokers/traders called ODIN) to market the newly launched commodity contracts. Its initial membership fees were kept low and in a pay-as-you-trade mode, unlike the large membership fee based model, to induce the broking community to test out commodity trading. The equity broking community brought in speculative trading volume, and the old gold traders shifted from the global exchange to MCX for managing their price risk. A quick assimilation of a significant trading volume reduced transaction costs (bid–ask spreads) and brought in more traders. As volumes picked up, it became increasingly difficult for NCDEX and other rival exchanges to come back in the metal segment. A quick assemblage of several related assets brought in transaction volumes in an unfolding market, while craftily denying rivals access to the key assets (recall the exclusive deals with global exchanges).

---

[16]COMEX specializes in the facilitation of metals futures trading. Originally an independent exchange, COMEX was purchased by New York Mercantile Exchange (NYMEX) on 3 August 1994 and merged.

We now would move to a discussion on star resources, with an example from the film world. We hope to have convinced readers of the need to look at star assets as a separate category, quite unlike a resource that is homogeneous and thus replaceable with each other. Stars, in contrast, have individuality or uniqueness.

2.4.1 Star assets

Why should a movie venture pay so heavily for a star; contrarily, could a movie without a star expect to generate a revenue stream? If you stretch a little beyond the world of movies, you would notice that the typical lead characters described in books by 'management-gurus' or those by the 'management wizards' and characters such as a Nobel laureate, a hugely salaried scientist, a CEO or a rugby-player all belong to this class of 'stars'. Do all these forms of businesses require a 'star' to generate revenues, or do the requirements vary across fields of businesses? And, above all, does the business need the prop of a star or, conversely, is the star in need of a business? If you look around the business milieu, particularly in India, you will find several areas where the 'star' as an asset is a powerful influencer of business dynamics. Recall the tiff between one of the leading hospital chains in Delhi (Escorts) and its 'star' doctor whose (global) reputation brought patients in hordes.[17] The hospital chain (and its management) apparently failed to bind the 'star' professional to a strong employment contract, allowing him to set up an independent health-city while working for his current employer hospital. Can the 'star' be bound to an organizational mode or would a 'star' remain mobile across a large network—freelancing, so to say?

Once an asset is a star, investment in that star locks up the star for the contracted period with the contracting business. So, you have created a monopoly—at least a temporary monopoly. Further, the investment is lumpy. You cannot believe that a thousand stuntmen could compensate for the loss of a star actor. Or well designed systems and standards could compensate for the 'star' doctor, who the patient expects will spin the magic wand. Then, the star is unique and hence cannot be substituted by another star. In other words, a business or a product (such as a movie/TV serial)

---

[17]Some relevant news articles on this issue of Escorts Hospital and its 'star asset': Indo-Asian News Service (2007), Sreeraman (2007), *Indian Express* (2007) and Subramanian (2007).

may expect to generate a barrier, even if for a while, that is insurmountable. In our age, one of the most important strategic objectives relates to how to generate uniqueness. In the face of extreme standardization and commoditization that sets in decreasing returns dynamics, generation of uniqueness that is valued would lead to an increasing returns mode of profit realization. A star achieves this for the business or for the product.

Stardom as a belief can be sustained just as series of canards could be; however, a star must have a birth and a death. The star is just like a product or an asset with a life. In order that a business could have a star, its birth must remain accidental and enigmatic. To the degree that this birth is unpredictable, the value of that stardom could rise. This uncertainty on the emergence of a star is important. Contrarily, fixed assets would be accumulative and would have little uncertainty. In other words, a star happens by accident and is no different from the discovery of a hidden treasure. Another way of appreciating this could be to look at a star as an antithesis of a commodity. Brilliance and novelty, that a star is prized for, need therefore a short life. No wonder a star should be proverbially mercurial, despotic or unpredictable during its period of stardom. So it makes great business sense to propagate that its star-CEO takes decisions by not following rules yet making surprising profits. An interesting aside is that a governing-contract as per the requirements of the agency theory cannot be designed for a mercurial star. So, how can you bind such a star to the organizational mode?

2.4.2 Star as an entrepreneur

Stardom in this sense is entrepreneurial. An entrepreneur cannot be an agent; so too a star cannot be an agent. Moreover, it would be close to impossible to design a 'performance standard' for the star. In other words, the institution of star asset must sustain enough incentives for the star in order that he (or she) can garner enough influence (or votes) on sustained basis. Star value thus would depend on the mechanism of garnering enough influence (or votes) in favour of self. A business could thus discover these mechanisms such that it can sway influence (or votes) from one star asset to another potential. Strategic capability to manoeuvre influence (or votes) would thus be most coveted. What are these mechanisms or what are the institutional landscapes of the influence (or voting)? Now probably you could appreciate the importance of clubs and the elite pools. Further, a star must engender envy in others who have not tasted the stardom. Conversely, those who do not know a star must be pitied. Hence, you have a good world of fashion where not belonging to the fad can lead to exclusion and that itself generates the increasing returns dynamics which lead to a quasi-monopoly position. Does ideology also play a similar role, or a 'belief' around a particular stance of business?

Another alternate perspective argues that, as for example in a movie, a star is a shock absorber. Risks of a business or of a product are somewhat reduced if there is a star. In this sense, you can indeed consider the star as insurance or as an asset with expected future series of revenues with known present values. Try to employ those models in calculating the present price that you could pay for a star asset. Please observe the shortcomings of these models. Should you expect to capture value of a star asset in terms of predictable revenue stream? If it is possible to capture value in that sense, a star can be provided an employment contract that can be lucrative for the star to accept. Why does the star prefer, particularly in the Mumbai film-making world, to remain a freelancer? In the next section, we explore why it may help us better understand the film-making world of star assets if we embrace a risk-taking rather than risk-aversion attitude.

2.4.3 Risk-taking institution

We argue instead that risk-taking is very important. Several authors, however, have emphasized risk-aversion as the explanation to the emergence or the evolution of an institution. A common perception based on risk aversion would argue that a trader (say in commodities) engages in a hedging transaction in a futures market to insure against risks of price fluctuations—a risk-aversion mode. This was the view propounded by even Keynes. But several trader accounts testify to a limited hedging interest, which came about only when exporters got into fixed price export contracts. The risk aversion then is contingent on a requirement to conform to certain specifications. It is systemic. Production of, say corrosion resistant steel, would demand a conformance to a specification and hence variations must be controlled against. So, the production engineer's risk aversion arises from the specific task that is on hand—it is rather a property of the production system. Production of a film has no need to stick to such specifications. If one appreciates this systemic requirement of adopting a risk-aversion stance, then one also can possibly realize that risk aversion is not any innate human property. To the extent such systemic requirements do not remain (such as in the art market, where final products remain unspecified, quite unlike steel), risk aversion may not be a favoured mode to adopt. Traders would, in contrast, engage in active speculation and the futures market can be then seen as a specialized market trading in a risk—this specialization is what makes a futures market attractive to the trader who wants to trade in a particular risk.[18]

Risk taking, in fact, can be quite commonplace. Betting is very well known. Can you find out the turnover in the betting market—in cricket and different other sports, in India and in other countries, or the size of the global lottery business? Estimates in the media suggested that the betting circuits generated a transaction volume of INR 2,000 billion, across UK (where betting is legal) and other markets including Dubai and India (where it is not legally allowed). Organization of industry sometimes could be better understood in terms of risk acceptance (rather than risk aversion) and creative industry, as it is in the film-making in India, particularly in Bollywood, might have its foundation in acceptance of risk. Accounts of film-making in Hollywood and much of Europe, however, concentrate on risk reduction as the motive that guided formation of contracts on the production and distribution side. The rise of multi-divisional large (Chandlerian) firms in Hollywood is also explained as a risk reduction move. In contrast to this account, Bollywood (and its stars) seems to have revelled in taking up risks.

2.4.4 Star and organization of film-making

Stars play possibly the most significant role in the making and the success of a film. Costs owing to a star are a disproportionately high share of total production costs. Moreover, increasing the share of cost in favour of the

---

[18]In fact, undertaking insurance in lieu of self-insurance could be explained in terms not of risk aversion, which is traditionally emphasized, but of a cost reduction strategy strengthened by the fact that the insurer provides for cross checking of arrangements in place within an organization that reduce chances of, say, fire hazards. Thus, insurance industry provides the third party governance through creation of classification system of risk classes, benchmarks of investments required to control, say, fire hazard, and so on. Self-insurance, in contrast, would not succeed in bringing such strong governance. Industrial history of the rise of insurance industries provides several instances of such an articulation.

star might increase the chances of the film becoming a blockbuster 'hit'. Cost on star is dangerously endogenous. On the other hand, a star can bring in very large revenues or nearly nothing. Uncertainty in the revenue outcome can be extremely high. A possible suggestion could therefore be to produce low budget films with no star, since now the environment would be more stable. However, increasing number of films from Bollywood continue to engage stars. Risk and uncertainty increase thereby.

Film-making in Bollywood, however, is organized quite differently from how it is organized in Hollywood. In Hollywood we find several large integrated firms—such as Sony Pictures or Warner Brothers—while Bollywood offers a large number of small production houses, often organized as sole proprietorships or simple partnerships. Directors, producers, financiers, syndicators of finance and, most importantly, star actors remain mobile and engage in project mode to work on particular films as freelancers. Film-making continues through the continuous process of formation and dispersal of project teams. In Hollywood, rise of stardom of the actor and the rise of large firms as controllers of the production process were simultaneous. Bollywood, however, shows that it is not inevitable—or, in other words, stardom can coexist with networked modes of production. Scholars studying Hollywood film-making have seen star costs for a production house as an investment in branding, and thus as risk reduction. Further, that because expenses on a star are endogenous and it is sunk cost, concentration or market power might not reduce even if there is an increase in the size of the market. Few production houses also attempted hoarding rights to a star actor for limited periods of time through exclusive contracting.

Bollywood, contrarily, exhibited a process where stars existed and stardom prospered without causing the business of film-making to adopt the structure of a large firm. A star in Mumbai costs at least as much in proportion to the total cost as a star in Hollywood would. Increasingly over the years, both the cost of film-making and the cost to a star have been rising. Moreover, numbers of films produced from India have been increasing as well. The model suggested from a reading of Hollywood cannot possibly be extended to understand the Bollywood phenomenon. Risks did not deter participants in film-making to spend increasingly on star (or risk did not force the participants to organize a large firm as a risk-reduction move). No less important has been the fact that Indian films have been increasing the size of market, including revenues from exports, and this increase too did not necessitate the formation of large firms in India.

In Bollywood risk-taking appears to be an important aspect of this production process. Unlike in Hollywood, a star in Bollywood is an investor. A star invests in intangibles and sometimes in tangibles, sharing the risks and uncertainty of the outcome along with other groups of investors. film-making in Bollywood is based on thick network of joint production. Competition in film, we would moreover argue, shares greater similarity with version-based competitions in areas such as software with increasing returns. Hence, to extend our argument on star's role, a star in Bollywood is more like a platform (like that of Windows) than a brand shared across products. Several investors in a film, holding distinctly different types of assets with different risks and uncertainties, can join in the film-making severally without affecting mass distribution of a film. Specifically, Bollywood provides a structure that retains the incentives for holders of distinct asset types to invest in own asset and engage in self-insurance. Several practices in Bollywood, particularly its difference from that in Hollywood, point towards such incentive structures.

2.4.5 Star as the investor

A star has great stake in a film. In Mumbai, there are agents who go out and negotiate with the producers and directors on behalf of a star. These agents set a price on a star and, in return, the agent receives often a commission of about 10 per cent. An agent, being an independent rating agent, keeps a tab on the market for tastes, the marketability of the star and on the quality of the total project including its background singer, the story, the director, the co-star and others. There are both dedicated and floating agents. With the falling marketability of a star, desertion by agents would commence and the fallen star would then negotiate through informal network channels. A star must keep appearing on the screen, however. A long absence surely would indicate that the star, notwithstanding her/his current market appeal, would soon lose the future market appeal. Asset value of a star, while uncertain, is strangely related to the rate of appearances, which must not shoot up beyond certain preferred limits though. Increasing returns is experienced since more appearances ensure increase in star rating as well as potential scarcity (due to unavailability of the star for a future film project); however, beyond a limit of appearances, the star might appear too easily available. The fad of 'star asset' market thus exhibits an interesting phenomenon.

Attempts to bring a star under an employment contract would undervalue the star, who is expecting to reap increasing returns from successive future films. This portent of undervaluation acts as disincentive to the star who reaps benefit from film-making in two modes: first, as the current revenue and second, as the potential increase in future revenue. The asset that a star is has these two values, current and the future. The star is more concerned about the appreciation or at least non-depreciation of its future value. A star, therefore, prefers to remain as an independent investor in film production. An employment contract undercuts this incentive of a star. Property rights to the asset in the person of the star, underemployment, would ultimately as a residue reside with the firm. The star expects to increase in future its own asset value, and this expectation acts as the strongest incentive for this star to act as an independent investor in a film-making project. In Mumbai, therefore, the star is an investor. Several other advantages follow this model. Employment contract is known to suffer severely from costs and hazards of monitoring. Even a contract structured around performance and bonus attached to revenues earned by a film, in short the dual contract, cannot compare with the gains that the star stands to acquire in future. Moreover, risks and uncertainties that are peculiar to stardom and that cannot be equated with financial risks remain with the star as an independent investor. In Bollywood, therefore, unlike Hollywood, different modes or types of risks and uncertainties prevail.

Self-insurance is then afforded in Bollywood. A star, in order to reduce her risks, determines the number of appearances she should make in a period or the genre of film she should act in or the emotions she should elicit. Uncertainties remain, however. Such uncertainties cannot be covered by these self-insurances. Lurking behind the uncertainty is supernormal entrepreneurial profit from a blockbuster. A single blockbuster would elevate the rating of a star for a future period. Profit from a blockbuster for the star is in future period. In contrast to the risk premium as a profit to an investor, an actor or any resource earns a Knightian[19] profit owing to uncertainty. This profit is speculative in nature and cannot be predicted even over a short horizon—it is like a jackpot. It arises from uncertainty, rather than risk. Readers would recall the difference we made between risk and uncertainty, risk being probabilistic and uncertainties

---

[19]Frank Knight was an early 20th-century economist who argued about a mode of profit that was accompanied with uncertainties. It is beyond and different from a rent that is more predictable (Knight, 1921).

more in the nature of sheer ignorance. The director or the producer of a film and several other important gatekeepers of the production process, unlike a wholesale trader of a commodity like grain, cannot accomplish quality gradation of resources completely. Profit earned by the producer is thus partly from uncertainty arising from sheer ignorance and partly as a premium to more conventional notions of risk.

Networked world of production in Bollywood offers a few other modes of risk-taking and risk-sharing. In the simplest instance, asset holders join in severally (in syndicates) for different film productions during the same period; typically a star as also a studio would work on three or four films. Network reduces risk and thus self-insures. Reducing time to produce a film is another instance of such insurance. Typically, a Telugu-language film from Hyderabad would take 3–6 months to produce. In a Tamil-language film from Chennai, this time could vary from 4–12 months. For example, in Ramoji Film City at Hyderabad, one can enter with money and exit in the shortest possible time with a film. Hollywood, in contrast, would take several years to complete a production process. Hollywood also would produce much fewer number of films—it under-produces as risk hedging; while Bollywood proliferates production.

There had been a couple of network nodes, similar to a venture capital manager from the Silicon Valley, such as the syndicator, the producer, the director or the sole distributor. These nodes could encourage retention of differences in the quality of resources while allowing a minimal exchange of competition-reducing information amongst extant resources. Such a minimal common knowledge took care of fashions such as changes in inter-generational choices of dialogues or dances. A typical market would demand maximization of information for efficient functioning, and in cases of absences of information leading to market failures, Hollywood offered the chandelarian firm. Indian films offered in lieu an intermediate network-based solution, based upon minimal common knowledge.

Sharing a circuit (or network) of information leads to multiple forms of investment. Typically, a film-family would be engaged in financing, starring, lead singing, cinematography and even up to distribution. A large firm can at most offer a bimodal contracting for risk sharing, with a bonus kind of financial sharing of revenues earned. In Bollywood, most importantly, multiple modal contracting (most often unwritten and based on trust) prevails. Often in a Tamil or Telugu film, a star would be accepting distributorship in lieu of cash payment for starring. A good example is the Telugu film star Chiranjivi, who is reported to be charging INR 40 million, paid partly in cash and about 75 per cent in distributorship rights in 2007. The loss to the producer under such circumstances are often made good by the reputation effect of the star and by extra amounts made from other areas of rights selling. Often a star would be a producer, and in many cases also own theatres. Multimodal investment, in several distinct asset varieties, constitutes the other important mode of risk insurance in Bollywood.

2.4.6 Ownership institution of several asset and valuation

Readers may recall our earlier discussion regarding organization as a homunculus and risk bundler and the alternative of developing autonomous risk profiles of each sub-homunculus level asset, including possibilities of trade in it (see section 2.3.3). A large firm in Hollywood is a risk bundler; and hence all assets must be homogenized for control to be exercised and visualized as a financial asset at most. Hollywood then can offer only a bimodal risk contract—a current compensation and a revenue-linked future bonus. Bollywood, in contrast, offers multimodal contracting because the network mode is retained. Our earlier reference to the tiff between Escorts and its star doctor also shows how a star (the doctor in this case) makes a multimodal investment (hospital asset along with practice-based reputation) as a risk insurance (see section 2.4.1); this ability to retain the freedom to engage in self-insurance is crucial to the network participant—without this ability, risk has to be given up to the organization as the only point capable of taking it. Readers would also realize from the account of the conflict why an organization is so wary of such multimodal risk investment rights of its employees. So long as such possibilities remain, the holder of the expertise would not be bound by an employment contract and would remain mobile like a networked freelancer.

For managing risks then, network needs often specific practices that support transactions that an organization would not require. Differences in practices in Bollywood from that of its peer production system in Hollywood may be seen from this perspective. Earlier we had pointed to certain specific practices in distribution systems in Japan (right-to-return norm) that help networks to bear unbundled and specific risks at different points in the network. Bollywood, thus, retains multiplicity of ownership around different types of asset holders, including the star actors, who engage in different types of self-insurance. The risk articulation of each type of asset remains distinct and different from a mere financial risk, which also points towards different mechanisms of insurance afforded to each type of asset holder—assets are thus several and not reducible to a sum of money.

How does this network transact and tackle a project specific risk? Our discussion above points towards ways of handling risks of each distinct asset holder over a period of time, that is, the risk related to sustenance of asset value over time. Understanding of the project risk would take us into a discussion of the network mode of transaction. At the background of the production process is a set of financiers taking high risks in investing. We will discuss the mode of transaction of what we are calling thick networks (which are also found in Silicon Valley), which differs from the mode in a vertical large organization, as well as that of the proverbial price-based market of standard commodities (like a commodity spot or futures market) in Chapter 4. Here we now move to a discussion of other types of assets and the specific demands that it makes on governance.

2.5.1 Common pool assets

As we look beyond the organization into the social space in search of assets, an important category that comes up is common pool assets. Businesses oftentimes piggyback on such common pool assets. Culture, which provides certain widely shared beliefs and attitudes (and often certain specific skills), can be used to one's advantage. Japan's Tokyo Metro, for instance, has an enviable record of operating at the highest levels of punctuality, with a more complex optimization to achieve. Appendix 2A provides a detailed account. As you read through it, consider the following: (*a*) does Tokyo Metro rely on a shared cultural asset as a key element in its design of the system, and (*b*) what would be the cost of setting up a governance system, along with record keeping, punishing/penalizing in a culture that does not value punctuality? Would it at all be possible? Many a time, these common pool assets become crucial for a business milieu.

Let us take another instance. Look at a village lake. Do you observe a management committee in charge of maintenance? Without a costly structure of governance, do you think the common village lake is wasted? You can have several variations where you would not find a governance structure around a common pool asset—in other words, it is not managed at all—and such arrangement seem to be sustainable and value adding. A discourse on free-rider type problems would possibly dispute this claim. Often what we do not consider while invoking the free-rider problem is the costs of governance, or the cost of working a private property right. If the cost of governance (in other words, the transaction cost) becomes prohibitively high, then players with a strategic interest in an asset might prefer a common pool stance. Failure to realize this may also lead to non-growth of other markets or nondevelopment of other linked assets. As a matter of research, can you find out why the growth of m-commerce is getting stunted; or, why broadband penetration is much lower in the US than in Europe or Japan? Would Google be worried about it and what would be its stance or strategy to solve the problem? In the first chapter, we talked about Google's interest in forcing commoditization of basic voice-based mobile telecommunication.

A pool can be publicly owned, such as river water or the spectrum. Contrarily, a pool can be created cooperatively, again through two modes: first, as in cooperative research between competing firms or between public and private entities—a pool gets generated through cooperatively induced pooling in of knowledge or other assets; in another mode, the second type, a pool gets created by withdrawing from exclusive ownership or by withdrawing from exclusionary power. In the cooperative pool, agents pool in fragmented assets or rights to assets in order to enable each participant an extended right to all fragments. In the domain of scientific research, a cooperative pool, often known as the public space, is formed by a mode of social contracting whereby each researcher contributes to the common knowledge by generating experiments and data or by providing for conjectures and theories and sometimes even by offering prototypes, protocols, organisms or experimental physical entities. Withholding of one or a group of such offerings would reduce mutual gains; and often, by offering, the offerer generally enjoys the privilege of deciding the course of development of a new knowledge/object; hence, the offerer has privilege of precedence over others as well as a privilege over others in enjoying benefits from complementary assets, under the control of the offerer.

In many industrial districts, a leading firm offers to the public several proprietary intellectual properties (IP), such as Motorola offering free to other software firms in Bangalore a set of IP on software business processes. There are several gains that the large firm might like to enjoy out of the offerings; for example, often the offering generates the basis of a standard or the basis of developments of all future products and no wonder, the offerer large firm has several complementary assets that would gain disproportionately from all such future products developed by other firms.[20]

In another mode, such as at the knit garment producing hub in India at Tirupur, small exporting units pool several types of resources including, sometimes, IP resources. In this case, a pooled resource is a common service or a common order book or a common input. Can you reason why individual business entities (in many industries), instead of moving towards vertical integration, remain independent while sharing several horizontal as well as vertical resource pools? Typically, a cluster shares common pools. In clusters, often equipment—such as tool rooms—that require a size of investment that is far too large for any single firm to make are invested as common pools. In cases where a few firms make such investments, others participate in it through an active rental market. In fact, any industrial geography must enjoy such increasing returns opportunities, otherwise also captured through the notion of 'spillover', through sharing of resources, rights and opportunities.

In the second mode we discussed, the pool is formed through the withdrawal of the 'exclusionary power' of a powerful blocking asset—so, a dominant asset holder gives up power already achieved to engage in a greater game. As an instance, you can think of a patent pool, where firms with blocking patents and enjoying immense blocking power might withdraw from the exclusionary power of blocking in order to allow other patents holders with perhaps complementary intellectual properties joining in the pool (initiated by the blocking patent holder's withdrawal of the blocking right). In the two modes, then, the temporal arrival of the pool differs—in second mode, a current dominant power holder gives up exclusionary power to create a wider milieu over which an influence is sought in future, while the former mode starts from a cooperative stance and power is derived from contributing to the pool. The difference is subtle, but is important.

2.5.2 Patent pool

A holder of a patent enjoys a private right to benefit from the IP. This is fairly well known. However, this private right can be a problem for innovation and the advancement of technology. Few (or actually no)

---

[20]Participation in 'public space', through an offer of an asset, then leads to a power to set the direction of asset development—this is a significant element of academic or scientific power.

patent represents *de novo* (or fresh) knowledge—usually it builds on earlier patents; similar to the 'stack' arrangement in contemporary software. So, most patents are of the 'improvement patent' type. A patent holder, thus, can hold a next-stage incremental innovator to ransom by not licensing the patent to one working on the next generation improvement patent, so to say. Patents that are called 'blocking patents' or 'essential patents'—which is something like a 'compulsory stack' and cannot be built around through an alternative route—become particularly powerful and can stunt the growth of the next-stage solution.

This blocking threat would be of special concern in an ex-post sense; that is, when the costs of development are already sunk-in, it makes the next-stage innovator especially vulnerable to the gaming possibility. In another case, if a next-stage solution requires several patent licences from several holders, in a sequential negotiation game, even a minor patent holder would wield disproportionate power, holding up the licensing of the 'bunch of patents' from proceeding further. A patent pool, in various forms, withdraw this ex-post blocking right among a set of pool participants—where the rules of licensing (can be free licensing or a pre-announced price schedule with terms and conditions) are announced by all pool contributors ex-ante—removing the possibility of the ex-post gaming.

> One of the major innovation of early 20th century—radio—could be commercially produced only when the several patent holders were forced to license technologies (at a royalty) to Radio Corporation of America (RCA)—the company formed to implement the patent pool arrangement at the instigation of the US military services, who required the product. Under US antitrust law, patent pools enjoy a reprieve from the purview of antitrust enquiry allowing competitors to cooperate in joint licensing, provided they follow a few important guidelines. It might be interesting for the reader to visit any patent pool website such as Moving Picture Experts Group (MPEG) or numerous such standard pools in telecommunication or IT space. In a different mode that is not as warring, the blocking patent holder, in order to induce several 'improvement patents', can design a pool with a mode of licensing that would allow joint sharing of the improvement to both original and improvement patentee. An examination of patent pool arrangements would reveal a wide variety of licensing terms. Most contemporary electronics and telecommunication technology standards include a patent pool.

2.5.3 Variations in rights and increasing pool-asset value

Most common elements in a cooperative pool without costly structures of governance would have: (*a*) no one singly or even otherwise, no team or club owning in full or part of the whole; (*b*) however, a large number of rights of use exist; (*c*) such rights are transferable, sometimes; (*d*) often, rights are mutually dependent or some rights could be used preferably together though, in most instances, users of such complementary rights are unique individuals; (*e*) there exists even rights to rights; (*f*) perhaps all rights-users enjoy the pool on inter-generational long-term sustained basis; (*g*) while use of one right could have a market or can be priced, there would be perhaps another right that fails to generate a market or create a price—in other words, market and non-market rights do not only coexist but are often complementary. A pool, however, has a boundary and an absolutely free entry is not usually allowed. Users of a pool asset also do not have a use right (or other rights) without any obligation—so that the free-rider problem does not arise. It is, therefore, best seen as a non-market mode of exchange of rights and obligations, where some or all of the rights might not enjoy a market and a price. So, it is a complex mode of non-market exchange.

Take up, for example, the common pool of music and songs from the Indian district of Bhojpur or the genre of painting style from a district of Rajasthan or the culinary styles from Turkey or the art of making wine from a district of France—in all such cases, we notice the cooperative pool of assets. Information on the genre or the style is shared freely in the pool. If you are in the business of music or entertainment, with a broad array of distribution assets such as satellite rights, TV channels, DVD and CD rights and distribution set-ups, you would possibly be interested in the formation, preservation of genres of music and possibly also 'star' asset generation in genres of your interest—your business is in an 'adjacent area'; you have what are called 'adjacent assets' in your organization. Let us now look into a genre of Bhojpur music or the North Bengal folk music forms.[21] In the domain of inter-genre contests, is creation of a 'star' in the genre important—so that genres that fail to throw up such 'stars' would lag in its influence and genre valuation? Contrarily, can the star in a genre stand alone without a minimum density of assets in that genre—and, in that sense, is the star indebted to such widely dispersed

---

[21]This inspired Sachin Deb Burman and his lineage in Bollywood film music.

folk assets that do not necessarily have a high monetized value? How can this debt be repaid, given that monetized repayment would possibly not work? Now you can appreciate why a common pool is crucial—expertise cannot be sustained (and stars created) without a common pool of more mundane assets.

No doubt if you go to centres with a high geographic density of assets of certain genre, such as medicinal plant knowledge assets in Uttaranchal, you will find that a large part of that knowledge also lies diffused with the local folk population, intermeshed with several daily life practices. Contrarily, you will also find several assets, such as pieces of historical monuments that can be valorized through a tourist value chain, which lies totally neglected and mostly you would find scanty little knowledge of (or about) such assets among the local population, who might even be involved in defiling it. Does free-riding explain this phenomenon, or does a common pool (or its lack) possibly explain it better? Does this difference in interpretation lead to a difference in action (or strategies) that you would evolve? So, when you take private rights over such a monument (out of your tourism business interest), would you adopt a strategy of alliance with local asset holders or would you govern the asset through your agent managers from a distance—in particular, what would be the transaction cost implications of the difference in stance?

Does this situation on the need of a common pool change if more information is both generated and supplied at no cost, including very cheap information on infringements? Suppose you have launched a business of placement agency, using the above questions and leads, suggest as to what types of information on applicants or 'manpower' (or the detailed professional bio-data) you ought to share and with whom to share and how much—in order that you could increase the size of placement market as also in order to raise your credibility.[22]

Consider another example of the intra-organizational common pool—a large vertically integrated business organization. Suppose you

---

[22] Open source software milieu provides a public logbook (or an indexation) of contributions of code contributors—rating it in several dimensions of coding skills. Generally, coding achievements of this type inside an organization would not be capable of being signalled to a wider market across multiple organizations. But coders working on open source software pieces can often signal achievements through the public credit system. How does the signal of the public credit differ from that of, say, recommendation from the boss in the former employer organization? How does this difference affect the manpower common pool?

have to design an information system for this organization, what should you do—design a cooperative pool as above or design an incentive-based and quasi-priced restricted access system of information? Try to conjecture on the consequences of free access to all information generated internal to an organization. Could you still retain the old mode of hierarchic governance, or should the governance improve to other forms? How far the milieu of this organization would influence your decision; that is, if, for instance, your competitor organizations are hierarchic and large as well as there are only a few of them, would you still open up access (inside the firm) to the common pool of information?

2.5.4 Patents and open source software

Open source software works on the basis of sharing of the source code—so that any user remains free to alter the code as he/she deems fit in the context of application of the software. Its stance is against that of proprietary software policy. The open source software is, therefore, a common pool asset which can be used, leveraged, modified by other business interests to offer innovative software service solutions that would build on top of the common pool resource. However, the open source is a threat to proprietary stance in the same software space and there have been threatening litigations encroaching into the common pool.

The common pool—because it does not have costly governance (and a financially well-endowed firm as a holder of the asset!)—would find costly litigation impossible to pursue. A few interesting countermeasures have been the announcement of litigation support budgets from financially powerful firm and interest groups, such as IBM, who is basing its service strategy on the open source building blocks. Governments in Korea, Japan and China also have an interest in preservation of the common pool—worried with defence (security!) implications of proprietary codes during times of potential wars.

Would formation of a rival patent pool, with uniquely crafted licensing terms of the pool, be a good solution? Thus, boundaries of a common pool asset may be threatened or redefined and firms/organizations with an interest in an adjacent field might have a deep interest in protecting and preserving such common pool assets. In light of this discussion, do you think that documentation (digitally) of the traditional knowledge on medicinal property of plants/herbs that exists as a treasure trove in the hills of Uttaranchal (a province in North India) a good idea? Does digitization open up the knowledge assets—what is the counter to a possible appropriation? Does digitization change the dynamics of who belongs to the pool and who is a de facto outsider—or, in other words, does the boundary of the pool change as a result of digitization? What would be the access restriction to the digitized information? Who would (or should) control such gateways of access? You may also analyse the National Innovation Foundation, created by the Government of India and discuss your findings in terms of areas of success of the initiative and its failures.[23]

Inter-organizational common pools belong to another type. Take, for example, the case of a standard or that of the flux of human resources transiting between competing organizations or the results of an experiment such as the genome. In fact, information disclosed through patents is perhaps the best example of such pools. The institution of a patent was created with this precise motive, which is often missed in more simplistic articulations of the patent concept. Patent, first, is a disclosure of information on the novelty—and the monopoly right (temporary) granted (to exclude others) is in lieu of such a disclosure of valuable information rather than as an incentive to invest in research. The incentive is aimed, therefore, at creation of a common pool that would be inter-organizational and public—freely shared and used or reused or modified by a wide network of several innovators.

2.5.5 Marshalian agglomeration-based common pool

If you think of the leather industry or some of the globally acclaimed brands, such as Gucci that dominate the industry, you would note that they owe their origins to a few clusters in Italy, where there would be a geographical concentration of a particular industry (in this case, leather). Silicon Valley would be another instance of a cluster that is contemporary. The financial world would also provide several examples of International Financial Centres (such as London or New York), where there is significant concentration of major players and key assets in the industry.[24]

---

[23]For a rich description of the open source software, interested readers may look at the work of Steven Weber, all available freely on the web.
[24]Can you think of reasons how, even in a globally connected world, such few centres have been able to retain their hold as the core of the global financial system? What is the nature of assets held in such concentrated locations?

Alfred Marshal argued that such clusters get created because of agglomeration economies, where firms can get an advantage of several positive spillovers. Other way to look at the spillovers is to see it as a common-pool asset which proves useful to the firm in its transactions. We must here realize that geographic concentration alone is not enough for spillover generation; common-pool asset creation requires inter-organizational flow of information and flux of assets—so, it requires considerable inter-organizational transactions. Generally, such powerful clusters would be characterized by great amounts of intra-trade of various kinds—so that a complex mesh of transaction gets created within the geography. Spillover realization rides these networks, intermeshed in transactions. So, geographic concentration alone does not suffice. Geographically concentrated clusters would differ on the intensity of intra-trade as well as on the types of transactions that occur in the intra-trade mode. Can you look at Silicon Valley and Bangalore in a comparative perspective? Would it be right to equate Bangalore with Silicon Valley? Intra-trade in Silicon Valley is very rich—a wide variety of assets change hands and it presents a very dense transaction (including of subcontracting) network. In Bangalore, in contrast, it appears that the 'shilled manpower influx' constitutes the most important 'common pool asset'.

2.5.6 Network shared club-type common pool

So far we discussed pools that are relatively open—or similar to public assets in nature. But an asset perspective in strategy would recognize a wide array of common pools, with varying degrees of exclusion ranging from a completely open (public) asset to a totally private asset. A common pool amongst a small network or a club would represent something in between. Contemporary businesses would throw up several such examples of network-type common pools. Alliances of various forms between two or more organizations would be prime examples. Contemporary information intermediaries often are a mode of creation of club-type common information pools that are owned by third-party platform owners or database companies. Such third-party intermediary business interests often force release of the data and form rules of sharing that enable the release of information amongst cooperating organizations.

CASE STUDY 2.7: Intermediation of Priceline.com

Priceline.com was one of the celebrity firms of the dot-com era, shooting into prominence riding an aggressive brand campaign and its business process of providing customers of airlines to bid (or rather make binding posts) the prices at which they wanted to buy a ticket. Airlines then could either accept or refuse the offer. In practice, airlines also bid their supply schedules into the portal and price matching was accomplished algorithmically. It reversed the algorithm of a purchase transaction as would happen in regular commerce, where the supplier generally has the right to quote and the buyer can then decide not to buy or to proceed with the transaction. The transaction details are something like this. A customer (usually pre-approved member) would log on to the website and define the source and destination cities, the day of travel and post a price that he/she is willing to pay. If the deal is acceptable, that is, if it finds a matching supplier, the electronic payment mode is automatically activated and the ticket is issued. Customers could not bid more than once on a particular route, so that the best price remained undiscovered to customers—except through extensive sharing between successful customers.

Since Priceline.com attempted selling to the budget-conscious price-sensitive sector, its ticket contract is not the most comfortable one—there are several frictions designed in to put off the business traveller. Customers would not have cancellation rights and would not be able to choose the number of hops or the exact time of day (only very broad ranges such as early morning or evening can be specified) of the travel. Partners of Priceline.com include Delta and a few other US airline companies; the airlines obviously are supplier partners of the portal. When launched, within a few years, it was selling close to 6–8 per cent of air tickets. Airlines were interested in Priceline.com because it enabled them to sell excess capacities (unsold tickets) at very cheap prices to the budget-conscious traveller, while maintaining price discrimination for the less price-sensitive customer category. Airlines' bids into Priceline.com, moreover, was not visible to each other—unlike if they published some of the low fares in, say, their own websites or through the shared reservation systems such as Sabre (where prices are visible to each other and to travel agents by regulatory mandate after an antitrust case in the 1990s), which would have been matched immediately by rivals. In Priceline.com, airlines could choose to be far more aggressive in pricing and bid just based on capacity utilization in a particular flight. The bidder does not take into account possible bids by other airlines protected by the

(Case Study 2.7 contd.)

(Case Study 2.7 contd.)

> information shield created by Priceline.com. Without such a shield, an aggressive bid by an airline with low utilization in a particular flight might have been matched by another airline that faced lower empty seat pressures. The availability of the rival bid information itself would change the bidding behaviour to a joint function of rival bid and own seat utilization. So, information release into a common third party by design of a rule of the shared (or jointly created) database enabled airlines to compete more vigorously in a segment and increase utilization of capacities without hurting their other pricing interests or stances. Cooperative creation of the shared database (or a joint definition of a common turf) introduced a new mode of competition, which could allow the firms to quote low prices in a rather coordinated way.

In several industries, such as shipping or airlines, you would have other kinds of shared assets—such as common reservation systems—where just as Priceline.com (see case study 2.7), you would have complex rules of sharing and encapsulation among different parties. Such shared assets are of the club-type and, in many cases, denial of access or access only under restrictive conditions can be used as a discriminatory, exclusionary mode against non-members. Jet Airways of India recently announced that it would route its US flights through a new international airport hub, that is, Shanghai, bypassing the more common Singapore hub—and the point of contention was the ticketing access rights granted to it in Singapore in the common reservation systems that was not acceptable.

2.5.7 Governance and management of joint/common assets

Our discussion in the last section brought out the importance of joint or common assets. Writing the rules of sharing, defining the boundaries of the pool and such activities are very important. Our discussion in the introductory chapter (see case study 1.3) talked about the conflict over the joint assets between the French group Danone and the Chinese group Wahaha over ownership of bottled water brand that has grabbed the top position in the Chinese market for bottled water. Known more as the battle over Wahaha, in this case Danone alleged that the Chinese group responsible for management of the brand (developed through the IP from the Danone) had swallowed up the brand asset. This has been a case of developing an asset jointly. There are hundreds of similar other cases in recent times where assets developed through joint investments soon ran into conflicts over sharing (or the mode of governing the joint asset) and erstwhile cooperators soon developed deep fissures and distrust, leading even to bitter legal cases. In the Wahaha case, piggybacking a large global brand to develop both a market (for the type of drinking water asset, that is, bottled water, vis-à-vis other forms of drinking water) and a network of marketing of water bottles initially under the brand of Danone by the Chinese business, showed an opportunistic seizure of a potential business; the successful Chinese group lost no time to piggyback Danone to develop assets under their own control. The business literature would provide you with a plethora of examples of alliances gone sour.

CASE STUDY 2.8 Joint Pool Assets of Rambus, Inc.

The Federal Trade Commission (FTC) announced on 5 February 2007 that it had at last delivered a penalty ruling in its long-running prosecution of memory technology company Rambus Inc. for illegally creating a monopoly in certain standards-reliant technology by abusing the Joint Electron Devices Engineering Council (JEDEC) standard-setting process in the early 1990s. The stakes were high for Rambus while awaiting the Commissioners' decision, since that decision could influence the outcome and damages assessed in the multiple private cases that are ongoing between Rambus and the various semiconductor companies that have refused to pay royalties to Rambus. These royalties relate to patents that the FTC had already held were illegally hidden by Rambus from the working group members in JEDEC that created the Synchronous Dynamic Random Access Memory (SDRAM) standard at issue. At least one judge had already delayed further action in one of these cases in order to learn what penalty the FTC might conclude would be appropriate under the circumstances. For the standards community, the FTC's anticipated judgement would also be significant, because if Rambus were to be let off lightly, gaming with the standards system could appear to offer better business returns than playing by the rules. Such a perception could tempt other companies to try the same gambit and also lessen participation in standard setting overall. Clearly, if there is more to lose than to gain by helping create, and then adopt, a standard, then standards development could become a

(Case Study 2.8 contd.)

(Case Study 2.8 contd.)

> process in which only the unaware—and those that wished to prey upon them—would participate.
>
> In a somewhat similar case, Dell Computer acquiesced in 1996 to an FTC consent decree,[25] under which it surrendered any right to require payment of royalties by implementers of a Video Electronics Standards Association (VESA) standard. Like Rambus, Dell had been accused of failing to disclose a patent during a VESA standards development process and then later asserting that patent against implementers of the same standard. Dell was also required to subject itself to oversight in its standards-related activities for a period of 10 years. Most obviously, then, the FTC could decide to limit the royalties that Rambus could charge to implement the SDRAM standard or to bar Rambus from charging any royalties at all.
>
> > [W]e find that a maximum royalty rate of .5% for DDR SDRAM, for three years from the date the Commission's Order is issued and then going to zero, is reasonable and appropriate. We also find that a corresponding .25% maximum rate for SDRAM is appropriate. Halving the DDR SDRAM rate reflects the fact that SDRAM utilizes only two of the relevant Rambus technologies, whereas DDR SDRAM uses four. (Updegrove 2007)
>
> Significantly, the order also prohibits Rambus from charging more than these rates on any outstanding licence agreement. This element of the order would seem to automatically diminish the damages that Rambus could be awarded in any ongoing litigation based upon alleged infringement of the patents in question.

2.5.8 Governance of future asset formation

Common asset should best be looked at, therefore, as a dynamic proposition to wrest larger part of a future asset to be developed through the currently proposed and jointly owned asset. Thus, entering into a joint

---

[25] In a consent decree with antitrust authorities, a firm against whom a proceeding is on agrees or commits to either follow certain practices or more frequently not to continue certain business practices, without legally admitting to having ever done it. In return, antitrust authorities drop the investigation. If in future, it is found that the decree was violated, courts can take it as a contempt of court and serious penalties can be levied. The onus of implementing the decree is on the one accepting it.

ownership is a step towards a game of strategy, the objective of which is to: (*a*) develop and expand the current asset type or develop a novel type of asset and (*b*) to seize control of the full or larger part of that new asset from the partner and/or from others at a future date. Engaging in the network mode in governance of shared assets or even jointly creating such assets has a dynamic connotation—conflict and cooperation inhere together, albeit with temporal differences. The first step that you should instruct yourself in is that an asset is never static. Take, for example, the value of an asset. What is the value? Let us, for simplicity, assume value would be what potential buyers might be expected to pay. One could enhance, thus, the value, provided you could arouse the expectations of most non-owners or partial-owners. For example, the value of a condominium increases as the co-investments in the associated infrastructure, including of the brand of the lifestyle that the condominium espouses, also increase. This owner did not invest directly in the infrastructure, which has mostly been paid out of public fund, albeit the owner gains in handsomely. Do you think if public investment in infrastructure such as roads/expressways, and so on, were rolled out uniformly across, say, a large city and its periphery, that is, without any distinction in quality levels across space, valuation of real estate space in currently favoured locations would have gone up? Is not the temporal dynamics of infrastructure development out of public funds an important factor shaping valuation of private real estate assets? In the same manner, expectations on a stock or on a brand or on a product such as the iPod could be built up.

In order to build this up, a single owner would need a club; alone, it would be impossible to whip up the frenzy of expectations. In fact, owning an asset implies you have to grow this. A good strategy is to grow the asset under your control relative to and, perhaps, at the cost of another asset. Several strategies might follow: (*a*) price of your asset is increased, (*b*) you acquire the control over an alliance-partner's asset or over a contiguous (or adjacent) asset or (*c*) volume of asset under your ownership increases. All the modes, however, would need the context of assets under others. In recent times, forming alliances has proved very satisfactory; forming asset-class clubs is another strategy; further, raising price of asset primarily through institutional contests has perhaps become most important and provocative. Unlike the normal discourse where current market share of a product would determine winners in a race/contest, or where cumulative market share shape up potential of deriving learning-by-doing based cost advantage, an inter-temporal institutional race which aims at shaping valuation is crucially influenced by the *expected size of the ultimate network in contrast to a rival network*, which defines the market and shapes the valuation. The importance of expectations drives the strategist to attempt coordination of expectation of complementary investors. In our chapter on markets, we would look into a few instances of how such expectation-shaping occurs through the use of linked investments in complementary assets. For our purpose here, it should suffice for the reader to appreciate the fact that a move to transfer an asset into the common pool can be dictated by a strategic concern aimed at growing the size of the network of users of, say, a technology standard in order to influence valuation of assets linked to the particular standard.

Biomedical industry and asset class contests

In the biomedical industry, there are several kinds or classes of assets. Think of knowledge assets related to devices, such as Computed Tomography (CT) scanners, clinical practice based assets and pharmaceutical assets. Is there often a contest between these different classes of assets? A rapid development of CT scan-related assets can make certain doctor-based clinical practice asset redundant or vice versa, where a clinical skill would often make referral to a CT scan usage quite redundant. If you think a bit, you will realize that doctor-based clinical practice assets would be extremely variegated—there would be severalties—where case reports and exchange of cases reports would be crucial. Device or pharmaceutical assets would be based on standard solutions—either a standard pill or a standard image pattern (to which each case is benchmarked). Such assets are usually exchanged through mediums such as journals or through meetings/conferences. Shift of the journal space from an emphasis on case report kind of knowledge pieces to large sample pattern studies, also called random control trials (RCT) (through editorial policy changes or introduction of a flood of new journals focusing on RCT type of research), would influence the relative asset valuation of the different classes of assets by enhancing the exchange of assets of a particular mode while suppressing the exchange of the other kinds of assets. This rivalry between asset classes is therefore not fought on prices but on the institutions that will determine the pricing mode. It influences the framework of pricing (based on detailed account in Banerjee and Anand, 2007).

2.5.9 Nodal governance and agreed coordination for asset valuation

There are several types of common assets. For example, often a 'standard' is a common asset. Why should the common asset class be so pervasively common! You must not forget that one of the most fundamental assumptions underlying a business is that a few undertakers of business agree to transact a good under an agreed set of conditions. In the simplest case, even transactions along a value chain need such prior consent. All such cases of business transactions, including that of competition, need what is described as 'coordination' of the rules within which the game of competition is played. Such coordination assumes that parties involved agree to and adhere to a common governance framework involving, among others, the framework of price determination of assets being transacted. Without such implicit prior consent, the market will fail to transact. We can appreciate, therefore, how necessary it is for an agent to achieve a coordination among other assets, first, and then to acquire a control over the framework in order that relative prices could be altered in favour of own business. Change in the framework, however, is difficult and a matter of contest—simply because it challenges a (or several) node(s) of power of the coordinator.

A theoretically pure market, however, would not need such social contracts. Real markets although are always under coordinated states of affairs, and especially in a globalized world, clubs appear even more necessary because otherwise a very large number of uncoordinated and fragmented businesses would enter the fray, leading the scenario to a chaos of too intense competition. There are several coordinators. Typically, you would like to believe that the regulators (or other entities of the state) are these coordinators. Most often, however, tacit agreements between business firms and otherwise a governance mechanism managed by a club of investment bankers, mutual/asset funds and similar other entities undertake coordination between different business entities. As an example of the former type, you could imagine how Microsoft's products created coordinated offerings by a very large number of vendors; and as an example of the latter, you could imagine how Morgan Stanley or CSFB organizes buyers and sellers of assets and how they partition assets, previously under unified control, as in the recent case of ABN Amro. Such coordinators, naturally, would enjoy immense voice or power, and strategy must take note of such power emanating from these nodes. An asset revaluation or re-architecturing can scarcely be achieved without negotiating with such nodes of power.

There is, of course, a bilateral mode of coordination. Several examples could be cited here, such as between most large pharmaceutical firms and the small biotechnological start-ups. Several different types of contracts have been entered into, ranging from control over the R&D (say, over the process of asset creation) through control over marketing rights (say, over the valuation of assets created, potential bundling and construction of portfolios) to the right to disposal of a particular product (say, over the process of asset partitioning and exiting). Often large firms with the power and voice attained through venture financing retained greater control in the contracts, although there are cases where smaller entities wrested significant freedom.

One should not overlook, though, the fact that even in bilateral negotiations the investment bankers, the stock traders/analysts (particularly star analysts) and the rating agents, for example, often enjoy voice. As a strategist, therefore, the task is to choose an appropriate asset as a potential prey and with what one would like to join in collaboration—one would need then to choose a milieu of certain clubs of asset owners and, therefore, certain rules of asset valuations. The goal is simply to enhance the value or the volume of asset under control. Alliance strategy informs on such modes of transference.

One should never forget that assets are not homogeneous and are also not often amenable to breaking down in size. Moreover, a large number of assets are sticky and not amenable to transfer either. The size of a marketable asset, however, depends more on the institutions in the market and no intrinsic worth defines the asset size. For example, only under certain external market–institutional influence does an asset under a vertically integrated large multi-divisional firm become a saleable unit of asset that is completely alienable from the integrated firm. Given the fact that most assets are not perfectly homogeneous, can you reason out under what conditions you can create a market and a price for an asset! Is homogeneity of assets crucial in creation of a market (and a price) of the asset; or, in other words, would the heterogeneous idiosyncratic quality (or properties) of an asset need to be suppressed to generate a market? In the case of technology, what should determine your price?

2.6.1 Modular assets

The other significant aspect about networks of assets that concerns a strategist is the question of modularity. A module, as you all know, fits in smugly with its complementary. In a production process, wherever such possibilities are there, a set of interface standards must also exist, at least implicitly if not explicitly. Modules adhering to 'interface standards' can then smugly fit into each other. To modularize a system, then, interface standards have to be created and enforced within the production network. A 'standard' is a social contract enforced sometimes by a regulator, else by a government executive. It is close to a legal document but without enforceability. Therefore, in order for a standard to come in vogue, it is desirable for at least one business firm to be sufficiently large; often a group of large firms enforce a standard, assisted by a regulator, and this the large firms enforce by virtue of their power of procurement and/or power of complementing.

Modular systems are characterized by low inter-module dependencies so that a partitioning between different modules is possible. Dependencies get captured in the rules of the interface or the standard that would connect different modules. Design changes within the module then can be made easily without bothering about other modules, as long as the interface rules are obeyed—this being captured through the notion of design independence or autonomy of the module owners. In case of an integral product, it is only the integrator who can lead and initiate any product development or new product designing initiatives; component producers would need to very deeply collaborate with the integrator to initiate any change. The integrator, in all such cases, would retain almost a veto power over the component producer. In practice, under such integral architectures, component producers would not invest in product development capability at all. Modularization of the product design, by reducing interdependencies across modules to a minimal set of shared interface rules, reduces the hold-up possibilities, allowing module owners to have autonomous development strategies. If you think of an automobile, you would realize that it is an integral product, quite in contrast to the personal computer (PC), which is very modular. Automobiles, thus, use very few common design components across cars of different firms or even cars across different platforms of the same automobile firm. Automobile components are thus non-standard, or were till very recent times when attempts at modularizing the design started off in the industry. A personal computer uses, in contrast, several common interchangeable components that are standardized.

In an information sense, modularization leads to encapsulation of module-specific information within the module owner, while releasing information about the interface into a public or quasi-public domain (that is, shared only amongst a limited club of firms). A large firm, through adoption of modularization, can encourage sharper competition amongst the suppliers or the complementary assets; competition at the module level can go up. Suppliers can also increase batch size of production (hence achieve scale economy) thereby reducing cost. Overall, modularization leads to cost reduction, as production processes are largely homogenized and requirements for costly and specialized information exchanges between supplier and procurer firms are reduced. Network modes of production in contemporary industries, as in mobile phones, computer systems and old industries such as furniture use modularization extensively.

2.6.2 Governance by module integrator

A lot, however, depends on how system integration takes place at the procuring or assembling firm. A firm can design a system with no modules but instead have a highly integrated set of closely enmeshed sub-systems; in such a case, strategic moves and innovation take place at both the firms and in joint consultation—when such production spans multiple firms. In the converse case, the procurer might keep system integration a closely guarded secret and a sticky as well as a specific asset, while keeping for open competition any module that fits in with port characteristics satisfying integrator's or assembler's requirement. A module supplier can of course be innovative but necessarily have to satisfy the standards. The nature of the modular system would differ depending on how public the interface standards are—that is, it can be fully public or can be shared amongst a closed set (or club) of suppliers. The literature makes a distinction between modularization in production systems and in the product architecture (or design) (Cusumano 1985, Takeishi and Fujimoto 2001). An integrator firm often can keep system integration (in a design sense) deeply enmeshed across sub-systems and hence integral, but might make production systems more modular and even outsourced in order to reduce module costs through commoditization. Production system modularization does not aim at and hence does not lead to product development capability build-up at module-owner level. Their role remains limited to module production and drives it towards commoditization. The integrator derives power out of the integral nature of designing and to the extent that in an inter-temporal game, newly innovated design continues to be of significance, the integrator maintains power over the network.

In the case of an M-form or a similar hierarchic large firm, a division or even a process could be thought of as a module but surely at a significant cost. In other words, it is costly to make modular asset or convert an integrated asset into a modularized form. It is usually a long engineering project that is required to achieve the feat. An asset that is modularized can easily be distanced from deep coordination that is exercised within an organization. Typically, outsourcing of business or knowledge processes (that would remove a module to an outsourced business partner) assume that those are, as it were, modular assets. Can you reason out what are the costs to modularizing of assets! Only a few years back experts used to praise integrated M-form asset.

What interests within an organization would like to partition such an integral asset into saleable modules? How do you think the price would be determined? Would you therefore need a divisional or a process asset to maintain own accounts, own cash-flow measurements?

In another word, is an integral asset just as an arithmetic sum of several divisional modular assets or is it the intermeshed nature of interrelationships between the different divisional modules that constitutes the essential nature of integral asset? In contemporary industries with extreme outsourcing, such process assets are often called 'governance assets' and is a key asset that allows the firm to exercise control over the wide network. Modular outsourced engagements would often fail without the creation of such assets. Finally, modularizing production processes could have driven commoditization and cost-leadership strategy; what gains would you have by modularizing organizational assets—are they of an increasing return type? Are the gains similar to what is sought through modularization of production assets?

2.6.3 Modularization to access sticky customer information

Traditional thoughts on production system designing through much of the last century did not think of customer specific information as too important. Think of different forms of consumption of tobacco—many readers would probably recollect modes of tobacco consumption when consumers could get their flavour of tobacco and roll their own cigarettes—much like the contemporary smoking (or hookah) joints. Compared to tobacco consumption as cigarette sticks, the other modes provided greater space to consumers to partly define consumption. Cigarettes, in contrast, provide for a standardization of the product—customer choice being limited to a short menu as provided by the producer. Differential customer preferences (regarding, say, variety or flavour of tobacco consumed) would be much less valuable to the cigarette mode compared to the tobacco (or hookah) mode. The cigarette producer's interest in variety in the consumption space is limited by the length of the menu of differentiated products that its FMCG style distribution can handle. A firm might have a larger (such as ITC) compared to a shorter menu of others, but no large firm would possibly want a massive proliferation of varieties at an increasing rate.

If you think of another important business function—pricing—you would notice that producers generally would post prices based on costs, partly because they have the information on costs while, at the same time, not having information on the utility value at the customer end. So the easiest thing to do is set uniform cost-based prices; if now you can devise a mechanism to reveal the preferences and utility of a product from a customer, then price discrimination becomes possible. That would increase profits, but it would require the design of a mechanism that makes it possible for producers to discover customer information. This is not easy. If such dispersed (sticky) customer assets are to be valuable to the producer, it has to devise a means to get access to such assets. Modularization provides one way to do that—something that several companies pursuing a user-led innovation strategy adopt.

The semiconductor industry provides a good example. Sometime during the evolution of the industry, few key technologists felt that customization of chip designing would become valuable, particularly since semiconductor applications were becoming multifarious—in a wide diversity of user contexts that differed in terms of what was required in performance. Telecommunication applications on a mobile set dealt with real-time problems, while an application in an extremely computation intensive application might not have the sensitivity to real-time requirements at all. So, user-specific sticky information and expertise would be valuable, but the architecture of the product then did not allow such a possibility. Repartitioning of innovation process tasks (into modules) had to be achieved through fundamental changes to the underlying architecture. Traditionally, manufacturers of custom semiconductors had carried out all chip design tasks themselves, guided only by need specifications from users. And because manufacturer development engineers were carrying out all design tasks, those engineers had typically incorporated need-related information into the design of both the fundamental elements of a circuit, such as transistors and the electrical 'wiring' that interconnected those elements into a functioning circuit.

The brilliant insight that allowed custom integrated circuit design to be partitioned into solution- and need-related subtasks was that the design of the chip's fundamental elements, such as its transistors, could be made standard for all custom digital circuit designs. This subtask required rich access to the manufacturer's sticky solution information regarding how semiconductors are fabricated, but did not require detailed information on specific user needs. It could therefore be assigned to manufacturer-based chip design and fabrication engineers. It was also observed that the subtask of interconnecting standard digital circuit elements into a functioning integrated circuit required only sticky, need-related information about chip function—for example, whether it was to function as a microprocessor for a calculator or the voice chip for a robotic dog. This subtask of 'wiring' the circuit was therefore assigned to users—the parties already in possession of the relevant need-related information. In other words, this new type of chip, called a 'gate array', had a novel architecture created specifically to separate problem-solving tasks requiring access to a manufacturer's sticky solution information from those requiring access to users' sticky need information. Tasks involving sticky solution information were then assigned to chip manufacturers, while those involving sticky need information were assigned to users.

This scheme is superior to general mass-customization modes, which is limited to a mix-and-match choice from a menu (maybe a wide menu) of parts, or elements. Here, the customer defines partly the product (the proverbial last mile), with the variation possibilities through designing in the customer module being immensely higher. While this re-architecturing helps producers tap into valuable customer information, realization of the new architecture that achieves the modularization through a technology (the gate array technology in this case) also poses a challenge to the old non-modularized mode of producing custom-chips.[26]

Readers would have noted that modularization in production often aims at commoditization and the inducing of a trajectory of decreasing returns reducing costs of modules, while modularization of product design aims at inducing an increasing returns flight—the change in governance attempts at inducing investment in product development to be shared between the integrator and the modular asset holders in novel ways restricted so far by the veto clout of the integrator. A flurry of

---

[26]You would recall our discussion of the Toyota governance system (see case study 2.3) that enabled the organization routine (the rules of coordination) to continuously transform itself through use of 'sticky micro-information assets' that would usually lie untapped at the worksite. You can now look at the design of rule-writing as a shared right at Toyota as a mode of seeking access to such 'sticky' assets. Implementing such a shared mechanism would usually require a modularization of tasks, so that interdependencies are minimized across modules. That would bring about role clarity. Negotiations under a shared right mode would not succeed without the aid of modularization.

new product, much larger product variation, and shorter lead times of development are then what is hoped for—a gain which would accrue over a longer time period than one achieved through the decreasing returns path of module commoditization.

Case Study 2.10: Rivalry in automobile industry and differential adoption of modularity

Automobile industry has been one of the pillar industries of the last century; yet, automobiles, unlike computer systems or mobile telephones, are not at all modular in either its designing or production. Is it possible to think of modular automobile systems—one condition you would recall is the growth of interface standards (such as Institute of Electrical and Electronics Engineers [IEEE] standards)? In the early years of the automobile industry, the Society of Automotive Engineers did attempt creation of such interface standards, so that component parts could become interchangeable (or have compatibility) across models and assemblers, but it did not find support among the large assemblers of the US—Ford and General Motors. Common component development, or interchangeability across products/platforms/ organizations, remained almost non-existent in the industry. Non-modularity, naturally, strengthened the organizational mode, creating the vertically integrated firms or at most (as in Japan) firms that shared interface standards within its own supplier system. The increased competitive intensity and financial crisis in several automobile firms have set off a search for new solutions—part of which is a rather slow attempt to embrace the concept of modularization.

Two German automakers—Mercedes and Volkswagen—set off the modularization process in the auto industry in the mid-1990s, setting up several plants following the new principles. Plants of both these firms departed from the traditional practice of assembly of a large set of small components on a long assembly line to assembly of a few larger sub-assemblies (new modules) on a shorter final assembly line. Few of these larger sub-assemblies were also outsourced to component producers—with significant production and designing responsibility. Mercedes, in a JV with a Swiss watchmaker, set up a plant for making 'Smart'—a new generation car that has different product architecture (that is, a new mapping of function to component or sub-assembly) obtained with important design inputs from the component producer Bosch.

The drive towards modularization is particularly strong in Europe due to a few factors. Modularization has been accompanied by outsourcing to leverage on much lower wage rates prevailing with component producers

(Case Study 2.10 contd.)

(Case Study 2.10 contd.)

providing an immediately achievable advantage, unlike in Japan where such wage differentials are far lower or even non-existent. Modularization along with outsourcing of production and designing would also reduce investment risks, which the Europeans are hoping would help them get back to profits. European component producers, over the past few years, have engaged in M&A and emerged as important forces shaping the evolution of modularization of the industry—taking greater control of design functions as they emerge as sub-assembly suppliers with enhanced design capabilities. Readers may note that the evolution of the module boundaries itself is a dynamic contested process and component maker M&A often aims at taking control and defining a module at a significantly large sub-assembly level. What kind of advantages might accrue to the European system that can depend on module owners' product development investments for introducing new products with shorter development lead times?

The Japanese automakers, in contrast, have not proceeded with any significant module outsourcing. Modularization has been driven by worker ergonomics and remained limited to own plant layout reorientation—to provide better work conditions as a way to attract workers (in great short supply in the 1990s) by having shorter assembly lines—and a system of several short lines for assembly of modules and a final assembly line to integrate the modules. Moreover, it has remained restricted to production system modularization, with attempts to move design to a more integral architecture. Along with this has been a desire to bring down quality control to the sub-assembly stage, which required a remapping of functions-sub-assemblies sets (product architecture), so that quality parameters could be clearly articulated. Product design remained, however, highly integral, and interdependencies among components even increased as the Japanese firms sought to strengthen the organizational mode of coordination. The Japanese have been driven by two major considerations in keeping themselves limited to component level outsourcing. Decades of component level procurement had allowed the managers of the Japanese assemblers to develop rich understanding and information on detailed cost structures of component-makers; such information built over years have been assetized and are used in supplier negotiations, which are often with dedicated suppliers and hence the pressure of commodity competition cannot be used as a bargaining tool. The Japanese had engaged in this kind of procurement much more effectively than the European Union (EU) automakers. A sudden shift to procurement at larger sub-assembly levels would

(Case Study 2.10 contd.)

> make the supplier internal process transparent and the historically developed negotiation asset irrelevant. Large assemblers were not prepared for that. Additionally, they also did not want to lose the utility of the distinctly Japanese multi-skilled workforce that can be redeployed across assembly lines and functions, which would be not as valuable if assembly gets reduced to putting together much larger sub-assemblies that are under supplier control. Both these sets of assets were distinct to the Japanese; Europeans, in contrast, never felt constrained in moving to sub-assembly procurement due to these kinds of considerations.
>
> Modularization in Europe has been led by redefinition of the inter-firm boundary and has been associated with increased outsourcing, while in Japan it has been a firm-internal process and has proceeded without significant changes in supplier relations. Outsourcing in Japan remains at the component rather than the larger sub-assembly levels at which design independence can possibly be thought of. Modularization of product architecture has thus been influenced significantly by component suppliers in Europe. Will Europe shift faster to common interface standards and interchangeable components shared across models and manufacturers?[27] (Excerpts from Takeishi and Fujimoto, 2001.)

2.7 A SHORT SUMMING UP

This chapter was an exploration of different modes of creation and valuation of assets. The strategist is not a passive actor in the resource market at all, procuring or selling at prices, implicitly behaving like a price-taker—descriptions based on a resource perspective often misses this important point. The resource world is not a world of power—it does not tell us much on how power is wielded. If at all there is a dimension of power that is important in the resource-based view, it is derived out of quantity commanded, such as procurement volume or through hoarding of scarce and valuable resources. An asset perspective, we argue, is richer then—for it often helps point towards the mechanisms of exercise

---

[27] Interested readers may explore the International Motor Vehicles Programme (http://www.imvpnet.org/) for more details.

of strategic voice. A strategy preserves its own assets—its volume as well as value—and in this project has to engage with other assets and asset owners, either contesting the rival asset to reduce its value or sharing it in different joint modes that we explored or even, in several cases, simply expropriating it from other asset holders. A particularly important point to note about contemporary businesses is the importance that asset sharing or establishing joint governance has assumed—this is one important mode of network-based strategies. Since assets get valorized increasingly in plays in wide networks—a strategy of simple resource hoarding often fails—it fails in extending governance over a wide milieu and over other assets. The reach of governance of the asset goes down. A simple deterrence mode, thus, often would fail to increase asset value. No doubt you see today a great intermeshing of businesses and value chains in complex webs, enhanced alliance activity, a frequent recourse to subsidiary modes and a plethora of public standards and races and contests around such assets.

APPENDIX 2A

Legendary Efficiency at Tokyo Metro

Visitors to Tokyo marvel at the ultra-modern appearance of much of the subway network and are baffled by the sight of young (Japanese) men openly reading cartoon porn during the rush hour. Crime is almost unknown on the network, as is vandalism. Prices are modest and begin at Y160 (US 1.35) for a single journey, with an all-month all-lines pass costing Y16,820.
—Views of a German executive travelling frequently in metros across the globe (on his weblog)[28]

One day, a friend of mine commented that 'after living in Tokyo for quite sometime, I have learnt that even crowded commuter trains run to the second. I have literally set my watch by a bullet train's scheduled arrival time' (Pilling 2007). Tokyo has not one but two subways. Teito Rapid Transit Authority (TRTA) which runs eight lines is owned partly by the national government and partly by the metropolitan government. Table 2A.1 compares TRTA with the London Underground, Kolkata Metro and Delhi Metro for the years 2006–07.

What is more, Japanese attention to comfort and convenience is simply a bonus to the efficiency. Several stations have individual jingles play when the doors open, so that those who have nodded off during the ride (as many commuters do) will recognize their station's tune and alight

---

[28]Andrew Stevens, 'Tokyo Metro: The World's Cleanest and Most Extensive Subway System', available at http://www.citymayors.com/transport/tokyo_metro.html (accessed on 28 May 2011).

Table 2A.1: Metro Railways in Different Cities

	Tokyo Metro	Delhi Metro	Kolkata Metro	London Underground
Stations	164	65	17	253
Route (kilometerage)	177	59	16	408
Passengers per day (in millions)	5.58	0.45	0.34	2.53
Number of carriages	2,455	640	NA	3,954

Source: Compiled by authors from various sources.

when necessary. And the distinct scent of a Japanese subway train is lovely. The train cars are always climate controlled and comfortable, but this added touch is noteworthy, an only-in-Japan oddity.

Compared to the London metro, Tokyo has fewer stations, fewer track miles, fewer cars and yet carries more passengers. How does it do it? Actually, a part of the answer is possibly right there in the table above. Fewer track miles means fewer trains idling along with a small number of passengers. It also helps that Tokyo is more densely populated than London. TRTA is also well-run. According to its handbook, it makes a profit (after interest payments) of about USD 110 million a year. So, what is going on here? A consistently well-run profitable enterprise managed by the state.

There is another aspect that really helps. At an early stage, TRTA decided to build its tunnels to a standard (for Japan) track gauge and loading gauge (that is, the size of the car) and a standard power supply. This has meant that it has been possible to allow through running from and to private and Japanese National Railway tracks. While other countries including Britain and India have been debating the merits of Cross-Rail, that is, a mainline railway running underneath, for over a decade, in Japan they designed in that possibility almost at the start. In other words, at an early stage of its existence it made decisions that have had extremely good effects decades later.

A few experts reason that the existence in Japan of a large number of well-run private railways has provided a discipline for and competition to state-run railways. Perhaps we can also argue that Japan's legendary efficiency has also little to do with technology—as is sometimes supposed—and much more to do with people's attitude to work. If you watch Tokyo's subway guards, you will notice that they run everywhere, as if they were on army manoeuvres. So do many others in Japan. Everywhere you look, the Japanese work with an unmatched speed and efficiency.

The railway system is sustained not only by the rolling stock and railroad tracks, but also by specialists in various fields such as electricity, communications, station management, train service planning, and so on. If even one of these elements is missing, the trains will not operate. For smooth railway service, the people in charge of each part of the system must perform their work to the same high standard. If even one individual in any one section of the system tolerated slight delays occasionally, there is no way the railway system can achieve an average delay of less than one minute. As is often noted in the field of business studies, the 'excellent companies' that enjoy consistently outstanding levels of performance and success are never just superior to the rest. In most cases, they are significantly better. Furthermore, such companies always have a corporate culture dominant enough to guide employees towards these outstanding achievements (see Mito, undated). The same applies to Japanese railways as well.

The Japanese railway companies have devoted so much money, time, labour and passion to ensure on-time service. The on-time service is assumed on the passengers' side as well. Japanese travellers plan their holidays as if train schedules act as the pivots of the entire itinerary. That is why passengers in Japan are often incensed by a rare delay of merely five minutes. But on the other hand, Japanese passengers are unbelievably cooperative when it comes to ensuring on-time service. Even in Japan, you will be hard-pressed to think of an industry in which the 'valued customers' cooperate so well with the service provider. Passengers just intuitively know they have to play a part in ensuring on-time service. On the cleanliness aspect of the Japanese Metro, a globetrotting American executive commented on a traveller's blog:

> Having spent a respectable chunk of my lifetime riding metros in New York and Boston, in my mind, "subways" are automatically synonymous with "soil." The fact that I should never touch the railings nor be surprised by trails of trash and waste in American subway stations is a given. In Japan, you could eat off the platform floor if you had to, and don't expect to see an empty coffee cup or pages of newspaper come rolling down the train aisles. These train cars are as sanitary as hospital waiting rooms.
>
> I was recently amused by one of my train's conductor's obligatory nighttime trek down the length of the train to pick up any trash. He had a small plastic bag shoved in his pants pocket and wore a pair of sanitary gloves.

I watched him walk down empty-handed and walk back the exact same way. I laughed internally and shook my head in disbelief. How is it that a public subway system remains spanking clean all the time?

I soon learned just how much the Japanese value the cleanliness of their subway after a friend and I accidentally dropped a few papers onto the floor of the subway car without noticing. The man next to my friend and the woman sitting next to me both gave us a bit of a nod toward the floor and an expectant look. Nobody eats on the subways out of respect for making a mess in such small quarters. Rarely will I even see someone drinking on the subways.

Everyone uses the subway, and I mean everyone. This is perhaps the first subway line I have been on where doctors, university professors, and corporate head honchos use it on a regular basis. There is absolutely no shame in riding the Tokyo Metro. Simply put, the Japanese are proud of their mass transit.

Yet, there is an aspect of the subways here that falls on the complete opposite end of the spectrum and into a category entirely unto itself: the issue of men ogling pornographic magazines and comic books. At six in the morning, at eleven at night, it happens regardless.

How the Japanese choose to draw the line as to what's respectful and what's not is something a foreigner like myself needs time to digest and understand in due time. Luckily for me, I have hundreds and hundreds of hours left to spend on the subways to draw closer to some sort of conclusion. (Roeser 2004)

While we can give accolades to the Tokyo Subway for its efficiency, on the other hand, it would be unfair to blame the Indian Metro authorities completely for their poor show, that is, for the relatively low utilization and frequency of trains (see Table 2A.1). The Indian metro systems have to compete with cheaper modes of public transport such as buses and trams. In addition, one should also consider the fact that Delhi and Kolkata, unlike Tokyo and London, have a very large percentage of poor people. Quite often, they cannot afford even the fare of the Metro, which appears more than reasonable to the upper and middle class users. Kolkata Metro is also often hit by strikes.

Furthermore, experts point to the absence of composite ticketing in these cities, which is prevalent in many developed countries, where the same ticket can be valid for the underground as well as for buses, trams and even suburban trains. For instance, a traveller from one corner of Kolkata, who has to go to work to another corner of Kolkata, will be in a quandary during office hours if he has to change from the Metro midway and take a bus.

Similarly, it can be argued that residents in London have good access to public transport, and buses and trains run frequently with good off-peak service. But like Indian Metros, London has poor punctuality[29] and the worst waits for bus service. A recent report on the London subway also noted that the London system is in need of renovation and modernization because of its age.

What would you ascribe the success of Tokyo Metro to (in terms of punctual train running)—its own elaborate planning and control system or on a successful piggybacking on the cultural norm of punctuality in Japanese people? Can you view such cultural norms as a specific asset that is socially generated (in wider social system, such as schooling system!) and like a common pool asset can be piggybacked on by businesses? Should a firm's strategy be influenced by such specific cultural assets? (See also Sosnoski, 1996.)

---

[29]Well, you might think that the countries in Europe have railways that boast of punctuality. However, a closer look at the figures shows that the definition of 'delay' is very different. In most European railway systems, a 'delay' is defined as '15 minutes behind schedule'. In other words, for example, '14 minutes behind schedule' is still counted as 'on time'. This is how European railway companies are able to obtain high punctuality. On the other hand, the definition of 'delay' in Japan is more severe; only trains with less than a minute's delay is defined as 'on time'. Therefore, the sense of punctuality is fairly different.

3

Strategy and Organization

3.0 INTRODUCTION

Strategy literature in the last decade often made a distinction between strategy formulation and implementation—in fact, in terms of pedagogy and the way the discipline is taught in (at least) India, that divide is still retained. While formulation interfaces with the external world, implementation looks inside the organization; and the classical texts would generally follow formulation. The division is conceptual. It also separates the terrain of enquiry and discourse. Implicit in the division is also a salience granted to formulation as preceding implementation in the world of practice—a notion that many in the mainstream discourse would carry. This has several implications, one of which was the classic formulation of Alfred Chandler that 'structure' of the organization (or the creation of the bare bones framework of reporting relations, information flows and control mechanisms) would flow from the strategy adopted by the organization.

His studies of the giant American corporations of the mid-20th century also pointed towards such a phenomenon.[1] Most organizations studied were extremely intensive in fixed assets, and were quintessential manufacturing firms, mostly producing commodity-type products. Like the classic example of Du Pont, they diversified in the scope direction, forming separate divisions under the common authority of the

---

[1] See, for example, Chandler (1962).

corporate structure, as their (manufacturing) process led to generation of new product lines—often by-products of a common process whose markets had to be created. By-products often required different downstream assets compared to the main products, such as distinct marketing or distribution assets to be built up. A business division provided such partial autonomy to create differentiated assets through which such markets could be reached, created or controlled. This is what has come to be known as the multi-divisional (M-form) corporate structure, and a separation between corporate (domain of corporate headquarter) and business (domain of the business division) strategy. In the account then, the Chandlerian organizational structure (in its multi-divisional form) evolved from requirements of specific strategy pursuits. To put it in another way, the organization is viewed then as a tool of implementation of a specific strategy. If seen as a tool for fulfilling strategy objectives, implementation can only follow formulation. Organization design and strategy then fits together. It is, as readers would understand, a very rational account.

This view has been contested from several perspectives and a contemporary account does not recognize the distinction between formulation and implementation too strictly, particularly in terms of its ordering. It is perfectly plausible to imagine a scenario when an internal organizational initiative (of, say, restructuring) is set off not from a preconceived strategy or an external positioning that is sought but from something else—maybe a desire to seek dominance over internal nodes of power which thwarts the CEO—and the strategy unfolds only ex-post, through a process of destruction of old nodes of power and the formation of novel nodes that were just in a germinal state (often dormant) in the old organizational formation, unconnected to other complementary nodes. Progressive strengthening of such alternative internal nodes then engages in a search for a sustained business model. Several successful BPR initiatives are actually of this type. Change in this perspective, then, is not driven through fiat which would first require a clarity on the strategy to be adopted—leadership in the change process is rather like unleashing a novel force or sets of forces, and then stand as a sort of bystander, enjoying partial fruits through shared cash flow rights or even control rights as the novel turf evolves through the activities of the unleashed forces.

There was another problem as well. While formulation could move towards a more systematic formalism—through generation of frameworks—implementation remained a sticking point; articulation of a theory of implementation seemed extremely difficult. This difficulty created the imagery of strategy as 'crafting'; and implementation was the domain where craft imagery remained most pronounced.[2] Implementation remained the domain of 'star' implementer as the 'dramatis persona'—beyond the analytical rigour that the discourse on formulation sought to embrace. Formulation, in contrast, could be analytical. In this chapter, we explore the organizational world; but we do not conform to the formulation–implementation divide. In other chapters, we contested the formalism in the domain of strategy formulation as well— arguing that the simpler formal frameworks, on deeper deconstruction, turn out to be manifestations of particular problems faced in practice during a particular point in history—so it is institutionally contextual and limited to management of certain types of assets (mostly heavy on fixed assets) and decreasing returns product markets alone. It was also institutionally specific to the design of legal/regulatory framework that was rooted in what we called 20th-century notion of equity as the sole carrier of bundled business risks. Multiple specific risk markets were absent in such institutional milieu. The notion of a strong organizational boundary that separated one from another organization was an outcome of such an institutional design. Therefore, looking at a formulation–implementation divide or at extra-organizational (or market environment) and intra-organizational concerns as separate domains made perfect pragmatic sense.

Our discussion in the earlier chapters argued that a different context, such as an increasing returns product market or systemic product markets (we discuss systemic products in detail in Chapter 4) or the business of platform provisioning (such as stock exchange business!), would need us to articulate different kinds of frameworks or even concepts to capture the dynamics of what we earlier called the external market. For instance, we argued that a contemporary networked business world would require the strategist to adopt an asset perspective—looking at own assets in relation to other assets, influencing relative asset valuation frameworks, and so on. This is especially important since nodes of power and the modes of wielding of power get altered more frequently today—such as through novel use of informatics-based intermediation or disintermediation moves that necessarily span a network of firms.

In this chapter, organizations are looked at as one mode, often in contest with other modes of linking transactions—such as a network of

---

[2] See, for example, Mintzberg (1987).

several partners bound by contracts, or a thick network of business relations loosely bound through inter-temporally formed trust assets. Organization agendas then are today very deeply driven by agendas in wider extra-organizational networks of asset holders. This is a kind of deep influence—quite distinct from the analytical perspective of looking at the extra-organizational environment as a background that provides opportunities or threats to business. This influence goes deep into the very core of intra-organizational practices—it is disruptive; the protective mask of the fixed organizational boundary that often ensconced such practices in the intra-organizational field alone lies punctured today.

3.0.1 Organizational or extra-organizational power

Would the concerns of a platform owner, such as a commodity exchange, conflict with the interests of the holder of organizational power in a firm that is in the business of production of a commodity? The organization interest may want control over pricing—in traditional producer set (cost plus) pricing systems; that practice would itself limit the trading volume of the exchange. Exchange business would go up if all producers of a commodity agree to participate in the trade in the exchange and such competition sets up market clearing prices. The exchange venture can then stand as the purveyor of such Walrasian competitive pricing system.[3] Note how the producer firms now have to reorganize their pricing function—practices such as pricing schedules (that remained stable for long horizons, and a change in it was a news), or of discount-based marketing would be unstable. Pricing on the exchange would even have intra-day fluctuations and the notion of a single price would go. The trader in a trading desk of the producer firm sending bids in the computerized terminal that provides access to the exchange would be a key pricing point, rather than a more central high level pricing committee manned by senior managers in marketing and finance functions. The exchange venture, in their business interest, would go and set up such trading desks in the commodity producer organizations, deeply effecting core organizational practices. Could you imagine a scenario when

---

[3]Walrasian competition refers to price clearing markets that elementary textbooks on 'economics' deal with.

producers outside a cartel arrangement in a commodity industry would want to strengthen such a platform as a way to undermine cartel power? Control over pricing, i.e., who sets prices, alone or together with several others, following certain rules (or loose criterion), appears to be a key area of conflict. Those familiar with states of affairs in contemporary organized retailing in India would know how this ability to set prices is the point of contention between FMCG-type producers, such as Hindustan Unilever, and organized retailers like Big Bazaar and Spencers Retail. Maximum Retail Price (MRP) type regulations in India, which makes printing of MRP in packaged goods mandatory, ensure that Hindustan Unilever Limited (HUL) has a control over setting price (at least the maximum price) at the point of final consumer purchase. Unilever in the US, in contrast, does not enjoy this privilege; final retail point pricing there is in the domain of the large-scale retailer there. In private label brands, however, organized multi-store (multi-brand) retailers in India enjoy such privileges of being able to set prices at the points of purchase.

Unlike other accounts, which seek to look at organizations from an efficiency perspective—as if reaching of efficiency is the purpose of the organization—we argue that the basic premise of an organization formation must lie in the desire for dominance, over internal nodes of power as well as those lying outside the organization boundaries. Only in certain cases would efficiency be the objective or purpose of such an organization. As we argued in the introductory chapter, our account is rooted in the individual subject—the strategist subject who thinks and acts. From such a standpoint, the organization is just one element in a wider canvas—often with only a hazy boundary between the intra-organizational and the extra-organizational. Power and the desire to dominate pervades across this wide canvas. But organization surely differs from the outside—in terms of how power and control are wielded. Thus, we argue that the story of an organization, from a strategy standpoint, must be relative to this difference with what is possible or feasible outside the organization, in terms of means and levers of control and influence that a strategist can use, in pursuance of the motive to win.

Our discussion in this chapter proceeds as follows. We first engage with the notion of organization as a coherent unit, which is the dominant view, arguing in the process that pragmatically an organization can be better visualized as a temporary coalition of fractured domains of power (see section 3.1). Organization has multiple stakeholders, in contest, often in explicit violent conflicts, with each other in a sort of balance that is dynamic over time. It is like a field with a balance of power that the leader seeks to influence and modulate. That takes us to a discussion on the modes of formation of nodes of power in the intra-organizational field (see section 3.2).

One dimension of our discussion seeks a distinction between power in the intra-organizational and the extra-organizational fields (see sections 3.0.1, 3.1, 3.2 and 3.3). We visualize intra-organizational exercise of power as a kind of executive authority. Node formation inside an organization then seeks to create such positions of executive authority and generate a legitimization around the exercise of executive authority. Formation of an organization then is a contested choice on whether certain transactions would occur under executive authority or under governance forms that are in the extra-organizational domain (see section 3.3).

We discuss a few dimensions of such contest; in particular, we argue that retaining tacitness of transactional practices (like a tacit process asset!) or, in other words, limiting its transparency to certain thick intra-organizational networks serve to strengthen the claim of the organizational executive authority as the preferred mode of governance of a transaction. (Readers can refer to case study 1.9, where we showed how coding of design expertise was a precondition for inter-organizational collaboration in ASIC industry, removing certain processes beyond the organizational boundary.)

We then discuss the structure of an organization, visualizing it as an inter-nodal balance of power inside the organization (see section 3.4). Restructuring then is a tinkering or an attempt to chart out an alternative path to a new balance of power. Restructuring is a dynamic process, power infused and almost always heavily contested, either through explicit opposition or through tacit subversion. In emphasizing the dynamic element, we argue that the path chosen—and the temporal ordering—is most important rather than a rational static account of a coherent structure. Restructuring, as a reorientation of the balance of power, then is not purely an intra-organizational affair; nodes of power outside the organization remain enmeshed in such conflicts as allies or rivals. The intra-organizational and extra-organizational fields then constitute a continuum shaped through the acts of the strategist leader. We illustrate each of these arguments with instances of restructuring episodes. We end the chapter with a brief summary of the dimensions of organization as a specific mode of exercise of power (see section 3.5).

3.1 ORGANIZATION AS A HOMUNCULUS OR AS FRACTURED COALITIONS

Several descriptions of organization from a strategy perspective assume the organization to be a homunculus—that is, it has a unity of purpose or intent. Such an organization can be deployed to the achievement of a strategy or, from the other side, such an organization can evolve, through visioning, a coherent strategy, which then can be executed.[4] Formulation can assume this description of the organic whole in terms of unity of intent; while the implementation domain can then be the vehicle to ensure that deviation does not occur—rogue intent working at cross purposes can be smoothened out through effective design and execution of intrusive control tools. The 'homunculus' assumption is too simplistic and it is plausible and more fruitful to view an organization as a collection (or a coalition) of several conflicting motives and intent even in the best of times of its organizational life. Such incoherence, politicking, factionalism, interdepartmental and inter-divisional rivalries, personal fiefdoms, and so on, constitute the staple of managerial gossip; it is an important part of the lived life of managers. Such incoherence of purpose is normal, therefore, and is not an aberration. The internal canvas of the organization is as chaotic as the external one, where the organization faces a wider network or a market. The organization can then be viewed as a site of numerous negotiations—and just as outcome of negotiations remain unpredictable a priori, organizational outcomes also remain so.

Multiple agenda and nodes or the coordinators inside who set such agenda for both negotiation and subversion constitute the organization of a firm. In the first chapter, we discussed the notion of a 'node' of power—as a seat that has a power to effect a denial. We also identified

---

[4]This should warn readers to the possibility that a codified or formally articulated vision statement often does not capture the de facto strategic stance of an organization—something that one would often feel in practice inside an organization. Mostly, such statements remain quite nebulous—without a clear articulation of threats or a clear delineation of the novelty sought to be created or a clear articulation of the turf excluded. Only under certain conditions when clarity exists and a dominant coalition of the holders of a particular intent takes note of the threat or agrees on a novel state of affairs that they jointly want to move to would a codified vision statement more closely align with practice. In certain cases, codified statements might not reveal the main perceived threat, since a public signalling into the wider milieu is not desired at that stage. Readers are suggested to visit websites of some of the popular companies and see their articulated vision statements (and critic the same).

several means through which such nodes get formed. If we have to move away from the notion of the organization as a homunculus—a rational whole—then we have to search for such nodes inside the organization. Formation of nodes, strengthening of existing nodes, decimation of rival nodes, and such acts of balancing amongst contending nodes constitute the organizational agenda of a strategist. If we recall our argument developed in the first chapter, nodes were formed through three broad mechanisms—one was of information encapsulation or asymmetry, the other was through agglomeration in the resource or asset space that creates a lumpiness that provides a voice to the seat that holds or controls access to the lump and the third was through effective bundling of several assets that defines a power over the assets thus bundled.

> Think of a BPR initiative that seeks to link directly actors/managers along a process path that spans across divisions enabling direct transactions between them. Divisional heads have often been against such moves; it undermines the power of the divisional heads. If you think of the nature of this power, you would have to think of the agglomeration—the division as a lump—over which the divisional head would command control and often would be able to negotiate with other division heads on the basis of such lumpy nodal power. Inter-divisional negotiations then provide a key tool for generating organizational dynamics. If a process-based coordination is instead instituted following BPR consultant advice on, maybe, grounds of improving process efficiency and reducing coordination cost, what would be the alternative node formation mechanism in the organization that would drive its dynamics? Would the organization disintegrate without adequate node formation? We provide narrations later on how lack of control over assets (or alternatively non-formation of a node) reduces the top management's ability to act. Imagery of an organization as a rational homunculus would not let one understand and appreciate such concerns that seems to dominate top management minds.

In our earlier discussion in previous chapters, we had argued that a strategist manoeuvres across several such nodes that constitute the milieu—or the turf of strategic action. Our emphasis on the intricate linkage between the intra- and extra-organization fields would also mean that nodes spread across the whole canvas, including those outside, often act like a continuum over which the leader's action pervades. If we view the organization as an outcome of a tussle, then necessarily we cannot subscribe to the notion of a static organization as well. Several accounts of organizational coherence, such as the McKinsey framework,[5] which seek a jigsaw-like fit, are simply incapable of providing any account of this dynamic aspect. An organization is then a dynamically evolving entity, and negotiations across several nodal power holders provide it the dynamism that sets it in motion over time. Contests over control, cornering of resources, setting and shaping of agendas, tussles over contesting institutional paths, and influencing voting of others in favour of one's own assets would constitute a concrete story of this dynamism.

Thus, negotiations and conflicts may be seen as dynamic phenomenon and like our earlier notion of asset, this temporal dimension is important. Negotiations may often be kept protracted over long horizons with intra-organizational nodes in tandem with nodes that lie outside the organization. One may think of the 'Apple Store' as a platform to a few million suppliers; does such immense support from the extra-organizational 'voters' shape up internal organizational dynamics inside Apple Inc.?

Readers may also appreciate why it is so important for the senior managers of a spun-off entity to immediately seek outside business, so that parental control over revenue remains at most moderate. Without such balance from outside forces, the spun-off entity will hardly command the power to reform and reshape parental organizational practices and nodes of power and their interrelations that might be required for driving its business growth.

> Readers may note how the business portfolio of Bajaj Finserv Limited and Mahindra & Mahindra Financial Services Limited have changed with a larger chunk of business coming from outside the group/parent firms, Bajaj Auto and Mahindra & Mahindra. On the other hand, Ashok Leyland Finance Limited (a subsidiary of Ashok Leyland Limited) and Nagarjuna Finance Limited (a subsidiary of Nagarjuna Group) have portfolios dominated by group business. Would you think that the faster growth of Bajaj Finserv and Mahindra & Mahindra Financial Services, compared to the other two firms, can be ascribed to this difference?

---

[5]In the early 1980s, the consulting company McKinsey & Company proposed the McKinsey's 7S Model. Structure, strategy, systems, skills, style, staff and shared values were the seven *levers*. An organization was analysed in terms of its fitness and coherence across these seven elements. For more, refer Peters and Waterman (1982).

Extra-organizational nodes, in partnerships, can strengthen certain internal nodes and weaken others. Contrarily, in an intra-organizational power tussle, extra-organizational nodes are valuable potential allies or rivals.

The strategist thus has to engage with the chaotic canvas described above. Taking this perspective removes the (intellectual) desire to seek coherence (and robust explanations) and opens up several apparently irrational organizational moves to new interpretations that can, in turn, inform action. Can you think of moves inside the organization which otherwise would appear quite irrational—except when you note the conflict it induces? Can a CEO deliberately induce such a move to open up the proverbial Pandora's box to seek a negotiation with an erstwhile power node that had so far remained beyond grasp?

How does the strategist engage in this series of negotiations, so to say, inside the organization? Briefly recounting our discussion in the first chapter, such moves must be informed by an understanding of the process or basis of node formation, nature of assets of nodal power holders and interrelationship between different nodal power holders. Acts of the strategist must seek the fourfold levers of: (*a*) punishment or the threat, (*b*) encouragement, (*c*) reward and (*d*) differentiation to modulate the negotiations and seek a winning over of nodal power holders. Readers may go back to the first chapter for detailed understanding of the fourfold strategic acts.

We now move to discussion on different aspects of an organization and how a strategist may look at it in pursuit of the win within the organizational field that is sought.

3.2 RULES, ROUTINES AND AUTHORITY IN ORGANIZATION

Coordination achieved inside an organization amongst several complex tasks requires a set of rules that bind several activities together in a coherent way. In classic large organizations, such coordination led to generation of a unified product—such as an automobile that enshrined the complex coordination in a single product. Each task needed to link up, in a rather smooth fashion, to the larger whole in such an organization. Rules were the formal definition of these linkages, often enshrined in written work documentation (often called Standard Operating

Procedures [SOPs]). Design of intra-organizational coordination, in most accounts, would seek a coordination of multiple tasks that need to be performed to generate, say, an automobile, a product flowing out of integrated organizational effort! Such accounts root coordination within a rational purposive discourse linked to certain objectives of production/profit. Departure from an account of organization as a homunculus that we argued for would lead us to viewing rules as a governance tool instead. We detail several dimensions of our argument below.

3.2.1 Rules, routines, tacitness and organizational power

Apart from formal codified rules, organizations also possess a 'way of doing things or getting things done' that may not always be written down explicitly. A large literature called these 'routines',[6] or habitual ways of doing things, which included, apart from the rules, certain epistemic capability (to provide answers or solutions only on a query) of the work participants (or managers) that were a part of the knowledge repertory. This type of knowledge cannot be fully described and gets accessed only on a query or in the face of a context or a problem. This difference between the rule and routine is important, since the non-codified element of the routine has been argued to be an organization-specific sticky asset (also called tacit knowledge); it cannot be accessed from outside the structure of the organization. If you recall our discussion of the Toyota Production System (in case study 2.3), where work rules were written in a shared mode with the workers—the governance mechanism was aimed at engaging the worker (you can visualize his/her knowledge as capable of responding as an epistemic engine) who would bring such tacit knowledge.

This tacit, sticky knowledge has been seen as a unique organizational asset which can define an advantage for the organization; recall how we argued that the several Japanese automobile companies are trying to retain the integrated organizational mode in contrast to the Western manufacturers emphasizing modularization with an intent to outsource. (See the section on modular assets.) Between codified and tacit knowledge then lies a boundary, on something like a continuum that is of concern to a strategist. Codification of an erstwhile tacit knowledge can lead to the formation of a process asset (such as process software) that can then

---

[6]See, for instance, Nelson and Winter (1982).

be disembodied from the internal organizational setting. Recall how this disembodying through software tools was crucial to the transfer of relevant producer-specific information to customer engineers in the early years of the ASIC industry that enabled joint product designing (see case study 1.9). This 'unsticking' was the most crucial step in the evolution of the industry. Contrarily, letting information lie in a tacit state would diffuse it in the dense communication networks internal to the organization—such process assets then remain hidden from potential hijack by organizational outsiders. Internal nodes of power in the organization remain the purveyors of such tacit assets.

3.2.2 Rule-following organization or rules as context for negotiation

Rules, however, raise another question—who writes the rule? Power, in fact, would lie in writing the rules. One can also ask what ensures that rules are followed while minimizing opportunism, i.e., at very low transaction costs. A rule-following organization is a myth flowing from the image of an organization as an organic whole; in fact, more than rules, rule changes are important (or changes in routine) and that process involves negotiations throughout the organization. Contemporary understanding of rule brings out another reason to doubt the notion of rule-following behaviour. If one simply asks what it means to follow a rule, one can realize that rule following can be most easily cognized through instances of breaking of the rule alone. Following a rule is more unclear and inexact. Workers on assembly lines understand this very well—and work-to-rule is quite a common form of protest over management decisions, where non-violation of rules ties the management ability to wield the penal threat and yet the coordination process inside the organization gets subverted.

It is in fact possible to show that a rule-following organization is a myth—such an organization, if it existed, would not have any dynamism whatsoever. Rules, then, can at most define the boundaries—like an injunction—of what is not to be done under certain circumstances. Inside the boundary remains a huge grey zone of action that would constitute organizational life, where rules do not provide a leverage of influence to a power holder. So, why does a power holder take interest in rules? Rewriting of rules is often an act of redefining the boundaries of action—and it provides a means to reorder relations between the multiple nodal power holders inside an organization.

Those who have worked in organizations would also realize that such negotiations over rule changes are difficult and are politicized and quite susceptible to subversion as well. Power holders often use tools such as influencing committee formations or modes of decision-making or setting agendas (often bounded mandates) of committees where contests over 'rule changes' are staged. In other words, taking control of or influencing the voting process appears to be the key. Many observers of managerial processes—constructing theories out of detailed studies of work-life—argued that the political processes are central and it was noted that a strategy as 'intended' by the senior management team does not necessarily get implemented; what emerges is something quite different—called the 'emergent' strategy—pointing towards an implementation slip. So, the top management, especially in a large organization, cannot hope to run its fiat through the organization—the organization as a homunculus fails. This important insight (primarily from the works of Henry Mintzberg[7]) is missed by several structuralist accounts that view organization as a smoothened rational construct.[8] One way to understand this apparent lack of power of the leader of the organization lies in the fact that cooperation of the nodal power holders is crucial for the leader. They are key organizational gatekeepers and enjoy agglomeration power in several senses.

It is impossible then to view the key power holders (or the top management team) as resources—such as human resources (HR)—in a market. They often are quite irreplaceable, unlike a market resource. In other words, they are not often tradable and the threat of the market often does not work as a governance tool in the intra-organizational field of power. Authority inside an organization, in this sense, is quite distinct and is a kind of executive-based authority not witnessed in a market. This notion of an executive authority as a point of control over assets that do not enjoy a market (and we referred to several such assets in our discussions earlier) needs to be clearly understood. We explicated earlier the notion

---

[7]See Mintzberg and Waters (1985).

[8]Such description emphasizes the aspect of symmetry and fit (as in a jigsaw puzzle) between the different elements. The frictions, or power tussles, are not emphasized. It also does not inform an actor on how to act—what would drive what? Would the infusion of a new skill (or skill-holder) drive the change to a new system (or rule set), or would it be otherwise—a system change generating the organizational demand for a new skill which is then inducted? The temporal order would be crucial in a dynamic story, while a static account would not worry much on it. By neglecting the dimension of power, it undermines the description of the process of change that is of greater concern to an acting strategist.

of tacit knowledge assets as one such type of asset over which executive authority dominates. In our contemporary times, several forms of executive authority may be witnessed, not only inside organizations but also in large financial institutions, such as sovereign wealth funds (see Appendix 5D). Executive power is a counterpoint to the market, such that creation of a market in an asset would undermine executive authority over the asset. It 'unbundles' the marketable or tradable asset and by taking it to the market (or its transaction to the market or extra-organizational network mode), removes it beyond the exercise of intra-organizational executive authority. *This point is most crucial.*

Linking up to our discussion in the previous section, we argued that an organizational intervention is often conceived over a wide canvas that includes several extra-organizational nodes. With the notion of executive power as distinct from and a counterpoint to the market, exercise of organizational authority can look at creative ploys, such as moving a conflict with an internal nodal power holder into the market domain or, say, involve an outside executive authority in the negotiation process by creating mutual business interest. Several (business) projects are in fact conceived with such motives of shifting the turf of negotiation, sometimes broadening the turf to include several more nodal power holders or otherwise constricting it to narrower turfs. Particularly important is the joint management of executive authority and market discipline; market often provides an objectivity that can be usefully leveraged in a negotiation process by an executive authority inside the organization. Markets and competition around market processes make information transparent or, in other words, generates profuse information. Readers may now appreciate why business process outsourcing, by creating an outside organizational node (the outsourced business process owner) or more often a process asset market (where the process asset is commoditized with several offerings), redefines the way an intra-organizational conflict and its negotiation unfolds. Our discussion on DoCoMo's launch of the i-mode business would provide an illustration later in the chapter (see case study 3.5).

3.2.3 Organization and executive authority

Following from our above discussion, we argue that an organization can be viewed from a strategy perspective as composed of the following elements, which can help one grasp better the exercise of authority inside an organization:

1. The 'chief' of the organization, and his/her lieutenants. Two aspects need to be considered. The intent of the 'chief' and the mode through which he/she hopes to win or 'enjoy the fruits of a win' is extremely important. A general description of a profit maximizing individual does not suffice. The several dimensions of cognition of a win are important. We explore this aspect below. The relation between the 'chief' and the lieutenants is also extremely important—such as the relation of CEO of business group (BG) companies and the family patriarch.
2. The structure of the organization, which is an assemblage of several nodes of power, defining through their interrelationships (such as through reporting relations) a form of information sharing and encapsulation—a hierarchy of privileges such as budgetary sanction rights.[9] Such cathedral type constructs, by their very design, induce information asymmetry and provide a pan-organization view to certain privileged vantage points while denying it to others, which supports the exercise of authority inside the organization.
3. The mechanism of grant of reward by the chief or the power holder; several organizations would have an incentive system to address this. But we must note that the incentive system, so much as it is a fully coded system (with no uncertainties), cannot be a lever of power. The node of power must have uncertainties inherent in it—it must be a site of discontinuity. (Recall our discussion in section 1.7 on the concept of a node, and power as a voting right at the node that can induce a discontinuity in outcome.) An incentive system is then part of a routine, while redesigning of incentive system would be a strategic act. The incentive system therefore immediately would raise the issue of lobbying, since incentive system is always a scale, whose design can never be neutral to different parties. Power, therefore, is exercised around the allocation of such incentive systems—that is, a domain of negotiation. You can see the case study on Citibank

---

[9]You would note that in organizations such as Reliance Industries, important powers such as budgetary sanctioning authority vary widely among managers at similar levels but handling different roles, such as in different projects. Several privileges in such organizations remain contingent, subject to frequent changes, reversals and negotiations. This would be quite unlike a typical US multinational corporation. This difference clearly locates the executive power of the owners and the small core group.

restructuring (case study 3.4) as an instance of how the top management used incentive reallocation as a tool of change—a tool with the power holder must be noted by the milieu (intra-organizational in this case) to be an effective tool.
4. The exercise of threat inside the organization and its mode.
5. The exercise of discrimination inside the organization and the power holder acting as the arbiter of such 'internal tournaments'. Promotions, access to key projects and roles, provide such occasions. An organizational life of wins and losses—several rounds of such temporal races played out with vigour—retains the rationale of the organizational life and the mode of exercise of power. Are wins in internal tournaments, which define the ladder up an organization, based only on performance? Lived experience of organizational life would tell you that proximity to several power brokers inside the organization would also be important. Tournaments and hierarchy are important in the exercise of power inside the organization. So, sudden acts of delayering—often seen as a fashionable concept nowadays—can potentially destabilize an organization, reducing the micro-wins that people contest for. It might have a demotivating effect on the managers; but importantly, it would also lead to a loss of a lever of exercise of power by the chief of the organization. While the first aspect is usually understood, the second aspect of the loss is less appreciated. What would be the alternative mode of exercise of power inside such a delayered organization with enough authority to hold the organization together?

The discussion above summarizes the elements out of which the organizational life as a contested field of power gets manifested. Acts of nodal power holders create the organizational field.

3.3 CONFLICTING INTENT, MULTIPLE STAKEHOLDERS AND VIEW OF THE FIRM

Our discussion in previous chapters has shown how the contemporary organization is severely penetrated by numerous ties with an extended extra-organizational domain. The image of neat separation of organizations, each owned by different sets of owners, hardly can capture the reality of contemporary organizations. Who anyway owns an organization, in the sense of having an abiding interest in the assets of the organization? Shareholders are a mobile set of owners, exiting and entering a stock/scrip at will, driven by fluctuations in a secondary market, while financial institutions are themselves owned by a mobile set of owners. Senior managers and the CEO and a large part of the workforce are also mobile across a set of organizations.

> Who then is the bearer of the intent of long-term survival of the organization—over a long period or a very long period that includes an inter-generational sense? Without the holder of such intent, can an organization survive and prosper over long periods of time? Routines of an organization are often like an asset that is built over time and can potentially remain an asset over a future horizon. Can routines define a continuity of an organization over time?

An inter-organizationally mobile CEO can hardly be expected to always be the 'organization man', so to say; the assignment is like a project, a temporally delimited part of an extended series of such assignments that he/she expects to engage in. The elevation to a position of CEO often puts him/her in play within the wider milieu for such assignments. The CEO can, thus, be expected to pay heed to the milieu that would generate for him the next assignment, and performance in the current role can be expected to be delimited to what can be demonstrated as a signal of capability to the wider milieu that would generate the next assignment. Especially in the US, this is a serious problem—one of the dimensions of corporate governance crisis. How can you tie the CEO to the organization? Attempts in this direction have sought to link CEO compensation to profit or stock market performance of the firm through bonus or equity ownership—trying to implicitly move towards an owner–manager position. In a pure incentive sense, can such compensation designing create an owner out of a CEO? Or, in other words, would such an incentivized CEO act in a similar way to a small firm owner, who intends to hold the organization (as an asset) over the long term—and possibly in an inter-generational sense of bequeathal to heirs (to the wealth) as well? We discussed several such issues, and the incompleteness of bimodal compensation in the case of 'stars', in our discussion in the second chapter.

3.3.1 Business family/group and shareholder as different stakeholder groups

With this description, you can look differently at family-owned businesses, which is, in any way, the state of affairs in most parts of the world, except maybe in the Anglo-Saxon economies. Business families would often organize their multiple business interests in several legally independent firms, which together would define the BG. Business groups are then a special institution in themselves and we need to distinguish them from the notion of shareholders. In most economies across Europe and much of Asia, such BGs constitute a significant part of the business landscape. BGs and their portfolio of companies have come under great criticism in recent years, particularly from analysts who took a financial market perspective—pitting often the interest of the financial investors (including small retail investors) with the controlling family BGs. The existence of BGs have, in some accounts, been ascribed to the weakness or non-development of markets, particularly of finance, in developing countries. From a strategy perspective, however, it needs to be emphasized that BGs play a very important governance role; a role that a financial market possibly cannot replace.

A reading of the financial history of the United States, done in some detail in Chapter 5, would show several instances where market modes of (hands-off) governance was required to be supplemented by the active governance role played by entities such as private equity, venture capital or the leveraged buyout firm. As we will argue, private equity brought in this element of exercise of executive power in the Boards of the large corporations to induce changes that financial investors wanted but could not achieve through the market (influencing valuation in secondary market or through takeover market). Our general description of the notion of executive power would have alerted the reader to its ubiquity, for most assets would not have markets, even in the United States. Executive power gets exercised through commissions, regulatory systems, antitrust authorities, tax systems, legal systems (through exercise of judgement on laws and statutes) and several such bodies that are pan-organizational. The forums at which it is exercised and the way it is exercised or the institutional constraints, such as the specific voting mechanism that it relies on, differs quite widely; but it would be wrong not to clearly understand the difference between executive authority (which may take several specific forms) and market-based governance.

Bank-based governance earlier in Germany and later in Japan and public executive dominated governance in the US, Japan, Korea or in France and Germany point out the importance of non-market executive-based governance that are not always linked to finance or credit. In fact, the executive ambition in Japanese Ministry of International Trade and Industry (MITI) in terms of creating globally competitive domestic enterprises and acquiring technological capability as part of their notion of state power of a rising Japanese society regaining global pride was very important in shaping up investment direction of several large Japanese BGs.

The intent of the business family and the financial investor cannot thus be equated. We would rather argue that the two groups connected to a firm constitute different stakeholders and the primacy of the financial stakeholder cannot be overriding. Corporate law on this displays huge variation across jurisdictions, and several domains such as Germany, France and other areas of Continental Europe do not subscribe to a shareholder-based governance system. In Germany, the supervisory board sits above the board of directors (in what is called a two-tier board governance system), with representation from non-equity stakeholders of the organization. Each interest group throws up constraints on the other, and we would prefer looking at the literature from such a vantage point without normative considerations.

A group of legally independent firms closely controlled by a business family would constitute a BG. In some cases, one or more than one firm of such groups of firms under common control may be listed in stock exchanges as well, in which case they would have firm-specific financial investors with a firm-specific interest. BG, thus, is a supra-firm institution—its writ runs across several independent firms that constitute a closed group network. The institution of the BG, thus, throws up a unique set of governance issues. Design of several practices in BG firms, including its mode of deployment of assets, is driven on the one hand by the business family interests and on the other, by the requirement to respond to the constraint imposed by 'firm specific' financial investors. The family's perception of threat, its modes of imagination and ambition become vital. Consideration regarding bequeathal of assets, sharing of assets during inter-generational transitions, constitutes a few amongst its important concerns which might not interest a financial investor.

If you note, you will find that in India, most BG firms would be concentrated on narrow product/business lines and yet the group, as a whole, would be quite diversified. The practice of organizing the family business in multiple legal entities is not restricted to large groups alone—it is a ubiquitous practice in India—and even fairly small businesses that would fall within the global definitions of small and medium category would have such group structure. Several reasons, including tax considerations, play a role. Often, new businesses are started in new entities to separate the risks of the different businesses; this separation enables outside investors (including equity investors, banks, and so on) to participate in financing separately. In many cases, external financiers, including banks, prefer new business venturing in separate entities to prevent conflation of risks between the established and a new line of business controlled by the same family.

How does a BG structure differ from an M-form diversified business? At one level, the BG structure retains common control but affords a possibility of unbundled risk participation of outside non-controlling financial stakeholders at the level of each independent firm that usually has a specific non-diversified business. In the M-form instead, the financial risks of several divisions remain bundled together in a common balance sheet. If one looks at the evolution of the Reliance Industries group (Mukesh Ambani group), one would notice that the diversification along the vertical petrochemical value chain was almost always accomplished initially through a new entity, separate from the more stable former businesses (see Appendix 3B). The financial instruments used to raise resources were different, and it allowed a differential participation in large risky ventures of these new projects—as distinct from the risk in the established business. After the new business stabilized and differences in project risks no longer remained important from the perspective of external financial stakeholders, it was often merged back into the larger corporate structure within some kind of divisional arrangement. Contrarily, external investors, such as a bank, might force a merger between a financially weak and a strong BG firm as a hedge against what it feels to be an impending bankruptcy—effectively extending its rights over the cash flows of the healthy business line.

> Can you now think how Citibank, as large multi-divisional organization, differs from a BG that organizes businesses in different independent firms (rather than divisions) under some form of common control? Does it lend more autonomy to the operating firms? Look at the Softbank case described in the next chapter (see section 4.3) and try to reflect on it. Does the group structure provide a possible vehicle for unbundling of risks and for differentiated and shared control?

How does a BG control its vast empire of multiple group companies? Intricate financial mechanisms, including cross holding across companies, exercising control through friendly trusts and other such modes are quite common. Developing and deputing a group of loyal managers across group companies is also important. You can now think of development of Tata Administrative Services (TAS) as an attempt to develop a group of managers, loyal to the BG and mobile across group companies. In fact, the Tata group provides an instance where considerable autonomy can be devolved on the CEOs of group companies—within a framework of trust and loyalty to the BG.[10] Such empowering of professional managers, not necessarily at the expense of the family or the group interest (such as the *kieretsu*), has also been a feature of Japanese big business—where professionalization of management actually occurred even before the US. We look at two Indian BGs in the cases in the appendices to this chapter (see Appendices 3A and 3B).

3.3.2 Other stakeholders

Who are the other stakeholders of an organization? A stakeholder needs to be viewed as a power holder capable of influencing through a 'voice' exercised through negotiation, the strategies of an organization. A few important categories of stakeholders are as follows:

1) The professional who enjoys power in a professional circuit, quite independent of the power within the organization. Auditors, lawyers or technologists with a strong guild-type association that can set limits to and influence practices of the organization are a few examples. An auditor inside an organization is, therefore, under simultaneous governance of the internal organizational administration as well as that of the guild (the chartered accountants' association). Power of such professional bodies reach deep into

---

[10]You may also recall the skirmishes in the Tata group in the 1990s, when an old set of (group) company CEOs—who were the loyal lieutenants of the earlier group chairman JRD Tata—failed to strike a chord of trust with the new group chairman Ratan Tata. Establishing leadership over the group companies was possible only with the removal of the 'old stalwarts' and the rise of a new set of lieutenants. The details of the crisis would inform you about the possibility of breaches of trust between the promoter group and the cohort of senior power holders in the organization.

the organizational domain. Several corporate governance norms of financial disclosure in the US have been brought about by auditor and financial analyst bodies that enjoy quasi-legal status. The professional thus wields a countervailing power to that of the organization with which the organization has to engage and negotiate.

2) Unions often are another important node of power that influences the governance of the organization. If you have noticed the recent contest for takeover of a few business units of Ford Motor Company, the United Auto Workers Union came out in support of the offer from the Tata group, while they opposed the offer from the Mahindra group that was along with a private equity partner. Can you find out the reason?

3) Civil society groups, including non-governmental organizations (NGOs), constitute another important power node, particularly in contemporary times. Several groups such as green trade groups, fair trade groups, anti-child labour groups not only influence regulatory processes, but also act as watchdogs for enforcement of certain norms.

In many cases, the professional as the power node becomes important, especially when we think of rivalry between firms—say between Germany and the US—with a difference in the nature of such professional power nodes. The German or the US job classification system, with an elaborate, finely grained job classification system enforced through unions across the industry, meant that organizations did not exercise control over determining skill typologies. Japanese firms, in contrast, without an elaborate job classification system, could resort to multitasking of its workforce. Firms, because of differences in the institutional context, that is, in the mode of exercise of power of the professional nodes, evolve through different paths that can provide a potential for distinctiveness. These stakeholder nodes need to be considered in a strategy story and power in these nodes challenge the primacy of the financial investors. If we take a broader stakeholder view, then we can take a stance of negotiation—and possibilities emerge of viewing the external nodes even as allies in greater conflicts. The nodes also provide a mechanism through which an institutional influence can be wielded—such as skill categorization in a software milieu to influence skill development of its manpower that remains in an inter-organizational state of flux. Should a milieu of organizations often create or encourage the creation of such nodes as a strategy initiative?[11]

3.4 STRUCTURE OF AN ORGANIZATION

After our discussion on organization as a coalition of nodal power holders, we move on to a description of the structure of an organization that would explore a means of gaining a balance of power inside the organization or in tinkering with it. The mainstream account would argue that structure flows from strategy and hence is a rational outcome of strategy. This was the stance of Alfred Chandler. His studies of large US corporations of the mid-20th century, mostly around manufacturing or integrated process industries (such as chemicals, Du Pont being a classic case), placed the rise of large corporations on the efficiencies reached through economies of scale achieved, principally in a large sunk asset—a physical plant in most cases. The plant produced, in most cases, an integrated product which also had a standard specification (such as a chemical from a process plant). One would need a large organization to run the fixed asset to realize the potential economies of scale that plant size made possible. The standard product, in turn, required a tight coordination (to check deviations) that was achieved through the managerial fiat inside the organization. This description is that of a Chandlerian organization. However, multiple products created out of a common process often created problems that were resolved by separation of such new product businesses into separate divisions and we had the M-form organization, or the multi-divisional firm, with each division geared towards quasi-independent mass production/distribution. The bureaucracy of a large organization appears then to have limits on the extent of diversity it can handle.

---

[11]Early history of the Tata group would inform you that when the first steel factories were set up, not only were formation of unions encouraged, but training institutes were also built to provide workers with skills of negotiation, wage bargaining, and so on. What you must realize is that such initiatives were needed to institutionalize a mode of negotiation, that is, a rule or a code of engaging in negotiations (or even conflicts). While the negotiation would hover around several contentious areas—such as wage hikes—the fact that the negotiation happens within a certain framework is itself an implicit cooperation between the two parties—management and union, in this case. You may look at such 'frameworks' or 'rules' as a common asset.

This description is just of one type of structure. Several other organizations in similar businesses, such as automobiles, in other geographies did not subscribe to important elements of this story. Toyota as well as Mercedes accepted umpteen product variations; and a typical Mercedes plant would churn out several hundreds of variations of cars. While Toyota devised rigid rules—as we argued, it did not standardize it, leaving it open for worker negotiation—Mercedes, in addition, retained considerable unspecified autonomy with the workmen in creatively fashioning their work, including design freedom. Mercedes was not a Chandlerian organization; it retained entrepreneur craftsmen inside its organization. Also, think how the structural requirements would change if you enter a service industry—where the customer interfacing (such as doctor-driven surgeries) are individuated solutions from specific men of the organization rather than an integrated organizational outcome. What would be the organizational structural implications of IBM shifting from the 'product' to the 'service' mode; in addition, if IBM starts peddling of small micro-assets (proto-products that would be a sort of an intermediate tool in software production processes) in addition to its customer interfacing with mega-service projects negotiated centrally with the client? Would all these descriptions generate requirements for similar structural arrangements inside the organization or pressures for deep changes to be felt?

In numerous cases, one would find today, organizations going through too frequent restructurings; a new round follows even before the old one has taken roots and one is not sure if the first restructuring really was effective in achieving its goals. Importantly, real organizations seem to have different kinds of purposes, quite unlike Chandlerian mass production. Small market sizes and several kinds of resource scarcities dictated different kinds of optimization in much of Europe and elsewhere in the world as well. Toshiba, in the early years of its technology catch-up, provides a valuable counterpoint to the Chandler story. A reading of its design would tell us that a factory—as a concentrated space of production—does enhance control; but that control can seek different purposes. In Toshiba's case, the focal factory was an intensified and hastened coordination on new product development and rapid technology learning (see case study 3.1).

As we argued above, an organization story based on structure often searches for a right structure—or for a fit. In contrast, we are arguing that the organization design as well as the structuring of the processes inside an organization must be seen as part of a series of action that a strategist initiates in search of power (and thus it cannot be an objectively rational fit)—to preserve the dominance attained and to gain additional ground.

Case Study 3.1: Toshiba's focal factory

Even an organization in a relatively stable business with an old organization may use this basic mode. Toshiba's concept of a 'focal factory'—the Yanagicho Works—provides an instance. A factory mode is generally thought of as a means of concentration of production—so that mass manufacturing advantages can be taken care of. But in the case of Toshiba focal factory, the factory mode started playing (or was designed to play) a totally different function from somewhere between the war years and the last quarter of the 20th century. It was designed to be a concentrated site of product development, where geographic concentration in a factory could allow strong coordination to evolve integrating R&D, manufacturing, distribution—every aspect of the product, so to say. Multifunction and multi-product, the focal factories were categorically different from mass-production factories with distinctive management styles and structures to integrate planning, design, product and process engineering. Organizational flexibility, technological adaptation and mental labour are institutional traits of a focal factory and liveliness and a deeply negotiated hierarchy in the workplace are some behavioural features. They were mandated to produce a continuing stream of innovative products rather than a stable mass-manufactured product. Multi-specialization teams would work on projects, building prototypes, scaling up production and setting up the tooling, negotiating the distribution and sales coordination mechanism in a series of temporal activities as product idea evolved. At any time, several such projects would be on and several products would be manufactured in the factory with different degrees of maturity. In other words, the focal factory did not concentrate on a product; in fact, there would be too much variety in the product basket, which would change and evolve quite rapidly over time. But it was concentrated and specialized in another sense—that was very contextual. It was a focal point of learning of technology and experimentation, largely with Western technologies, but providing unique spins to it—where engineers, technologists and skilled workmen would have the creative play of tinkering, experimenting and learning such tools. It was a specific outcome of late industrialization and the intense urge to play a fast catch-up under conditions of resource and skill scarcity that defined the context. The focal factory is the site of generation of increasing returns—where structural fluidity allowed learning to happen very fast, generating novel solutions, some of which reached high volumes of mass manufacturing and became blockbuster products, while a much larger number remained low-volume limited-period offerings. Those reaching mass production reached

(Case Study 3.1 contd.)

(Case Study 3.2 contd.)

> more stable structures of mass production and was managed in a more traditional mass-production mode. The world mostly noticed the products that reached large scales, but more engineers and skilled workmen in Japan worked on low-volume products than the mass-volume ones, experimenting and learning. It constituted the core on which organization learning and evolution was based and was the key organizational differentiator in terms of coordination modes (summarized from Fruin, 1992).

The intent of the power holder is therefore crucial—so is that of other contesting nodes both inside and outside the organization. The mental note of the threat as well as the domains that are sought to be conquered shapes the processes. Formation of structures may then be seen as a dynamic evolving process—a process that is often a priori unpredictable in terms of its outcome—but conceptual understanding of the processes centring on the wielding of power can provide us a guideline to act, which nevertheless would not be prescriptive. Uncertainties would arise from the incomplete reading of the intent—or the milieu—as well as through the discontinuities induced by uncertain outcome of negotiations. Between a successful and an unsuccessful negotiation, the difference in outcome can be very substantial. A description of a process, particularly those of change, possibly captures best several elements of exercise of organizational power, as well as its failure, that is, the failure in the wielding of power and the intermediate opportunistic alliances that are often struck on a subversive note. It was this possibility that a Mintzberg account hints at. Below, we provide three different accounts, or stories of change. One can notice, as one reads through, the similarities and the differences in the accounts.

CASE STUDY 3.2 — **BPR project in a large Indian bank**

A large Indian public sector bank, 'B', undertook BPR while under transition to a regime of liberalization. It has a large branch-based structure to acquire local savings, where processes of banking add little value; in other words, there is little local lending as well as bank intermediated transactions. Value is added at the head office through treasury-like financial operations and

(Case Study 3.2 contd.)

(Case Study 3.2 contd.)

through providing credit to industry. 'B' faced a transitional dilemma: BPR implies retaining only value-adding processes and deleting non-value-adding processes. Regulatory guidelines and structural considerations would not allow this bank to implement a big-bang BPR. Yet, appreciating that competition was sharpening in the value processes with the entry of new global and private entrant banks, two successive chairmen and a few senior managers initiated change management by engaging an international consultant. *The consultant failed to appreciate the wealth of knowledge that grass-root banking had provided. How that could be valorized did not occupy their attention.* The chairmen and the team of managers could not choose between structure, business process, strategy and technology—what could be the driver of change and in what sequence of change the best outcome could be secured! Negotiations on change management between the stakeholders and the consultant resulted into tacit opportunistic alliances. Enthusiast managers through self-taught understanding on BPR offered certain novel solutions to change, which were rejected.

Environment and the bank

Structure, business processes and management systems of 'B', similar to other nationalized banks, evolved under the controls by several machinery of the government. Since 1991, the system of controls over banks and over 'B' began weakening. 'B' too began preparing itself for managing the change. Set up in Mumbai about a hundred years back, 'B' has remained in the forefront of innovations. With nearly 2,500 branches, it has a large network across cities and the countryside and compares very favourably with the best and the large banks of India. Regulatory structural constraints imposed limits and deformed business process. A bank competes with other banks or other financial agents through its branches reaching out to the customers. This can be called a branch-based, spatial, retail customer centric competition.

In contrast, a bank also competes for credit disbursal or for export or project-based businesses. This latter-type competition engages the head office or other select offices only and does not involve the branches. Or, in other words, within the current constraints of structure, bank-based competition for credit disbursal does not involve the branch network. This we define as bank-based competition. It follows that these two types of competitions bring about a structural disjunction, or a cleavage. Can a banking business

(Case Study 3.2 contd.)

(Case Study 3.2 contd.)

process be defined so that it can alleviate this problem of disjunction, through joint work between the head office dependent banking-based structure and branch-based structures? Such a process integrates several structures. The non-relation (in a deep business process sense) can then be overcome.

With branches in plenty and an average branch serving only 12,000 people (in 1990) yet burdened with a very large number of small deposit accounts, branch-based competition lost its credibility. 'B' has more than 1,200,000 accounts (for credit) whose value is less than a meagre INR 25,000, about 700,000 in the range of INR 25,000 to 200,000, and about 75,000 such accounts above INR 200,000. Typically, a branch serving retail customers would receive deposits in three categories, savings constituting about 12 per cent of total deposits, current (mainly for business) about the same, and term deposits about 75 per cent. A typical branch would lend little of its deposits, if at all. Part of its fund would be lent through the zonal/regional special credit divisions and the rest would be transferred through a transfer price mechanism to the head office, which while disbursing credit to the profit-earning businesses, transfers a part of the profit to the region back. A region would in general disburse about 65 per cent of its deposits as credit in its region, out of which only about 20 per cent or about 12 per cent of total deposits would get disbursed to the profit-earning businesses, the rest of credit goes to several weaker sections. As a result, almost 90 per cent of income of a region would flow from 'interest income' category, which comes because of fund transfer to headquarter, and only about 10 per cent from non-interest income.

Dependence on interest income at the branch or region level implies that the bank follows a retail branch-based strategy while priority of non-interest income implies a bank-based strategy. Branch-based strategy, however, cannot preclude the other altogether. A branch or a region, thus, in order to remain competitive and earn profit, remains limited to interest income category and towards this goal it attempts to maximize the total deposit and a branch fails to implement strategies of the business organization. Skills set that thus get developed in a branch and the regional/branch goals and strategies that are nurtured are for deposit mobilization. Regulations prevented 'B' from specializing in specific areas of deposit mobilization or in credit disbursals or other forms of business such as merchant banking. The result was that interbank branch-based or intra-bank inter-branch competition was hazy and the market had no knowledge of what special interests or special skilled services they could expect from 'B'.

(Case Study 3.2 contd.)

(Case Study 3.2 contd.)

Structure of 'B' has been hierarchic and regional/spatial as well as functional. It has not been based on business processes. Incentive to an employee in 'B' has never been special pecuniary benefits; it has remained as promotions across a long chain of seniority. If the career movements are lost, the incentive system breaks down. 'B' having little manoeuvrability in business options was also thus burdened with little scope to restructure its organizational structure through reengineering of incentives. Personal initiatives of the middle level managers were to be unleashed since that appeared to be the best course for raising productivity/profitability. In 1995, the then chairman of 'B' recognized that strategy, structure and culture had to be changed, but for managing change, its sequence was most important. The question was: what was the driver of change and what sequence of transformation could bring best desired outcome? 'B', typical of a nationalized bank, has been having its successive chairmen for an average period of one year to a maximum of two years. The board of 'B' too keeps changing its composition; senior managers of 'B' get regularly, and often in about a year's time, transferred to another position located perhaps in a distant place. Middle managers too have a similar fate. Incentives targeted to individual performance thus could not be designed in this system. A long and complex structure of rules, the latter having substituted individual predispositions with strict rule-following, defined the environment.

This first chairman conducted a strengths, weaknesses, opportunities and threats (SWOT) analysis around 1995, results of what was shared with association of the officers and the union of the employees, who both soon became active agencies of transformation consisting of four aspects: transformation of organizational structure, introduction of novel organizational processes, restoration of financial health and induction of customer orientation. Results were to appear soon. 'B' posted profits of INR 500 and 2,760 millions in the following years of 1995 and 1996. The first chairman offered a vision of 'B', bypassed several rules, set himself and other super-performers as the 'role models', set up performance benchmarking, identified and then nurtured talents inside the organization by way of providing them with rewards, challenging tasks and recognitions. Overall, he encouraged a culture of cooperational work, risk-taking, accountability, especially to bank customers, with customer satisfaction as the end result of performance, and an innovative attitude towards 'rules', which were to be interpreted anew. This set the norm of recognizing new and novel banking processes through recognition of new interpretations on those rules.

(Case Study 3.2 contd.)

(Case Study 3.2 contd.)

By 1996 there was a new dynamic chairman with knowledge of BPR. Simple activities of novel interpretation of rules would not take 'B' far, and the second chairman thought of two alternative modes: incentives reengineering or changing the culture of work. Reengineering of incentives amounting to declaring publicly a new set of rules regarding novel incentives might attract unwanted criticisms and even refusal. Incentives should be part of the written code of rules and a reengineering of incentives would assume changes in the rules then. The second chairman, thus, thought of a culture, unwritten and formally unannounced, in which an employee could take risk or the employee towards achieving greater customer satisfaction could remodel rules. Culture relied more on 'roles' played out by individuals. A culture would encourage roles differentiation and betterment of roles on the one hand and on the other, a maximal alignment of individual with several roles.

The second chairman could appreciate knowledge gaps and incentive mismatches in his own organization. He, however, did not have the answer to the riddle: which amongst 'structure', 'strategy', 'process', 'technology' and 'individuals and roles' will be the best driver to effect transformation? Who could be initiated first in effecting change-leadership, and then how and which elements of these five aspects would form the sequence of change? Structure was saddled with regulations by outside agencies. Strategy was burdened with imposed banking objectives and the severe schism internal to bank structure reflected in branch-based banking versus total banking. Business process as such was amiss. Technology was not easily accessible and individuals represented the greatest challenge offering both greatest resistance and strongest support to change.

The second chairman and a small team of a few middle and senior managers noticed, however, the gaps in knowledge as the common denominator to these five aspects. These gaps can be represented on the four corners of a diamond, in which the left entries, namely, 'branch', 'structure', 'rule following' and 'individual' depict the existing states of affairs in 'B', while the right entries, namely 'bank', 'process', 'value maximize' and 'roles' represent the desired states of affairs. *This chairman and his team understood that there were gaps in knowledge between banking through a branch or through the entire bank, or between knowledge about the rigidity of existing structure and the fluidity of desired banking processes, and so on.* Transformation of 'B', they felt, would involve a knowledge reengineering. However, the chairman and his close team were undecided about the engine of change and about the sequence of knowledge reengineering needed. Culture, they felt, could be the

(Case Study 3.2 contd.)

(Case Study 3.2 contd.)

driver and it would do away with big-bang changes and the sequencing, and emphasize 'individual and roles' as the key to change management. Culture, however, was too fuzzy; and since the stakeholders would appreciate a set of signals of change, they thought of formal change rituals. The chairman chose BPR, value chains and benchmarking as the change rituals. He convinced the board that 'B' was in need of a BPR, to be more specific, a business processes and information systems reengineering (BP&ISR). This proposal that a BP&ISR was needed and that an international consulting firm be appointed as a consultant was approved. This second chairman left before the consultant was to submit its 'Report'.

Technological states of affairs at 'B'

Domestic banks including 'B' continued branch-based computerization and forgot to plan information system globally for the entire bank and for strategic objectives, with emphases on key business areas. Branch computerization based on piecemeal legacy systems was limited to functional tasks, ignoring processes.

- Computerization thus was not at all targeted to bring higher values to customers and was not also targeted to bring to the branch information required for participating in the profitable finance businesses, resulting into serious weaknesses in the new profitable areas of bank-based banking.
- Over the years, these *islands* spread over from select branches to the regional, zonal and then the head office, though never connected through communication network or through business processes, establishing a ramshackle framework of management information system (MIS).
- Technology could not become the first driver of change.

Transformation of 'B'

Current knowledge in 'B', separated in *islands* of functional practices does not add up to the knowledge of business process. 'B' has been following a personnel policy of transferring regularly its managers across tasks on the same functional line. It has also erected a long hierarchy of promotional avenues. Board of 'B' believed knowledge management was accomplished through integration of functional and spatial skills. However, second chairman argued

(Case Study 3.2 contd.)

(Case Study 3.2 contd.)

that knowledge ought to have related to processes alone. A reengineering can initiate transformation choosing a key factor, the driver of change, out of the five factors: 'structure', 'strategy', 'process', 'technology' and 'individual and roles'. Driver takes up in a definite sequence other four factors. In Massachusetts Institute of Technology (MIT) framework, strategy is the driver which takes up in sequence structure first, followed by, in parallel, both the management processes and technology which converge on individual and roles. In Fujitsu framework, technology as the driver impacts first upon individual and roles which change structure, followed by causal changes in management processes and finally in the strategy of the organization. A change is not linear. It is the outcome of a series of negotiations transacted over a long period between several agencies with varied power and controls. Initial proposed solution often takes a beating.

Negotiated contour of change

The international consultancy organization submitted its report nearly after a year, based apparently on the MIT paradigm, but which was a mixture of everything. The consultant presented seven 'modules' on strategy, organization structure, business process redesign (for credit management, and for branch operations only), treasury, HR, Management Information System (MIS) and information technology (IT). The consultant was not to take part in the change management process. Managing change is an act of negotiation and an act of 'doing'—a theory or an advice on the same without a commitment to be part of the change activities turn out to be meaningless, and such advices fail. The consultant knew that 'B' was not as serious in changing as 'B's' agents were in building images. The consultant found it convenient to shirk off its restructuring mandate. All the agencies thus acted as opportunists and the alliance of win–win for all was too convincing. Senior managers initially felt threatened, apprehensive about their future in the organization. A compromise was reached early. Middle managers could not get the number of positions enhanced or could not secure a faster track of promotion. A new 'B' with a strong brand-presence and definite competitive edge over others would be desirable; and so, many middle managers proved the most active change agents.

Consultant's suggestions

The consultant proposed key strategic services from 'B' should be under: corporate banking, small and medium business banking, personal banking, retail

(Case Study 3.2 contd.)

(Case Study 3.2 contd.)

and mass market banking, and rural and developmental banking. It suggested a new functional–divisional structure under reorganized functions to be managed by different 'heads'. Personal banking, corporate banking, banking for medium businesses and for cooperatives were the new functional thrusts. No process defined by value chain across functions and along the vertical line from branch upwards was identified. Strategy was identified with a reorganized functional structure alone. Suggestions included defining of clear reporting lines, ensuring that existing processes remain well controlled, roles defined and business structures set up around target markets. The branch-based and bank-based diarchy in 'B' was left untouched by the consultant and business processes that could integrate the functional structures of branch with the head office remained uncharted. Most importantly, the report did not identify the 'driver' of change and the sequence with which the driver would effect successive changes.

Fear of change and technology to control

Uncertainty regarding change arouses fear for loss of control; the consultant suggested a rigorous and invigorated MIS while keeping the role of technology only as an adjunct. Suggested MIS should reduce time to collect information from the branches, get centralized and collect right information on clients, defaults, risks, and so on. Such a centralized MIS function should be part of the function of finance, induce a stronger functional/divisional control structure, and remaining within the function of finance, it would be guided by the old strategic planning. MIS with strong functional emphasis would, by way of enhancing the power of planning, reduce 'B's' exposure to the changes induced through technology (like end-user computing) in the financial market. Opportunist internal agencies thus liked this idea of the consultant. The consultant's IT strategy was to support the strategic initiatives of anytime anywhere banking for personal and corporate customers as the most important objective. IT support to the redesigned processes, the MIS and HR renewals, improvement of customer service and ensuring uniformity of service, and improving efficiency of housekeeping were ignored. Most importantly, end-user computing was simply forgotten.

Change management as compromise

In short, suggestions on IT fell far short of any contemporary and comparable IT project in a large bank abroad. Suggested implementation schedule

(Case Study 3.2 contd.)

(Case Study 3.2 contd.)

kept 'PC/LAN' automation and selection of IT system at the beginning of the eighth month. Interestingly, 'establishing new senior management team' was the first task on the first month, followed by 'developing business plans and marketing strategies' and 'defining roles and responsibilities for key positions' on about the second month, to be followed by 'reconfiguration of branch network' on about the third month. These were to be followed by 'identification of existing skills and staff reassignment' on about the fourth month, succeeded by 'management of staff transition' in the next month, and so on. Phases of identified 'change management' were successively as following: organization structure, process redesign, HR and change management, management information, and IT. Interestingly, while the initial approach to transformation appeared to have been driven by considerations of strategy, the implementation schedule conveyed the hint that the change was to be driven by structure. It meant creation of new structures, with budget heads as the first acts. Such incongruities appear to be the result of a complex negotiation process. Departmental MIS was now replaced by a centralized MIS reporting directly to the Chairman and the board overlooked end-user competence.

Conclusion

'B's' operations failed it in buying out strategically positioned banks abroad. Size matters in banking. Integration of several types of banking, too, matters. Such an integration of a large number of banking processes in a large corporate entity is the foremost long-term challenge ahead of 'B'. Its BPR never laid out clearly the processes or set up a process performance measurement system (PPMS) to monitor the progress of process reengineering. The puzzle of what constituted the driver of change remains unsolved. Absence of a strategic position in the market and an edge over others in productivity, in market presence or even its failure to establish a dependable brand name have rendered 'B' unattractive in the long term. It has successfully met short-term targets and its stakeholders in the board are happy, but after a very brief period, insiders started believing that the BPR had failed. The most significant gain from a BPR is that processes are visible, identifiable and synergistically integrated rendering passage of information or signals, especially from the top management, quicker and uninterrupted. However, signals inside 'B' face road jams. A simple strategic control over the processes or functions by the top management ensures compliance with strategy but it does not ensure

(Case Study 3.2 contd.)

(Case Study 3.2 contd.)

> creative participation by the end-users in the organization. Negotiations and dynamic formation of opportunistic alliances between several teams inside 'B' with the consultant subverted the turnaround possibility time and again. A complex negotiation skill alone can guide. The consultant and the board did not understand the design implications of IS/MIS and of the BPR. Managers felt that the project should have given importance to incentives reengineering, to harnessing core knowledge competencies and in bringing competitive pressures down inside the business processes through a thoroughly overhauled IS/MIS, a high degree of training in computer use with subsequent training in attitudinal changes, a better software and a better computing platform. The core problems of branch-banking versus bank-based banking, gaps in knowledge and inability of the structure to offer an incentives system remained unsolved. IT needs to be in the driver's seat. Would adoption of a Fujitsu philosophy have helped? Who or what interests inside the organization could have owned it up?

The failure of the above initiative to bring about a structural change appears interesting. What do you think are the reasons for it? Structure creates silos inside organizations—they are, as we argued, points of agglomeration. So, the head of a division commands power out of this agglomeration. Several such nodal power holders in a balance of power, along with an inter-temporal tournament of promotions that over time promise access to such points to a waiting pool, appears to be what sustains the organizational life. As long as business or adoption of a particular strategy does not require a deep coordination across such silos, it offers a successful recipe. The classic Chandler organizations were all of that type—where coordination and interdependence between silos could be defined at a high level. If, in contrast, interdependence needs to be defined and mapped at several levels between multiple such silos—as is the requirement for a process level coordination running across several silos—the structural elements act as a major barrier to achievement of a strategy or a business need. Several contemporary accounts thus challenge the 'silo' mentality and exhort management to adopt more fluid process-based coordination. Few such process-based realignments, however, demonstrated sustained strength, challenged mostly by the agglomeration based power of the silo heads. When structures were broken with force by the leader as the *dramatis personae*, the organization regrouped quickly enough to traditional silo-based types. The description below of a rather well studied episode of restructuring at hearing aid manufacturer Oticon provides one such instance.

Restructuring at Oticon

Oticon is a Danish hearing aid company that was the leader in the industry for a long time. By the 1990s, it had, however, slipped into third position behind industry leader Siemens (a division of Siemens was in the business) and another US firm. The decline of the firm was palpable to any insider—it lacked the drive and the energy to move forward; for a long time, it did not have new product lines and was unable to negotiate with the advent of new technologies that enabled the design and manufacture of miniaturized inside-the-ear hearing aids. In 1987, the company experienced financial catastrophe, with half its equity being wiped out. It was also hampered by a rigid organization. Functional departments such as marketing, finance and manufacturing were led by directors who also made up the senior executive group responsible for all strategic decisions. A governing foundation that owned the company was composed of the same people as the management. Concerned about the future in the face of the debacle, they looked outside the company for new leadership. Lars Kolind was brought in to lead the company. Kolind was an interesting personality. An active member of the world scout movement, Kolind had a short stint as general manager of a market research firm, which he left after building it to a leadership position in Denmark to join the Danish National Science Research Academy, also simultaneously holding an associate professor's position in Copenhagen University. Kolind initiated a big-bang change at Oticon. He felt that the milieu of the organization presented severe challenges and a very interesting opportunity.

Oticon's rivals, such as Siemens, were well endowed with financial resources as well as technology depth. It would be difficult for Oticon to match either—so oligopoly type growth based models would lead to further entrenchment of the dominance of Siemens type of organizations. With all its strength, Siemens had a problem—it was a large organization and part of an even larger BG; it was structured and information moved slowly inside the organization. Oticon was also structured similarly—as organizations emulated structures that were celebrated around the early days of manufacturing success. But being much smaller—an R&D centre of 120 persons and a

(Case Study 3.3 contd.)

(Case Study 3.3 contd.)

slightly larger manufacturing set-up—Kolind thought that restructuring to have profuse generation of novel information and hastening of intense internal transactions and exchange could be achieved far more easily at Oticon. This novel organizational mode would lead to a long pipeline of products/concepts and a marketing strategy on 'novelty' in design and functionality, 'short-product-life' and proliferation of variety; Kolind hoped this would lead the market away from its current stance on emphasizing the product to a focus on the holistic (integrated) user experience. Novelty in user experience could come sometimes from a technology tweak, sometimes from packaging, or sometimes from novel features—several possibilities remain that cannot be ex-ante predicted. The clarity thus was on an underlying process of product development—and an integrated product that interfaced with the user experience cannot be developed in a departmentalized set-up, implicitly admitting the stickiness of information at departmental nodes. The temporal order of his steps was as follows:

1) Meeting most people inside the organization individually; identifying in the process the leaders of the informal world—the gossip-mongers as well as the party leaders, as he said.
2) Putting his personal wealth in the company to buy a stake, which the board approved—even though quite surprised at it. He then went to a bank and pledging his stake opened a large credit line from the bank.
3) Announced a restructuring that created the image of a spaghetti organization—a dense mesh of internal transactional and informational arrangements that would evolve and morph and always be on a contingent mode. The whole organization would be built around such temporary projects—executed in a guerrilla mode.
4) The internal décor of the R&D centre and the headquarters was changed and a paperless, wall-less, office-less office was created.
5) The restructuring initiative was announced to the external world and academic observers were made part of the initiative from very early days of the change process through a large government grant on building of futuristic organizations. The experiment, thus, was in a wider play.
6) The restructuring idea was put up internally and those who did not agree with the new mode were given an option to seek jobs outside the organization within 18 months.

(Case Study 3.3 contd.)

(Case Study 3.3 contd.)

> 7) The largest resistance came from middle managers, who were the key people involved in running the internal tournament up the organizational hierarchy; there was a sense of loss of control at this level. The middle manager layers were also points of sticky information, which thwarted a massive information movement that could guide transactions.
>
> 8) A single window project clearance body was created for projects above a particular size through a single project approval board. This became the new power centre, which Kolind himself influenced. Smaller projects could be carried out much more easily without the approval of the board.
>
> This experiment has been studied quite widely. It did lead to an intensification of idea generation, leading to new products that helped the company turnaround. Within a very short span of time, ideas that were lying around in hibernation due to sticky information flows took shape rather quickly leading to market success. The restructuring initiative took this form because of the 'clarity' of what was sought. That clarity was not on certain product concepts; the products and the technologies evolved. The clarity was on a process of unleashing of forces that would generate an organizational distinctiveness with respect to the milieu and a particular reading of the weakness (organizational) of the rivals. (Summarized from information in various sources; HBS Case No. 9-395-144, written by John Kao; work of Nordic scholars of new forms of organization are particularly useful.)

But, what would one expect, as the new spaghetti structure worked for some time? With deep interconnections across all levels, and contingent teaming up and subsequent dispersals it would prevent the buildup of powers of agglomeration. It thus effectively destroyed the silos inside the organization. In contrast to the narration of the bank BPR case, where the commitment of the top management to any change was virtually non-existent (and hence a superficial presentation of few nominal changes drove the agenda of the chairman and the board), in the case of Oticon, the leader had staked personal fortunes on the change, much to the surprise of his board colleagues. And it did succeed in generating a stream of novelty rather quickly. It was the perfect recipe that an innovation-driven outlook (romantic!) often desires. But rather quickly, trouble started—the expectation raised on information symmetry, equal opportunity and free play of ideas faced disillusionment. Initial believers turned sceptics rather fast. The Central Project Committee became the focal point of criticism—it was seen as opaque and, more importantly, organizational members felt that the old silos were effectively recreated through the powers of the project committee and it worked out through the grant or non-grant of approval (and budgets) to projects. Who the project-lead was mattered more than the project idea! That was the common refrain. A massive rule-set was drafted to guide the project committee to remove aspersions cast on the Committee's working. The pure form of spaghetti structure was partially abandoned and several division type intermediate positions and nodal points were created.

This raises an interesting issue. Readers can think now why we were arguing that an organization hardly can be conceived for purposes of intra-organizational governance as an efficiency-enhancing or profit-maximizing machine. It is importantly a political coalition; and wins and losses in such political contests—micro-wins even—and a series of them over the temporal horizon constitute a plausible description of an organizational life. Organizational restructuring needs to meddle with such structures of temporal contests; it is only to that extent that an organization transforms over time. If one thinks back on the case of the BPR failure in the bank (refer case study 3.2), one can ask whether a sustained change process would have unfolded if a more committed management had chosen a Fujitsu-type approach and sought to empower through technology tools the weak current voice of the change favouring group (the middle managers with a longer term interest in the organization!). One would have noted how quickly the entrenched senior management team short circuited the process of change through opportunistic alliances that silenced the weak middle management voice. Would a more active Chairman, a more committed one, have prevented that? The Oticon story leads us to doubt it.

Is it then that organizations always necessarily would fail to deeply transform themselves? One interesting possibility seems to be a dynamic process where organizational nodal power holders are set up in a temporally evolving envelope of conflict and negotiation with several other extra-organizational power holders—who would be business partners. Joint generation of business then sustains a gradually evolving new structure within the organization. Our story of the reorganization of DoCoMo around its i-Mode business provides such an account (see case study 3.5). Before that, we discuss a restructuring episode in Citibank—again a well-studied one—that brings out the notion of incentive realignment (or reallocation) as a tool of internal change.

CASE STUDY 3.4 Citibank organizational restructuring

Citibank has been one of the highly successful global banks, which expanded from its US roots across the world, following the expansion of American corporations and business interests. Till the 1990s, Citibank had a geographic divisional structure, organizing its multiple businesses in different countries as geography-based profit centres that were almost like silos. A narrow cadre of senior managers moved across such geographic silo organizations establishing organizational control at the global level. In the early years of the 1990s, Citibank's Organization for Economic Cooperation and Development (OECD) banking business was under serious crisis; it was in the red—with high profits from emerging markets providing a cushion. But a staring crisis forced a fundamental re-look in the bank. Most standard banking solutions faced increased competition and decreasing returns in OECD markets. What could be the way out of this trap—could an increasing returns dynamics be induced? Financial liberalization had opened up the market of cross-border investments, financial and treasury management as well as risk management of various hues. Several multinational companies (MNCs) now were placed to engage in more active cross-border arbitrage and integration of financial functions. But how could Citibank reorient its processes and internal assets towards this new evolving market and what would be the structural manifestation of the change? What would be the source of value addition in the new mode—or the new market? One way was to search for possibilities of potential spillovers arising from current activities that can be captured with either a process reorientation or a structural change; the novel assets created through capturing of the spillovers can then be a source of value addition.

Internal projects and deliberations revealed that for most activities that Citibank then engaged in, potential spillovers lay along the customer dimension; that is, spillovers would be sticky to a customer context. This called for a customer centred mode of organizational and incentive deployment as the primary coordination device. Citibank, in its new strategy, decided thus to focus on a list of around 1,400 global customers alone—leaving the rest of the market; since the value of the new modes of value addition could be appreciated and leveraged only in this segment. It changed its structure to a customer-centred mode, with various processes and asset holders across multiple geographies, expertise areas and industries linked (or coupled) strongly along a particular MNC customer. This internal group of Citibank often would just mimic the structure of the client with respect to location of roles and

(Case Study 3.4 contd.)

(Case Study 3.4 contd.)

> functions in various geographies and several variations would be tolerated across such multiple customer teams.
>
> The incentive system (or the rule) was changed to hasten information exchange and transactions (on a shared mode) based on profuse information assets. Frontline bankers facing the client were expected to share business leads (that would generate new deals) across several geographic sites—so, an initial engagement with Citibank customer in Italy might lead to businesses in Portugal, France, and so on—in a continuous evolving series of fresh transactions. Bonuses were based on high-powered incentives, tightly linked to own business (rather than corporate profits); revenue recognition for the same transaction was often done twice or thrice in different units/divisions to provide credit for passing on of crucial business leads to other bankers in different locations; role reversals were made and the top management started talking about profits from French customers—a set of global customers with French headquarters—rather than profits from the business unit in France.
>
> The OECD business in which this restructuring was carried out started yielding results almost immediately; there was a fast turnaround. Interestingly, immediately after the restructuring, Citibank started entering the syndicate loan market in Europe, participating with other banks in syndicated and consortium modes of lending. It had earlier exited this mode (or the specific market) as margins were too low for a rich organization (with a large overhead) such as Citibank in that market. The new entry was driven by a different motive—syndicated loans provided the first point of entry into a client MNC. As a standalone proposition, syndicated loans were not attractive at all, but it acquired a fresh meaning under the new dispensation at Citibank. A profuse generation of customer-specific information, which followed from the customer premise entry through participation in the syndicated loan market, led to new businesses; Citibank—unlike other participants in the syndication—could leverage this potential spillover because of its intra-organizational structure/process that gave it a cross-national coordination capability at the level of exchange of micro-information (summarized from Baron and Besanko, 2001: 10).

The Citibank restructuring episode thus shows a different sequence (and a clarity as well) from the other episodes described. Strategy led the change, with a clear understanding of shifting from the current market to a new market of evolving customer requirement of just a select group of 1,400 MNCs. It drew a clear boundary of what it was excluding from the scope of what the organization would engage in. This reframing itself, driven by the crisis looming large, would weaken, in a sense, the nodal power holders of the geographic silos. In each geography (country), the new strategy restricted an expansion of customers beyond the select group of global clients. But is such clarity always possible to arrive at? Even in Citibank's case, was it a good idea to have such a clear articulation? Did it not rule out other possibilities that might turn out interesting in future? Strategy was followed by change in incentive system or reallocating incentive around a new set of activities that would use a set of dormant information assets lying inside the organization. Process-based coordination followed—creating a process capability to handle, track and work on the profuse information exchange that the new strategy espoused. Structural issues took a back seat, and it changed the last and possibly the least as well. Citibank continued to be the classic Chandler structure. The old nodal points of power were not decimated—they were negotiated into a new relation, where such nodes also benefited from wider business generation that inflated the compensation of the geography-based power holders as well. In contrast, you would note that in the bank BPR case (see case study 3.2), without a control over incentive reallocation, top management was severely constrained to act in effecting any deep structural change.

Under what conditions would incentive reallocation have failed? It is quite clear that the organization had an internal note of the nature of potential spillover that was not being acted upon because of a lack of a specific coordination mode that the restructuring provided. This novel coordination asset created is the contribution of the top management and one must note that two of the most important organizational functions (in a strategic sense) of senior managers inside an organization refers to preserving the sanctity of the exercise of 'organizational fiat' and provide a mode of coordination that other modes, such as a market mode, cannot provide. Specificity of the coordination asset to the organization lends it distinctiveness—a sort of sustainability, in other words—while the dispersed nature of the information asset (which in addition is sticky to the customer organization) also makes imitation difficult. The frontline bankers, as observers of such information, are potential generators of increasing returns as well. The point to note is that the observation of this market can only be done in the context of the internal organizational milieu of the client. So the frontline bankers receive information from the market (in this case, a partial market defined by the client internal organizational context) and act to modulate it as well, as they interface with the internal organizational dynamics of the client organization to generate novel business for the bank.

The exercise of executive power of top management was in reallocation of incentives—it is a rule-setting right. So one can now look into incentive(s) as a kind of reward offered—it is closer to a cash flow right and quite far removed from a control right. The right to set the rule is closer to a control right; it allows the top management to set the terms on which organizational races would be organized. It is a mode of control, therefore. But for it to work, the sanctity of the rule must be preserved—just as 'an internal tournament' of promotions would require a preservation of the sanctity of the rule of promotion (and a sense of justice around it). Otherwise, the tool would fail in its control function.[12] You will also realize why even a highly incentivized manager is different from an entrepreneur, who enjoys control rights and possibly greater degrees of freedom.

Both the narrations above reflected scenarios when the milieu could be read—and a move devised to seek a new position. What happens, however, if the milieu cannot be read, or it is yet to evolve and the organization seeks to be an agent in the process of evolution? Such an image can capture the world of Google in its early years or that of mobile computing (say Nokia) in the mid-1980s. How would a strategist design an organization in such a context of fluidity? Recollect that we argued that a rational organization design is a mythical concept; designs of organization are relative to structures that are relevant—the rival's organization structure, for instance. Without that, the design would lose its point of reference. In such scenarios, as the future evolves, jointly created by the strategist and other allies or partners in complex dimension of rivalry and cooperation, the internal organization also changes. We explore a specific instance of such dynamic creation of organizations at DoCoMo (see case study 3.5).

The interesting part is to realize that the organization evolves dynamically as an outcome of several negotiations led by the lead coordinator strategist. Power of the partner (or outside) organizations and its

---

[12]You will hear of several stories where elaborate performance management systems—grading mechanisms and such devices—fail because the wielders of power often fail to discriminate amongst contestants; so, the contest fails, possibly because of other considerations such as the threat exercised by the contestants to leave the organization or the specific project team. Internal anthropological accounts would inform you about the 'jokes' around several such control tools.

resources often might be useful to bypass or negotiate through nodes of recalcitrant power holders inside the parent organization and vice versa. Organizations in the partnership, thus, breach each other's organization structures and processes as the milieu evolves—this structural fluidity is also an essential requirement for the generation of increasing return dynamics. This joint management of resources and interest of power holders across intra-organizational and extra-organizational turfs offers a creative possibility to the top management to drive an organizational change process. One can now possibly look at joint ventures that do not achieve any level of deep integration and fail even when there is no conflict of interest (or intent!) at the broad partner level. An evolving joint venture would succeed in achieving integration only when there is mutual organizational destabilization as the basic driver of generation of increasing return dynamics. This needs to be driven through engaging in a series of conflicts and negotiations across organizations.

CASE STUDY 3.5 DoCoMo and i-Mode creation

Data communication over mobile phones has contributed to major progress in the feasibility and availability of the mobile computing. The internet access technology implemented over mobile phones represented by 'i-mode' of DoCoMo has stimulated an evolution from today's mobile phones into portable terminals. Japan outperforms America and European countries in the use of mobile internet technology by 2–3 years. The company registered an operating income of USD 7.3 billion (consolidated) for the financial year that ended in March 2001, becoming a high-return company, second only to Toyota. Since 1992, when DoCoMo was spun off from its parent company, Nippon Telegraph and Telephone (NTT), as an independent mobile communications entity, it has been endeavouring to open a large door to the mobile phone market in Japan.

Mr Oboshi, who was CEO of the company in 1997, predicted that the growth curve reflecting the increase in the number of subscribers of mobile phones in terms of voice communications would become saturated in the near future. As a result, he felt a sense of impending crisis over the returns and growth of DoCoMo. Focus was placed on the data communications market that would eventually take over the voice communications market. In January 1997, Mr Enoki, who was serving as Corporate Business Director at the time

(Case Study 3.5 contd.)

(Case Study 3.5 contd.)

(currently Senior Vice President, Senior Manager of Gateway Business Department [GBD]), was appointed by Mr Oboshi to develop non-voice communication services over mobile phones targeting general users. Mr Oboshi then assigned Mr Enoki to the task of building a new organization by means of recruiting HR within or outside the company and empowered him (with personnel and financial management) to start up the new service. With diverse and talented HR recruited from both within and outside the company, Mr Enoki started a new project (responsible for Gateway Business) staffed by some 10 persons, a unit that by August 1997 had evolved into the GBD staffed by 70 employees. GBD was then at developing a new service dubbed 'i-mode'.

Positive feedback of the elements through which information providers (IP) would continuously provide useful content to end-users of i-mode compliant mobile phones was urgently needed for the business model that was planned for successful i-mode service. This model was designed to expand the number of end-users as well as enhance the content provided by IPs. DoCoMo retained about 9 per cent of usage fees of the content, along with the communication charge; fees from each transaction was very small for DoCoMo, but proliferation of content providers as well as large user base contributed to revenues. A strategic community was established with hardware and software competencies inside GBD and other DoCoMo divisions, and also the external IPs, who were seen as the most crucial partners. The aim was to devise a new innovative business and revenue model that would be win–win for partners in the community. Leadership assumed a 'servant' role, listening and, when possible, acting to facilitate dealmaking.

The project adopted a three-pronged strategy. The first was the 'portal strategy' for developing new, useful content for the i-mode service. The second was the 'terminal strategy' with the aim to develop new i-mode mobile phone terminals including add-on features. The third was the 'platform strategy' to break ground for i-mode users using platforms for other than mobile terminals. Furthermore, these three business strategies were interactive with each other, thus capable of triggering a major synergy depending on the strategy concerned. In order to promote these business strategies, an important task was to proceed with the strategic alliance with many outside partners so as to yield practicable results. When i-mode service began in February 1999, the GBD formed the communities in succession through strategic alliances with outside partners in order to sign up end-users at an early stage of the project. The first step was to form a 'portal community' to act as the core of the portal strategy and enhance the details of the i-mode

(Case Study 3.5 contd.)

(Case Study 3.5 contd.)

portal operated by DoCoMo through which diverse risks and interests would be shared with IPs while enhancing the value of the contents so as to provide new values for the end-user. In addition, the advertisement delivery service was promoted on i-mode portal, and a top-flight financial service was also implemented at the birth of the net-based banking business. This strategy was recognized as an important positioning of services prior to the launch of i-mode sales. The second step was to form a 'technical community' linked with terminal manufacturers, which would become the core of the terminal strategy. This strategy was intended to trigger new demand for end-user terminals and to motivate users to replace their terminals by periodically adding new features to i-mode mobile phones. For IPs, the development of new mobile phones (such as JAVA-compliant phones) opened the possibility that content could be developed under new applications with the advantage of attracting new end-users. DoCoMo could also enjoy an increase of new revenue from increased communications traffic due to a greater penetration of mobile phones equipped with new features. The third step was to form a 'platform community' to serve as the core of the platform strategy in order to expand the scope of i-mode availability. Combining i-mode mobile phones with game machines, car navigation systems and other platforms would further expand i-mode availability. Process definitions evolved from negotiations in the respective communities and then were integrated across divisions. Issues of reliable service delivery, uniform customer experience, fast response to customer requests, maintenance of facilities and its expansion to handle the growing traffic volume soon cropped up and then integration with the tightly controlled process assets of DoCoMo's old voice business was sought. Unlike the fluid community-based loose governance in the strategic communities, process reliability required old-type competencies that were honed up in the traditional organization within its culture of tight control. This negotiation led to new capacity creation and expansion of the old organization; revenue sharing arrangements were often redefined to take care of the old interests. For instance, in March and April 2000, the traditional organization promptly increased capacity for the subscribers to i-mode centre, launched i-mode Service Stability Project and continued to enhance the reliability of the service on an organizational basis. The effort was to enable the old organization, facing the threat of decreasing returns, to experience volume based growth riding on the increasing returns generated by the innovative i-Mode project.

By promoting this sort of strategic community management, in March 2002, the GBD achieved the target of signing up 32 million subscribers

(Case Study 3.5 contd.)

(Case Study 3.5 contd.)

> (end-users) in just two years after start-up of the service. The success of i-mode raised the status of GBD. It was made into a new division named i-mode Business Division in July 2001 and it became vested with greater powers. Aiming to achieve further innovations, the new division began to work hard at preparing for a new i-mode service known as IMT-2000, a third-generation (3G) mobile service that will be marketed under the Freedom of Mobile Multimedia Access (FOMA) service brand name. Among the services being planned, high-speed data transmission as a trial i-mode service was launched in March 2001, and the world's first moving picture clipping service for mobile phones was slated to start in November 2001 (excerpts from Kodama, 2003: 307–30).

3.5 ORGANIZATION AS A MODE OF EXERCISE OF POWER

In the beginning of this chapter, we argued that the rationale for the existence of an organization may be sought in the desire for establishment of dominance—over both internal nodes of power inside the organization as well as nodes that lie outside the organization. How else would you make sense of such famous whips—such as that of Jack Welsh (of General Electric [GE] fame)—selling off businesses if it is not in the top few slots in a particular industry! For the buyers of such GE disposed assets, a lesser proposition might as well be quite attractive. Other accounts would explain the existence of organization from either scale economy perspective or from transaction cost minimization perspective. While scale economies are important, you must realize that it requires a large indivisible sunk asset to produce economies of scale; so, the source of the scale economy must be searched for. Consider a very popular description (almost an article of faith): that bulk procurement leads to lower costs of procurement. Is it true—or rather, necessarily true? Bulk procurement, as Porter argued, definitely leads to a bargaining power that can lead to lower negotiated rates. Does this cause a disadvantage to a smaller lot buyer? The problem is more complex here—in the presence of independent wholesalers and bulk integrators, small purchasers would not have a disadvantage; it is as if bulking is outsourced by small procurers to the wholesalers. But in the absence of such wholesalers, small procurers would face a price disadvantage in terms of bargaining power. You can note here the distinct advantage afforded to a host of small Japanese producers due to the presence of giant wholesale trading companies—the *sogososhas*—that carried exports into foreign markets. The larger firms and groups relied less on these wholesalers; but smaller firms needed them much more. The transaction cost perspective also provides important insight, one of which is the observation that coordination faces costs of transaction—through monitoring of rule/norm-following; so, a decline in transaction costs of coordination in a network mode can reduce the requirement for organizational mode of coordination. Both perspectives appeal to efficiency grounds. Our argument is that the efficiency ground represents an incomplete (or rather a partial) description; the strategist notes the existence of nodes of power, and action is driven by that. And for the strategist, apart from the outcome, the process of arrival at it is more important; outcome is uncertain from a strategist's perspective.

In our contemporary times, there have been few important changes that were reflected throughout our discussion. It has implications for organizational mode of exercise of power—both in its contest with other (maybe smarter!) modes as well as in terms of exercise of power inside the organization that we would briefly note here before closing this chapter. First, other modes of coordination have become powerful—such as in a network of smaller firms organized in a quasi-hierarchic mode of different levels (recall the several tiers of suppliers in automobile or software service industry). So, a large organization faces stiffer contest today; wholesale type of firms or platform providers can play effective coordination roles at low transaction costs. And such platform providers would thrive by the slicing up of the integrated assets of the organization to create the trading opportunity that would valorize the platform asset. It is important to note this dynamics.

Inside the organization, the power afforded through a 'sunk fixed asset' and the control tool built around it (such as the conveyor belt) as well as the premise of structural smoothness as the goal of coordination is under challenge. Managers inside a firm are expected to more closely mimic entrepreneurs, especially when the organization seeks to grow along increasing returns modes. Managers at fairly low levels of the organization then remain in close relation with extra-firm networks. To countervail this new-found power that one would draw from the networks, the organization has to search for new modes of exercise of organizational control. This is a difficult challenge, especially for an (Chandlerian) organization, built with a different purpose. Design of organization based on executive power is aimed at reducing the transaction cost through its exercise. We noted how the power wielder inside an organization works in a balanced field with other nodal power holders inside the organization. Within such a pragmatic description, can a manager mimic an entrepreneur? Is an incentivized manager, who can gain through exertions on a specific path (often specified through the Key Performance Indicator [KPI] specifics), similar to the entrepreneur whose domain mostly lies in deal-making?

In making that argument, we are not taking a position on the irrelevance of the traditional mode of organization—with its hierarchy and power wielding executive authority. Businesses require reliable execution capabilities that are built on tightly controlled process execution. Too often businesses fail because this simple fact is not realized. Several businesses, especially start-ups, fail because of elementary business management mistakes, such as inadequate attention to cash flow management. Our narration in the appendix to this chapter (on a start-up, Bangalore Labs) provides an interesting counterpoint, lest one believe that the fluidity afforded by the network and the deal-making possibilities to realize increasing returns gains constitute the future domain of business (see Appendix 3C). Bangalore Labs began as a high-profile start-up, made up of only deal-making people. It had the right connections, and funding from India's most celebrated venture capital (VC) firm. Yet, it encountered a disastrous failure. Was it because it neglected operations, or was inability to manage asset-heavy businesses a reason? You can read through the narrative.

The DoCoMo narrative possibly brings out what we are hinting at most clearly (see case study 3.5). It emphasized the role of the authoritarian 'old' structure rather than obfuscating issues through a general rhetoric on innovation. The projects handled by the strategic communities (note the use of the term community and not group or organization) were loosely governed—ideas evolved amidst very loosely guided process of conflict and negotiation. The new services and its detailed process map then required integration with the tightly controlled old organization, where the purpose of low transaction cost through tight hierarchical control was admitted openly. DoCoMo then provides a paradigmatic case of a partnership between decreasing and increasing returns models, one that several organizations are attempting today under the threat of break-up under the burdens of pursuing a decreasing returns path.

APPENDIX 3A

Cross Holdings as a Control Tool: Case of Tata Group

BGs/*chaebols*/*keiretsu*s are a group of formally independent firms under single common administrative and financial control, owned and controlled by either families or trusts or foundations. These business networks are usually owned through investment firms with cross holdings in affiliates. In most countries, industrial scenario continues to be dominated by these business houses. They often diversify across different product lines with many divisions under them, similar to US conglomerates. For example, in Korea, the Samsung group controls a host of firms predominantly in heavy engineering, construction and electronics. In India, the House of Tatas is one of the oldest BGs. The group is largely operated through a holding company, namely Tata Sons, with a very diverse product portfolio.

Historical Overview

Established by Jamsetji Tata in the second half of the 19th century, the Group has grown into one of India's biggest and most respected business organizations, largely due to the entrepreneurs' vision, their commitment and its fortitude in the face of adversity. In 1938, at the age of 34, Jehangir Ratanji Dadabhoy (JRD) Tata was elevated to the top post in the Tata Group. Over the next 50-odd years of his stewardship, the group expanded from just steel and textiles into many other areas including chemicals, automobiles and tea. Right from the beginning, JRD stamped his style of working on the organization. Breaking with the Indian business practice of having members of one's own family run different operations, JRD pushed to bring in professionals. Even as the Tata companies became legally independent under the dismantling of the managing agency system in 1970, a semblance of unity was maintained by a network of inter-corporate shareholdings, weekly cross-company directors' meetings and JRD's dynamic personality and moral force. JRD once commented on his role as chairman of the company:

> Today the companies are free to operate independently and in fact they do. Today, except in Tata Sons I do not wield any kind of executive authority. But because I am senior in age, I operate more on the basis of influence and confidence ...
> There is something absurd in so far as we have no more interest than any other shareholder in most of the companies. We get nothing extra for managing them. For example, till 1978, 90 percent of my time went between Air-India and Tata Steel as the chairman of both, and what did Tata get out of it? ... we get nothing. (Lala 1981: 192–93)

JRD encouraged his hand-picked chairmen to operate their companies autonomously within the perimeters of the Tata philosophy of professionalism and ethical business practices. As a result, the chairmen of larger Tata affiliates had grown accustomed to ruling their domains without interference from the Tatas for decades. Although these affiliate commanders all traded on the Tata name—one of the most respected brand names in India—they cherished their independence and vehemently protected their empires.

The Leadership Change and the New Moves Made

Ratan Tata, the son of one of JRD's cousins, was an open, trusting man and a shy, soft-spoken individual. He was called back from the US in 1962, where he worked as an architect, in order to work for the Tatas. In 1981, he was elected as chairman of Tata Industries Ltd (TIL), which he was to turn around from a small company into a group strategy think tank. In March 1991, Ratan was nominated by JRD to the Tata Sons chair. Ratan found himself as the head of a conglomeration of companies that were described by one Tata director as 'no longer existing as a group except in their culture and name ... It is only because of the financial institutions which are the major shareholders that Tata management is allowed in these companies'.

This resulted in Ratan Tata, at the helm of the then stodgy Tata group, setting out to unite, refocus and modernize the sprawling group of almost 100 largely independent businesses. His ways have been critiqued at by a lot of sceptics as also the righteousness of his means. But finally when he managed to put the group together and launch it into a high growth spiral, he did gain respect and acceptance as one of the most capable and strongest personalities to have led the group. In one of his first moves, Ratan lowered the retirement age for the heads of Tata affiliates, resulting in his victory against the old guard. Ratan Tata also implemented a number of other strategies including the following three:

- In 1994, ignoring the concern of many experts over the entry of foreign firms, Ratan sold a 20 per cent stake in Tata Industries Limited (TIL) to the Hong Kong based Jardine Matheson group for INR 1.26 billion. Ratan planned to use this capital influx to fund venture start-ups. The group also anticipated that Jardine would contribute expertise in a wide range of upcoming businesses activities such as retailing and financial services.
- Ratan Tata decided to undertake the responsibility of promoting a unified Tata brand which could be used by all companies which would subscribe to the Tata Brand Equity scheme. Each company that subscribed to the scheme would derive the benefits of the centrally promoted Tata brand. Ratan proposed that the subscribing Tata companies each pay a small contribution, the amount of which would depend upon each company's association with the brand. Participating companies would require subscribing to a code of conduct ensuring uniformly high standards of quality and ethical business practices.
- The group went on a restructuring exercise. The objectives included: (*a*) each company must be the industry leader occupying one of the top three positions and (*b*) the business identified must have potential for high growth and should be globally competitive. There was a break from the earlier sentimental approach to businesses that have been built over decades. Hence, the group exited the businesses of toiletries, cosmetics, consumer electronics and pharmaceuticals among others.

Fund Raising by the Holding Company

Through its primary holding company, that is, Tata Sons, the Tatas held minority shares in group companies ranging from 0.01 per cent to 15 per cent. In order to increase its stake in its affiliates, Tata Sons determined that they would need to raise a total of INR 7 billion in 1995–96 to realize a 1 per cent increase in stake in each of the major Tata companies. To raise the necessary funds, Tata Sons invited subscriptions to a INR 3 billion rights issue. The shares were made available to Tata group affiliates (at a premium) through the renunciation of shares by various charitable trusts (having the rights). The additional money was raised by internal generation, debt and other strategies.

While it was legal for Tata group companies to purchase Tata Sons shares and vice versa, collusion between the companies to exchange shares would be a violation of law. The media queried Ratan's plans; concerns stemmed partly from debate that the selling price of Tata Sons' shares had been overvalued. From an analyst's point of view, the deal seemed to lack any benefit for the investing companies. Ratan argued that the shares would appreciate immensely if Tata Sons were to go public, and no shareholders had yet officially complained of the illiquid nature of the Tata Sons investment. But one foreign investor admonished the participation of the Tata companies in the Tata Sons rights issue stating: *'This (diversion of capital) won't do the Tatas any good.'*

Increase in Cross Holdings

The infusion of funds in Tata Industries Limited and Tata Sons resulted in change in the cross holding ownership structure as displayed in the tables below:

Table 3A.1: Ownership Structure of Tata Sons

Stakeholder	Stake FY 1994 (%)	Stake FY 2005 (%)
Tata Trusts	78.0	65.9
Tata Group Affiliates	Less than 1	12.8
P. S. Mistry	17.5	18.4
Tata Family	3.5	2.9

Source: Compiled by authors from various sources.

Table 3A.2: Cross Holdings after the Tata Sons Rights Issue in 1996

Major Group Companies	Value of Tata Sons Shares Bought by Companies (amount in INR in million)	Tata Sons' Stake in Group Companies		
	FY 1996	FY 1995 (%)	FY 1996 (%)	FY 2005 (%)
Tata Iron & Steel	688	2.3	8.5	19.8
Tata Motors	688	1.8	2.7	21.9
Tata Power	370	5.6	6.3	28.7
Tata Chemicals	569	7.9	8.2	11.2
Tata Tea	n/a	7.6	8.6	14.7
Indian Hotels	250	13.3	13.3	12.3

Source: CMIE-PROWESS and ISI Emerging Markets Database.

The rights issue was a crucial step in the overall strategy. It does provide Tatas a lot of comfort by increasing their management control and also in avoiding hostile takeover battles. But if we combine information of Table 3A.1 with the information of Table 3A.2, we observe that it was using the funds of group-affiliated companies with significant non-promoter shareholdings (herein, Tata Group affiliates) to increase Tata Sons' stake in the company itself. Consequently, Tata Sons used this money to increase its stake in these Tata group affiliates.[13]

---

[13] One way to argue in favour of cross holdings is to state that this benefit will give access to the affiliate company shareholders by giving them access to the upside of high growth Tata affiliate concerns such as Tata Consultancy Services. This they would receive by way of dividends declared by Tata Sons in future (after the rights issue). But, the counterargument would remain that portfolio diversification of assets and investment management can be done by individuals/institutional investors on their own (or by investing in the mutual funds). This is so if we look from the viewpoint of a financial investor—in terms of cash flow rights.

Capturing the Changes in Ownership Structure

A glance through the financial numbers of Tata Motors, the biggest of the Tata group affiliates, over this 15-year period, gives an understanding of the cross investments (Table 3A.3). We observe that over this 15-year period, Tata Motors' investments in group companies had risen phenomenally. Similar was the pattern observed in other major Tata group affiliates.

Table 3A.3: Group Dealings of Tata Motors (INR in millions)

	1991	1995	2005
Sales	25,508	56,403	202,765
PBDIT (Profit before Depreciation, Interest and Tax)	3,704	7,527	23,369
Assets	16,975	41,369	139,946
Net Worth	5,831	14,203	41,113
Investment in group companies (mainly Tata Steel and Tata Finance)	0	1,909	19,422
Investment in group companies as a per cent of Assets	0.0%	4.6%	13.9%
Investment in group companies as a per cent of Shareholders Funds	0.0%	13.4%	47.2%

Source: Compiled by authors from various sources.

Figure 3A.1 gives the emerging cross holding pattern of the group in the year 2005. Apart from the primary holding company (Tata Sons), we observe that there are many other Tata group controlled investment firms which are part of this complex holding pattern (say Tata Industries, Kalimati Investments and Aftab Investment Corp). The ownership structure of Tata group shows signs of both 'pyramid' and 'cross-shareholding' structures in group firms. A 'pyramid' denotes a hierarchical chain by which a family controls a firm, and cross holding happens when a controlled firm owns any shares in its controlling shareholder or in the firms along that chain of control (including any indirect means). A few

Figure 3A.1: Structure of Tata Groups Listed Firms—2005

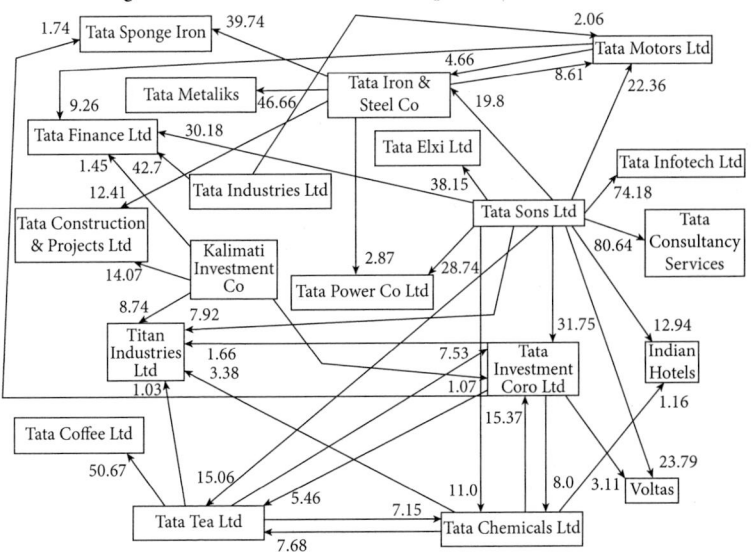

Source: Compiled by authors from various sources.

other points can also be concluded. First, we observe that the group has largely increased its indirect holding over its affiliates during this period. Second, we also observe that the ownership of these Tata group affiliates is becoming more dispersed, that is, the number of holding companies is increasing.

Getting behind the Cross Holding

Prior to restructuring, in 1991, the Tata group was a loose confederacy of 300 companies having sales of around INR 86 billion and controlling an asset base totalling more than INR 85 billion with very small ownership stakes. As a consequence, the chairmen of larger affiliates had grown accustomed to ruling their domains without interference from the Tatas and once in a while competing with each other in a similar line of business. Using increasing cross holding structure along with other strategy tools, Ratan Tata made the Tata group affiliates more cohesive and controllable. For example, there have been no rumblings among the Tata group affiliates during the period 2000–05 and onwards. Surely, a stake of at least 26 per cent would have made it easier to manage the group affiliates against hostile takeover bids. An increase in the cross holding structure of group companies beyond this point combined with pyramidal structure provides a mechanism for the Tata group to control firms within the group without necessarily having significant equity investment. An increased complexity in the cross holdings among group companies is a classic counter takeover defence strategy.

Cross holdings is a common phenomenon across Asia. Within a BG, cross holdings amongst group affiliates are often used to fund a group's (unstated) empire-building objectives. There are many BGs which have adopted cross holdings and intra-group transactions. Cross holdings entrench the position of the BG—creating a strong defence against possible attack (a takeover) from outside or a secession from within. From the perspective of a strategy thinker, a lot of issues can be pursued, such as: (*a*) What are the ingredients which made this cross holding structure route successful for Tata Group (while it became a bottleneck in the case of a few other large BGs such as Bajaj and the Nandas of Escorts)? (*b*) Is this model sustainable for other BGs? Would a BG with multiple family units (several sons and heirs, say) create such a unified interlocked structure or should cross holding be devised differently? Can this model work in other countries? (*c*) Going forward, is the increase in cross holding structure going to be beneficial or a bottleneck to the group—say, in terms of other perceived threats?

APPENDIX 3B

Reliance Group Subsidiaries

The Reliance Group, founded by Dhirubhai H. Ambani (1932–2002), is India's largest private sector enterprise, with businesses in the energy and materials value chain. The group's annual revenues are in excess of USD 27 billion. The flagship company, Reliance Industries Limited, is a Fortune Global 500 company and is the largest private sector company in India.

Backward vertical integration has been the cornerstone of the evolution and growth of Reliance. Starting with textiles in the late 1970s, Reliance pursued a strategy of backward vertical integration—in polyester, fibre intermediates, plastics, petrochemicals, petroleum refining and oil and gas exploration and production—to be fully integrated along the materials and energy value chain. Today, the group's activities span exploration and production of oil and gas, petroleum refining and marketing, petrochemicals (polyester, fibre intermediates, plastics and chemicals), textiles and retail.

One of the standard strategies adopted by the group to grow has been to create manufacturing plants of massive capacities (compared to the peers at that time). Typically, the group would identify an area to get into (say, a backward integration project), create a subsidiary to execute the project, and then raise finances using a combination of innovative financial products from the retail investors using the initial public offering route. Given that Indian capital markets have a developed equity market but a weak debt market, Reliance Group would ensure that it would typically raise equity-related instruments from the retail investors while the company would raise debt from the institutional investors in international debt markets. Once the group completed raising money from these new entities, the group would then execute the project at a fast pace without facing any resource bottlenecks. In other words, these mega projects would go on stream ahead of time with minimal cost overruns. Once these new mega projects go on stream and stabilize their operations, resulting in generation of steady cash flows, the group would then merge the subsidiary company into its flagship company.

The following table gives details of the major projects undertaken, the names of subsidiaries created and then merged with the parent entity.

Table 3B.1: Reliance Group and Its Companies: Over the Years

Name of the Firm(s) Created	Year of raising finances from retail investors through the newly created firm; Primary Products of the Project	Year of merging it with parent entity
Reliance Textile Industries Limited (flagship company)	1977; Textiles	Flagship firm renamed as 'Reliance Industries Limited'
Reliance Petrochemicals Limited (subsidiary company)	1987; Polyester staple fibre, linear alkyl benzene and related intermediate chemicals	1990
Reliance Poly Propylene Limited (RPPL) and Reliance Poly Ethylene Limited (RPEL)	1992; Polyethylene, polypropylene and other petrochemical products	1995
Reliance Petroleum Limited	1994; Petroleum refinery and oil exploration	2002
Reliance Petroleum Limited (a new entity with similar name)	2006; New petroleum refinery (export oriented unit)	Project under construction

Source: Compiled by authors from various sources.

As of 2007, Reliance enjoyed global leadership in its businesses, being the largest polyester yarn and fibre producer in the world and among the top five producers in the world in major petrochemical products. Table 3B.2 shows the Mukesh Ambani-managed group companies in 2008.

Table 3B.2: Mukesh Ambani's Reliance Group in 2008

Nature of Company	Name of the Company
Major Group Companies	Reliance Industries Limited
Main Subsidiaries	Reliance Petroleum Limited, Reliance Retail Limited and Reliance Industrial Infrastructure Limited
Other Subsidiaries and Associates of Reliance Industries Limited	Reliance Netherlands BV (including Trevira), Ranger Farms Limited, Retail Concepts and Services (India) Private Limited, Reliance Retail Insurance Broking Limited, Reliance Dairy Foods Limited, Reliance Retail Finance Limited, RESQ Limited, Reliance Jamnagar Infrastructure Limited, Reliance Haryana SEZ Limited, Reliance Industrial Investment & Holdings Limited, Reliance Ventures Limited, Reliance Strategic Investments Limited, Reliance Exploration & Production—Dubai Multi Commodities Centre (DMCC), Reliance Industries (Middle East) DMCC, Reliance Global Management Services (P) Limited and Reliance Europe Limited

Source: Compiled by the authors.

From a strategy perspective, a lot of interesting questions arise, such as: (*a*) What makes the group use the subsidiary mode of raising money, executing project and merging it with flagship so successful? (*b*) What are the ingredients which made this subsidiary route successful for Reliance group (while it failed for other large BGs such as Essar and Usha Rectifier)? (*c*) Is this model sustainable for other BGs? Can this model work in other countries? (*d*) Going forward, how can this organization grow?

APPENDIX 3C

Bangalore Labs[14]

Bangalore Labs was a company founded in December 1999 by a team of professionals who hailed from the field of technology and networking. The company was founded with the mission of networking as religion and the stated purpose of providing network consultancy and solutions to its clients.

Comparisons of Bangalore Labs with another start-up which came up around the same time—Mindtree Consulting—abounded, especially with both firms having a founding team comprising successful professionals in their respective fields. Given the buzz around the profile of the founders, it is only prudent that we understand what this profile was all about.

The idea of Bangalore Labs was originally mooted by T. G. Ramesh (Tiger) (in his 40s), who was heading sales for an important region of Nortel Networks. He had come up with this suggestion in a cocktail party where he bounced this idea off another IT professional from Infosys Technologies Limited—an *Infosys crorepati*[15]—to be precise, Umesh Malhotra, who was in his early 1930s and who had a successful track record with Infosys. Umesh also came with sales background, but with some project management experience and was part of the early team of Infosys. Umesh has expressed his desire to Infosys to move on and do something on his own, but had not come up with what exactly to do.

---

[14]This case has been contributed by Rama Subramanium. Rama was part of the Bangalore Labs experience.

[15]One crore is equal to 10 million. Infosys *crorepati* means making and owning a wealth of more than INR 1 crore due to benefits of being associated with Infosys (say, through employee stock options).

Tiger's selling skills were legendary and he was a person clearly endowed with the gift of the gab.

With the seed of the idea finding fertile ground, the two drummed up a team comprising Joy Nandi, who was working under Tiger in Nortel Networks and was another brilliant technology sales person, V. Natarajan (Natty), who headed South Asia sales for Lucent Technologies, and Shriram Ramdas, who was a common friend to Tiger and Natty, and was a successful sales professional with FedEx, the logistics multinational. Of the five founders, Natty, a father figure with lot of grey hair reflecting his experience and stately personality, was chosen to be the CEO of the organization.

Observing the developments in Bangalore Labs, a keen observer commented that entrepreneurial business always leverages a network (social/political/business). Novelty of the offering, which may not be technological and can be business model innovation as well, can be deciphered and marketed in the network. It is this insight that enables partners to build business ideas, sell to each other and transform each other in the process. It just looked as if Bangalore Labs was missing this.

Interestingly, Mindtree Consulting also had a profile of founders which reflected experience in the field of software development. But, there were some clear differences between the two players: one of the founders of Mindtree Consulting came from an operations background, another from a sales background. It also had generalists with a streak of the maverick who could slip into any role ranging from finance to HR. And it also had its choice of a grey haired CEO, who in his earlier role had experience in managing and building one of the most successful software stories of the nation. In short, it was a full rainbow of expertise. In comparison, the Bangalore Labs initial team was a sales team—a team specializing into selling black boxes. No one was, for instance, a product architect, a traditional role. Product or business model articulation is the domain of these architects—a creative job.

The name Bangalore Labs was interestingly picked up among other reasons for its 'Great IPO value'. Networking was seen by the founders of Bangalore Labs to be an uncluttered uncrowded market in an era of IT start-ups and dime a dozen dot-coms. This was partly driven by the fact that between Nortel and Lucent—two companies that owed their existence to networking—came three of the five founders. The promoters sounded bullish right from the word go. Shriram, one of the promoters, said in an interview to *New York Times*, 'India is on its way to being the back office for the world' (Landler 2001). Nandi wrote in an IT weekly:

All of us were successful in our respective businesses and wanted to see how we could create an organization in the services space. We saw a phenomenal disconnect between people who understood networking and those who understood business processes. There was a great divide between small IT firms on one hand and the Big five consulting firms on the other. So we launched India's first Managed Services Provider (MSP) with an NOC (Network Operations Centre) called IMARC. (Rao 2002)

Media coverage of Bangalore Labs was flattering and this company was expected by most people to go places and was even spoken of as the potential Infosys of networking. This positive media coverage helped Bangalore Labs attract funding as well as talent. Funding came from ICICI Ventures, a VC subsidiary of ICICI Bank. It was a time when ICICI Venture had loads of funds at its disposal but very few good opportunities to invest. It raised USD 4 million from ICICI Ventures in the first round of funding, of which USD 2.5 million was being spent on putting in place backend infrastructure for the new facility.

Talent came in the form of successful professionals from blue-blooded corporates and consultancies—chose to join Bangalore Labs in the dream of creating an organization from scratch.

So, Labs began life in 1999 as a Managed Services company with its primary focus being on remote network management. Network performance, security and management of a network set-up were part of a second level of services that were launched mid-2000. To be specific, Bangalore Labs started with two broad service offerings. The first was that of providing e-business solutions to corporates. And the second was to provide remote network management services using its state-of-the-art NOC which it was setting up. The NOC was a capital-intensive, technology-heavy business, which required an upfront building up of capabilities and infrastructure that was then used to pitch to customers.

The e-business consulting was a people-heavy business for which the key ingredient was the profile of the consultants that Bangalore Labs would deploy on an assignment. In this, Bangalore Labs was on a strong wicket with people from premier management institutions and with work experience from big five consulting companies, respected MNCs and technology companies willingly joining the company. Narendra, Vice President (HR), stated in an interview that the start-up veered from the traditional in its efforts to attract and retain talent by creating a well thought out career management system and employee stock ownership plan (ESOP) package. The bench strength of Bangalore Labs was the envy of any start-up. In fact, Leena, the HR Head, in an interview to a newspaper mentioned, '*An example of our success with creating the "PULL" is that we go to campuses only by invitation ... Last year 80% of all hiring was done through internal referrals*' (Hindu 2001; emphasis added).

Right from genesis, Bangalore Labs had striven for a non-hierarchical structure in the organization. Nandi pointed in an interview that 'there was always undue pressure on work in our earlier jobs' and 'so we aimed at having fun while doing work to get greater productivity (Prashant 2002). We have impromptu KM (i.e., Knowledge Management) sessions. On the last Friday of each month we have a Coke and Samosa session where different locations dial into Bangalore and the management team sits in'. However, business was not easy to come by. Essentially it appeared Bangalore Labs' service offerings, of consulting, was too broad based and anybody willing to pay for such services would rather go to an Accenture or PricewaterhouseCoopers (PwC) who had a significant experience in this area. However, smaller projects which an Accenture or PwC wouldn't pick up could have been a starting point, but the founders who had started the company with e-business as a stated area of focus felt their service offering was weak.

During this phase came up an interesting opportunity. Deloitte and Touche had won a big project for one of its clients in the US and was looking to outsource a specific piece of that work. It was looking for someone to programme, manage and complete this piece of work which involved process design. Tiger, who was heading sales at this time, saw the opportunity this presented and pitched for this. However, in the process, it also appeared that process design was a specialized area of consulting and that there was merit in focusing our offerings on process design. It was hence announced that there will be a restructuring of the business portfolio and Bangalore Labs now had four sharply defined business segments, namely Process design, Technology solutions, Security solutions and NOC. Security solutions came about because of two reasons: (*a*) there was an existing project that Bangalore Labs was working on which had to fit; and (*b*) there were also a good number of enquiries in that segment, albeit of low value. Having a sharper business focus, it was felt that this will help Bangalore Labs win the Deloitte contract.

The Deloitte contract came through, but the scope of work that fell to Bangalore Labs was quite limited, and the expectation that it would get a larger share of the process-design pie did not come through. Unfortunately, during this time, some enquiries for small opportunities in the e-biz space had to be turned down, citing the new direction of Bangalore Labs as reason.

Around this time, the founders were also looking at the second round of funding which was soon to be required as the NOC operations were yet to start, and, moreover, it was felt that the ability to scale up NOC would be an important determinant in getting business. Hence talks were on with venture funds who usually also express opinion on what strategy the company was to pursue. In one such discussion with a promising funding opportunity came up the idea of xSPs—this in short stands for service providers in the technology space of various types. Hence it was decided that the focus will be on specific technology clients in the service provider space. This, however, meant that the consultants, typically with experience in areas like supply chain management, were to learn an area which was new to them. Nevertheless, this was announced as the new strategic direction of the company. It helped that the only process design and technology consulting contract that Bangalore Labs had won after Deloitte and was still working on happened to be for a data centre which fitted the xSP description. Hence, the team of consultants working on this assignment need not have to be disturbed, while the sales force had to realign their offerings.

One of the problems faced by the sales team was also that the consultative nature of offerings required highly tailor-made solutions which could not be read out from a product sheet or learning about a specific product. All sales people came from an environment where they sold 'boxes', which meant products with clear well-defined specifications. Consulting was a different ball game. What we offered was not well defined. What the customer wanted was also not well defined. This essentially meant that every sales call had to happen with a consultant in tag. Hence the sales manager was reduced to doing the tasks of opening the door, chasing a client, setting up meetings and follow up. The real task of convincing was in the hands of the consultants. This also resulted in the clients expecting the same person who sold him the project to work on the project, which was not something that was always possible. Most of the time, the best people were already on a project and they were also on call for key sales pitch. This meant they were in more demand. This also resulted in the sales managers feeling their talents being underutilized as the key selling job was no longer theirs.

Almost all of Bangalore Labs' revenues accrue from India, with a small percentage coming from the US and Australia. Unlike most start-ups, where the network of the founders drums up the initial business, few of the enquiries subsequent to the first 2–3 opportunities came through the network of the founders and almost all of them came through either the painstaking sales effort of the sales personnel or through contacts of the consultants themselves. The list of customers included Pidilite, Hathaway, Hughes Telecom, Jasubhai Digital Media, Larsen and Toubro (L&T) IT, Net Decisions, Skumars.com, Spice Telecom and Vysya Bank. Consulting, security and enterprise management gave good revenue in India. The break-up has been roughly 50 per cent of consulting revenues coming from security, 30 per cent from enterprise management and 20 per cent from networking solutions.

Box 3C.1   From Start to End: Important Events for Bangalore Labs

November 1999: A start-up promoted by five professionals, the company was born with venture funding from ICICI Venture Fund. It was the first to offer managed services in the country and to offer remote network management.

February 2000: The firm announces a partnership with Aprisma Management Technologies to utilize *Spectrum* management solution to manage enterprise networks. In addition, the firm will be an authorized Spectrum training partner.

May 2000: The firm, India's first vendor-independent networking services company, has been chosen by Vysya Bank, *Dainik Jagran* newspaper and Ezeepoint.com as their networking partner with the task of designing connectivity solutions.

September 2000: The firm announces its ESOP. The company sets aside 15 per cent of its total equity base towards ESOP for its employees.

April 2001: The firm kicks off a new service called Vulnerability Assessment wherein it offers customers 'Ethical Hacking', a service to expose potential vulnerabilities in the Information System Infrastructure.

November 2001: The firm formed a strategic alliance with Singapore-based USD 100 million technology holding company Planet One Pte Ltd, for providing IT solutions to the Asia–Pacific market. A few in the media report that 'Planetone acquires Bangalore Labs'.

December 2001: The firm announces a partnership with IBM India Limited to implement and maintain IBM's Tivoli software solutions for their customers in India.

January 2002: The first CEO, Natarajan, together with another promoter, Shriram, quit.

June 2002: The second CEO, Ramesh, quit the company, together with another promoter, Umesh.

December 2002: Nandi, the last of the original five promoters put in his papers. He was the third CEO to quit.

(Box 3c.1 contd.)

(Box 3c.1 contd.)

> **February 2003:** New management appoints a new CEO, Jim Timmons.
>
> **June 2003:** Bangalore Labs changes its name to Net ProActive Services Pte Ltd., with immediate effect. Net ProActive Services Pte Ltd. came into effect on 13 June 2003 in the US.

Source: Based on the following news links:
http://www.thehindubusinessline.com/2002/12/27/stories/2002122701050700.htm (accessed on 3 November 2007);
http://www.domain-b.com/companies/companies_b/bangalore_labs/20011109_planet.html (accessed on 3 November 2007);
http://www.prdomain.com/companies/I/IBM/newsreleases/20021517327.htm (accessed on 3 November 2007);
http://timesofindia.indiatimes.com/cms.dll/articleshow?art_ID=1359277082 (accessed on 3 November 2007);
http://www.netproactiveservices.com/content/blinnews.htm (accessed on 3 November 2007).

The xSP service offering unfortunately did not take-off well due to two key reasons. First, Bangalore Labs was not clear of what it was offering in this space and was trying to be everything. Second, service providers themselves were caught in a serious problem wherein overcapacity in the market and unprofitable business models left most of them strapped for cash.

Meanwhile, the NOC was operational but Bangalore Labs was unable to obtain clients. However, since it was a guzzler of cash, Bangalore Labs had almost entirely run out of cash for these operations and was desperately in need of more funds. What was looking very attractive in a presentation as a business model for the NOC was proving a problem in getting clients to sign up. The NOC was touted as a service offered entirely remotely. However, clients preferred to have at least a few people onsite to manage the network, which Bangalore Labs was unwilling to do. Bangalore Labs felt it can outsource this task to other organizations that traditionally offered this service, but clients ended up being more comfortable with doing business with just the company providing onsite support.[16] It was also partly a case of an idea ahead of its time, as most networks today with greater bandwidth and network pervasiveness are indeed managed remotely, but that was not so obvious in year 2001.

---

[16] An excellent experience of the technology issues faced by a customer of Bangalore Labs is provided in the book *Annals of Cases on Information Technology* by Mehdi Khosrow-Pour (2002: 157–62).

Initially, the company's focus was on international markets with the US being the biggest potential market and an offshore delivery model. Bangalore Labs invested a lot in the US only to retract due to the slowdown. It shifted focus to India. 'Even today we are considered a thought leader in the security space with the widest breadth of consulting, security and technology architecture services. From 2002, Bangalore Labs is looking at the Australian, APAC and US markets', said Nandi in an interview to an IT magazine (Rao 2002).

Interestingly, during all this, it was believed ICICI Ventures considered Bangalore Labs as one of the gems in its crown, at a time when it had taken some beating due to the dot-com bust. By May 2001, the founders of Bangalore Labs were engaged almost full-time in scouting for venture partners, spending very little time on actual business development. There was a sense of hurry prevailing in having to do something fast, and the feeling of a sinking ship had set it.

By August 2001, Bangalore Labs was seriously strapped for cash and had to sell off to a company in the network management space called 3D Networks. By November 2001, popular national newspapers, such as *Times of India*, were rife with rumours that that the firm had no focus and was heading nowhere. Ironically, most of the people in Bangalore Labs' NOC ended up joining larger companies like Wipro and Infosys, which were setting up their own NOC service offerings, and which today are highly successful businesses for these IT giants. By 2002, people from the consulting business unit moved on the strength of their earlier experience. This left Bangalore Labs with just a skeleton of infrastructure investments with hardly anybody from the start-up team. By end of 2002, the last of the five-member founder group and the third CEO of the organization, Nandi, also quit the organization.

Key issues to pick up from the failure:

- Lack of clarity of purpose.
- Lack of steadiness in pursuit.
- No balance in the profile of the top team—all sales.
- Not unlearning enough—sale for box-selling is fine, but not for consulting.
- Governance mechanism of ICICI Ventures seems to be lacking (or weak).
- Founders from the beginning were after valuation and sell-out, and not into building a business.

4

Markets and Regulation

4.0 INTRODUCTION

This is a rather short chapter on a strategist's perspective on markets and regulation. We discuss a few aspects of the concept of a market (see sections 4.0, 4.1, 4.2, 4.3 and 4.4) and then move on to discuss about regulation (see sections 4.0, 4.4 and 4.5). First, what is a market? Our earlier discussion pointed towards an institutional view of markets. Institutions or underlying rules support transactions in a market. In contrast to an abstract market defined by demand and supply, our description would concretize the specific rule structure within which the market operates. Readers may recall our earlier discussion on the norms of electric utility pricing in early 20th-century US in the first chapter (see case study 1.2). Consider the market for central processing unit (CPU) chips—the one dominated overwhelmingly by Intel. Does not Intel have enormous power over the market—not only in the sense of setting the price (or commanding a large quantity or market share)—being almost a quasi-monopolist, but more importantly as a rule setter?

> Intel's top management set the pace of technical change in the CPU space by making clock speed the most preferred dimension of performance and committing to a rate of improvement on it over time. This pre-committed rate of technical change along the single dimension of clock speed (also known as Moore's law in popular descriptions!) achieved a coordination of *dynamic expectations* of a whole ecosystem consisting of computer makers, software

> application writers—whose investments were shaped accordingly. How did it acquire this power? Importantly, it led the whole industry to believe in the fad that processing speed—megahertz—is the only relevant variable of concern in measuring the advancement of the CPU/chip industry, leading the industry along a one-dimensional trajectory. In other words, it focused the industry on concentrating technical developments along a chosen/preferred trajectory. This dominance has only recently been questioned by several contenders, such as Advanced Micro Devices (AMD), NVDIA and a few others who have proposed alternatives. This dimension of dominance in being able to set rules or standards that are adopted in an ecosystem would be most crucial from a strategic perspective.

Intel would engage in transactions with PC manufacturers through a series of contracts. Is not it imperative for a strategist with an interest in this market to look for the specific contract structure as shaping the market—such as exclusivity clauses imposed on the buyer that force buyers to have single sources of procurement. Later in the chapter, we would revisit the case of Intel's contracting practices with key customers. If we subscribe to this institutional view of markets, then implicitly we would have to accept the idea that different asset holders in the market space enjoy nodal power—power to effect a denial, in different senses. We explored this dimension of acquisition of nodal power through different modes in the first chapter (see section 1.7). Such asset holders also would have powers to shape up, change or preserve the underlying rule structure that supports transactions in the market space.

It would perhaps be easier to visualize the market space as endogenous to the acts of the nodal power holders; that is, the market as it exists is not exogenous or lying outside the world of strategic actors; it is rather shaped up by their very acts—acts of conflict, contests, cooperation, and so on. We then depart from popular readings that convey a sense of markets as given—as exogenous. Our emphasis on an institutional view of markets in contrast to the hypothetical 'free market' (with its *invisible hand*) is again very pragmatic. It helps us focus on the numerous acts of coordination that occupy managerial time and energies—acts such as syndication, cartelization, joint prospecting, joint venturing, contracting, and so on. The market as experienced practically by acting strategists is deeply institutional. It is through these institutional practices—such as, say, contracting—that a strategist/manager gets a feel/sense of the actual market. It is again through these institutions that market dominance or a win over the rival is sought as the ultimate goal of a strategist. Our exploration in this chapter would revolve around different dimensions and types of coordination in specific institutionalized markets. By coordination, we refer to the convergence on certain business dimension across a set of agents. In our discussion at the beginning of the chapter, the agreement within a wide milieu on the salience of clock speed as the most important parameter of computing power represents a coordination. Coordination thus has a functionalist motivation. Discussion on acts of coordination naturally would bring out aspects of governance as well. Governance refers to the dimension of motives, including possibilities of slippages that agents under coordination have to solve. Governance thus explores the motives, incentives and its compatibility, the power of agents, and so on, as they strive to maintain the coordinated state with respect to certain dimensions of business interest. A state of coordination would implicitly require a rule-set to which the coordinated agents would abide by. Such rule-sets would need to be governed, first, in arriving at a rule-set and then in preserving it. A state of coordination thus would always need to be governed. Hence our exploration would span these twin dimensions of coordination and governance.

In the process, we would provide several descriptions of markets that differ in their institutional moorings; specifically, we would talk about:

1) markets as interlinked contracts, mainly of differentiated but highly specifiable products, where contract enforcement and relational assets provide the governance mechanism;
2) markets of homogeneous products or commodities with price clearing characteristics, where governance is organized around the threat of competition afforded by the rival vendor of the standard product; and
3) thick network markets (where transactions on highly differentiated and uncertain assets occur in dense networks, such as in Bollywood film production or Silicon Valley tech-start-up financing). Such markets depend crucially on inter-temporally created assets for governance, in the face of failure of governance modes common in types (1) and (2) above.

In each of these types of markets, we would explore very briefly the nature of inter-organizational coordination involved in strategic acts, specifically focusing on the differences that coordination seeks in each type of market. Markets of type (1) and (2) above would mostly have decreasing returns characteristics and deterrence motives would shape up the governance sought, while (3) primarily would lend itself to generation of increasing returns and market-making would gain primacy. Markets of type (2) above depend on the proverbial price clearing or price-based coordination, but require acts of coordination that create hubs or central market places that underlie the Walrasian markets. It is, we argue, a necessary primitive for the existence of markets of type (2).

We would also distinguish markets on the basis of whether the product (whose market we are talking of!) is: (*a*) standalone, (*b*) systemic or (*c*) platform, with systemic products and platforms generating increasing returns. We would explain each category along with illustrations and significance from a strategic perspective as we move on. Specifically, we would argue that systemic and platform products demand a 'dynamic coordination', where the final coordinated state cannot be specified exante, in the face of massive uncertainties. Coordination seeks to influence the expectation and investment of a bevy of complementary asset holders. Coordination and hence governance can only be designed around a minimal convergence. These markets would mostly also have 'thick network' characteristics. Such markets also lend themselves to generation of increasing returns dynamics, and coordination seeks to release the unfolding of such dynamics from existing institutional constraints. One particular form that such acts of coordination take involves transformation of a set of linked assets connecting them through novel modes of transaction.

We would then induce our reader to think of a market, not as an abstract concept of demand and supply interaction, but rather as a specific one, shaped by the institutional details of the market and specific nature of the product. We argue and show that this approach provides a more pragmatic path that can illuminate action. That would draw our discussion on markets to a close and we shift to a brief exploration on regulation.

If, as our description above indicates, all markets have underlying rule structures, then the difference between market and regulation does not seem so obvious either. Regulation, after all, is a rule set by the executive authority with the regulatory power. Regulation, usually, is associated with the government's executive powers; but in the contemporary business world, several regulations are enforced through non-state bodies, such as standard setting bodies that are like clubs of private businesses, or by a private exchange, such as a stock exchange. So, regulation by the government regulator must be just one class, albeit a special one, amongst different types of regulation. We do not think regulation is unimportant or even less important in contemporary businesses. And, to reiterate, regulation emanates from several quarters in addition to that of the government. It may be useful, then, to see regulation as a manifestation of the power of an executive authority whose jurisdiction runs over multiple organizations; and when the state does that, it is backed by the sovereign—which, in a sense, is a higher authority than a business organization.

In our discussion in the chapter on organization, we viewed organizational power as a kind of executive authority (power of a CEO inside the organization) limited to intra-organizational affairs, and we pointed towards several other points of exercise of non-organizational executive authority that lies in the broader social/political space. The span or jurisdiction of a regulation and/or the executive authority that shapes the regulation, its temporal stability, means and mechanisms through which regulatory contests are waged with proponents of alternative regulations—all of these would constitute elements that would interest a strategist. Any asset holder with a temporal horizon over which an ownership over the asset is sought to be enjoyed would be interested in the dynamics of valuation of the asset. Our discussion in the chapter on assets pointed out how asset valuation is dependent often on the institutional structures. Thus regulation, as one major element of the institutional structure, creates vested interests that eye either preservation or change in regulation. We discuss, in particular, two distinct inspirations behind regulation—one as countervail to the dominance of powerful interests (such as antimonopoly regulation), and the second as a support for enabling creation of distinct institutional structures for supporting the growth of novel technology/business models.

Regulation, by the government, if viewed as the manifestation of executive authority, points to several other interesting areas that a strategist needs to take note of. Is regulation through the executive authority in a Ministry of the Union (or Federal) government similar to that of an independent statutory regulatory authority (such as Telecom Regulatory Authority of India or Securities and Exchange Board of India [SEBI]) or that of the local/provincial government? Does regulation through uniform national statutes, or regulation through a series of temporarily effective 'executive orders' issued by local government authorities create different institutional structure of markets that can lead to differences in strategic response? While the US provides a close instance of the first type (also called Anglo-Saxon Common Law tradition), China seems to be closer to the second type (often called Civil Law tradition). Does this difference affect the structure of the market in a particular country that the strategist needs to understand and possibly work on? For instance, does it lead to a difference in the sites of the government machinery (federal or provincial power holders) where regulatory tussles are played out? Our engagement in this chapter aims at organizing our thoughts around these issues.

4.1 RULE-BASED MARKETS AND REGULATION AS RULES!

The concept of 'free market' has become particularly popular in the last two decades. It is often visualized as an economic system based on supply and demand with little or no government control. Privatization has become a part of the economic programmes of many countries since the beginning of the 1980s that has shifted the control of several types of productive assets into private ownership. Almost all Russian big business today is the creation of such massive asset transfer. But does that mean the role of the government has vanished? Quite contrarily, one would find that a key role of the government as rule-setter has increased—as setting regulations and such. The rules and modes of privatization, the bidding process, the kinds of agreements the privatized asset holders enters into with the government—all appear to be of great interest to the business world. Businessmen across the world obviously understand this particularly well. The ruling of the regulator is binding on a business, which points towards a superordinate authority of the regulator vis-à-vis business organizations (see illustration below and case study 4.1).

> Readers may recall the 2009 Department of Telecommunications (DoT) ruling regarding Tata group telecom licence. Telecom policy requires that a licensee in a circle cannot have more than 10 per cent stake, directly or indirectly, in another licensee in the same circle. Tata Tele/services had a Code Division Multiple Access (CDMA) licence in Mumbai and Idea Cellular (jointly controlled with A. V. Birla group) had Global System for Mobile (GSM) licence in Maharashtra. Idea Cellular applied for a Unified Access Service Licence (UASL)

in Mumbai, since a presence in Mumbai was crucial from the growth perspective of Idea. Idea Cellular, during that time, was also a contested property, with the A. V. Birla group and the Tatas each trying to take control. Its subscriber base was also larger than that of Tata Teleservices. Tatas tried arguing that Tata Teleservices and Idea Cellular are different companies, and Idea Cellular does not control Tata Teleservices. But DoT interpreted the common group ownership by the Tata group as implying control over another licensee in the same circle. Tatas finally sold their stake in Idea Cellular and held on to their ownership in Tata Teleservices.[1]

CASE STUDY 4.1 Regulatory role to resolve matters between provinces: An instance

Over the last few years, there has been a dispute between two states/provinces in South India, that is, Tamil Nadu (TN) and Karnataka, over power supply that brings out the issue of jurisdictional conflict. The regulator had to play a role of arbitration.

Case facts:

- Tamil Nadu Electricity Board (TNEB) entered into a contract with JSW Power Trading Company for supply of 300 MW of power from January to May 2010. The concerned power project is in Karnataka and is falling within the jurisdiction of Southern Region Load Dispatch Centre (SRLDC). SRLDC controls the southern states and is part of Central Electricity Regulatory Commission (CERC).
- Due to shortage of power in Karnataka in April 2010, Karnataka state government ordered JSW to stop supplying TN and instead feed Karnataka.
- TN moved Madras High Court and the Court ruled in favour of the contract (that is, TN).
- Karnataka High Court supported the state government in its stoppage of the power to TN and its verdict put SRLDC in a fix.
- Before the matter was heard in the Supreme Court, CERC and the two state governments amicably settled the matter out of court.

---

[1]Sourced from *Business World*, 'Whose Idea Is It Anyway?', available at http://www.businessworld.in/index.php/Whose-IDEA-is-it-Anyway.html (accessed on 20 November 2009).

One may also recall the US antitrust authority's ability to break up American Telephone & Telegraph Co. (AT&T) in the early 1980s. The period saw the dramatic conclusion of a historic monopoly case against the telephone giant. The US Justice Department settled claims that AT&T had impeded competition in long-distance telephone service and telecommunications equipment. The result was the largest divestiture in history: a federal court severed the Bell System's operating companies and manufacturing arm (Western Electric) from AT&T, transforming the nation's telephone services. The recent problems for Microsoft over its proprietary source code in Europe is another case in point.[2] Regulation by the government is then ubiquitous. The instances above indicate why a strategist with business interests has to take note of regulation—as emanating from various executive authorities in the government with different jurisdictional ambits. Although, then, large amounts of assets have in recent years moved to private hands through privatization and a withdrawal of the government, rules set by government constitute one important set of rules that underlie the markets.

Conceptually, then, rules are ubiquitous in markets and are essential for its operation. Rules emanate, however, from various sources—private contracts between parties to a transaction, rules by clubs such as standard bodies, or rules from different executive authorities with differences in their jurisdiction. Thus market institutions, such as private contracts, and government regulation type rules constitute something like a continuum or possibly a hierarchy. (A private contract that violates a state statute can stand nullified.)

From the strategist's perspective, it is the turf over which rules are set (and contested), the procedures used in rule setting, the process of negotiation and conflict resolution, the actors involved and the nature of constraints under which they negotiate, jurisdictional ambit of an authority and such other facets of rule-making that are important.

It leads to a pragmatic understanding of the mechanisms of influence that one can bring to bear on the rule-setting process. Readers may recall our discussion regarding the open spectrum group's attempt to engage

---

[2] It is a case brought by the European Commission of the EU against Microsoft for abuse of its dominant position in the market according to the competition law. It started as a complaint from Novell over Microsoft's licensing practices in 1993. In 2008, the EU announced that it is going to investigate Microsoft Office's Open Document format support. In 2009, the European Commission announced that it would investigate the bundling of Internet Explorer with Windows operating systems from Microsoft, saying, 'Microsoft's tying of Internet Explorer to the Windows operating system harms competition between web browsers, undermines product innovation and ultimately reduces consumer choice.'

in a regulatory contest (see case study 1.7) and reflect on how it differed from the instance of a software firm's (making telecom handset software) engagement to change the contract terms (see case study 1.5) to move to selling software to the handset integrator on a risk-sharing royalty rather than an upfront payment basis. Transforming a bilateral contract, participating in a standard setting process, such as MPEG (see illustration on p. 116), engaging with an executive authority of the state for a redefinition of certain statutes are thus quite different forms of engagement. They require different skills, different assets. The stakeholders involved and the milieu differ as well. We explore these issues briefly in the section on regulation. Before we move to regulation, however, we will take a look at concepts of markets—trying to make a distinction between various types of markets.

4.2 MARKET

Often, the words 'market' and 'competition' bring to us the narrow view of product market and competition therein, where the product in question would normally be quite stable, such as, say, cement or toothpaste. Mainstream strategy discourse would mostly concentrate on strategic acts in such product market. But take the case of large business groups such as the Aditya Birla Group or Thapar Group—they not only compete (and once in a while collaborate) in the product market but also compete in other 'factor markets'[3] such as labour (including intellectual capital), financial and, most importantly, the market for corporate control. The business organization thus lies at the intersection, so to say, of numerous such (different) markets. Several strategy moves, thus, make sense only when we look at the firm as an entity that flexibly makes moves in such interconnected markets. If, then, several markets are linked from the perspective of the strategic actor, how are they linked or, in other words, what is a pragmatic way of conceiving of such linkage? The neoclassical stance looks at several such markets linked through price-clearing modes. Our description below argues for an institutional view of markets and thus several markets are linked through sets of constraining rule structure. The interlinkages are not therefore smooth; the canvas is rather highly fractured. One can visualize

---

[3]Factor markets can be described as markets of factors of production like labour, capital, raw material, and so on.

several nodal points. Movement across markets is then movement across several such rule-sets. Price fails to signal across such fissures of fragmentation. The strategist works in and across such fissures. We elaborate it below.

General accounts of markets as described and discussed in the preliminary courses of economics, finance and even strategy domain would be associated with an image of the *invisible hand*—a market is supposed to just exist out there. We depart from such notions, primarily because of our pragmatic concerns. Businesses and managers are preoccupied with numerous acts of inter-firm coordination or attempts to arrive at a coordinated outcome or a state of affairs. A motive of dominance seeks an influence, or seeks to shape up and/or modulate markets by acting in different ways on the coordination sought and achieved. The rhetoric of *market power* is an instance of a form of such desire for dominance. It refers, in the simplest sense, to the volume dimension of the market of a product that a firm may control; of course, such volume share leads to a pricing power. A firm with market power has the ability to individually affect either the total quantity or the prevailing price in the market.[4] They have, what we called in Chapter 1, nodal power through agglomeration, in most cases through lumpy fixed assets required to produce/distribute a product (see section 1.8).

Traditions in industrial organization literature and in several tracts of strategy literature look at such volume dominance and distribution of market shares as a crucial element defining the market structure. The number of competing firms, their size, distribution, as well as the number of buyers in any given industry, influence the market structure. The major factors that impinge on the market structure existing in a particular industry are: the levels of seller/buyer concentration, levels of product differentiation prevailing in a particular market, and the entry and/or exit conditions in the prevailing market and the nature of information flows. Based on the concentration of the buyer and seller and the barriers to entry or exit the market structures can be summarized as in Table 4.1.

---

[4] Market power gives firms the ability to engage in unilateral anti-competitive behaviour. Some of the behaviour that firms with market power are accused of engaging in include predatory pricing, product tying, and creation of overcapacity or other barriers to entry. If no individual participant in the market has significant market power, then anti-competitive behaviour can take place only through collusion, or the exercise of a group of participants' collective market power.

Table 4.1: Market Structures

Market Structure	Seller		Buyer	
	Entry Barrier	Number	Barrier to Entry	Number
Perfect Competition	None	Many	None	Many
Monopolistic Competition	None	Many	None	Many
Oligopoly	Exists	Few	None	Many
Oligopsony	None	Many	Exists	Few
Monopoly	Exists	One	None	Many
Monopsony	None	Many	Exists	One

Source: Adapted from Bello, Sepiriti and Letete (2009).

Thus, degree of competition and control over a market (both by sellers and buyers) determine the structure of the market. But the structure of a market must not be seen as 'state of nature' that exists, but as arising out of strategic action by the participants in the market. Oligopoly-type contests and strategies of deterrence built around it refer to this aspect. Most such markets of a standard product would be subject to decreasing returns—a strategy of deterrence executed amongst a set of such organizations can delay the advent of decreasing returns, bringing in stability to a prolonged rent stream. The existing players in the industry would neither permit any new entrant nor would like to disturb existing market arrangements. The existing players would enjoy 'rent-like returns', and this is an important dimension of large contemporary corporates.

For example, Coca Cola and Pepsi have created an oligopoly that controls more than 75 per cent of the entire global carbonated soft drink industry. Direct price wars between the main rivals have been kept to a minimum, and the volume dominance gained has been leveraged in negotiating supplier prices as well as dictating terms in the distribution contracts in their own favour. Stable markets do not always emerge and the firms can always challenge one another by cutting prices. Instability can arise on several accounts—the simplest of which would be price wars that disturb existing price points. One may think of the Indian mobile telecom market. The average revenue per user which has been declining at a rate close to 10 per cent for several quarters has been attributed to the price wars between telecom players for gaining market share in a saturated urban market. Faced with fierce price-war scenario, the marginal revenue per additional user of the telecom sector for the second quarter of FY 2009–10 has been just 16 paise. Several of these episodes of price wars have also been precipitated by new entrants into the industry, as new licences were provided by the department of telecommunication (ASSOCHAM, 2009).

Instability in pricing would not still disturb the broad industry boundary—the product definition and the institutional structure that supports the market. We argue that a deeper level of instability arises when such boundaries are subject to acts of redefinition. That is usually accompanied by institutional changes. Our primary concern, as we proceed, would remain with understanding such acts of redefinition. Implicitly then, we would not consider a market as given—with formed and stable boundaries—but would induce the reader to think of how the market itself is constituted through numerous acts of the strategists. Such accounts would be useful when new markets are sought to be created. One may recall that the business volume of several billion dollars in European Football Leagues, Indian Premier League and such other sporting events are quite a contemporary phenomenon. Those markets did not exist even just a few decades back. Then there is example of Microsoft Windows. It has not only created a new market of home PCs, but also created a whole ecosystem of application developers (can see them as several complementary asset holders) amongst whom Microsoft sits as a king, a global coordinator (and a bundler). These examples raise a simple question in our mind—is creation and stabilization of a novel market so simple? Importantly, can a simple description of the market structure as the distribution of market shares (or in other words, market concentration) capture dimensions of market-making that is of concern to a strategist?

4.2.1 Market-making and market institutions

While discussing markets, we generally focus on the buyer and seller and tend to overlook the role of the market institution underpinning the transactions in the market. There is a pragmatic reason for that—for stable markets, such institutional structures are already in place, possibly through numerous acts of the pioneers in that market. Current participants, thus, scarcely need to take note of that in executing the routines. However, to create a new market, such as the European Premier League with a billion dollar valuation, pioneers face a different problem. The markets are nascent when pioneers venture. The institutions that would become well-accepted norms and would be taken for granted by all and sundry involved in the transactions would not be in place yet. Since such institutions would be missing, transactions would not occur till they are put in place. Two quick illustrations are provided below:

> One might have noticed the executives of Airbus, as part of their marketing initiative ahead of the launch of Airbus 380, a much larger jet that requires longer runways, engage deeply with airport authorities and infrastructure operators in order to initiate investment in upgradation of existing airport infrastructure. Lack of complementary infrastructure can decelerate the growth of the new jet market—small delays can be very costly, as competition catching up would reduce the profits of the novel product. So, it is not just the investment and hence the build-up of the infrastructure, but its timing and synchronicity with targeted production and development plans that may be crucial.
>
> Those of you who have followed development of e-commerce markets and auction systems of industrial commodities—such as, say, steel—would know how crucial it is to ensure that the steel on offer in an auction has certified specifications. Much investment, through certification agencies, often private certifiers, is involved to guarantee to the bidders that the product definition is tight. In other words, credibility of the certification (or strength of certification assets) determines how truly the physicals map into the digital representation on which bidding happens. Only a tight product definition allows one to concentrate on price and quantity in a traditional auction sense. The potential of reach that digital media affords at a very cheap cost faces often the barrier of reliability of certification. Locally sticky information on quality that can be gauged through inspection depends on the strength of certification to get broadcast widely through the digital mode. A failure of certification often disrupts the potential of expansion of reach of digitized media. Market-making in the digital space needs to work assiduously to get around such deep institutional bottlenecks.

To create any new market, we not only need respective buyer and seller but we also need a bevy of complementary products and infrastructures in place. We need to bring together the actors, define the rules of the transaction and facilitate the transaction. Markets, to work as they should, need institutions. Market institutions define the rules of the game. They put constraints, formal and informal, on the actors in the market. In the absence of supporting institution, markets will falter.

> In Chapter 3 (see section 3.0), we discussed about the importance of a credible settlement price determination process as a key asset for the commodity futures trading ecosystem. (Settlement price is the exchange-announced price at which the outstanding contracts at the end date of a futures contract are closed or settled, in cash.) Exchanges generally provide it. But, establishing credibility of the settlement process is a difficult issue—it requires the exchange to have a huge control over the trading system. It is generally built over time. Exchanges such as the London Metal Exchange or the Chicago Board of Trade (CBOT) have this crucial asset. It is a simple institution, but its absence is most damaging for the prospects of the market.
>
> Readers may reflect on another dimension of commodity futures markets. One essential presumption in such markets is the homogeneity of the underlying product, say wheat; in India, contrarily, 120 different varieties of wheat are grown even now. In the US, the story of the rise of the CBOT is simultaneously a story of the homogenization of the product space in heavily traded commodities. Would the agricultural futures trade volumes in India then remain essentially limited: the Forwards Market Commission and the futures trading ecosystem might like the idea of a homogenization of the product space to hasten commoditization, but the ministry in charge of biodiversity resources might have a different view altogether.

Often these institutions are woven together and preserved through the legal mandate in the form of state regulations. SEBI regulations were crucial in forcing the Indian equity trading ecosystem to move to digitized transactions with Straight-Through-Processing (STP), where data entry happens only once in a full trade cycle from order initiation to settlement of trade. The power of the regulator hastens the coordination required. But, many a time, this role is taken by large firms or groups of large firms, who command the market power to drive these changes through.

Recall Intel's ability to achieve dynamic coordination of technology investments across a wide set of firms, modulating it to particular rates of processing power improvement in CPU chips—and it took upon itself the risk of delivering the expected improvements in computing power. Thus, creation of the market requires the exercise of coordination by the lead coordinator or the king of the network. To summarize, strategies of market-making, essential in a story around a novel product or a technology, would require the strategist to take interest in the institutional dimension of markets.

Having pointed out the importance of looking at the institutional dimension of markets, we would examine how decreasing returns and increasing returns stances affect how one looks at institutions. Specifically, we argue that the deterrence motive in decreasing returns settings push a strategist to look at the institutional structure as props of the deterrence motive; while the increasing returns motive built around market-making seeks novel institutions as support for a new market or new types of transactions.

4.2.2 Deterrence and institutions under decreasing returns

In our earlier discussion in the first chapter, we argued that in decreasing returns contexts, pressures towards commoditization are immense—and it is like a trap then. Deterrence motive seeks to delay the eventual commoditization and loss of rents that would result from it. Dominance attained in a market then needs to be guarded or preserved. While industry structure accounts help us understand the state of affairs of such dominant position in different industries, it does not provide enough cues on how such a state may be or actually is preserved over time—or how it is sustained. We argue that one major instrument to achieve sustained deterrence arises from the institutional structure that the strategist creates and preserves. Contrarily, a challenger has to contend with subversions of the entrenched institutional structures. The simplest of such rules include several bilateral contracts or sets of agreements between several firms that aim at preserving the status quo and the current balance of power that it represents. The brief narration in case study 4.2 on the marketing practices of Intel provides one such instance. Rival entrants such as AMD, engaged in technology catch-up, found entry blocked by the strong agreements that Intel was able to preserve with important customers in the market. Years of attrition and long legal dispute cost the litigants and the insurance firms (who insured the legal liabilities!) a fortune and finally led to an out-of-court settlement between the two firms in 2009, with Intel agreeing to a consent decree to desist from engaging in such practices.

CASE STUDY 4.2 AMD–Intel conflict

AMD and Intel, two of the world's largest chip manufacturers, have been locked in a bitter legal battle for several years now. AMD had filed for antitrust action against Intel in Japan, Korea and Europe and in all jurisdictions had won a favourable verdict from the respective antitrust authorities. AMD has alleged various claims against Intel in the Actions, including without limitation that Intel has been leveraging dominance in the supply of x86 microprocessors through the use of exclusionary pricing, discount and other practices that unlawfully restrict AMD's ability to compete. As the antitrust cases proceeded, both parties also filed court cases alleging violation of the relevant standards related to retention of evidence that could have been used in the case. A series of these legal tussles finally led to an out-of-court settlement in November 2009, where both parties agreed to withdraw and mutually settle all pending litigations (on antitrust and IP violation fronts). Intel agreed to pay USD 1.25 billion dollars to AMD as a consideration for the agreement. Intel, without admitting to the conduct of the disputed trade/business practices, agreed to commit to not adopt any of the specific disputed business practices that are described below. By the time the agreement was signed, Intel had spent several hundred million dollars on the litigation across the globe; much of the legal expenses, however, were insured and recovered from the insurance company.

The antitrust complaint covered several Intel business practices that were believed to be acting as restrictive trade barriers to market access for AMD.

1) Intel offered customers very deep discounts in exchange for being the sole supplier of microprocessors to an Original Equipment Manufacturer (OEM).
2) Intel often forced/induced customers through offering of a deep discount to limit or delay its purchase or use of specified AMD products on either a geographic, platform, market segment, distribution

(Case Study 4.2 contd.)

(Case Study 4.2 contd.)

        channel, volume, share of purchase or some similar basis, effectively excluding AMD from the market.

3) Intel often offered benefits to customers for limiting, depositioning or delaying its marketing, promotion, launch, advertising, production, distribution, sale or branding of any product containing an AMD microprocessor; or abstaining from participating in any AMD promotional activity, virtually leading to a boycott of participation in AMD events.

4) Intel often implemented in its technology or forced manufacturers to include what was christened 'artificial performance impairment', which were designed deliberately to impair the functioning of AMD products if included in the product system.

Given that till early 2000s, AMD was a follower or a catch-up kind of player, the exclusionary trade and technology practices of Intel led to elongation of the period of monopolization of the chip market—providing Intel more time to develop and then graduate the market to the new generation technology.

Intel and AMD had severed business relations for a long time. In 1976, AMD and Intel signed their first comprehensive cross-licence agreement, where AMD and Intel both agreed to license to each other all patents each company held. In 1982, after IBM selected an Intel microprocessor for its PC but only on the condition that there is a reliable second source supplier for its PC processor needs, AMD renewed the comprehensive cross-licence agreement with Intel. In 1987, Intel notified AMD that it was terminating the second source agreement, an aggressive move to prevent AMD from producing a 486-compatible microprocessor. That began years of legal disputes between AMD and Intel, and limited customer choice to a single source for PC microprocessors for a long period of time.

AMD began an independent programme of chip development and in 1990 released the Am386 microprocessor family, based on Intel's 80386. Sales of the Am386 were strong. In October 1991, Intel commenced a federal court action for copyright infringement. An arbitrator subsequently awarded AMD full rights to make and sell the Am386. The Supreme Court of California upheld this decision in 1994.

This legal intervention was crucial in freeing up AMD to pursue its own chip development without the fear of patent infringement litigation from Intel—a powerful behemoth by then. Meanwhile in 1993, AMD introduced the

(Case Study 4.2 contd.)

(Case Study 4.2 contd.)

> Am486® microprocessor; and it powered Compaq computers and thousands of other manufacturers' PCs, bringing competition into the 486 market.
>
> In 1994, however, Intel and Hewlett-Packard (HP) announced the development of a proprietary 64-bit microprocessor architecture that was incompatible with the millions of existing x86-based PCs and software applications. Intel senior vice president Albert Yu then had declared, 'If I were competitors, I'd be really worried. If you think you have a future, you don't.' In 1995, AMD introduced the AMD-K5 microprocessor, its first independently designed, socket-compatible x86 microprocessor. In 1997, AMD introduced the successful AMD-K6 microprocessor, a pin-compatible alternative to Intel's Pentium microprocessor. Its introduction heralded the return of competition and helped drive PC costs below USD 1,000.
>
> In 1998, AMD launched the AMD-K6-2 microprocessor, featuring 3DNow! technology. Invented by AMD, 3DNow! was the first x86 innovation to significantly enhance 3D graphics, multimedia and other floating-point-intensive applications for Microsoft Windows-compatible PCs. In 1999, it introduced the world's highest-performing x86 microprocessor, previewed the first x86-based, 64-bit architecture and announced its multi-core strategy. In 2005, it started winning major market successes with leading PC makers such as Lenovo agreeing to source chips from AMD.
>
> Over the last few years, AMD had adopted a differentiated path—moving towards optimizing its chip design for graphic intensive applications. In December 2009, after the agreement with AMD was signed, the US Federal Trade Commission began an investigation into the global dominance of Intel, alleging in particular that Intel was, through unfair means, trying to extend the dominance in its current CPU chip market to the emerging graphic processor unit (GPU) market through product bundling, restricting licensing and interoperability so that standalone GPU developers stand at a disadvantage. New entrants, such as NVIDIA, with a focus on GPU market was likely to be more severely affected than AMD that has a sizeable presence in the CPU market as well.[5]

The narration of Intel–AMD conflict above brings out certain important issues. It shows clearly how dominance in a market (in terms of

---

[5]Compiled from Intel–AMD agreement available at http://www.sec.gov/Archives/edgar/data/50863/000005086309000213/exh101.htm and FTC complaint available at FTC website (accessed in November 2009).

current market share) is preserved by creating entry barriers that enhance the power of deterrence. Unlike products such as cement or aluminium that remain quite stable over a long period of time (in terms of its specifications, and so on), CPU microprocessors are on a trajectory of technological improvement—so that each version has only a short period of existence after which a large part of the market would upgrade. In such a setting, entry deterrence needs to be effective only for very brief periods—sufficient to provide the designing time for the launch of the new version. Marketing practices of Intel then may be seen as a lever to preserve dominance for a short period only—delaying the entry of the rivals that would commoditize the older version. Such delay allowed Intel massive profits, but for a short period, in a particular version. Interestingly then, we observe a dual play of decreasing and increasing returns. Engaged in market-making for its novel versions (technologically advanced), it cooperated with several ecosystem partners engaged in complementary businesses attempting a fast growth of the new version; at the same time, through crafty design of contracts and marketing (and other technical) practices, it attempted blocking entry for short periods in the older version. It is also interesting that growth of new firms, such as Acer and Lenovo, in OEM computer manufacturing allowed customer space to AMD to enter in a big way. These new firms were more willing to break away from Intel dominance. Market growth made it difficult for the current entrenched leaders to co-opt the new ambitions of the entrants.

Readers may note that the deterrence motive of a firm often forces it to adopt market limiting strategies, since a loss of control is feared. In earlier manufacturing-based cartels, it always led to output restrictions as a mode to drive up or control prices. Would a faster growth of computer market, such as through faster price/cost drops (which Intel delayed), or faster entry of new players have reduced Intel's profits? This counterfactual question is most difficult to answer. But, anecdotal evidences from experiences of cartels and several such market limiting deterrence arrangements showed that when the agreements collapsed, the incumbents also benefited financially from the market growth that resulted. But, analytically, one must realize the difference between actual ex-post events and the ex-ante expectations. It is expectation that shape action—and deterrence has a particular motive—preservation of a current rent structure. It can make one turn a blind eye to the potential of novelty, laden as it is with uncertainty. The difference between the certainty of a current rent and uncertain possibility of a future payoff from novelty may be significant, especially in the ex-ante sense.

Our reading of the case above does not relate to legality or otherwise of Intel actions or its legitimacy; our sole concern is to point to the significance of the rule structure crafted and then enforced as a key pivot to preserve the dominance. Literature on strategy often totally misses this crucial aspect of pragmatic conduct of business. The constraining rule structure also needs to be preserved by the entrenched market leader by managing the expectation and payoff structure of the ecosystem. Very fast growth or entry of new actors/firms often disturbs such balances. Entrant strategies then would need to either work around such rules in place or contest it by engaging with other points of executive authority (each of which would have its own idiosyncratic mode of operation, its own logic, so to say, and would usually involve significant expenses as well; just think of the antitrust lawyers' involvement in the Intel–AMD conflict). In the Intel–AMD conflict, the alternative point of authority that AMD engaged with was the antitrust authorities in several national jurisdictions, appealing to the notion of 'abuse of dominance' as defined in the legal statutes and the practice of anti-monopoly enforcement. The anti-monopoly regulation, in that sense, serves as a counterpoint to acts of deterrence of an entrenched entity. The Intel case above shows deterrence exercised by a single dominant firm. Often perpetuation of dominance is exercised through agreements between several firms, or clubs of firms, led by a dominant one. Several commodity industries demonstrate such cartelization or other forms of business coordination that has a deterring effect on competitors outside the club. We provide an instance of the global aluminium cartel in case study 4.3.

Alcoa's dominance in the global aluminium business

The roots of dominance of Alcoa in the global aluminium business lay initially in the patent on the production process of aluminium. Two Americans, Bradley in 1885 and Hall in 1886, received patents for two closely similar but slightly different processes for extracting aluminium from alumina through the electrolytic process. A Frenchman also received a similar patent around the same time. These inventions became the basis of four independent companies. Bradley assigned the patents to Cowles Brothers who organized the Electric Smelting and Aluminum Company. Hall's patent rights were obtained by Pittsburg Reduction Co. (eventually Alcoa) led by Arthur Davies, with the

(Case Study 4.3 contd.)

(Case Study 4.3 contd.)

financial backing of the Mellon family. The French patent was assigned to a company for commercialization in France and to another firm with rights across all jurisdictions except France. As all started producing (similar product through slightly different process), two in US and two outside, especially in France, prices of aluminium dropped sharply to less than a fifth of what it was five years earlier. After five years of active competition, the industry shifted to a period of litigation. In 1893, Pittsburg Reduction Co. filed an infringement claim against the Hall patent worked by the rival. Cowles produced no aluminium after that date though the Court ultimately held the validity of the Bradley patents and adjudged Pittsburg Reduction Co. as the infringer from the very outset. Pittsburg Co. paid the Cowles Brothers a tidy sum of USD 14 million for an out-of-court settlement, partly as liquidated damages, partly in consideration of their promise never to enter the aluminium industry again, along with a discounted special price for purchase of ingots for their rolling operations (Cowles operated a downstream unit). Pittsburg Co. (rechristened Alcoa in 1907) became the sole producer of aluminium in the US till World War II.

Alcoa's ability to retain this dominance was an outcome of simultaneous preservation of monopoly in the US market and its ability to manage the export market. In the US, it vertically integrated, particularly into power production (hydel, which was cheaper), through buying up of riparian rights along the Long Saute of the St Lawrence, and mining through acquisition of bauxite mining assets so that very quickly it became the sole owner of all bauxite mines in the country. It also integrated forward into manufacturing of cooking utensils, extruded products, cable, castings and gradually building the market for aluminium products. In buying up firms in bauxite mining, Alcoa would obtain commitment from the other party not to enter the aluminium industry, for a hefty price often. It also required its suppliers not to deal with other competing producers. In 1912, in an antitrust consent decree, Alcoa agreed to abrogate these covenants in restraint of trade. Later, however, it continued to exercise a price squeeze on downstream aluminium sheet-rolling mills, creating hurdles for independent rollers.

On the international front, European producers had also grown considerably and, in 1893, Alcoa granted a French concession to its patent to a small French firm. This was an open challenge to the operator of the Heroult-process group of producers. A bilateral agreement was completed in 1896, inaugurating the first global cartel in aluminium. It included commitments not to enter each other's home and tributary markets. In 1901, just before

(Case Study 4.3 contd.)

(Case Study 4.3 contd.)

the Heroult patent expired, a second more comprehensive cartel was organized for a period of five years. It included almost all other producers—each member's home market was a protected market, while the rest of the world market was divided according to an agreed quota (or share). To eliminate competition in price, a governing committee set prices for sale in open market periodically. During this period, US prices remained stable (it was already high, possibly at monopolist's revenue maximization levels), while European prices rose sharply. Both European and US producers doubled capacity.

In 1906, the third cartel agreement was struck. It included, in addition, a requirement of each member to post a guarantee equal to the open market sale quota, which can be forfeited if the agreement was broken. Detailed submission of sales and volume data in members' home countries was also mandatory. Capacity addition in Europe was slow during this period. High profits and expiry of the patent drew in VC-backed entry. Internal dispute over continuing the high price policy led to dissolution of the agreement in 1908. Prices declined almost 50 per cent immediately in Germany. However, Alcoa entered into a bilateral deal with Automotive Industry Action Group (AIAG)—the main exporter from Europe, restraining each other from entering each other's home market. The US market remained shielded for some time.

In a year, however, the US market was flooded by imports from other exporters; prices collapsed and volumes of consumption went up by more than 50 per cent in just about a year. Alcoa also reduced prices, and its profits in 1910 stood at higher levels than what it earned during the period of cartel control. Alcoa's expectation on the price elasticity of the product was evidently wrong.

Late in 1911, A. V. Davies of Alcoa began negotiations with the European producers to organize a new cartel. There were two hurdles to reviving the old agreement. The American market had grown too large and was by far the most attractive market to sell aluminium in. It was too difficult to keep out others from exporting into it. Europeans had also built up capacities, and when Mr Davies went to negotiate to Europe in 1911, European exports met a large part of the US domestic demand. Alcoa also was under investigation with antitrust authorities in the US. The second hurdle proved easier to manage. Eventually, Alcoa accepted a consent decree and settled the case with antitrust authorities on 7 June 1912. The next cartel agreement was signed on 12 June 1912.

Agreement with the Europeans was more difficult to arrive at. The mechanism which was agreed to was interesting. Instead of uncontrolled (and

(Case Study 4.3 contd.)

(Case Study 4.3 contd.)

uncoordinated) competition in US market, a more orderly sharing of the fruits of the US was proposed. A syndicate of several companies producing aluminium in France was to invest in a venture in US/Canada, where Alcoa would also take an interest. This venture would jointly invest in production and also in joint market development to expand the use of aluminium. If they wanted, other European producers—the British and the Germans—could also participate in this venture. The JV started plant construction, but World War I intervened. War orders forced capacity expansion in all countries and cartel agreements broke down. However, large government orders itself shifted the industry to another regime of coordinated pricing, quite different from the cartel arrangements.

After the war, however, the US market was faced with a deluge of European imports; prices steadily fell and Alcoa started responding in the early 1920s. Its strategy consisted of the following: massive investments in Europe for over five years. It purchased a 50 per cent stake in Norsk Aluminum Company in Norway—one of the rogue exporters into US market, who defied cartel controls. It acquired equity positions in Italian producers. With the Germans, it failed because of the German government's unwillingness to relinquish control; however, it signed agreements to the effect that the Germans would limit their exports into the US market. Prices at which they would export was also set, in relation to Alcoa posted prices. It started buying up or taking equity positions in bauxite mines, hydroelectric power producers, aluminium reduction plants and fabrication facilities across Europe. By 1923, the concerted investment-led attack started paying off—and Europeans had softened up to sit for the sixth cartel agreement negotiations. It was first a simple gentleman's agreement on pricing restraint, with no strong mechanisms as quotas.

The seventh cartel came into existence in 1926, and had an elaborate quota system that parcelled out global markets to different producers—on both ingots and metal sheets and other prefabricated forms—so as to integrate the rollers into the fold. With an interim extension of three years, the arrangement lasted for almost five long years. Members were penalized for exceeding the quota, and they received compensation for underselling their quota. Although Alcoa did not formally participate in the arrangement because of their consent decree, it controlled the cartel through another firm Alted, where Alcoa had control through director interlocks.

The period of the global depression beginning in the late 1920s led to tighter controls and coordination, as excess capacities came up all around

(Case Study 4.3 contd.)

(Case Study 4.3 contd.)

> with falling demand. At the core was the Aluminum Alliance, incorporated in Switzerland. The company issued a stock of 1,400 Class A stocks. The subscribers were cartel members—one stock for every hundred metric tonne of their annual capacity. Detailed calculations were provided in the agreement. In addition, there were 1,200 shares that were authorized and remained unissued—for future allocation to non-members (if they joined) and to members if they expanded capacity or acquired non-members. It, however, required approval from the Board of Governors of the Alliance. At the beginning of the Alliance, all accumulated stocks of members in excess of 40 tones per alliance share were required to be removed from the market (inventory lying at various points) and members had to pay GBP 55 per tonne for them. Alliance directors periodically fixed minimum prices. To make it effective, the Alliance was allowed to buy and sell metals. If a member could not sell the full quota at the minimum price, the Alliance stepped in to buy the excess. Thus, Alliance buying price became the effective price floor. Alcoa, again, did not participate in the arrangement formally nor did it take shares in the Alliance, but remained involved informally. Alcoa chairman Davies continued to be the 'star' in the global aluminium industry—the unquestioned leader for close to 50 years. The World War II brought demand explosion and cartel arrangements were not found useful again. Thus, for close to 40 years, the industry coordinated through various forms of inter-firm agreements that achieved differing degrees of coordination. The agreements were supported by asset structures, investment parity and occasional use of threats, and had to be craftily managed. Co-optation of member interests led to success when it was effective—divergences led to break-ups (excerpts from Stocking and Watkins, 1946).

Our discussion in this section so far points towards a general direction. One pragmatic way of looking at markets would be to view it as shaped by a set of interrelated contracts or business agreements. It is on the basis of these sets of agreements, so to say, that goods and services move across transaction parties. It provides the basis for governance of the transactions, either horizontally amongst competitors or vertically with value chain partners—roles and responsibilities of each party, restrictions on each and liabilities of each, and so on, get defined on that basis. In all markets, where one finds significant concentration (buying or selling side, and most often on both sides), one can understand the market from this perspective. Market power finds its expression in such contract and agreement structures. This description of a market is quite different from the hypostatized price-clearing market (Walrasian market), in a specific sense. The contracts and agreements provide several clauses that influence each other's freedom to act, binding them for periods of time that may vary in length in various different ways. It also introduces numerous variations in the relationships that can be appreciated only from close quarters. Thus, unlike a pure market of standard commodity where price can be assumed to contain all information since everything else is standardized, markets such as the CPU processor market described earlier presents numerous complex variations. The firm's acts note the complex contract structure when acting—and naturally the acts are quite different from a pure Walrasian auction market participant. Business negotiations also concentrate less on the price in such markets, but often much more on fine and detailed contractual obligations and mutual restrictions. Such rule structures are power-infused and are a means to renegotiate relationships as well.

> Readers familiar with technology transfer licences would know that such transfers impose several different (and quite common) kinds of restrictions on the licensee. The licensee would generally have restrictions on the markets where the licensed technology may be applied—either defined as product groups or as geographic markets within which the licensee's business may be limited over a specified contract period. Licensors of technology often coordinate the use of such clauses to shape up a global market with restricted competition in each domain. Licensors may also impose restrictions on the licensee's right to improve the technology or work the 'self-improved' technology or apply the technology in a different field of use. In several cases, it might be in the licensee's interest to get away from as many such restrictions as business relations and negotiation may permit. Readers may appreciate how such a product market based on several licensed producers would be hard to fathom without an understanding of the underlying contract structure.

4.2.3 Types of market and nature of products/assets

We can now conceptually look at two types of markets as counterpoints: (*a*) a Walrasian market—where transactions are based mainly on price—because everything else, including the product specifications, business terms and conditions of warranty, various liabilities, and so on, covering all other aspects relevant in a business relation, has been standardized and hence commoditized and (*b*) a market consisting of interlinked agreements, contracts and procurement processes, where complex negotiation on multiple dimensions of business, apart from just the price of a deal, would be of great concern. A Walrasian market would generally have several buyers and suppliers, usually showing low concentration levels, while the second type of markets would show high concentration.

A third kind of market also is quite common. It is a kind of fragmented market, but is extremely non-Walrasian, in the specific sense that that the goods/services exchanged is non-standard, that is, goods retain considerable variations in its specifications, qualities, properties, and so on. Examples would be Bollywood film production, knit garment manufacturing in Tirupur cluster and high-tech financing in Silicon Valley. The examples would have clarified what we mean by non-standard goods. Information on quality of a film project (vital information for a participant in a financing syndicate), technical capability and reputation of a start-up technocrat in Silicon Valley are highly non-standard. Film, as a product, is also non-standard—in the sense that no two films can be compared like, say, one can compare two different lots of steel (of the same technical specification). Generally, it is believed that all such non-standard products lead to vertical integration where complexities (of say information) become firm-internal and the firm/organization as a whole bears the full risk. But several examples we see around actually point towards a different practical state of affairs; and in our discussion on film-related assets, we pointed out how such highly differentiated asset holders can transact in what we called a 'thick network market'. Amongst the three examples we cited above, Tirupur presents a difference from the other two. Information or products in Tirupur possibly does not carry as much uncertainty as information related to films or high-technology start-ups. How does such fragmented markets manage to transact and not get mired in opportunism, without using the threat of competition (price competition offered by another producer of the standard item in a Walrasian market) or the threat of the large firms who have powers arising from agglomeration (size in the current market)? We briefly provide some hints using the example of Bollywood film production (see case study 4.4).

CASE STUDY 4.4 The financiers of Bollywood

At the background of Bollywood, the financiers, a hoard of them, often arranged and informally syndicated by an individual, take high risk in investing. Classic market share and concentration figures would display very low levels at both syndicator and financier levels. Bankruptcies consequent to successive productions of 'flop' films have never been uncommon. In fact a large number of actors, singers or other associates who, believing that they had access to the information on quality of the film being produced ex-ante, invested in such syndicated finances to discover ex-post that their funds disappeared rendering them bankrupt. Information, then, is of highly uncertain nature—quite contrary to the certainty which a certified product offering in an e-commerce auction, say of industrial steel in mJunction.com. Sometimes the reputation of a film star or of a family having many members in the film-making industry assures the potential investors ex-ante about the reliability of the quality of a film being produced, which in turn acts as network-based information to potential investors. Repeated losses are surely dampeners and are replaced regularly by average quality films that get produced in large numbers with near-sure prospects of just break-even revenue earning. Occasional blockbusters made good not just the losses alone but the faith in the system of networked funding. Personalities in film earn in cash often not disclosed to the tax authority, and such cash, given the privileged access to information that these personalities enjoy by remaining in networks, are therefore reinvested in the production process. The market including the not-networked informal market does not enjoy such privileged access to information ex-ante on quality of film, including the reliability of film-project production schedule. Money from the informal market therefore is arranged through the syndicators, who are inside the network. This network we call a thick network—in the dual sense that it is densely connected to each other and it exchanges several different kinds of quite complex expectation based information (or information that is rich in possessing several, often interrelated dimensions).

A syndicator is comparable to the venture fund manager. Such a fund manager enjoys privileged access to the quality of projects seeking funds, and such managers share information amongst them on competitive prospects of each project. Finally, such managers get replaced regularly. As a result, a manager in such funding fail to reap extra benefits from agency-related moral hazards. Finally, the entrepreneur hides certain information from the

(Case Study 4.4 contd.)

(Case Study 4.4 contd.)

manager, who in turn too hides some other encapsulated information. Unlike in the large firm where the senior manager controls cash flow, in Bollywood, very similar to the venture financing of Silicon Valley start-ups, the producer does not control the cash flow alone. In Bollywood, cash flow including milestone payments (which are in vogue in Bollywood) and the total budgeting are determined primarily by a bevy of arrangers, or syndicators, and the role of producer remains subdued. However, many producers are arrangers or otherwise many producers invest substantially in a particular film project and then they have dual roles.

In the Hollywood model, the firm handles fund. Hence, a particular film can be considered as a capital machine that produces a stream of revenue. Such a firm can manage flow of cash both over multiple film projects and across divisions within the organization such as between the subdivisions of production or between several modes of distributions. In order to retain and exercise greater control, the senior manager reduces several types of capital inputs into a common form, the cash. For example, a star is reduced to a wage earner. In Bollywood, separation of ownership, along with the retention of severalties of properties, affords distinct and different incentives for each owner. Therefore, property owners do not look for return in terms of cash revenue alone. In turn, this implies that a common market does not exist. Such a market enables exchangeability of resources including selling of resources against future receivables of cash, such as contractual wages over a future period. Moreover, such a market would not provide enough incentives to networks through which information ex-ante on quality of resources or of outputs flow. Contrarily, in Bollywood, owners of several assets exchange information on respective resource classes or categories.

A typical production arranges for multiple types of resources, such as directors, actors, stuntmen, cinematographers, costume designers, funds, and so on. A producer or sometimes a fund arranger keeps close information on resource availability as well as respective qualities in each network of resources. Owners of such resources are in keen competition with each other to get into better and higher-rewarding projects which is realized over time. The producer, as a venture manager, negotiates with each holder of assets, and similar to a wholesaler, sorts resources, schedules arrivals of resources and rearranges resources. Prices paid or future rewards assured therefore do vary across types of resources as well as across the quality judged ex-ante. The syndicator with intimate knowledge and information on the quality of

(Case Study 4.4 contd.)

(Case Study 4.4 contd.)

> resources as well as with a pulse for the popular likings enjoys advantages owing to information asymmetry.
>
> Resources of actors including both existing and potential stars, singers, lyricists, screenplay writers, costume designers, directors, editors and such others float in the Mumbai bazaar. In early years, a few professionals remained unionized or had guilds. Most such resources as directors never had guilds. Film production takes place even now on a project mode with resources including cameras or studios getting hired daily or on a period basis. Sometimes, even the shooting scripts or the dialogues is changed or gets written on the shooting floor. Possibly the most important benefit of such a system of production is its readiness to adapt to changes in the market of resources or the markets for film-tastes. Indian film-making is possibly amongst the most agile. In fact, rather often, a project right from inception to complete execution, takes just about a year. Longer projects could go up to, say, two years and rarely would a film-making project cross this limit. Typically, regional films take shorter time and budget. Hindi films would often cross the one-year limit. A typical Hollywood film takes much longer time to complete.
>
> The distribution circuit remains separated from production both in terms of organization and ownership. Regional or countrywide rights to distribution followed multiple norms including a single down payment to payment based on the number of weeks exhibited. The local owner of the projection theatre too shares the risk since part of the earning depends on the number of tickets sold. This state of affairs, however, have not changed much with technological changes and with the rapid spread of television, the DVDs, the satellite broadcasting as also with changes in the technology of film production. The bazaar of resources, the organization of production and the making of reputation, however, remained nearly the same as previous.

A few aspects relating to the description above requires reiteration. First, it is important to realize that in such thick networks, it is the inter-temporal build-up of reputation and other assets that keep an actor/asset holder away from opportunism. The threat lies in the inter-temporal access conditions to the network—the system is held together in the shared belief of increase in future asset value, loss of which is feared. The most interesting dimension of this form of governance through thick networks is its ability to generate and transact on hugely differentiated assets, without recourse to either the threat of commoditization or that of the executive authority wielded inside an organization. This then is a particularly important aspect of thick network forms of markets for strategists with an eye on managing increasing returns contexts. Before we move on to the next section, it may be worthwhile for the reader to appreciate the differences in governance problems or the way it is handled in the three types of markets we described. In a Walrasian market, what prevents opportunism is the price competition afforded by rival offerings in what is a standard product. In a market on interlinked contracts, such threats are not effective. Opportunism is often handled through contracting (about which we explore in some detail below) and through other relational assets which may be under threat of decay under opportunism. While governance through contracting is afforded under conditions where transactions can be specified, under extreme uncertainty (such as we described in Bollywood film-making) contract specification often would be hugely cumbersome and ineffective. Reputation and other such assets that have a build-up along with expectation of a future stardom hold the system away from opportunism in such 'thick networks'. Thus, the form of a market is also, at the same time, a form of governance—and this must be realized. And the form of governance influences the kind of assets that would get built up or would be valorized. Moves to take transactions from one type of market to the other are primarily, then, a reengineering of governance that a strategic act seeks. In seeking such reengineering, the strategic act would also possibly redefine the nature of asset formation amongst the market participants. For instance, think of a procurement process organized under Walrasian type auctions. Such procurement would fail to put a value on non-standard specifications (or properties in a product) a supplier may develop, even when it is valuable from the point of view of the production process of the procurer. The procuring firm may then want to shift the supplier away from Walrasian procurement. Yet that very act would release the vendor from the threat of Walrasian price competition that was the countervail to opportunism. Alternate governance that is effective must then be designed. A strategy account that privileges the notion of governance, either in preservation of certain institutions or in its subversion, must take note of such differences.

4.2.4 Products, platforms and increasing returns institutions

We now shift attention to another dimension of markets by attending to the product or its nature. In particular, let us reflect on whether the specific nature of the product in a market is important in lending it special dimensions or properties. We would try and understand if certain key dimensions of a market (or its dynamics) can be described for a typical (or representative) product without wasting energies in thinking of the specificities of a particular product. We are then implicitly looking for certain typologies that would help us appreciate the differences in market dynamics across the different types or categories of products. Let us think of a pack of toothpaste and, say, X-box as two products. Are they similar or quite different? A little reflection would tell us that X-box, quite unlike a pack of toothpaste, is what you may call a systemic product. An X-box cannot stand on its own; it needs a bevy of games (complementary products) that would run on it to have any utility at all—it is part of a whole system of products; we would call it then a systemic product. We can also call it a 'platform', on which an infinitely differentiated and profuse series of games can run, offering possibilities of extreme differentiation in terms of consumption. Powers of a pack of toothpaste appear much more subdued in comparison. Surely, a toothpaste to be useful requires a toothbrush as well—but such assembling is accomplished at the level of consumption. An X-box offering is mediated by the producer—in a sense that game developers deeply interface and interact with the X-box vendor in order to develop a game that would be consumed along with X-box at the final point of consumption.

Readers can also reflect on several other products—such as films, softwares like Windows, entertainment events like a sports league (say English Premier League). They all appear quite different from the archetypical products represented by a pack of toothpaste or corrosion resistant steel of a particular Bureau of Indian Standards (BIS) specification. So, the specific nature of the product seems to matter then, and we seek to capture just one aspect of that. One way to look at the difference is to ponder on the boundary of the products. Can our product be clearly and fully specified, and in that sense, does it have a clear boundary to separate it from other products with equally distinct boundaries? Steel or a pack of toothpaste is highly specifiable and complete in itself. The specification is also stable over time; and a consumer or the market would expect a reliability of conforming to the specifications on all batches of production across time periods. Stability is valuable in the market. In contrast,

X-box along with the multiple versions of popular games that might run on it, constitute an incompletely defined product—in a great flux, admitting of high levels of differences. The variations in subsequent versions appear important to the consumer.

If we take the sports league as an example, such as the Australian Rugby League that we discussed, what would you think would be a good description of the games? Would you like to call it a 'product'? In other words, would you call it a product, and what would be its specifications? What is valuable in a game appears to be the uncertainty in outcome that generates the excitement in a game? In some sense, uncertainty is consumed (leaving apart the game connoisseurs who also consume finer technical aspects, but possibly such enlightened spectators do not drive contemporary valuations!). The difference with consumption of steel now is possibly clearer. So, we propose three archetypes: (*a*) standalone complete products that are fully specifiable; specifications remaining stable over time, a series of minor variations generally introduced; (*b*) systemic products or proto-products, which can be valuable for consumption or have utility only as part of larger product systems that are often jointly produced (and often designed) through interaction amongst a network of firms; they are then incomplete products; (*c*) platforms that are a special category of systemic product that remains stable over time, but allows extremely variegated complementary systemic products to work in tandem with it. The three archetypes are not watertight; neither would one expect products to tightly conform to this classificatory schema. Each archetype has unique properties that are of concern to a strategist, since it alerts one to different dynamics inherent in markets of each archetype. We offer some more details below.

A standalone product is the simplest and we need not spend much time on it. A systemic product, by its definition, introduces a network of producers as the unit of production—that is, a network offers the product to the consumer. You may think of X-box along with blockbuster games. While an automobile also is produced by several firms (or a network), the network lies hidden to the consumption side; the integrator or the assembler presents a sole face and as integrator bundles the components and assumes all liabilities (including that of after-sales service under severe market restraining conditions nowadays) on the product—from the perspective of the consumer, it is the auto assemblers' product. A systemic product lends itself to a series of variations introduced very quickly through different assemblages of the product system. A platform, in addition to being systemic, provides a stable continuity over temporal episodes of infinite variations in the final product (as viewed from the consumer perspective). A large e-commerce site peddling thousands of variations of products from across the world produced by millions of small and large producers represents something like a platform-type distribution asset through which several micro-products find a market. It is quite distinct from the typical brand-/firm-specific distribution asset that restricts itself to a single firm's brands and product offerings. From the strategy perspective, a platform benefits immensely from extreme variation and differentiated offerings; in pursuance of its growth, it would want such proliferation. X-box wants a large range of variations of the games, possibly sourced from a very wide range of suppliers—not for inducing price competition, but from the perspective of bringing in variety and width in what the platform offers. The content strategy of platforms, such as Apple Store (see p. 152) or the DoCoMo i-mode portal we discussed earlier (see case study 3.5), are of this type.

Now, what is the strategic significance of the difference we are trying to point out? Strategies built around systemic products and platforms admit to increasing returns. Let us illustrate through an example. Think of the distribution assets of a typical FMCG firm with territorially delimited exclusive relationships with a set of distribution partners who are often specific to a single FMCG firm/product line. Clauses in distribution contracts restrict the distributor from contracting with competing firms/brands in the same product class/category. In contrast, think of a general distributor, or rather wholesaler, who would not have such specificity and would engage in general distribution. A general distribution asset holder owns and offers a platform, whose valuation would increase through proliferation; in contrast, FMCG-type distribution assets are brand-tied (and bundled) and would allow only a limited product proliferation, and preservation of own brand dominance. The motives and strategies adopted by a platform distributor and a typical FMCG-based distributor is thus quite different. Now you would possibly appreciate why the Indian FMCG space offers such limited varieties, compared to that of, say, Japan, where a typical food store would have close to more than 10,000 stockkeeping units. Informal accounts suggest that the Indian production space offers more than 100,000 brands, only a few of which enjoys access to quality distribution assets, and even fewer access to assets of mass media (just around 10,000 brands can access TV) and brand broadcasting. For an innovative small brand with new products, distribution access is a major problem in the Indian market. Japan, in contrast, has a long history of robust general trading companies that offers distribution access—like a platform—not only nationally to small brands, but globally through its extensive global distribution network. Would you then think the Japanese and Indian markets to be structurally different in terms of their architecture of assets and their interrelationships?

The second dimension of increasing returns dynamics in the context of systemic products involves the inter-organizational acts of coordination. The systemic product can stand only as an outcome of intense inter-firm coordination. Such acts carried out across organizations often blur organizational boundaries. In our earlier discussion, we pointed to the blurring of boundaries of organizations as a key contemporary development, often aided through innovative contracting, particularly in the financial domain, but also through development of several types of risk markets. The discourse on uncertainties of contemporary times is fundamentally not because of technology, as is often made out, but because of blurring of erstwhile stable boundaries—boundaries in its multiple senses. Stable organizational boundaries, stable notions of risks bundled through simple equity, stable products—constituted together a paradigm. Just as organizational boundary redefinition is a frequent act today, so is product boundary redefinition. Product boundary redefinition often would induce or get support from acts of organizational boundary redefinition. Stable boundaries, in these several senses, made deterrence the most important strategy stance. With boundaries in flux, deterrence suddenly appears less attractive—innovation appears to be the buzzword. But, we think, in focusing on innovation and losing sight of the deeper issues related to boundary redefinitions that anchor such process, several accounts have just missed the most important dimension of the contemporary increasing returns world. Our earlier discussions across several chapters had tried bringing out how the acts of boundary redefinition, operating under boundaries in flux, present a different set of problems to the strategist. The lack of stability takes away the moorings on which the old modes of governance were based; and that, we argue, is the fundamental source of disruption. We provide an example of what is at play and with that end this section.

Take a piece of real estate asset—a land in a commercial estate or a large building with valuable office floor space in a popular business area. Suppose this asset is purchased by a large intermediary or real estate company, securitized and sold off as a Real Estate Investment Trust (REIT) instrument, which investors subscribe to. REIT is a special purpose financial vehicle which securitizes the rent stream flowing from a real estate asset and like a mutual fund unitizes it. If the REIT is listed, its value would depend on the rent stream and expectations of its movement. REIT, in most jurisdictions, is also eligible for sizeable tax deduction on rental accruals, under the condition that a substantive part of it is redistributed to investors. If you reflect on the implications of this act, you would realize that the whole notion of demand of the real estate piece has been transformed. The distribution of risks has changed; the boundaries of the organizations involved have changed; the definition of what the product was and what it meant to the consumer has also transformed. Finally, the property rights to the asset has been transfigured beyond recognition—who owns is not clear—instead, we have several types of shared rights and accesses over the asset piece. To the REIT investor, it is an investment class—defined with a risk-return combination—that has different correlation with other asset classes. Exit is easy for the REIT investor—liquidity is high—and demand for the asset may well be driven by investor-risk views in the Singapore risk market; in other words, does the location of the asset matter anymore to the Singapore investor? Possibly it matters to the shop-owner who runs an outlet there. Who controls the asset piece? Does an REIT investor, owning a small cash flow right to the physical asset, actually drive the valuation mechanism? Who or what kinds of mechanism enjoy voice over the valuation process? Has the shop-owner lost control? Boundaries, in all senses, have been made unstable and susceptible to quick acts of redefinition. Note that in this act, technology is hardly involved. Uncertainty yet is huge—what has changed is that boundaries have become malleable. And this is noticeable across all dimensions—organization, product, risks and property rights. This is the source of uncertainty and of increasing returns. In a way, this is a central theme on which the narration in this book has unfolded.

That, in a way, completes our discussion on the different types of markets and why a strategist in contemporary times needs to take note of that. We now move on to a discussion of different forms of inter-organizational coordination in markets of different types that we discussed, interweaving our discussion with concerns on governance as we move on.

4.3 INTER-ORGANIZATIONAL COORDINATION IN A MARKET—A FEW TYPES

In our discussions in the last chapter, we had noted the importance of coordination across a wide network as an imperative of a contemporary strategist. The coordination we explore in this section is inter-organizational, as distinct from intra-organizational coordination to which we referred in the chapter on organizations. Under increasing returns, we have argued all along in several chapters and in several ways, coordination has to be sought by the fast growing firms across a vast milieu spanning several nodal power holders and several types of asset holders. We now very briefly dwell on such issues—trying to put across, through instances of different types of coordination, a few facets of such acts of coordination that lie at the root of increasing return dynamics.

1) Coordination in the simplest sense would refer to coordination in demand and supply through the price mechanism—as happens in a *price clearing* market. In simple terms, this means that markets tend to move towards prices which balance the quantity supplied and the quantity demanded such that the market will eventually be cleared of all surpluses and shortages (excess supply and demand). In fact, even when we talk of price-based coordination, we have already assumed coordination amongst participants on several other aspects—such as product definition, consumption meaning, and so on. Generally, this is too obvious to even draw our attention, but when such coordination is missing, it becomes more noticeable. Moreover, the type of coordination described above (price clearing) would work in a Walrasian market—instances of which remain few in practice. This price based coordination is not of much interest to a strategist in most contexts.

However, there is another dimension to such price clearing markets that is of interest to us. Hidden behind demand–supply dynamics is often an auctioneer who sets rules, broadcasts information, and so on. It also requires ensuring that all demand and supply gets aggregated at a single point for price-based clearing to happen. Otherwise how would the proverbial price discovery happen? This is an act of coordination—an accomplishment, in fact. If you look around, you will not find too many such markets—but in few cases, such as, say, the Tokyo fish market (Tsukiji), a remarkable demand–supply agglomeration occurs. Almost half of the global tuna production is routed through the market, where prices are determined based on bids from agents of buyers who are spread across the whole world. The agglomeration results from a monopoly of the site of aggregation. Now, possibly, you would understand the purpose behind the *Agriculture Produce Marketing Committee (APMC) Act* in India, which created a geographic monopoly of a marketplace—

the *mandi*[6]—within a territorial catchment area for pricing of agricultural produce. Recent amendments in the *APMC* have allowed agricultural procurement outside the *mandi*. Would that affect price discovery by fragmenting demand and supply? Given that there is considerable variation in agricultural production in India, would electronic price dissemination be effective in integrating demand–supply volumes, or would visual inspection in a common marketplace prove to be valuable? Please remember, aggregation provided by common marketplaces enhances competition and is thus a check on opportunism in transactions. Can one then look at several e-commerce initiatives as offering routes for private dealmaking as opposed to public auction based price discovery that one finds in *mandi*s?

Imagine a very large supermarket where all electronic gadgets from around the world are available. Does such massive aggregation itself affect competition? Can such global aggregation be achieved by e-commerce portals? You would find several such marketplaces in China. Why do you think such assets have not been created in India? Does this difference affect the nature of markets in the two countries? Such spatially concentrated places or hubs are of great importance as coordination devices. Just think of the fashion district of Paris or that of Harajuku Street in Tokyo; fashion statements emanating from those sites have a large broadcast, generating a huge fashion market—with the Paris fashion genre having a global influence on shaping consumption meanings. Harajuku Street was cultivated as a fashion centre by the Association of Harajuku Street that included several pioneer fashion retailers such as Five Foxes. There are no such central sites in India with a large broadcast capability—Indian fashion-conscious consumers thus would not be able to agree on a raging genre of fashion easily, and hence firms would have limited ability to modulate large fashion swings. Coordination acts involving creation of hubs or central marketplaces are important in creating the underlying structure of competition in the market. Creation of a marketplace where a centralized auction can occur—to enable the proverbial Walrasian price clearing—is then a reengineering of governance achieved through the successful coordination in centralizing all

---

[6]*Mandi* is a marketplace where the procurement of agricultural commodities is concentrated in India. The *APMC Act* provides the legal framework for the operation of such marketplaces in India.

deals that the operator of the marketplace achieves. This is the strategic dimension of the coordination one may be interested in. An important question is how the central marketplace operator (often an association of several firms) wields the power to assemble such central hubs and then prevent its fragmentation?

2) Coordination, in increasing returns contexts, however, is mostly of a dynamic kind. The task is to influence and modulate the expectation and investment of a bevy of complementary asset holders, so that a product system gets developed together. Systemic products, as our discussion highlighted, would have to stand together. This coordination is dynamic. Unlike the coordination described above, in creating a central auctioning hub, where the desired end 'state of affairs' is known and governance seeks to quickly arrive at such states and preserve it, dynamic coordination seeks a different engagement with the ecosystem. Often in such episodes of dynamic coordination, the end state is too uncertain—the task is to make a set of ecosystem entities coordinate a series of investments that would dynamically evolve generating a series or an envelope of products/technologies en route. Because of deep uncertainties in the eventual product architecture, its specifications or the nature of the market or the relationship between different ecosystem participants that would stabilize eventually, acts of dynamic coordination must allow considerable freedom to the participants, or, in other words, attempt to force a strong governance ironing out possibilities of opportunism would harm the prospects of the unfolding of the new 'system'. Coordination thus may be based only on certain minimum convergence that can then be governed strongly, leaving large terrains of choices under entrepreneurial freedom or acts of opportunism. We illustrate a few dimensions of dynamic coordination below.

As an instance you can consider the Intel strategy of setting up the venture fund Intel@64 when it was on the development project of the 64-bit Intel processor. The venture fund was created jointly with the OEMs, who would deploy the new upcoming chip and a few 'lead early adopter' users from different verticals that would implement solutions built on the new processor, leveraging its additional capability. A group of such firms together with Intel set up the fund. The aim was to finance start-up technology projects that would develop technologies, software, applications, and so on, that would grow the Intel 64 ecosystem. For Intel, it was aimed at speeding up the process of adoption, so that diffusion of the new chip is fast enough and a global sweep of dominance is achieved fast. Short product life of chips (it gets supplanted by new versions) and the threat of commoditization from imitators implied that benefits from hastened adoption would be significant for Intel. It was an act of coordinating co-creation of complementary asset pieces in a wide milieu, to hasten up the arrival of the market.

Our earlier description of Intel pointed towards another dimension of coordination—the ability of Intel to make 'processing speed' the sole criterion of evaluation of chip quality, foreclosing several other technically feasible options. But it succeeded in providing the broad ecosystem with a guided path of technological investment. It was only in the last few years that several other alternative evaluation metrics have been proposed by competing firms such as AMD. The lead network firm often acts as a focal point, and if it commands enough power, then it is able to coordinate the dynamic envelope of expectation around a series of novel products. Without such roles being played successfully, investments may fail to materialize.

3) Dynamic coordination concerns another type of intervention. Increasing returns moves often attempt, as we discussed in the case of MCX growth (see p. 103 for illustration) or the growth of the Australian Rugby League (see case study 2.1), a coordinated transformation of several linked assets that are then connected through novel modes. Access rights to existing assets are negotiated through and a new assemblage of assets quickly put together generating runaway profits. The case of Softbank below provides an instantiation of that approach.

Softbank: Proliferation of linked subsidiaries

Softbank is led by Mayayoshi Son, its president and CEO. It is an internet incubator and venture capital firm run along the lines of CMGI in the US, offering an instance of a novel mode of linked expansion through independent subsidiaries. Son, an offspring of Korean immigrants, made his first million when he sold Japanese arcade games to University of California at Berkeley, as a student there. His next venture was a lightweight electronic

(Case Study 4.5 contd.)

(Case Study 4.5 contd.)

translator—his own invention. He followed that success with Softbank, which began as a software distribution firm in 1981. Over the years, Son funnelled Softbank's profits to a mixed bag of technology firms, among them the US technology publisher Ziff Davies. The really big bucks came with the internet IPO boom. Son's early investments in E-Trade, Yahoo and buy.com led to windfall profits. Better than his many internet-mogul peers, Son could devise an effective mechanism to leverage his wealth globally. For example, a US internet firm E-Trade, funded early in its growth stage, could be brought to Japan to essentially repeat the process. Likewise, a Swedish or an Indian start-up could be cloned in China or Japan. To accomplish this, Son set up immense venture firms to scour the world for firms ripe for funding. Towards the end of 2000, he commanded the largest internet venture fund. Separate funds searched out internet opportunities in China. Son's business stance was distinctly un-Japanese in several ways. He had scant respect for geographic boundaries and encouraged a highly individualized empire built virtually from scratch. He was a high risk player—bringing to business a gambler's instinct that was more American than Japanese. Son began with IT distribution business (which continues as an important operation even today) and then moved, as the internet space evolved, into networking and then into mobile commerce and mobile internet. His growth of scope of the group was motivated by the need to touch different points of the ecosystem in order to develop the strategic capability to transform institutions—establish novel linkages between the multiple touch-points.

The core of the group is a holding company called Softbank Corporation. The group companies are spread across the communication domain—the expanse and scope of the group being designed to synergize operations. Investment in mobile networks, for instance, can be valorized by financing a start-up that would deliver technology for mobile-wallets, and so on. Investment in infrastructure—the portals and platforms provided over the infrastructure and the services and content deployed over those platforms—has been a chain of expansion of the group. The group in 2007 consisted of 127 large and small companies—consolidated and non-consolidated subsidiaries and affiliates—spread across 10 business categories defined as mobile communications business, broadband infrastructure segment, fixed-line telecommunication segment, e-commerce segment, internet culture segment, broadmedia segment, technology services segment, media and marketing segment, overseas fund segment and other businesses. Several of these group ventures are either listed or have equity partners. In each category, it has one or a few anchor enterprises, for instance, Yahoo! Japan in internet lifestyle segment.

(Case Study 4.5 contd.)

(Case Study 4.5 contd.)

Its business on the revenue side mostly has been concentrated in Japan, while for sourcing technology (particularly from start-ups) it has scouted the globe.

It is starting to expand and look beyond Japan for revenues—targeting the evolving internet, mobile lifestyle space in Asia, particularly China, where its efforts are led by the anchor enterprise alibaba.com. In 2006, it engineered a highly leveraged (by debts securitized through stable revenue streams) acquisition of Vodafone Japan in a bid to gain entry into the mobile infrastructure space crucial for the evolving mobile commerce and mobile internet space. Upon acquisition, it changed several existing mobile operator norms, for instance, the pricing norm. It moved pricing model of handsets to 'instalment based higher set-price, low service rates' model reversing the practice of selling handsets by heavy kickbacks to agents and recouping such costs through higher subscriber charges. The lower subscriber charges are aimed at market-creation of its mobile internet content, which it is driving by linking its lifestyle segment enterprises (portal technology and content creation expertise) to the erstwhile Vodafone business.

In 2007, the holding company had consolidated revenues of JPY 2.544 trillion, a 2.3 fold increase with an operating income of JPY 271 billion. Softbank's business model—particularly the role of the holding company—appears to have realized the synergizing effect that so many points of headquarter control aspire to realize. It has been achieved, however, through generally loose control over a large set of enterprises that create a global interconnected web of assets.

Figure 4.1: Softbank Group Enterprise System

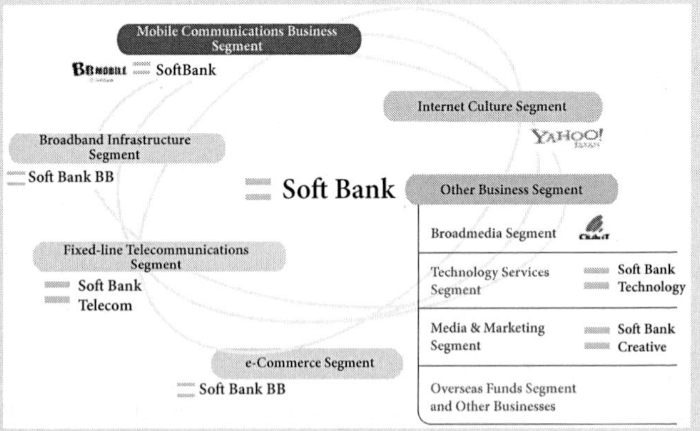

Source: The Softbank website, http://www.softbank.co.jp/en (accessed on 28 June 2010).

What is particularly interesting about the Softbank narrative is the span, in terms of width of sectors/industries, as well as the geographical scope of its coordination moves. There are two aspects of the coordination—an initial act to get certain sought-after partial rights (control or access) that enable changes in business processes that can then link up the asset with the transaction ecosystem of the Softbank Group, followed by a distanced governance that reaps simultaneously the cash flows as a result of the restructuring. It represents a kind of piggybacking—putting together quick assemblages of assets. Do you find such massive coordination moves in Indian business or does the Indian business milieu present you with coordination attempts over more limited spans of assets. We had earlier noted the failure of ICL (see section 2.1.6). Can you look at e-commerce moves in India, such as, say, mJunction.com, and compare their span of coordination with say alibaba.com in China?

Moves like that of Softbank presume the existence of a clutch of assets or nodal asset holders, like, say, a third-party payment gateway operator. One aspect of such assets definitely would refer to transaction efficiencies, process reliability and other such concerns that are close to the concerns in a typical decreasing returns organization. Such assets are also managed under strong hierarchical organizational governance and we emphasized this dimension in our discussion on organizations. These assets may be called traditional assets. On the other hand, the core of a group such as Softbank that drives the increasing returns moves was a lean, flexible, creative and only loosely coupled organization. This core drives the increasing returns by linking up in a novel way—or hitherto unexplored way—several traditional asset holders. The asset-heavy, process-based businesses that otherwise would have faced decreasing returns prospects also stand to gain through the linkages within the Softbank enterprise to get it connected to newly arriving transaction spaces. We hint then at a possibility of a synergistic relation between increasing and decreasing returns asset holders—a dynamics that we also saw in the case of DoCoMo's i-mode business and its traditional organization handling voice-based communication under the threat of decreasing returns and commoditization (see section 3.5). The task of the core is then to gain enough control to drive through the changes (in practices or organizational routines) in the 'traditional organizations', so that the new linkages are forged for a novel set of transactions to materialize.

Summarizing our discussion on markets, we have proposed three different types of markets—markets as defined through a set of interlinked contracts handling specifiable but non-standard complex products, Walrasian-type price-based markets and markets of thick networks exchanging highly non-standard and uncertain assets. Each market type is also simultaneously a mode of governance and each market deploys different means as a check on opportunism. We also argued that the product type—stand-alone, systemic or platform—creates a difference in market dynamics, with systemic and platform type products inducing an increasing returns dynamics that nudges a strategist to follow acts of boundary redefinition and engage in deep inter-organizational coordination of different sorts.

4.4 BRIEF DISCUSSION ON CONTRACTING

After our description of a market and several types of markets, we provide a short discussion on contracts that act as a privately agreed rule structures governing the business transactions between firms, typically two firms. A business manager, in writing such contracts, remains concerned with several dimensions. Since a contract imposes a rule structure, there are two issues—first, how parties can write what we would call good or optimal contracts; and second, how such contracts would be enforced, that is, its fulfilment ensured. Typically, in contracting (say, in an employment contract) it is assumed that an agent is completely rational and has full access to information. The contrary view, especially of the transaction cost, would assume limited or bounded rationality and access to partial or limited information. With such constraints, contracting can become complex or even fail as a workable means for governing transactions. The possibility of ex-post failure for contract enforcement can keep the parties away from the contract and hence lead to a loss of a transaction possibility. Opportunism then leads to contractual failure and transactional failure. The rise of organizational mode of transacting (inside the organization) under the administrative fiat of the organization 'chief' is premised on this failure of the contracting mode.[7]

---

[7] You may also note here that opportunism reduces substantially in transactions in an interconnected network that exchanges information very fast as it increases disproportionately the costs of reneging on contracts. Mechanisms equivalent to excommunication from networks reduce opportunism and hence transaction costs. Geographic concentration along with rich and intense intra-trade (features of a cluster) also makes transaction costs lower as trusted relations develop. In general, as game theory models would show, repeated transactions between known parties are far less susceptible to opportunistic deadlocks (for example, see Axelrod [1984]). The behaviour of various individuals inside a village (or a similar social community) or traders in a *mandi* is a case in point.

Otherwise why would we need an organization? All transactions could have been organized under contracts. In an organization, the leader (such as the CEO) wields an executive authority which, under threat, reduces the possibilities of opportunistic behaviour and hence transaction costs. But unlike two parties in an organizational hierarchical relationship under an executive authority, two parties in a contract enjoy greater freedom in negotiating contract terms or even acting opportunistic with due notice of the threat clauses in the contract.

4.4.1 Contracts—an introductory discussion[8]

Contracts define the rules within which parties in a business transaction engage with each other, transacting on complex exchanges. Contracts influence the price of a product/service. Wondering how? From the mid-1990s, infrastructure has been given huge thrust in India, particularly under the public–private partnership (PPP) mode, setting off a massive investment programme in highways and expressways, metro railways, airports, ports and power plants. PPP projects in the form of build, own, operate and transfer (BOOT) are sustained by a concession agreement (contract between the government and the private investor) for its life of 20–40 years. Considering the long duration of these projects, these contracts are very carefully worded, discussed over several rounds and legally vetted. Investors expect the concession agreement to address all tangible risks and address concerns of all stakeholders, namely investors, lenders, the government and users. An incomplete concession agreement often leaves investors demanding higher return due to the unaddressed risks that emanate from the possibility of challenge to the concession agreement that important stakeholders may mount. Users of the facilities (roads, airports, and so on) are made to pay higher fee.

Are these contracts sacrosanct? The answer is yes and no. Let us explain now. In India, major airports have been redeveloped on PPP basis and are successfully functioning. Real estate concessions (in and around the airport projects) subsidizes these airports and real estate revenue forms a significant portion (approximately 50 per cent) for airport concession holders. Concession agreements of these projects clearly define the percentage of revenue to be shared by the private

---

[8]This section has been co-contributed by M. Karthikeyan, an XLRI Alumnus.

developer (of airport) with the government year-on-year. In a select case, a private developer asked prospective real estate occupants to make substantial interest-free-refundable-deposits and in exchange offered very low rental payments on the property. The private developer stood to save huge interest cost that otherwise he would have paid for constructing the airport facilities. Most importantly, these deposits would not be categorized as 'revenue' as per contract and hence the private developer's revenue share (of the low rental) in absolute value would go down.

Should we conclude then that contracts are fragile? Not at all. The government plugged the above revenue leakage eventually, though the contract could not control that. Contracts are powerful references and the spirit is always seen even if certain words can be misinterpreted. With the backing of executive power, government could check the opportunistic flight, but would a private counterparty, possibly with lower business standing than the violator, succeed in putting a check on opportunism? Can contracts be designed to anticipate these ex-post risks of violation and opportunistic acts?

Within the transaction cost perspective, the basic element of explanation is a transaction, regardless of the fact whether the transaction was about a lumpy and sticky asset, or whether the parties entering into transaction are very dissimilar in terms of size or in terms of asset-ownership or in terms of access to alternative sources of information; in fact, a transaction cost perspective forgets that asymmetry in the power to transact between the parties or the degree of vulnerability (say between a daily labourer and a corporation of large size, or between a small supplier of perishable goods such as milk and a large buyer such as Nestlé) of one party in the transaction or that of high asymmetry in asset ownership between two parties—all these transform this otherwise powerful tool of analysis into a less attractive proposition. Our account, in contrast, has sought to locate transactions in the mesh of power. Asymmetries are crucial in our account. Opportunism has to be conceived, not in the abstract notion of a hypothetical transaction, but in the concrete contextualized transaction in a power-infused relationship.

Contracting has to deal with two different sets of issues in the design of contracts. Terms of a contract or the contractual arrangement reflect, on one hand, the outcome of negotiations where power inheres—so that the asymmetries of power between contracting parties get manifested in contract designing. This asymmetry would affect not only the prices of a product, but also the distribution of control rights, say over a joint asset. Another aspect of the contract designing would be to look at creative crafting of rules to ensure a cheap mode of joint enforcement—exchange of information that would check opportunism, partition and allocate risks between the contracting parties, and so on. An interesting illustration is presented below:

> Clubbing of sale of a catalyst to licensees of a chemical process technology often is an attempt to open to inspection (in an information sense) the production volume information of the licensee on which the royalty arrangements are based. Himont, a chemical company that decided to license out its cutting-edge technology for producing polypropylene (with superior characteristics) in the 1990s, had to craft a contract that would induce licensees to invest in the novel technology that was not yet fully demonstrated. The risks were high, with the potential to disrupt licensee investment. Himont's contract guaranteed performance of the technology, therefore. But taking this risk meant that Himont required certain control over the producer, since without that it may be exposed to moral hazard kind of problems, and for no fault of its technology, suffer contractually invoked damages. It bundled catalyst sales and offered turnkey construction of the plant to the potential licensee as two modes of gaining partial control over the production plant. In lieu, it guaranteed performance of the technology. For another class of licensees willing to take up the risk, Himont offered a simpler plain technology transfer at a lower cost, since risks lay with the licensee. Risk of the plant to produce to expected performance level was thus unbundled or partitioned into risk of technology (that lay with Himont as the developer) and risk of production operations or faulty plant design that lay with the licensee and was beyond Himont's control, except through the contract. Catalysts thus provided a technology solution to the contract problem—it was like a device. Such problems, however, might not be possible to overcome always. Controlling the production risk, Himont could offer risk insurance on the pure technology and hence take care of concerns of the licensee regarding the risks of the novel technology. Thus, contract design was aimed at pragmatically addressing the opportunism possibilities by separating roles and partitioning risks among the two transacting parties. In other industries, such as automobiles, one would often find contracts that shift the investment burden in costly tooling, such as jigs-fixtures, of a component maker if the investment is specific to a client model to reduce the discomfort of the supplier of getting exposed to high risk (of hold-up) after the investment is made.

4.4.2 Trust in community-based business networks[9]

Contract enforcement remains another area which we need to look into. One way would be to look at costs of enforcing contracts or the costs of accessing the enforcement institutions. Such costs are large. Recall the narrative of legal disputes between Intel and AMD. Apart from formal written contracts, much of the business also runs on simple trust. Small firms make deals with each other and get finance, using personal network and ongoing relationships to substitute for missing costly contracts and use trade credit to make for the lack of access to financial markets. Trust mechanisms, however, are not blind acts of faith. Traders and wholesalers often provide very large credit lines to the retail market participants that a bank cannot provide, since they can generate at very low cost reliable information on solvency of a trade partner. In markets where there are multiple actors working together, the mutual trust and network formation can be an essential part of the market transactions. Business networks, caste communities or religious communities often provide such support in building and enforcing trust relationships. If we look at the history of the Indian business community, the dominance of a few communities is easily visible. The old merchant communities in India have been mainly dominated by the Gujarati Banias/Jains, Marwaris, other non-Gujarati Banias, Parsis, Lohanas, Punjabi Khuranas, Travancore Christians, Bohras and Bhatias of the Kutch–Kathiawar–Sindh belt. Most of these communities developed their own formal and informal banking networks, institutions, in the form of cooperatives, and dispute resolution mechanisms that also regulated the behaviour of its members, checking any deviations.

Banking and credit facility created by these communities mainly catered to the requirements of their own community members, especially entrepreneurs. For example, the Andhra Pradesh Maheshwari Cooperative Bank Limited (popularly known as Mahesh Bank) supports in meeting the banking needs of most of the small and medium sized Rajasthan-based trading community members especially Marwari Maheshwaris in Andhra Pradesh.[10] Very similar is the purpose of the Catholic Syrian Bank Limited, a private sector bank with a strong presence in Kerala and nearby states. The business ties formed more along kinship and ethnic lines remains important in several businesses.

---

[9]This section has been contributed by Ankur Jain, an XLRI Alumnus.
[10]www.maheshbank.org/ (accessed in November 2009).

The story of rise of the people of Indian origin in the United States in the motel business explains this form of informal contracts. More than 50 per cent of all motels in the US are now owned by the people of Indian origin. And if we look deeper into the data, we will find that 70 per cent of these Indians (that is, over a third of all motel owners) are Patel, a Gujarati community surname of Indian origin belonging to a particular sub-caste. Outside India, the Patel diaspora has migrated worldwide (Varadarajan, 1999). Within the Greater London region, it is the third most common surname. But it is important to note that most of them are immigrants who migrated to the US for better opportunities. Buying a motel, even one that is in the red, usually requires a substantial down payment, one beyond the reach of most new immigrants. That, however, is one key to how this particular niche was captured. The down payment was seldom a problem for a prospective Indian purchaser, who was often able to turn to a network of relatives and friends to help him out. The unique kinship ties in the group unquestionably helped in other ways also—for instance, information about properties for sale to other members of the same community. One would find such ethnic networks based dominance in several industries, such as, say, global diamond trade—once controlled totally by the Jews and increasingly by Gujarati businessmen. These networks are close to the thick network markets we described earlier.

It is important to understand that the contract terms sought by a powerful party/organization also reflects the business model that is being driven. Often firms indulge in innovation and experimentation while designing contracts. Sometimes powerful parties intentionally allow entrepreneurial freedom to even the weaker party to encourage multiple asset development that would, in turn, benefit the core licensor. Organizations such as SAP,[11] for instance, is in relations with a bevy of implementing organizations/partners, with whom SAP would share rights to improvements done by the implementing agent. This ensures a constant reverse flow of knowledge assets from the customer site to SAP, aiding its subsequent development process that can reduce the cost of version upgradation.

Italian firms such as Benetton provide another interesting instance. Its business model, till a few years ago, consisted of a three-tier system—a

---

[11]SAP is a multinational software development and consulting firm. Headquartered in Germany, SAP provides enterprise software applications and support to businesses of all sizes globally. The company's key product is its Enterprise Resource Planning (SAP ERP) software.

lowest tier of several hundreds of small or tiny-scale producers of 'grey' garments, Benetton owning a centralized, highly automated dyeing plant, and several sets of franchisee dealers who created in an entrepreneurial mode a market for Benetton products. Benetton was linked to the two other tiers—one each in upstream and downstream part of the value chain—through contracting. While the contract with the grey garment producers reflected a stronger contract, more intrusive in nature, the contract with franchisees was looser, allowing encapsulation of local information at that level and a build-up of franchisee specific asset. In fact, when electronic data processing (EDP) systems linked up the value chain, Benetton chose to leave the franchisees very loosely coupled. Entrepreneurial role of the franchisee was important for the franchising firm. The control of the dyeing process reflected a mode of control (or coordination) over the value chain; it differentiated as well on the dyeing aspect with other rival brands. The stance towards contract negotiation then is also shaped by the underlying business model and the roles that each party seeks the other to perform within its business model. The contract shapes the role allocation between the contracting parties, influencing the types of assets that each party to the contract builds up or deems feasible to build up. Alternative asset architectures then often demand a reorientation of contracts and redefinition of the partitioning of roles and risks.

To summarize, therefore, and link up to our earlier discussions, contracts provide one alternative for governance of a transaction. It bears the mark of power asymmetry between the parties, and implicitly the business model followed, since it allocates roles between contracting parties. Contracts represent business transactions that are too complex (or multidimensional) for simple price-based governance; the pragmatic choice is then between contractual and intra-organizational governance through the power of executive authority enforced inside an organization. Contractual and organizational governance represents, in fact, a shifting boundary. Contractual innovation, development of devices enabling low-cost shared monitoring or transfer of information (sometimes backed by regulatory support) can shift a transaction that was notoriously difficult to govern through a contract (and hence undertaken inside the organization) to the contractual domain. The whole contemporary world of outsourcing represents such shifts. Contrarily, transactions and risks that current contractual practices cannot handle under current technology and regulatory conditions become a terrain for organizational expansion.

CASE STUDY 4.6 Japanese distribution system

In an earlier discussion (see case study 1.4), we referred to the contractual practice in Japanese distribution systems called 'right to return unsold goods'. It was introduced in the 1950s by apparel maker called Onward Kashiyama. For Kashiyama, this innovation in contractual practice was triggered by the possibility of releasing the retailers (department stores in prime locations mainly) from the burden of unsold inventory (or dead-stock) risk, hoping that it would induce department stores to give up their tendency to understock. Kashiyama could then leverage this enhanced retail presence for build-up of own sales. To take care of the resultant risk of returns, Kashiyama kept price control (resale price maintenance) and deputed its own (manufacturer seconded) employees to the department stores to access information as well as to act quickly on slow moving items by offering discounts. Department stores agreed to this arrangement, primarily because, in the boom of the 1950s, they were constrained in several senses. The market was shifting fast to what one may call Western clothing as Japan grew into an affluent society, creating a new kind of risk of a stream of novel products. Since patterns of consumer taste movement in these new categories were unknown, department stores were very cautious understockers. Kashiyama, with a national presence, had a better view of the whole market and a better ability to spot trends early. Under these new contracts, firms like Kashiyama virtually took control over several traditional retailer functions—reducing the department store to a sophisticated real estate infrastructure operator. Right-to-return spread very fast across distribution sectors in Japan. In men's ready-made suit business, for instance, manufacturers like Ayoma and Aoki used right to return to gain information on expected changes in suit market ahead of competitors and basing themselves on such insights could prepare production plans with a longer lead time that used the summer season (off-peak time) for manufacturing at low costs. The account shows how a contract can transform relations and lead to interesting and novel business model adoption (Miwa and Ramseyer, 2001).

4.5 UNDERSTANDING REGULATION

We began the chapter with a discussion on regulation that questioned the market regulation dichotomy. We instead posited regulation as a kind of rule structure that emanates from several executive authorities—

primarily from government, but also from standard-setting bodies jointly created by private businesses. And our discussion on markets and several types of markets (with their institutional differences) would have made it apparent that a notion of regulation as rules that thwart the free market is rather naïve and of little value to a strategic actor. Markets and transactions in markets are underpinned by elaborate rule structures—which we called institutions. Visualizing businesses as embedded in a network or more accurately a mesh of rules may not be inappropriate. All this together define the rule structure and the institutional context of a business enterprise; they are thus highly socialized and the free actor in the market is a myth we can give up. If one takes interest in this institutional dimension, a whole world of possible action points opens up; it does indeed provide a deeper understanding of market processes. Out of all the rules, government regulations constitute an important and a special class. Just like all other rules, including that of privately arrived at and mutually agreed contracts, regulations also constraint behaviour and options of an actor. Institutions always bind social beings. And a strategist thus takes a pragmatic interest in such rules, sometimes to enforce it, sometimes to slyly violate it and sometimes to wage a war to change it in own favour. Then regulations stand as unique rule set different from rules such as business agreements, since it has the powers of an executive authority that sets and enforces it, generally over a fairly wide terrain that is under its jurisdiction. If we agree to view regulations from this perspective, then without going into details and in-depth discussion on regulations, we just take a short detour pointing out a few aspects of certain important purposes underlying regulation that a strategist may take note of.

But before that, we would raise and just briefly touch upon the issue of jurisdiction of a regulation, particularly whether uniform regulation across jurisdictions is always in one's own business interest. Readers would be familiar with accounts in the business press, where foreign businesses continuously complain about idiosyncratic laws and regulations in China, implicitly making a claim for the establishment of a uniform global regulatory system. Such demands have been made on Japan and the European Union nations by the US, but in most cases, institutional specificities peculiar to each nation remain. In our discussion, we pointed to practices in the Japanese distribution system, such as 'right to return unsold goods' and 'resale price maintenance' that are illegal under Anti-Trust Laws on Vertical Restraints in the US, but are legal within Japanese Antimonopoly Laws. So what one considers right or wrong is partly an outcome of the vantage point—it depends on which system we are using as a reference point. Or think of corporate governance laws. While in India, the discourse generally revolves around shareholder right-based governance (such as Cadbury Committee-type system), corporate governance systems in continental Europe (Germany and France, in particular) continue to be quite different, although pressures for uniformity are also increasing. One important aspect relates to the two-tier board system in Germany, where several non-financial stakeholders, including employees of a large organization have significant control rights (and hence voice) in the supervisory board that sits above the board of directors. Shareholder rights are modulated through several other institutional restraints—representing one kind of a shared right structure. Businesses such as Siemens have not changed their structures, so far at least. In our discussion so far, it is clear that our account sees rules as manifestation of existing power relations and hence are carriers of interest; they are politically laden. Tussle over rules, often or rather always, are then battles for strategic control.

How should business interest then look at this issue? Case study 4.7 provides below an articulation around labour regulations in India.

Case of labour regulations in India[12]

Three major central Acts regulate industrial relations in India: *The Industrial Employment (Standing Orders) Act, 1946* (*IE* for short); the *Trade Union Act, 1926* (*TU*); and the *Industrial Disputes Act, 1947* (*ID*). Rules regarding lay-off, retrenchment and closure are far more restrictive. The *IE Act* permits certain types of lay-offs (such as contractual) or retrenchments (on disciplinary or medical grounds). But if it is instigated by financial reasons, then the *ID Act* comes into force. The *ID Act* since 1976 made it mandatory for employers to seek prior permission from the government to lay off or retrench any worker or close down the unit. Originally, firms with 300 or more permanent workers were under this requirement. But later in 1982 this requirement (codified in chapter V-B of the *ID Act*) was extended to all industries employing 100 or more workers.

(Case Study 4.7 contd.)

---

[12] This case has been contributed by Ankur Jain, an XLRI Alumnus.

(Case Study 4.7 contd.)

> A violation of this may lead to serious penalty on the employer as well as reinstatement of laid-off workers. This particular provision has been criticized as too restrictive and uncommon by international standards, given that the government has been conservative in granting permissions to retrench or lay off. For example, in 1997, the central government received 60 applications for lay-off/retrenchment/closure, but granted permission only in 6 cases. Because of this abnormally low rate of approvals, the provision of chapter V-B continues to be seen as a major stumbling block for the restructuring of loss-making enterprises. Lower flexibility translates into greater cost of employment, which often induces investors to shy away, or employ fewer workers.
>
> When India started liberalizing in 1991, many expected it to follow the path of the export-oriented low-wage manufacture, as charted by other Asian countries. But this proved impossible since the Indian political set-up did not allow liberalizing labour laws. On the other hand, small scale industries are, by and large, free of labour regulation, and present a free entry and free exit sector.

How can one look at this? Regulation in India has truly created a wedge in the labour market—through separation of the enterprises into categories that come under the ambit of regulations and those that do not. But, interestingly, such advantages of the small scale sector have not materialized into runaway growth of the sector. Data on small scale industries (SSIs) in India show up large incidences of sickness, low asset base, inadequate capital investment, lack of distribution and marketing assets, and so on. We earlier referred to the lack of general distributors, such as Japanese General Trading Companies (non-specific to brands/companies), which is an important feature of the Indian distribution milieu. Small firms also have great problems in accessing credit from the banking system and external equity markets. Small business owners have always been complaining about this.[13] Business prospects are shaped by a nexus of such institutions that intersect in a business, like a mesh.

---

[13]For details on the problems faced by the small scale sector in India readers may refer to 'Report on Financing of Enterprises in the Unorganized Sector' by the National Commission for Enterprises in the Unorganised Sector (Government of India 2007) and several other reports available at the National Commission for Enterprises in the Unorganised Sector, Government of India (http://nceuis.nic.in/).

Articulations based on just a single institution might not provide correct systemic insights. This would also help readers appreciate the fact that price often remains not the most important issue—access and control are much more important, and those are institutionally defined.

Let us move on to a high-tech sector, say telecom equipment. Is it always clear that a uniform regulation across the whole world or a country is a better solution than, say, jurisdictional fragmentation, and hence differentiated regulation, from the point of view of business? Case study 4.8 documents the Chinese experience.

CASE STUDY 4.8 The Chinese telecom market

Quite contrary to the scenario in India, the Chinese telecom market is characterized by jurisdictional fragmentation across provincial governments. Provincial telecom authorities retained considerable power over rule-setting, such as grant of licences and shaping up of procurement rules. The Chinese market then was not quite a national market—jurisdictional fragmentation would mean that in several senses, it was a layered market. Several telecom equipment producers existed because of this fragmentation. From the early 1990s, the Chinese government decided to provide a big push to developing telecom equipment manufacturing capability in domestic enterprises. Its first set of acts consisted of allowing several large MNCs to enter in JV arrangements with a few amongst the several domestic producers and using the large order/procurement size (due to a fast expanding network) to force technology transfer deals. By 1992, Shanghai Bell was the most dominant player in the market. Within a few years, the landscape changed—in 1998, domestic firms (apart from the JVs) controlled more than 90 per cent market share in some segments, like fixed line switching equipment. Firms such as Huawei who grew during this period adopted a dual strategy of provincial customization of technology, contracting and provisioning of service support along with manufacturing through a network of provincial manufacturers that it had acquired. It was a pan-jurisdictional asset structure that they created, cultivating support at multiple points of executive authority. We noted such asset building structure in the case of Wahaha (see case study 1.3) as well. The decentralized procurement market created severe competition and provincial manufacturers fought for national market share by moving beyond own province. Competition was then inter-provincial as well and fierce. The firms which emerged out of this competitive battle became the national firms, who were blessed with massive credit support for subsequent global expansion (excerpts from Saha, 2004: 3915–925).

The narration above brings out how entrepreneurial conduct by an executive authority holder enabled through jurisdictional cleavages can support a business strategy of a firm or a set of firms, shaping up key structural features of the market. How should business then look at issues of regulatory convergence? One way may be to look at the underlying reasons that force a movement towards convergence or demand one. Homogenization of markets, products, processes, and so on—standardization and commoditization across a massive territorial span require and create pressures for regulatory convergence. On the face of massive standardization, regulatory differences impose costly asymmetries. That is fairly well understood. But our narration here emphasized increasing returns—does an increasing returns stance based on generation of novelty also demand similar commoditization? Contrarily, it is based on institutional, often cultural idiosyncrasies. Readers may recall our discussions on the Tokyo Metro case, German CNC manufacturing, or Japanese auto industry practices, where culture-specific assets shaped up a differentiated strategy, practice or a process. It was the route out of the trap of commoditization, or a counter to the dominance of the current winner. So should business interests dictate a more nuanced stance towards regulatory convergence—a support for convergence where current strategy is to move towards commoditization while retaining institutional differences in domains where differentiation is sought, on the strength of distinct assets that have been generated due to a history of unique institution?

We end this section by identifying two broad types of regulatory roles: (*a*) regulator, as arbiter of conflict and as a counterpoint to the abuse of dominance and (*b*) regulator as arbiter supporting generation of differentiated assets. While the first type of function relates to limiting the harm that a current dominant firm causes to the market, especially rivals and customers, the second type of role concerns granting support to novel assets by enabling it to distinguish itself from older asset categories. We provide instances of both, very briefly.

4.5.1 Abuse of dominance and antitrust action

Although strategy seeks absolute dominance of the actor, most contemporary regulatory systems would not want a monopoly structure of an industry with an absolute dominance of a single firm. The state, therefore, enacts antitrust regulations or competition laws seeking to put in a leash against what is called abuse of dominance. Abuse of dominance is then a legal–societal notion that is defined in statutes and regulatory practice and differs in its specific form across countries. In a formal sense, the law may be evoked on any firm that has dominance in a particular industry, often called 'relevant' industry, to use the specific language in antitrust literature. (Relevant market definition, as can be expected, is often contested in actual practice.) The simplest measure of dominance is the market share that a firm commands in a market. Antitrust regulation in various jurisdictions usually has definite cut-off levels of market share, as threshold for triggering the antitrust laws. Usually M&A that leads to combined entity market shares greater than the threshold limits also require antitrust approval in several jurisdictions, including the US and EU. However, dominance by itself is not against the law. Dominance just provides the power, as it is understood in antitrust practice, for the abuse of the dominant position through exclusionary acts that harms the competitor in the same relevant industry materially by denying market access. The law would also have a range of prohibited exclusionary practices, which also gets developed over a series of case verdicts and judgements as a kind of case law. Law seeks to control the abuse. Practice of antitrust is complex legal terrain and is beyond the scope of our enquiry here. Suffice it to say here that antitrust enforcement (of course, shaped by the political system's tolerance for power of big business!) constitutes a counterpoint of executive authority that checks the exercise of deterrence power of incumbents. Rivals shut out of markets often appeal for redress—it is thus a kind of turf where a contest can be carried out.

A more nuanced sense of dominance, which is becoming important in contemporary industries and several judgements, is where a dominant firm in one market uses the position to thwart firms in other adjacent (and generally new) markets. The Microsoft case was tried on this notion of dominance of linked adjacent markets where Microsoft was seen as unfairly extending its dominance in the current operating system (OS) market to several other new types of emerging technology markets (see section 4.1). The recent FTC enquiry into Intel (see case study 4.2) has also been started on similar grounds.

4.5.2 Regulation overseeing inter-category contests

Handholding of incipient innovative business (or technology) moves, clear delineation of categories, exercising oversight over inter-category competitions (or contests) are other important roles of regulation. New categories often require creation of distinct institutions, such as separate labelling to prevent conflation (or mixing up) of categories. That helps in creation of a distinct identity. Such institutions might evolve cooperatively from within the business system, but it often requires supportive stance of laws to hold it against the threat of entrenched institutions and its stakeholders. The aim of this type of regulatory intervention is to lend support to an incipient differentiation of assets. So, it supports the creation of adjacent markets or niches, helping the process of boundary definition or redefinition. Regulation often holds the new boundary. Our discussion earlier on redefinition of boundaries of products would already have sensitized readers to the ubiquity of such redefinitions. The redefinitions are also at the root of increasing returns dynamics. You can think of genetically modified (GM) food labelling in Europe or that of wine regulation. Contrarily, you can think of the problems in India of GM foods and the conflation it creates in the consumption/distribution space without labelling and other category separating institutions.

CASE STUDY 4.9   US wine regulations

US wine regulations, much like its European counterpart, makes a distinction between varietal and generic wines as separate categories. Varietal wines require at least 75 per cent of volume content and its predominant aroma, taste, flavour and other characteristics to come from a specific grape variety. In addition, varietal wines are required to be labelled with an origin appellation as well. This unique labelling cannot be done by mass-wine-producers—who would produce sherry or port. Varietal wines have unique organizational forms—small owner (or winery) supervised vineyard with attached wineries, depend on non-capital intensive marketing (do not do costly mass advertising), wine-tasters (who mans the reputation gateway), boutique stores and boutique enclosures in general stores as channels to move their produce. In terms of production, they concentrate on getting a specific innovative winning combination of grape variety, soil and climatic conditions, and a specific maturation technique. Mass and varietal wines are engaged in inter-category contests—and the differentiation of the turf that aids this contest is enforced through law. Relative market shares between the two categories have shifted back and forth in interesting ways over time (Swaminathan, 2001: 1169–185).

Readers would note that separate categories of wine require different institutional assets. They use different distribution assets, capital equipment, skills and techniques. Differentiation of the product is an outcome of differentiation on several such counts, or in another sense, differentiation of the product requires differentiation on several other dimensions, including that of assets that go into its production/distribution. Each category thus accesses a different set of complementary assets. While those differentiated assets are created through complementary private investment in most cases, regulation grants the power to the category to specify itself as a special and different category, with certain sets of privileges that another category does not possess. Can you think of VC and its unique characteristics? A very simple and effective way to understand it would be to look into the regulatory definition—what are the special privileges or special rules for the VC sector, as opposed to, say, a bank or another kind of financial firm? Are such definitions uniform across countries? Usually not. This regulatory act is crucial from the perspective of an increasing returns strategist, who often has to engage in a regulatory contest to win such a vote in favour of creation of a separate category. Contests of this type are ubiquitous across markets. Global creation of a novel category often would require a global contest across several jurisdictions. We would end this section with a short description of a conflict between commodity derivative exchanges in India (see case study 4.10). It brings out the complexities in regulation to prevent 'abuse of dominance' under increasing returns.

CASE STUDY 4.10 Inter-exchange rivalry

In the 1940s, trading in commodity derivatives, forwards, futures and options contracts were brought under control through imposition of price controls (prices did not vary in the market). In certain cases, futures trading was outlawed for a few commodities, as part of the government's drive to contain inflation. These controls were maintained until 1952, when the government passed the *Forward Contracts (Regulation) Act*, providing the legislative foundation for the industry. Although restrictions on futures trade in essential foods, such as sugar and food grains, remained, the Act allowed futures trade in a limited number of commodities. The Forward Markets Commission (FMC) was created to supervise and regulate futures markets in the public interest,

(Case Study 4.10 contd.)

(Case Study 4.10 contd.)

but in effect, it gradually absorbed the exchanges' self-regulatory powers. In 2002, the Indian government decided to invite corporate entities to set up a commodities derivative exchange. In 2003, the Government of India recognized the National Multi Commodity Exchange (NMCE); NMCE was promoted by Central Warehousing Corporation and National Agriculture Cooperative Marketing Federation of India and Gujarat State Agricultural Marketing Board. A second commodity exchange named MCX was promoted by Jignesh Shah through Financial Technologies Limited (FT).[14] A third exchange, namely National Commodity and Derivative Exchange (NCDEX), was promoted by the National Stock Exchange (NSE) of India as another nationwide multi-commodity exchange. Among its promoters, NCDEX also had other large domestic financial institutions including ICICI Bank Limited (India's largest private sector bank), Life Insurance Corporation of India (LIC) and National Bank for Agriculture and Rural Development (NABARD). While NMCE and NCDEX were backed by institutional investors, MCX was promoted by a private organization/promoter (that is, FT).

Over the years, MCX had established a massive dominance in the exchange business in commodity derivatives, and thereafter in other markets such as electricity trading exchange. In 2009, MCX had close to 85 per cent market share of commodity derivative trading volumes. In terms of specific commodities, MCX dominated in metals (gold, silver and other metals) and oil—with the bulk of its revenue coming from gold trading. Trading in gold occurred mostly after evening hours, to synchronize with global trading in exchanges in USA and China. NCDEX, in contrast, was a leader in agri-commodities, but volume of trading was very small in agricultural commodity derivatives. In 2009, in order to capture the losing market share, NCDEX attempted reducing transaction fees. In February 2009, NCDEX issued a circular stating that turnover fees would be slashed to 5 paise per INR 100,000 worth of trade done after 5 pm, against the fee of INR 3 per INR 100,000 for trades done in the morning session. NCDEX's competitor, MCX, which has close to an 85 per cent market share, witnessed high turnover in the late evening session, and the move was targeted at capturing this market share. But FMC stayed the

(Case Study 4.10 contd.)

---

[14]FT was founded in 1995. Started with an initial capital of about INR 0.5 million, FT has present worth of USD 1.27 billion (as on 30 September 2009). FT provides technology solutions and domain expertise for digital transactions and financial markets across all asset classes including equity, commodities, currency and debt.

(Case Study 4.10 contd.)

move, on appeal from MCX. The FMC ordered the NCDEX to keep the new price structure in abeyance.

The classic argument in favour of regulation is to prevent monopolistic pricing by large players. The smaller exchange, NCDEX, cut prices in trying to gain market share. Ordinarily, in a duopoly, when one player cuts prices, the other is likely to follow, resulting in benefits for customers. Normally, a regulator would applaud a price cut, since elevated prices are precisely what regulation seeks to prevent. The matter was partially resolved when in late 2009 MCX reduced fees on its exchange and it ended the deadlock between the players. How do you look into this event? How do we conceptualize competition between exchanges? Is it a product, like a pack of toothpaste? It is like a 'platform' that we described above. And it appears to have increasing returns properties, in the sense that there is significant network externality operating. As more trading volume moves to an exchange, the bid-ask spread declines and hence the exchange becomes more attractive to others who have not joined. There is positive feedback operating. So, a small advantage has a potential to lead to a runaway dominance, a winner-takes-all kind of outcome. Was the FMC intervention fair? Or, was it a case of capture of the regulator by the dominant entity?

If exchanges are increasing returns platforms, are not monopolies preferable? Consumers would benefit from a monopoly marketplace in a single contract—that would enable better price discovery. So, how can multiple exchanges survive? One way could be through contract differentiation, so that growth of an exchange would depend on its ability to generate markets around new contracts, either in the same commodity (that can connect the market to new liquidity pools not accessible earlier) or in new commodities. Does our view change depending on whether we look at exchanges as products or platforms?

5

Institutions of Finance

5.0 INTRODUCTION: THE CONTEMPORARY ROLE OF FINANCE

Traditional strategy literature has mostly been woven around the 'firm' as an entity (or an organization) that is visualized as operating in a product or a service market—and hence a 'firm' or its 'product-specific' division would become the unit of analysis. Thus, strategy concerns remained bound to the product or the service offering. But the institutional story that we are trying to narrate cannot remain restricted to the realm of the product or the service—for the product or service market, embracing the consuming customers or rivals, constitute just one among several domains in which the strategist CEO of an organization remains institutionally embedded. Several other domains, such as that of technology and the world of finance in which the strategist necessarily remains embedded, crucially affect the choices and constraints faced by a strategist and shape up what the firm does. Let us take up, as an instance, a business group affiliate firm of the Ashok Garware Group (case study 5.1).

 Garware Marine Industries Limited — CASE STUDY 5.1

Incorporated in 1975 as a public limited company, Garware Marine belongs to the Ashok Garware Group of Companies. It got listed on the Bombay Stock Exchange Limited in the 1980s and has been engaged in the manufacture and

(Case Study 5.1 contd.)

(Case Study 5.1 contd.)

> marketing of fishing nets for over three decades using nylon yarn. The firm's website describes it as catering to the needs of a large number of fishermen throughout the Indian subcontinent and having sales of around INR 100 million per annum.
>
> The company's factory is located at Ahmednagar in Maharashtra with 24 imported net making machines from Japan. It has its own twisting division in the same factory to produce twine for captive consumption and produces around 30 tons of nets per month. The company has 15 employees at its head office in Mumbai and around 160 employees at its factory; it also has a ship repair division which employs five qualified engineers. Garware Marine markets its products through a wide chain of distributors/agents. As part of its investments, Garware Marine also holds 6 per cent equity stake of its sister concern, namely, Global Offshore Services Limited (earlier known as Garware Offshore Limited).
>
> Can we understand strategies of Garware Marine from an inspection of its product market only?[1] While Garware Marine and its fishing nets world remains important, one may explore several other dimensions, such as: the family tree of the business group; the use of this affiliate as a holding company arm of the Ashok Garware Group; to fulfil the internal capital markets objective of the business group; the use of this affiliate to ensure that the business group has control over other group companies such as Global Offshore Services Limited,[2] that is the group's largest and best performing firm (with market capitalization of above INR 3,500 million).
>
> In other words, we can say that Garware Marine, from a broader perspective of the business group within which it remains institutionally embedded, fulfils the financing needs of the Ashok Garware Group, acts as its investment arm and ensures that the family promoters have enough control over its business empire.

The narration in case study 5.1 reflects a rather simple institutional embedding of a firm in a business group that plays a role in the governance of the business group. This extra-firm institutional governance emanating from the larger world of financial institutions would be what we would explore. In this chapter, our attempt would be to narrate several such stories from the world of finance—which, in contemporary economies, stand as a partially autonomous milieu with immense powers

---

[1] Interested readers should visit http://www.garwaremarine.com/
[2] http://www.garwareoffshore.com/

to shape or de-shape strategic stances and modes of production or distribution. Modern financial systems, whether it is bank-based or based on myriad other financial instruments, have a capability to mop up financial resources (or savings) from a large dispersed pool of savers. One can think of the increased penetration of the banking network from this perspective, especially if one also remembers that most of the savings collection (or deposit mobilization in banking parlance) would get lent, especially in India, not at the local branch level but in central location such as the headquarters. Deployment of such large pools of finance (or financial resources) then becomes the task of the financial intermediary. Most contemporary firms/organizations depend on significant external financing, from the banking system or other financial intermediaries. So the financial intermediaries' own dynamics (and their rules of operation) deeply affect the interface it has with, say, the production organizations that it finances and consequently governs as well. For the organization, in contrast, gaining access to such large pools of financial resources through the mediation of the financial intermediaries would require them to share control and governance with the purveyors of the world of finance. Such access often remains crucial for growth of the business and the organization beyond what is permitted by own capital of the organization. Governance exercised from financial intermediaries would thus shape the strategies of the organization. It is this governance interface that would be of interest to us in this chapter.

The partial autonomy and the power of the financial world are evident in the imagery of 'financial capitalism', seen with awe or envy, with disdain or with appreciation depending on which side the observer associates oneself with and how he/she relates to this world. This power of financial capitalists that we are referring to is more than the pressure exerted to increase returns on capital that agency theorists would emphasize—it is the power to set the agenda of product or service businesses or the mode of profit generation—making certain strategic stances possible and others difficult to pursue. Thus, it is about *control*. In a sense, it is like a voting power—an institutional power to set norms which influence firms/organizations in the wider economy. *Fads, fashions and the belief-world are important.* Availability of financial resources around certain themes influences investment choices. Thus, the agenda-setting power of the financial world arises from their role as a kind of gatekeeper—allowing certain strategies to be financed while denying financial resources to others which then remain bound in its deployment to a puny resource raising capability. It is a kind of ex-ante screening power around trajectories of investments. Readers may recall our discussion on the contest in electricity industry (case study 1.2) around the norm of pricing. As we stressed there, the economies of large-scale central generating stations were realized ex-post after the institutional choice of producing electricity in central generating stations was already made. The other mode of decentralized generation lost out in an institutional contest—not because of inefficiency or its unworkable economics, but basically because it lost out in an institutional contest—that was framed in a specific way and was fought in a specific terrain/forum.

> Think of the White Revolution in India that raised milk production several fold retaining the dispersed small-scale ownership of milch cattle. One would recall the series of initiatives that pushed credit (banking) in small tickets so that households could get access to finances for expanding their holding of milch cattle. Can one imagine a change in structure of production—a movement into concentrated ownership (such as in large cattle farms)—if access to finance remained a problem for the dispersed household producers? The business model (production model) of large-scale dairies under cooperatives along with micro-scale ownership of cattle assets would not have fructified without this financial access!

The contemporary financial intermediation system is not a homogeneous institution working under common rules. It is rather characterized by multiplicities of institutions and norms of working—how possible investments are evaluated and screened, how investments are monitored, how different layers of control and cash flow rights are sliced up and risks parsed (or sliced) amongst different financial intermediaries, differ considerably across the financial spectrum. A bank and a VC firm or a non-banking financial company or a private equity firm—each is a distinct institution operating under differing norms (or rules), quite often also under different regulations. Imagine, for instance, the process involved in taking a loan against collateral from a bank branch vis-à-vis attracting an equity investment from a venture capitalist for an untested novel product idea. The bank and the VC would differ in several respects. A bank usually would lend against an asset and would be concerned with the repayment of the loan (and interests), while a VC would invest primarily to exit with a lump-sum profit booking at the end of a finite horizon. The bank and the VC would differ with respect to motives of investing, the incentives to monitor, the nature of monitoring and division of control rights between the financier and the financed. This difference defines the differences in 'practice' between these two types of financial intermediaries. We would explore these differences in this chapter. It is this dimension of institutional difference (in terms of the rules and practices of operation) that is the first aspect we explore in this chapter.

Case of 'Dosa King'

In early 1990s, R. Narayanan, chief executive and promoter of Gum India Ltd (makers of Big Fun and Champs chewing gum) came out with the concept of a chain of *masala dosa* outlets serving a *standardized*, economically priced *masala dosa* in a fast food environment using a machine that would make plain *dosa*s (and *masala dosa*s) automatically. A company was registered under the name and style of Indian Food Fermentations Limited (IFFL) and work commenced on developing the automatic *dosa*-maker.

A year later, after over 5,000 man hours of R&D effort, a machine was designed which could make *dosa* automatically. In this electrically operated machine, a dollop of batter would drop on the heated *tawa*; once *dosa* was ready, a dollop of *masala* would drop on to the *dosa* and the *dosa* would be automatically folded and picked up and inserted in a paper bag. The batter and *masala* mix would be made in a central plant at Butibori industrial area, Nagpur and supplied to the numerous outlets all over India.

IFFL's business plan document also stated that the company planned to give *dosa*-making machines on lease to the franchises all over India and eventually also enter markets in the Gulf and South East Asia which have large Indian population.

In 1992, Narayanan was confident that his Dosa King *dosa*s shall be of uniform, standardized quality and taste at all outlets and can be marketed at a very reasonable price of INR 5 per *dosa* leaving a 20 per cent margin for the franchisee. He hoped to have 100 outlets in few cities by mid-1993 and hoped to enter about 50 towns with a network of 500 outlets within three years. In 1993, IFFL also tied up with Nestlé India Ltd to market its *dosa* and *vada* batter in consumer packs in the country. The agreement stated that Nestlé would sell the ready-to-use *dosa*, *vada*, *sambhar* and unique *masala dosa* batter in consumer packs, under its own brand name.

IFFL was incorporated as a public limited company in August 1991. It obtained its Certificate for Commencement of Business in January 1992 to set up manufacturing facilities for making dry *dosa* batter and potato *masala*

(Case Study 5.2 contd.)

(Case Study 5.2 contd.)

> mix. The *dosa*-making machine had been accorded recognition as it received the Federation of Indian Exporters (FIE) award for the most innovative new products. IFFL also took funding from the Technology Development Investment Corporation of India (TDICI), a public fund for promoting technology start-up initiatives under a loan arrangement. It also got additional funding from the Tamil Nadu Industrial Development Corporation (TIDCO). The company issued equity shares to the public in January 1994 to part finance the project. IFFL started the Dosa King's commercial production of dehydrated batter on August 1994. It started manufacturing *dosa*-making machines with its unit at Nagpur. It also manufactured dehydrated batter and potato flakes from the same plant.
>
> But the *dosa*-making machine was not easily accepted by the target clientele and potential franchisees. The machine also had technical glitches. Both these issues reduced the *dosa* machine to a commercial failure. In 1999–2000, the company was declared sick under the Board for Industrial and Financial Reconstruction (BIFR) and the operating agency initiated steps for take-over/rehabilitation of the unit.
>
> Was dispersed equity investors (through IPO), the TIDCI or TIDCO (with a loan exposure) the right kind of agent to govern the initiative? Would a VC engagement, with milestone-linked payments, have better served the business cause? Was the finance availability around plant construction and expansion too early and did it take attention (and finance) out of the technology troubleshooting? Was it right for the firm to bear the full risk of technology (including the risk of technology failure during full-fledged commercial production as opposed to the prototyping stage)? Engaging with these questions takes us to the interface of the financier and the firm and the governance implicit in such relationships.

Our discussion in case study 5.2 brings out the differences in institutions of practice amongst several financial intermediaries. Such multiple institutions are also linked to each other as finance flows across institutions—say from banks to a VC fund where a bank may invest. A unit of financial resource originating in a commercial bank being deployed through a VC firm leads to a VC-type governance on the invested firm. The bank would have a cash flow right but not a control right on the deployment of the resource that originated within the banking system. This separation of cash flow and control rights—in its myriad forms—constitute the key to understanding contemporary financial intermediation, quite unlike the common equity of a single proprietor, where cash flow and control rights remain tightly bound together. We argue that finance, as *resource*, mainly refers to cash flow rights—the right to enjoy a rent-like return[3]—while finance as *capital* refers to associated control rights—the 'voice' in putting bets on the investment trajectory,[4] to speculate and to potentially profit. We would remain interested in several dimensions of control rights as it brings out sharply the governance that accompanies the deployment of a unit of financial resource. As a proverbial 'unit of financial resource' moves across such multiple intermediations, new layers of rights get attached to it and the governance exercised undergoes a change.

5.0.1 Modes of separating cash flow rights and control rights

Internationally, dual class equity is the most popular method. Dual class share structures give preferential voting rights to one of the classes. This may allow a company to raise money with, let us say, the class B shares while allowing the founder by owning much of the class A shares to maintain voting control. A case in point is the internet giant Google. Each of the class B shares reserved for Google insiders would carry 10 votes, while ordinary class A shares sold to the public would get just 1 vote.

In India, the pyramidal structure and cross-shareholdings enable the promoter family to control firms within the group without necessarily having a significant direct ownership. In pyramidal structure, for instance, the holding company at the top, say Goel Sons, has a 30 per cent holding in subsidiary Goel Steel. In turn, Goel Steel has a 30 per cent holding in subsidiary Goel Iron. As a result of this holding, although, Goel Sons has only a 9 per cent claim on the cash flow benefits of Goel Iron, yet Goel Sons is in a position to exercise full control over Goel Iron through this vertical chain. While pyramidal holdings are vertical chains

---

[3]Take the instance of investing in a 'real estate investment trust' (popularly known in the financial world as REITs) focused towards residential properties. The investor here is mainly looking for a stable cash flow rights, that is, 'rent like return'. This is exactly opposite to the position of fund managers managing the REIT funds, who have enormous control and veto power over deciding where these funds would go. Same is the case when investors invest in mutual funds and other similar funds.

[4]Take the example of investing in a holding company of a large conglomerate (say Tata Sons, the main holding company of the Tata group). The investor here is primarily looking for associate control rights and is less interested in the cash flow rights. This is opposite to the earlier example of investing in the REIT funds.

of equity positions, cross-shareholdings are horizontal equity positions in firms within the group structure, reinforcing the controlling shareholder's holding power. Readers might like to revisit the case of Tata's cross-holding structure case in Chapter 3 (Appendix 3A) to understand this in more detail.[5]

Instruments such as American Depository Receipts (ADRs), Foreign Currency Convertible Bonds (FCCBs) and Global Depository Receipts (GDRs) do not have voting rights. A most recent addition to this list is the Convertible Alternate Reference Securities (CARS), popularized by the Tata group with Tata Steel and Tata Motors issuing CARS. While all these instruments do not have voting rights, issuers such as, say, Tata Steel can compensate or reward investors by higher cash flows or reduced risks. Can one take a look at the financing of Tata Steel or Tata Motors recently—the ratings of the instruments, the backers who provided counter-guarantees and the return promised? One would observe in such instruments a trade-off between cash flow and control rights (for example, see Sivaraman and Anand [2008]).

Multiple institutions create fragmented domains of differentiated governance (and institutionalized practices!) that are linked together like a mesh. Each participant then stands on the support of others in the interconnected mesh. As financial resources flow through such meshes, participants across institutional categories would also constrain each other through different rules. The structure of the mesh is fixed at a point in time, constraining the set of possible action, but is inter-temporally more flexible as rules evolve. The fragmentation in governance means that resources do not move freely across different categories of financial institutions; it is sticky, at least over some period of time. This introduces the possibility of differential valuation dynamics specific to certain governance domains (or specific markets). Assets can have a component of valuation driven by such belongingness to a particular institutional market. Strategists in firms with links to this financial network would often profit from such dynamics, quite apart from profits generated in the product/service space.

---

[5]Academic literature points that the incentive and opportunities for controlling shareholders to expropriate wealth via the transfer of assets and earnings from minority shareholders of firms in which they have low cash flow rights to firms where they have higher cash flow rights increases as the distance between the control rights and cash flow rights increases. The phenomenon is often referred to as tunnelling (for more, please refer to works by Marrisetty, 2005).

> Readers may recall the large availability of private equity type investments (from Western PE firms) for buyout of fledgling networks of modern multi-brand retail outlets in India a few years back. Can one imagine an entry into this business and a quick rollout of outlets by promoter groups with an eye on the exit market through sell-off? Can such intent give a short shrift to concerns of sustainable profitability of the business and concentrate instead on dimensions used in the valuation of assets in this space by the private equity groups?

For a small enterprise without a linkage to the multi-intermediated financial domain or having no interest in the same, such opportunities do not exist and he/she lies tied to the product/service mode of surplus generation more tightly.

Financial intermediation then is not just about movement of money; crucially, it is about transformation in the governance of the finances that move thus. Acts of strategists occupying different nooks of the differentiated governance space in the financial domain influence the flow of financial resources across different governance domains. Such acts are mostly of novel rule-crafting and we explore a few such episodes in this chapter. It leads to a change in the quantity of financial resources that a particular mode of governance commands in deploying it in the proverbial real sector firm/organization. Organizational strategists, similarly, take note of such changes in financial resource availability under different financial intermediation mechanisms (and hence different governance modes) in choosing paths of growth they would adopt. We have then a deeply institutional market rather than a simple price-based market. Often financing would not be available to several types of borrowers, such as, say, small firms or very poor consumers, because within the rule structures, they remain unattractive customers. An innovative rule design, informed often by a deeper understanding of the field, can ease the flow of finances into such domains. We provide a narration below of an initiative to provide loans, mostly consumption loans, to very poor consumers in Bangladesh (also see Appendix 5A).

> SafeSave created in Bangladesh a network of financing system that provided integrated savings-cum-loan products (with a very simple design) to extremely poor people. Its system design, including the accounts/record

> system was developed to keep variable cost of transaction as well as overhead costs at the lowest. It departed from the practice of group-based lending (such as through self-help groups) made popular across the world through celebration of the Grameen Bank's model. Group-based monitoring excluded several people, particularly the poorest in a locality. For the non-bankable population who were slightly better off, Grameen provided a working model, but it left out a large segment. SafeSave was meant to address that segment. Instead of monitoring through peerage, SafeSave simply based itself on close governance among the frontline SafeSave employees, usually through intensified contacts. Would the model be scalable? What problems might it face as it grows or should it prefer retaining its small size? Does our discussion in the chapter on organization help you think through the problem as well? (A more detailed account is provided in Appendix 5A.)

This interconnectedness of financial intermediaries and the dynamics it generates is the second dimension we explore.

Our discussion in this chapter would bring out two different types of governance exercised by the financial world. On one hand, finance seeks an extreme form of commoditization or standardization across all asset holders in a particular class, such as, say, in a stock exchange-based valuation contest between firms in one industry. In this type, finance seeks to obliterate all distinctions between underlying assets and reduce it to price–quantity dimensions alone. We earlier argued in Chapter 4 about Walrasian-type competitive markets as similarly seeking this type of extreme standardization. On the other hand, finance on an increasing returns governance mode seeks to support the development of differentiated assets in order to release an increasing returns dynamics, from which the financier would benefit as well. This dichotomy between the two modes of financial deployment and hence governance—a decreasing returns mode that commoditizes and an increasing returns mode that generates differentiated assets—extends into the financial domain the implications of this fundamental difference we sought to argue on throughout our narration in this book. Increasing returns stance would not only seek new organizational forms and new forms of interorganizational dynamic coordination as we argued in Chapters 3 and 4, respectively, but would also need to be backed as well by financiers pursuing the increasing returns mode of governance. Without such support from the domain of finance, the increasing returns product stance, for instance, cannot stand on its own.

5.1 THE NOTION OF 'INSTITUTIONAL MOORINGS' OF FINANCE

Capital is often seen merely from a resource point of view, that is, to be accessed from the wider market that is external to the firm; the quantity dimension—volume and price—is what is emphasized in such a view. But capital, in several accounts, particularly in the works of the Austrian school of economists, has been viewed differently. Capital is a right to deferment of consumption—it is a 'voice' weaved around the provision of financial resources; it is a privilege therefore to choose or, more aptly, to place a bet on a particular trajectory of evolution of the future. It also then has a dimension of 'expectation' and would need to look into the future. This power and influence around deployment of financial resources is an act of strategy.

Exercise of this act cannot be accomplished through ex-ante rational justification alone derived from past experiences of investments—for that would only entrench old modes and remove the role of surprises. It cannot also be based on evaluations alone on which very wide consensus exists (or which is understood and voted favourably by all), for that would be merely going with the herd and the death of individual entrepreneur judgement. There must be elements of speculation as well—a suggestive discourse on build-up of a potentiality that the investment seeks to unfold, which is shared by an ecosystem creating the novel future. When a venture capitalist finances a technology proposition, or when Subhash Chandra finances the ICL, speculation on a potential new world, on unrealized possibilities, is very important and a part of the success of the moves lies in how ecosystem participants can get entangled in transaction meshes weaved around the novel speculative world. The proverbial entrepreneur, however, in the contemporary world is dependent on external financing sourced and secured from one or the other financial intermediary—making the entrepreneurial move contingent on gaining the support or the vetting from the financier intermediary.

As indicated earlier, contemporary financial systems are composed of several institutions, where the deployment of 'capital' is constrained by varying institutional norms of allocation that are relatively rigid over different time horizons. Financial resources can move only based on implicit compliance with institutions and underlying rules. Large swathes of the financial domain operate under such structured constraints; the relative asset category allocation under which a mutual fund or insurance fund manager operates, for instance, is flexible only in inter-temporal rounds when such allocation rules come under review.[6] Under a rigid rule structure, manager of financial resources often would seek to park finance in investments that generate higher returns. Such a discourse remains concerned with the quantity and price dimensions of transactions. Finance is in the resource mode, then. But the creation of spaces where such structures of inertia can be circumvented (to create a new rule or governance) is crucial to retaining innovative dynamics in the economy; such spaces also being the ones that would offer speculative profits that are beyond mere rents.[7] VC and other forms of private equity have been such institutions within the modern financial system. It constitutes innovative acts of financial re-intermediation—as we will demonstrate with examples of the leveraged buyout (LBO)[8] firm KKR or other VC firms—depending on the supply side for access to financial resources on the large institutions that were at the same time structurally constrained from acting in ways that the intermediary could choose to act. Such novel rule-making acts, or what we call innovative intermediation, would need to concern itself with the dimension of governance and a tweak in it that releases a new line of flow of financial resources.

So, in moving financial resources from the large financial institutions to the intermediaries, the mode of deployment of the finances changed; a relative unshackling of the constraints of the financial resource holder

---

[6] For example, a mutual fund reviews its criteria of creating asset portfolios no more than once a year.

[7] *Financial engineering, financial restructuring* often refer to such type of acts. A few instruments used in executing the same would include convertible instruments, asset-backed securitization, receivables-backed securitization, structured products, warrants, sweat equity, stock options, performance bonuses, Non Disposable Undertaking with Power of Attorney (NDU-POA) backed structures, and funding through overseas subsidiaries to overcome regulatory hurdles.

[8] A *leveraged buyout* (or LBO, or highly-leveraged transaction [HLT], or 'bootstrap' transaction) occurs when a financial sponsor acquires a controlling interest in a company's equity, financing it through leverage (borrowing). The assets of the acquired company are used as collateral for the borrowed capital. The bonds or other paper issued for leveraged buyouts are commonly considered high-risk assets. In January 1982, former US Secretary of the Treasury William Simon and a group of investors acquired Gibson Greetings, a producer of greeting cards, for USD 80 million, of which only USD 1 million was rumoured to have been contributed by the investors. By mid-1983, just 16 months after the original deal, Gibson completed a USD 290 million IPO and Simon made approximately USD 66 million. The success of the Gibson Greetings investment attracted the attention of the wider media to the nascent boom in leveraged buyouts. Between 1979 and 1989, it was estimated that there were over 2,000 leveraged buyouts valued in excess of USD 250 billion in the US.

occurring through the intermediation act—this mode of deployment and its change, we argue, is crucial from a strategy viewpoint. The personal supervision and board level governance played by VCs that enabled innovative products and firms (Apple or eBay) to unfold, or the role in direct governance played by LBO firms such as KKR to drive a new dynamics of efficiency in firms in old utility/manufacturing industries, focusing on asset-utilization (rather than asset expansion!), would not have been possible for bank-type financial institutions to execute within their extant norms (or institutions) of practice.

This mode of deployment of finances and the specific governance role it plays, we call the institutional moorings of finance—it defines the constraint to which the product market strategist has to pay heed. This 'institutional mooring of finance' not only has a diversity—variations of norms across a spectrum, as we argued—but is also in a state of flux, in constant evolution. Strategic moves in the financial domain, as we argued above, alter the quantitative resource availability under different modes of governance for investing in real projects. In what follows, we narrate a few instantiations of the diversity in 'institutional moorings of finance'. The narratives presented below—culled out of business history, primarily of the US—do not always lead to construction of a coherent, interconnected framework but provides an interesting interpretation which has been previously not highlighted in the domain of strategy.[9]

5.1.1 The role of finance in the rise of large corporations

The archetypical construct of contemporary economy is a large divisionalized corporation (often vertically integrated), exemplified by the likes of Ford Motor Company or Tata Steel. In the US, such large corporations have been hailed as entities that ushered in the era of 'managerial capitalism', where subject to the fiduciary obligation towards shareholders, managers would have significant control rights over the corporation. In much of the developing world, however, it is the promoter families that continue to be powerful in exercising control. While technological possibilities of large-scale production is viewed as an important reason for the rise of large vertically integrated corporations during the early years

---

[9]Of course, it provides a reading that does not claim certitude of being the only interpretation possible.

of the 20th century in the US, as Alfred Chandler explained—the role of Wall Street and the pre-eminent financier of those days, J.P. Morgan of the Morgan House, for instance, was equally crucial in the development of these large corporations.

The deployment of technologies of vertical integration required sustained capital asset accumulation over prolonged periods of time, and such 'system builders' often got into conflicts over utilization of current surpluses—shareholders often claiming enhanced dividend payouts. Theodore Vail, the genius of telecommunications, for instance, quit his job as head of AT&T in 1885, frustrated by the long squabbles over resources with conservative Boston financiers who enjoyed considerable control rights over the firms in which they had significant shareholding. The financiers could not understand or did not agree with the trajectory of system-building investment that Vail argued for. It was partly J.P. Morgan's genius and financial crafting that carved out a way for managers such as Vail to introduce the rational 'system-building' technology investments. In several restructurings led by the Morgan House, very high leverages were used to buy out independent companies. The capital structure of US Steel, one of the integrated corporations that J.P. Morgan helped put together, was more than 60 per cent leveraged. The purchase of assets was financed at substantial premiums as well. J.P. Morgan's ability to put the funds together by crafting innovative financing instruments effectively shielded managers from the pressures of quick returns. While a large number of investors provided the financial resources subscribing to various kinds of financial instruments—they lost 'voice' and control over deployment of the finances—Morgan as an intermediary took up such a fiduciary role on their behalf. Morgan's positive bet on the technology investment trajectory and vertical and horizontal consolidations proved crucial in the return of people like Vail to powerful positions.[10] The centralization of finances and the towering voice of financiers such as the Morgan family were as important as technology in creating the foundations of 20th-century US big business and its epitome—the vertically integrated corporation which soon morphed into the multi-divisional structure.

---

[10] J.P. Morgan was known for his appetite for industrial restructurings that would create mega integrated corporations and he presided over the creation of several such enterprises, starting with the consolidation of US railroads, over his lifetime. Not all of it succeeded and his most remarkable failure was the vertically integrated shipping and maritime services corporation, which floundered soon after its creation.

How crucial was the role of financiers such as J.P. Morgan in shaping the formation of vertically integrated behemoths? Scholarship is divided on this. The Morgan house definitely worked on a potential of new efficiencies that the coordination of large throughput (continuous output) provided to the new corporations. Recall our argument regarding the scale economy-based corporation as a mode of exercising control over a large fixed asset which can yield cost savings if its utilization is maximized. Are such high levels of coordination, required in large throughput production systems, possible without vertical and horizontal integration? It is more difficult to answer this. Experience with several contemporary industries, such as mobile phones, does indicate such a possibility, but it requires considerable activities of coordination to be carried out at inter-firm boundaries, at social interstices. Many activities of that kind—such as creation of shared database services, standards setting processes, modularization moves and public interface standards of such modularized product systems—were financed through venture capitalist activities close to a century later in the US. VC financing, in a way, chose a mode relying much more on a network of firms as the underlying architecture of 'real sector firms' rather than the vertically integrated form, radically differing from the pattern exhibited by the Morgan house at the beginning of the 20th century.[11]

5.1.2 The eclipse of financial capitalists

This powerful dominance of the 'financial capitalists' came to be questioned during the first half of the 20th century, and particularly as the US economy came out of the depression of the 1920s, a significant element of the political deal was to clip the power of Wall Street financiers. Several contemporary US financial institutions—the Securities and Exchange Commission (SEC) as well as the NASDAQ (which we will discuss later)—were creations of these times. One way in which the significant

---

[11]Take the example of the present mobile industry—there are multiple players interacting in a complicated business network to ensure a mobile value added service (VAS). The list would include a mobile equipment manufacturer, a mobile network operator, a mobile software application provider, a mobile content provider and a mobile content aggregator—the different activities taken up by different players, both competing and collaborating at the same time. In the Morgan era, it would probably have been the purview of a single firm ensuring all of the above using vertical integration strategy. Our discussion in Chapter 3 on organization of DoCoMo i-mode business provides a contrast (see case study 3.5).

sway that Wall Street held over the economy was sought to be countered was through creation of regulatory boundaries between activities of various types of financial institutions and restricting the discretionary rights of financial institutions and their role in governance of corporations. Managers in large corporations, thus, obtained huge amounts of discretionary powers—introducing the possibilities of opportunism on their part. Discourses around principal–agent problems, managerial hubris[12] and such other rhetoric began occupying the attention of much of financial economics.

5.1.2.1 Principal–agent problem

This refers to the conflict of interest between the principal (shareholder, in this case) and the agent (manager), who is to act 'in good faith' on behalf of the principal in taking decisions regarding the firm's activities and investments. The conflict of interest might lead to opportunistic behaviour—the manager acting in ways that lead to gains for managers at the cost of the principal (shareholders). This is especially so since asymmetries of information between the 'insider' manager and the 'outsider' shareholder (unfamiliar with the contextual nuances of the business) is intense, making monitoring of managerial behaviour extremely difficult. However, the articulation of the principal–agent problem rests on a limited legal articulation of shareholder as a holder of 'residual rights' after all contracted claims on the 'firm as legal entity' have been met. Residual rights, in an ex-ante sense, differ from the ex-post sense. Concepts of shareholders as lone residual-rights claimant, in an ex-ante sense, would deny any discretionary rights to managers either to decide or to enjoy partly the fruits of such decisions. Although such denial would be justified from the viewpoint of shareholders as a check on opportunism or more often fraudulent behaviour of managers; one may note that in the face of uncertainty, it is quite difficult to differentiate practically between wilful opportunism and an 'entrepreneurial-judgement-driven' speculative bet. Managers cannot therefore take a decision over states that are beyond contractual definition, yet control over decision-making in such states is precisely the domain of strategy. It implies, therefore, that managers can hardly strategize any more. Recall our earlier argument regarding risk

---

[12]'Managerial hubris' refers to managers' systematic overestimation of their abilities and making ill-advised decisions (especially on acquisitions) that expand their span and scope of control.

contracting with stars in Bollywood and how it differs from the corporate employment contract with managers. Possibly then, corporations were constructs for efficiency realization, since an incentivized manager can be an efficiency enhancing agent and not a creative dealmaker. A concern with efficient utilization can only lead along a decreasing returns track, albeit with a caveat that a powerful deterrence would delay the advent of such decreasing returns. Corporations, by design then, are decreasing returns structures.

Several contemporary forms of financial contracting, such as VC contracts, take a more nuanced view of residual rights and slice up control rights into various categories of rights (some of which can be contingent rights) and allocate it to different categories of investors, depending on who is best placed to execute a particular control right effectively.[13] Separation (and even unbundling) of cash flow rights vis-à-vis various types of control rights occur. This can be viewed as an attempt to get over the principal–agent type of problems. If we look carefully at economic systems, even in the US, the descriptions of corporate structures that we usually are familiar with refers to only a certain segment. Large areas of businesses that fed into and supplemented the decreasing returns corporate structures worked under quite different governance norms. Innovation was often fostered in dense network markets of Silicon Valley or in public universities or by executive power holders at nodal institutional points. It is only in the presence of such increasing returns spaces that the decreasing returns structures could renew itself and restructure with new assets that provided it, so to say, a fresh lease of life. Readers may recall our discussion regarding the DoCoMo i-mode case in Chapter 3 (case study 3.5).

5.2 PROFUSE DISCLOSURE OF INFORMATION: A GOVERNANCE TOOL USED BY THE SHAREHOLDERS

One way out of the problem of 'managerial opportunism' has been increased disclosures—seeking a profuse disclosure of information about the firm to reduce the information asymmetry. But outside investors far

---

[13]VCs make use of instruments such as optionally convertible debentures, warrants and stock options.

removed from the context of the actual product/service markets or the technologies of operations can have access only to de-contextualized information—which limits the role it can play in the monitoring of managers, who are insiders. The understanding or the dynamic reading of an information piece—which better captures its business potential—need not occur just with a release of new information; the contextual reading of the information piece is vital. The tool of governance, therefore, has been to set up comparative benchmarks across similar firms—contests on benchmarks can provide information that can aid the cause of monitoring and governance, even without the richness of the deep context which outside investors anyway do not have access to. Benchmarking and organization of efficiency races (or competition) around publicly visible and verifiable benchmarks then is a governance tool, quite similar to the Walrasian competitive marketplaces as a governance tool. Both reduce the contest to singular dimensions, forcing a low conformance on multiple other dimensions of an asset. This conformance around the 'other' dimensions that are thus given a short shrift is at the root of devalorization of such 'neglected' dimensions. We provide an example below:

> Morgan Stanley Capital International (MSCI) created the MSCI Emerging Market Index comprising of about 700 stocks in the emerging markets ecosystem: the 26 emerging economies ranging from Argentina, China and Hungary to South Africa and Venezuela. Emerging markets are countries considered to be relatively less developed, have less per capita income, and are considered relatively risky but have better growth prospects than the developed countries. There are several facets of this that are interesting. From an investor's point of view, the index provides a way of taking an exposure to the emerging markets at a transaction cost that is lower than the cost of holding/trading the underlying securities.[14] But the index also brings to focus the emerging economies in relation to other countries and the economy-wide benchmarks—a focus that can lead to more concentrated analyst monitoring of the emerging markets. For the companies whose stocks constitute the

---

[14]For a sample product, please see, http://ssga.com/weblogic/strategyDetailsPublic?st=/indx_eqt_strg_MSCM.jsp (accessed on 10 December 2008).

> index, this grabbing of investor/analyst attention would create an industry reputation, while races and contests amongst the companies[15] can generate firm-specific reputation as well. The move therefore is like creating a turf. Increased analyst activities and scrutiny would lead to development of certain emerging markets-specific, country-specific and even industry-specific indicators on which comparative races can be adjudged or ratings arrived at. Companies, in sending signals to the investor/analyst world, would remain constrained to the use of those rating indicators. Since it would influence valuations, indicators would also influence managerial decision-making within the firm as it brings in a mechanism of bringing in intense scrutiny. Readers may note that reduction of all underlying differences between assets to a unidimensional risk–return discourse (a homogenization or standardization, in other words) makes it amenable to price-based market governance.

Index construction then is a mechanism to bring the assets within the index under renewed vigorous governance. It expands the market of the asset as well—since index investors who otherwise could not have participated in the asset market also joins in to shape the demand. Such a participant in an index market would possibly look into the asset as only a part of the index and the risk–return performance of the index would be what would be monitored with respect to other indexes or investment options. Several other features of the asset, particularly specific features, say related to the governance of the particular firm, would not draw the attention of the index trader. Indexation is thus an extreme form of commoditization—generating a very liquid asset. Contrarily, one can note that a private equity group or a venture capitalist would be interested in such specific details and would play a role in its governance. In contrast to the pressures for homogenization generated by an index-trading market, VC profits from governance of novelty. It is thus an increasing returns institution, quite different from the index fund trader. We provide below another description of pressures from equity analysts and the equity trading ecosystem that pushed firms towards asset structure homogenization.

---

[15]Performance of the stocks relative to each other would lead in inter-temporal rounds in revision of the weightage provided to each of the stocks in the index.

Diversified corporations in the US currently face severe pressures from equity analysts who track the firm's performance to de-diversify and create asset structures that conform to the accepted industry categories. For certain purposes, the public corporation may be likened to a product. Traditional approaches to the issue of corporate control have generally regarded such sensitivity to shareholder wishes as unproblematic: since investors want nothing more than a high return on their investment, adjusting a firm's strategy so that it increases such returns was normal. But how does a shareholder or an outsider value the corporate product? This challenge is particularly acute because corporate shares are social goods in that they are generally valuable to their owners only if others come to value them highly as well. As a result, investors are highly sensitive to prevalent valuation methods and their associated categories. Such categories typically become entrenched as they are embedded in structures such as the analysts' division of labour. Each analyst would generally follow all or few firms across a few industries. Firms belong to industries and in that sense to a peer group and analysts would have excel models specific to industries that capture the financial interlinkage between different publicly available information pieces. On top of the industry excel sheets would be a few more relations that capture the firm idiosyncrasies. The benchmarks of the peer group provide the anchor in relation to which a firm can be valued. The equity analyst's role as crucial intermediary in framing financial performance information and the specific organization (or division of labour) in the industry shapes an institutional requirement of homogenization of asset structures of firms in a particular industry. Firms with diversified portfolio of assets (belonging to different industries) had a great disadvantage in not getting adequate analyst coverage, depressing the demand for their scrip in equity markets. A significant aspect of US equity market design has been the ability of the investor groups in forcing this institutional conformance that enhances the governance of outside shareholders. Such categories shaping valuation and benchmarking has been always there—in the early 20th century, such categories were differentiated as railways, utilities, and so on. From 1940s onwards, as corporates diversified, a new category arose called 'conglomerates' to which several firms belonged. They were difficult to value, but they had analyst following. Gradually as the 'diversified' category lost reputation, the category was deinstitutionalized, and firms faced valuation problems even if financial performance was good. In several other countries, including India, one would not notice

> such pressures for homogenization of the corporate product. It would seem, then, that control by public market investors is not a pristine state in which only issues related to a firm's income stream guide its actions but that such control introduces powerful constraints on corporate strategy. Accordingly, A. H. Stromberg of the URS Corp. summarized his feelings after having succumbed to analyst pressure to spin off its computer training subsidiary by saying, 'In a perfect world, I don't know if we would be public right now' (excerpts from Zuckerman, 2000: 591–619).

While the above description brings out the significance of the institutional structure of the financial intermediation mechanism in restraining corporate action, shaping basic acts such as choice of businesses to enter, it also points to a possible mode of creative engagement with the milieu of the analysts. Since pressures to belong to a category is what is significant, the process of creation of new categories would be required to bring about new asset structure combinations inside the corporate. In fact, several such category boundary redefinitions were carried out by star equity analysts during the dot-com boom towards the end of the last century. There was, for instance, a great tussle among two groups of analysts who proposed two models for valuation of Amazon.com type of firms—the conflict being what kind of a revenue/business model Amazon would have once it matured and realized the plans that it had on board. One group argued it would be like Dell (mass customization of consumer product), while the other felt it would be like Barnes and Noble (book selling industry). What would be a closest representative of a future Amazon was of concern! Of course, if one agreed to a close representative, valuation of future cash flows could be attempted. The large valuation of Amazon was supported by the group that proposed a Dell-like similarity (comparison to a similar asset). These proposed valuation models, or industry categories, are then dynamically formed—a few new propositions lose out and a few others get institutionalized as their star proposers win over the milieu over time, sustained by, of course, rounds of inter-temporal wins in this game of uncertainty. As a corporate manager, then, would one take interest in this dynamics of the equity analyst groups, and how would that constrain your investment horizons?

Such forces of homogenization would also require a profuse generation of information broadcast most often supported by regulation that forces disclosure. Information dissemination supports the external governance through price-based competition. In fact, it is an essential corollary. Take the instance of recent changes (from 2005 onwards) sought in accounting and disclosure standards that seek to force listed firms to release information on sensitivities of corporate earnings to variations in macroeconomic variables, such as interest rates, currency exchange rates, inflation rates, and so on. If such information is released, it leads to unbundling of information that points towards firm-specific performance from information that portrays the effects of macroeconomic factors. This is a loss of power for the managers. Yet, from the investors' viewpoint, the presence of risk markets for all such macro-variables would mean that a reasonably sophisticated institutional investor can hedge such risks (or take positions in it) in other risk markets and not depend on the firm managers to provide such risk hedging services bundled with firm-specific risks/returns. Unbundling and release of information allows outside financial investors in a firm to straddle multiple risk markets. Much of the Sarbanes–Oxley legislation introduced in the US a few years ago was conceived with a similar purpose to ensure more control to shareholders.

While information disclosure can serve the purpose of limiting the agency costs—reducing the possibilities of managerial opportunism—it tilts the management mandate significantly towards 'exploitation' of assets to an efficiency discourse. Exploration, as a mode, which can pursue innovative tracks, not yet widely shared amongst the 'group of firms' being benchmarked, becomes more difficult to adopt for any single firm within a group. Such moves would have to be taken up in something like a 'stealth mode', since the significance of it cannot be signalled to analysts/investors who would value the firm. Novel moves would need to have significant ex-ante coordination amongst a group of comparative firms to be pursued.

5.3 THE RECENT RISE OF PRIVATE EQUITY

The rise of private equity in the US (and globally) is another mechanism through which the institution of 'managerial capitalism'—the hall mark of the post-World War II economy (and the world of Chandler's visible hand[16])—has been breached. Private equity, in terms of definition, can refer to equity of privately held companies—where the owner manager desists from raising equity resources from the public equity markets, and hence as a corollary does not require publishing information, except when business considerations require such disclosures. Most family-based owner-managed enterprises are privately held firms. Unlike popular conceptions, the domain of such privately held firms is substantial and they constitute a wide array of types of firms in several businesses. Without the pressures of profuse information disclosures, such firms can pursue strategies unencumbered by the need to generate ex-ante agreement amongst 'large groups' of investors. But such firms remain relatively smaller.

The current connotation of private equity, however, refers to a distinct phenomenon that is tied to the modus operandi of firms such as Kohlberg Kravis and Roberts (KKR) or Blackstone. Typically, Blackstone or KKR would raise a fund for a particular purpose, say investing in the precious metal ecosystem or in a particular emerging market. Investors would subscribe to such a fund. The proceeds of the fund would be invested in assets in the indicated field and after a specified period, the assets would be sold and the fund liquidated, money being returned to the investors along with the capital gains. Blackstone would earn commissions on the funds managed as well as participate in the capital gains realized in the fund investments as a general partner of the fund. Partners of Blackstone or KKR would manage the investments actively, often sitting on the boards, using the voice to change key people or change investment and strategic direction of the companies in which they would invest. In terms of motive, therefore, private equity buys into assets with an explicit purpose of selling and realizing a capital gain on such sales; it constitutes a form of 'serial entrepreneurship', each assignment for a private equity partner being a 'time delimited project'. Private equity brings in the discipline of personal ownership (such as we witness in small private companies) ensuring low probability of resources mismanagement, yet can access huge amounts of financial resources through interfacing

---

[16]In his book titled *The Visible Hand*, Alfred Chandler argued that American business history can be separated into two phases: pre-1850 and post-1850. He contended that the first phase represents the market economy, that is, characterized by perfect competition. The second phase, continuing to the 1990s, represents what he calls managerial capitalism. The transition between these two periods constituted a revolution in American business enterprise, for it transferred operation of a company from the owner or partners to a full-time, salaried manager.

with large financial institutions who subscribe to its limited purpose funds. Case study 5.3 captures in some detail the exploits of KKR.

Kohlberg Kravis and Roberts (KKR) and its accomplishments

In 1976, a trio of dealmakers (Jerome Kohlberg, Henry Kravis and George Roberts) left their job with Bear, Stearns & Co Inc., setting up offices in New York and San Francisco, from where they started soliciting funds from banks and individual investors to execute their strategy of buying small companies with debt—a phenomenon that came to be christened as LBOs. KKR grew to become one of the powerhouses of big business finance and one of the more durable institutions in Wall Street. Their success was based on a somewhat novel, if not unique, approach that the trio developed over almost eight years of working together at Bear Stearns. They would buy well-established privately controlled companies with predictable streams of revenue and cash flow. In financing their acquisitions, they borrowed nearly all their money—and with the high debts or *leverage*, they minimized the cost of buying the equity—which in turn was shared with the target company managers. Assuming that the cash flows repaid the debt and the promotion of longer term efficiency was realized, in around 5–6 years, the leveraged equity could be sold for a substantial higher-than-average return.

KKR's LBO depended on several ecosystem participants and a kind of reciprocal relationship that KKR was able to forge through managing incentives and structuring of the deals. On one side were the providers of financial resources—debt managers at insurance companies and banks—particularly in KKR's case: Citibank, Prudential and First Chicago. Lawyers, accountants and attorneys in firms such as Deloitte Haskins and Sells were another group relationship with whom was crucial in crafting the deals. On the other side was a reputation that KKR built in establishing a trust and participation of the managers of the target firm who were invariably participants/contributors in the equity of the leveraged deal and whom KKR would always depend on to drive the change process forward. KKR partners themselves served as active directors on the financier dominated boards of the acquired companies, buying a voice into the company, ensuring that the strategic direction was aligned. Active monitoring was crucial to success—in a mode of partnership with the managers (who were part owners as well). The role of KKR was often to use the 'voice' to empower managers who had the energies and ambition to take the challenge of higher risks that large leverage posed. While the first set of relationships were crucial

(Case Study 5.3 contd.)

(Case Study 5.3 contd.)

in assembling the finances, managing the state and its regulators, structuring the deals to set the acquisitions up, the generation of long-term value depended on the second role that KKR partners played in internal governance of the firm—unlocking hidden value in under-managed assets, either by linking it to complementary assets or skills or unbundling it or removing cross-subsidies that hid underperformance, shifting internal control systems towards monitoring asset-utilization.[17] KKR's LBO activity reached a peak with the acquisition of RJR Nabisco in 1989, when KKR was overseeing USD 59 billion of corporate assets in 35 companies with just 6 general partners and 11 professional investment associates, supported by a staff of 47. Only four US corporations from the Fortune 500 list at that time were larger—GM, Ford, Exxon and IBM.

Crafting the design of financial structure:
Financial engineering at KKR
Crafty design of financial structures was crucial. We provide two instances. Fred Meyer Inc., which was a retail chain operating around 65 stores, mostly in Pacific North West, provides an interesting example. It required around USD 533 million in financing, but KKR raised it in two separate entities—one took up the real estate assets, while the other took control of retail operations. Since the real estate assets were the undervalued part of the

(Case Study 5.3 contd.)

---

[17] In many cases, the problem was how to force mangers to part with what Chicago school of economists—Michael Jensen being notable amongst them—called 'free cash flows'; cash flows from current operations that were in excess of the capability of managers to put to investments with an acceptable rate of return. Information on 'free cash flows' was difficult to fathom from outside and was known to managers alone inside the corporations. In a few cases, however, it could be seen from outside as well. T. Boone Pickens, who became notorious for launching a series of raids on oil firms—Cities Services, Unocal and Gulf Oil after the oil shock of the 1970s—argued that oil companies, who were then liquidating their reserves by producing more than they could replace (through exploration), were releasing a large load of free cash flows that managers were wastefully putting into asset acquisition. He suggested setting up of a 'royalty trust'—a financial arrangement through which oil companies could spin-off the reserves directly to its shareholders and thus unbundle the reserves as assets from other assets such as refineries and distribution assets. This unbundling would remove cross-subsidies that refineries or distribution enjoyed and force better asset utilization. The Pickens proposal did not, however, succeed. The conflict therefore was on how to share the rights to control the gains from a windfall profit—a sudden 'lucky' generation of immense surpluses.

(Case Study 5.3 contd.)

business, including the land under its retail stores, its revaluation provided scope for raising large amounts of financial resources. The unbundling, however, removed the implicit subsidies enjoyed by the retailing operations and induced managers to check asset expansion and concentrate on better operations and utilization of assets. The financing strategy, therefore, was crafted not with purposes of raising finances alone—but with an eye on the redesign of changes in managerial behaviour that KKR sought. Why did Fred Meyer's management fail to initiate this move on its own?

KKR's buyout of Union Texas Petroleum (UTP), owned by Allied-Signal Corporation, provides another instance of crafting of deals. When KKR was approached by Allied management for taking over UTP, it realized that the volatility of the oil business made a traditional LBO deal infeasible since stable cash flows on which to leverage was non-existent. So, KKR set up a joint venture with Allied, where Allied provided considerable risk financing under a clause that would lead to a lapse of Allied preferred stock if annual returns to KKR investors (the LBO fund) fell below 28 per cent over five years. With such a structure in place, the LBO fund could be raised. Crafty design of the financial contracts thus served to create an interface that could link up disparate groups, each with own concerns and constraints.

Expanding and nurturing the ecosystem
Hence, KKR LBOs started off with buying small good companies, mainly with a manufacturing business that would have relatively stable cash flows and the restructuring focused on increasing asset utilization. As it achieved success, its relationships with debt and equity investors evolved and it could raise larger pools of resources. As institutional investors (both on debt and equity side) gained confidence in the efficacy of the new mode, it led to creation of new asset classes in the portfolio of these institutions and it became easier for KKR to expand. In 1982, the first pension fund participated in KKR LBO fund; in 1984, the Harvard endowment fund[18] pledged finances, expanding the ecosystem both in terms of volumes of financial resources that KKR could access and the variety of institutional moorings (clauses and covenants) of such financial participation. By 1984, KKR gained access to another novel instrument—the 'junk bond', pioneered by bond specialist Michael Milken of Drexel Lambert.[19] Junk bonds were high-yield bonds that Milken started

(Case Study 5.3 contd.)

---

[18]See Appendix 5E for a write-up on University Endowment Fund at the end of this chapter.

[19]An account of Drexel and Milken can be had from Connie Bruck's *The Predators' Ball* (1988).

(Case Study 5.3 contd.)

placing within a large financial network that operated on 'trust' in a rather unbureaucratic way. Milken had a remarkable 'personal sway' over this network; Drexel's 'highly confident letter', though not a guarantee, had become a virtual assurance to the markets that the debts for a certain transaction would be placed and Milken almost never reneged on it. He also could have an enormous influence in striking deals amongst participants in times of financial distress—reworking debt schedules—that considerably brought down the bankruptcy costs. Through the second half of the 1980s, KKR's large LBOs increasingly depended on Drexel's ability to place junk bonds, including the Nabisco mega deal, till the junk bond market collapsed around the early 1990s.[20] As the pool of fund expanded, KKR deals increased in size and it became involved in the merger wave of those times, taking over large publicly listed conglomerates. KKR, in the Nabisco deal, played a role quite unlike his earlier ones—it supervised an extensive restructuring exercise, with asset sales and spin-offs of the huge unwieldy assortment of businesses which was built up by the group—a mega break-up of a huge conglomerate.

KKR, therefore, is a classic intermediary—a link between the financial institutions and the corporate boardroom that filled an institutional void that could carve out a specific mode of solution to the governance crisis, which literature has characterized as the agency problems. The financial institutions' incapability in exercising effective governance over corporations, to which it was a significant source of funds, was partly because of their own conflict of interest and the stance that regulation in the US took to try ameliorating that conflict, which influenced the practices of these institutions.[21] The net effect of that, however, was a problem of enhanced agency conflicts at the corporations

(Case Study 5.3 contd.)

---

[20]The banking crisis in the US in 1987 (debt defaults on Third World loans, crisis in Savings and Loans [S&L] institutions) led to the enactment of *Financial Institutions Reform, Recovery and Enforcement Act*. It required banks to increase their capital adequacy ratios. It also required S&L institutions to offload 'junk bonds' by 1994. They then held around 7 per cent of 'junk bonds' in the market and their offloading led to crisis of confidence, weakening the ability of Drexel—the key market maker—to maintain an orderly market. In 1990, Drexel filed for bankruptcy, while Milken was charged for securities law violations in 1989. Sometime later, regulations also increased the costs of out-of-court bankruptcy settlements by limiting the amount that bond holders could expect from informal exchanges.

[21]As part of New Deal arrangements and a series of regulatory interventions after that, the power of financial institutions to hold large equity blocks and influence managers was deliberately curtailed in the US. Banks could own very little of stocks; mutual funds,

(Case Study 5.3 contd.)

> as shareholders' control over managers diminished. The LBO technique—as financial engineering, therefore—can also be seen as an institutional innovation that brought back the financier's 'voice' into the boardroom of the corporation, reinventing in a way the personal supervision that early 20th-century financial houses, such as J.P. Morgan of the Morgan House, exercised when the foundations of the Chandler-type corporations were laid in the US. The crafty design of the financial structure and the equity participation of the managers created the cooperative milieu that would enable this strategy of storming of the boardroom, so to say, to perform the missing fiduciary role resulting in unlocking of shareholder value.[22] The rise of the institutional void that the KKR kind of move filled must, therefore, be understood only in relation to the concrete context that created the void. This specific institutional reading of a strategic move, in the richness of its context, is a theme that we have reiterated several times over the course of our arguments.
>
> The KKR deals also reveal how important a role financial engineering played in back-to-back linkages amongst different domains of finance. For the institutional investors, the KKR kind of LBO and private equity funds represented a new asset class—a new category that promised greater than average returns to the funds they were paid to invest. Enterprising fund managers and funds, such as the Harvard Endowment Fund that had the mandate to constantly scout for such novel alternatives, were the initial points of contact of KKR. To KKR, this was a story of gaining access to the financial pool lying in relatively conservative quarters and deploying it in a novel mode to fill an institutional void. Linkage of the two motives constituted the successful strategy execution. (Based on Baker and Smith, 1998.)

The rise of KKR and Blackstone epitomizes a particular form of this new phenomenon, which led to new pressures for exploitation of 'efficiencies' in organizations. In another form, private equity took the route of VC financing, where the focus was different—on seeking novelty, primarily attached to technology and its deployment. But VCs also shared a similar concern—investing to sell, the fundamental feature of serial entrepreneurship.

---

pension funds and insurance companies could not own significant chunks of shares in a single firm to have risk diversification through holding of wide portfolios, while pension funds often had the additional problem that they were substantially controlled by managers of the sponsoring corporations.

[22]Malcolm Salter of Harvard has christened KKR as the 'repair shop of capitalism'. The epithet well sums up their role as financial capitalists.

5.4 VENTURE CAPITAL AS A NEW MODE OF FINANCING INNOVATION

The VC model of financing, especially around Silicon Valley, constitutes another novel mode of governance driven by providers of finance who have unleashed a series of winning financing innovations in contemporary industries such as information technology, including computer hardware and software, biotechnology and bioinformatics. One specific feature of the VC model is the importance of personal supervision and control exercised by the VC on the start-up firm, both through presence in boards and management committees as well as crafty designs of the shareholder agreement (or contract). It differs from the weak governance exercised from a 'distance' by banks holding a debt contract or public equity holders who depend on price signals (of the stock) alone in a secondary market to indirectly exercise a control. Moreover, both these players lacked the wherewithal to understand and manage the dynamics of these then nascent growth sectors. VC control modes are direct, in contrast, and involve the exercise of business judgement not always defensible in a court of law—in a sense, it supersedes the mere application of rules/procedures. The first VC firms—such as Warburg Pincus—began out of a realization amongst sections of the investment banking community that traditional investment banking and financing activities had become impersonal and standardized, remaining limited to balance sheet information based financing, without any significant insights into operations or underlying strategies of firms. Investment bankers hardly cared for such detailed understandings of operations of firms they were financing. Such financing modes meant that novel moves and technology investments could not signal to the financial world for possible financing—a market failure loomed large as a result. Separate funds were formed, therefore, which were smaller and could concentrate in financing, with care and with personal involvement of fund partners, a smaller number of projects—the hope being generation of windfall profit streams.

Like other private equity funds, VC funds also engage in active governance, and invest in companies (start-ups) with the intent to eventually exit after a brief period—5–10 years in most cases—either through acquisition by a large firm or by sale in the public equity market through an IPO. The existence of the exit option—the presence of an equity market that encourages the listing of new firms with promising technology, such as NASDAQ—is crucial to the working out of the VC model. The focus of VC funds, however, is novel technologies and ideas; they specialize in financing projects that work on an 'exploration' mode in creating novel assets as opposed to 'exploitation' modes of utilizing existing assets, which we discussed in the context of the LBO firm. How does the VC fund manage the financial risk that accompanies such risky investments?

First, VC contracts unbundle cash flow rights and control rights in the design of shareholder contracts. When a venture capitalist decides to finance a start-up, elaborate financing and employment agreements are drawn up between the venture capitalist and the entrepreneur. At the beginning of a start-up life, the venture capitalist commits only a fraction of the capital needed to complete the project, with the expectation that additional financing will be made stepwise, contingent upon the project proceeding smoothly. This is a process that is called 'staged' capital commitment—the openness of future rounds of financing providing a significant control lever to the VC. They retain an exit option exercisable by refusing additional financing at a critical moment when a start-up firm needs an infusion of new funds to survive. Financing by venture capitalists normally takes the form of convertible preferred stocks or subordinate debt with convertible privileges. This means that they are paid prior to holders of common stock in the event of project failure. However, a typical shareholding agreement allows an entrepreneur to increase his/her ownership share (normally in common stock) at the expense of investors, if certain performance objectives (such as pre-decided technology benchmarks) are met. Fired entrepreneurs forfeit their claims on stock that has not been vested. In general, as the partnership evolves, the sharing of rights between the entrepreneur and the VC changes—in the event of successful meeting of interim targets and positive evaluation of outcomes, the VC tends to give up control rights to the entrepreneur desisting from intrusive monitoring/governance (which also increases his costs)—while failure to meet interim objectives by the founding entrepreneur leads to increase in control rights by the VC. The contract, therefore, has contingent clauses based on predefined milestone triggers[23]—enabling renegotiation of rights as the partnership evolves and initial uncertainties get resolved.

Venture capitalists are well represented on the boards of directors of start-up firms. In addition to attending board meetings, leading venture capitalists often visit entrepreneurs cum senior managers at the site of

---

[23]These milestone triggers are usually based on revenue targets, net income targets, technology development targets or even customer visit targets.

venture-funded firms. They provide a wide range of advice and consulting services to senior management, help to raise additional funds, review and assist with strategic planning, recruit financial and human resource managers, introduce potential customers and suppliers and provide public relations and legal specialists. They also actively exercise conventional roles in the governance of the start-up firms, often firing the founder-managers when needed, such VC induced change in management being quite common. Finally, in case of successful ventures, VC retains considerable say in deciding on the appropriate exit strategy. The range of roles played by VCs vis-à-vis entrepreneurial firms include ex-ante monitoring, that is, screening of proposed projects to cope with the possible adverse selection problem; ad interim monitoring; ex-post monitoring, that is, the verification of a project result and the controlling decision as to which exit strategy is to be exercised. The monitoring function of the VC is multifold. Ex-ante monitoring requires risk-taking entrepreneurial instinct and ability to draw road maps of technological development. Interim monitoring requires professional engineering competence in specialized fields and management skills. Ex-post monitoring requires financial expertise. Considerable sharing of information obviously occurs amongst VCs, such as through consortium modes of financing or through provision of expert advice/counsel in each others' projects. Because of the in-depth multilayered association that is required at each stage, it has been seen that VCs normally have a select set of industries/domains into which they would invest and on which they have built competencies over time.

VC financing in Silicon Valley has also been associated with modularization of product system designs. For example, emergence of the digital TV triggered off the whole modularization of the product development, an industry consortium joined hands to create a standard set of platform Application Programming Interfaces (APIs) that could be used by developers around the world in creating innovative modules for the digital TV. Very soon the development of the TV moved from an in-house start to finish exercise to a quick assortment of modules from various vendors who had developed the best competencies. Creation of standard interfaces allows module development without thinking about design dependencies with other modules and makes entry at the module level easier by making encapsulation of module level information possible. Sharing of interface level information and encapsulation of module level information constitutes the specific information arrangement. VCs generally remain the purveyors of interface designs, mediating information on systemic risks to the entrepreneur who specializes in the intra-module information. The VC acts as a bundling agent to the entrepreneur—

bundling the provision of finance with information and skills of marketing, insights on how the proposed innovation would link up to a wider milieu, financial and legal expertise that would determine the exit route to encashing the innovation effort. This bundling creates a node of power, which is crucial for the successful execution of VC monitoring.

To elicit maximum efforts from the entrepreneurs, VCs generally would run tournament-like contests, with winner-takes-all reward structures, amongst several projects in a specific module. The number of such parallel projects generally remains limited so as to retain incentives of reasonably high expectation of success of the participating entrepreneurs (since too many participants in the race would decrease the expected payoff!). As projects evolve and uncertainties get resolved, the VC often would reduce the number of projects that get financed in higher rounds of financing. For the VC, therefore, several projects represent 'real options' that are exercised depending on contingency of states of affairs as it evolves. This is also an effective way of minimizing risks using the proverbial 'eggs in multiple basket' route.

VC financing, therefore, is based on governance exercised over highly differentiated and specialized information; unlike financial information, information on the worth of ideas in evolution are far more difficult to elicit. Formation of 'clearing houses of ideas', gateway journals and elaborate databases provides a way out. Existence of a key journal, to which a large segment of the concerned technology ecosystem participants are hooked in provides a forum where races between competing ideas can be observed. An idea can also be thrown up for peer vetting and its outcome observed through the influence it is having on the trajectories of work in that area. In many cases, interim targets of VC financed projects might include publication in such journals to seek vetting of the proposed solutions.

> The main stages of engaging with a VC-type investor in financing a new innovative project would be as follows:
>
> **Stage 1:** Ideation stage/Prototype testing stage: The funding is generally through Angel Investors—largely, consisting of friends and high net worth individuals of entrepreneurs; the strategic association and direction from an Angel investor is vastly different from the other modes of funding.
> Most of the small time business start off with some kind of Angel funding; this was more unstructured in the past but of late, the Angel

> investment circuit is becoming structured (though very far behind when compared to the others). The funding volumes are low.
> **Stage 2:** Idea tested, Initial Expansion: Mostly its VC funded (we have covered the strategic dynamics already). Where would the VC exit?
> **Stage 3:** Growth Phase (or expansion of a particular division within the company): PE funding (amount of funding is larger compared to the other first two stages).
> **Stage 4:** Listing the company/tapping the Masses: IPO/stock market route.

5.5 EQUITY MARKET DESIGN, PRIVATIZATION OF EXCHANGES AND EMERGING INTER-EXCHANGE COMPETITION

The stock exchange—a centralized marketplace for the secondary trading of stocks—has been an important institutional innovation that has led to the rise of the publicly listed corporation. Exchanges, for much of the middle years of the 20th century, were viewed as natural monopolies—where trading of stocks could be organized at low transaction costs (see Mahoney 1997). Although the US had more than one exchange, most of Europe had only one stock exchange in each country. Stock exchanges were also, usually, controlled by brokers/traders and were seen as non-profit membership organizations. Within this framework, the relationship between stock exchanges and firms applying for a listing was viewed as giving rise to a long-term contract in which stock exchanges supplied liquidity, corporate governance rules, clearing and monitoring services and a signalling function to investors in exchange for listing fees. However, the globalization of securities markets has recently led to a growing number of companies seeking to raise capital across borders—breaching the geographic monopoly of exchanges in the primary equity market for listings. On the other hand, entry and rise of automated trading platforms, using electronic technologies, has introduced the possibility of trading securities without the intermediation of an exchange. This immediately introduces the possibility of decoupling of the secondary market and the primary market—or a decoupling of liquidity and clearance service from the provision of corporate governance and listing rules. The new set of players—the automated trading platforms—are privately owned and controlled, unlike the membership nature of the exchanges.

While in the US there has been strong competition between equity markets for a long time, competition among exchanges in much of continental Europe goes back to the mid-to-late 1980s only. The detailed evolution of the NASDAQ market, in Appendix 5B to this chapter, provides an account of the evolution of the market in the backdrop of contests with other equity markets and providers of liquidity services. Some have noted that the competition between exchanges in the US has been an important reason enabling financial innovation. In Europe, after competition was introduced from the mid-1980s, there had been significant reductions in trading fees—which have benefited investors—and a proliferation of trading mechanisms have increased market liquidity. But how do we conceive of the process of competition between exchanges? One way would be to look at competing exchanges as presenting issuers with a choice of listing requirements, trading systems, trading and listing fees and transaction costs (Foucault and Parlour 1999). These rules mean that on the investor side, each milieu with a set of rules of listing as well as mode of secondary trading offer different prospects of engagement. Exchanges would need to compete with each other in attracting investors to subscribe to the listings and provide liquidity to the share. These rules, so to say, are offered by exchanges seeking an expansion of business.

Contest in provision of rules, therefore, constitutes a mode of strategizing for the exchanges. The gamut of rules overseeing securities trading and listing therefore fragments into several milieus and several markets, which possibly can take care of the multitude of needs of different types of enterprises differing in size, risk profiles and lineages. These severalties in the structures of finance enable fund raising and capitalization processes with each milieu offering a specific mode and structure through a specific design of rule sets. The story of evolution of NASDAQ shows how the design of institution of 'market-makers/dealers' alongside its quote-driven trading system enabled it to create a market that nurtured the growth of high-risk new technology firms in the 1990s—a role that New York Stock Exchange (NYSE) failed to perform. In a different context, refer to our discussion in Appendix 5A on the experience of a microfinance agency (SafeSave) on inclusive financing that departed from the more celebrated and popular mode of group-based lending to poor consumers. Innovation lay in rule-setting.

Many believe that the effective absence of competition within countries between first- (or the large exchange) and second-tier (smaller) exchanges was a primary cause (along with inadequate investor demand) of the under-capitalized state of European small and medium-sized enterprises (SMEs), unlike the US, where such contests were always very strong. Moreover, it should be pointed out that the focus of Europe's first-tier exchanges on large, blue-chip firms reduced the attractiveness of the second-tier exchanges, which made it difficult for these exchanges to attract listings from firms that would be eligible to list on a first-tier exchange. Naturally, the most obvious way for the second-tier markets to compete with the rival first-tier exchanges was to become an independent exchange, like NASDAQ, which could provide a home for high-tech firms in Europe that would normally apply for a US listing. To a large extent, the emergence of the Euro New Markets (Euro.NMs), along with NASDAQ Europe (Easdaq) and London's Alternative Investment Market (AIM), is best seen as an attempt to pursue such a strategy. Appendix 5C provides a write-up on AIM.

In 1996–97, the Euro.NMs were launched in order to facilitate the financing of innovative companies with a high-growth potential, which were the type of companies that continental European listing rules would have excluded earlier (Pagano 1998). Consequently, the Euro.NMs established admissions, listings and disclosure regulation, trading procedures and operational standards as a means to achieve an efficient decentralized market which reduced the barriers to flotation for small and medium sized companies and provided start-up ventures with the best possible access to risk capital. The Euro.NMs also adopted a dual trading system consisting of a mix of a quote-driven and order-driven system, to ensure adequate market liquidity. By creating greater liquidity for the shares of SMEs and setting high listing and disclosure standards, the New Markets also aimed at attracting institutional investors.

The French New Market (*Nouveau Marché*) was the first to be created and commenced operating on 14 February 1996 as an alternative, independent investment market governed by its own organizational and operating rules while trading and clearing is done by SBF-Paris (*Société des Bourses Françaises*). Several other markets came up, of which the *Neuer Market* in Germany was most notable for its success in attracting IPOs. But most of these markets also collapsed along with the dot-com burst and the meltdown of technology stocks in 2000. Several of these new markets were closed amidst allegations of insider trading and fraud, which were features of those days. DAX, the German stock exchange, as part of an overhaul of the capital formation process in Germany is trying to set up a different category below its main market for small high-tech stocks to list and trade.[24] The new set of European exchanges set out by removing (or lowering) restrictive entry clauses/criterion, such as minimum enterprise size, but compensated it by design of extremely strict disclosure norms (that were often more intense than the main exchanges) to provide rich information to the investor base.

The UK, however, took a different track. It eliminated exchange-based listings rules and transferred authority to the stock exchange regulator, which establishes the minimum rules governing admissions. For example, this regulatory arrangement gives the London Stock Exchange (LSE) some discretion over which applicants, subject to their satisfying the minimum requirements, are admitted to trade on the AIM, which imposes less stringent disclosure requirements on the issuer. AIM delegates much of the monitoring role to its Nominated Advisors (see the write-up on AIM in Appendix 5C) who play the gatekeeper role that compensates for the lower compulsory disclosure. The disclosures are also tailored to each sector and the specific requirements of information from investors within that category instead of a standardized pro forma of information disclosure. UK regulatory stance therefore is a movement towards customized regulation and rules of disclosure in response to the rising costs of stringent disclosure norms, which has an adverse effect of raising transaction cost of listing of smaller firms. Following the recent success of AIM and its ability to weather the technology slump of 2000, several other exchanges are coming up trying to emulate the philosophy of regulation and rule-setting of AIM.

Thus, privatization of exchanges, which are no longer bound tightly with the interests of member brokers, has introduced novel modes of inter-exchange competition. Provision of rules that generate a market (or a trading platform) has become a major element of competition among exchanges.

5.6 A SHORT SUMMING UP

Several narrations in this chapter and the cases in the appendix demonstrate the variations in the institutional moorings of finance—the difference in motives and 'institutions of practice' that affects the mode

---

[24]One of the failures of the *Neuer Market* was in enforcing the lock-in period of shares of insiders so as to soften the impact of information asymmetry between old (promoter) and new shareholders and avoid what is called the 'lemon problem'.

of deployment of finance leading to pursuing of different routes to profit generation by different sub-domains of the financial world. The last few decades has seen immense changes in financial markets across the world. Regulatory changes have liberalized financial markets, introduced competitive dynamics in several ways and eased cross-border flows of financial capital, providing novel turfs for the strategic play of the financial domain. Pressures emanating from the financial domain would shape up possible strategic stances of firms and organizations in product or service business. Corporate assets can be broken or joined together or linked up in innovative ways through the intervention of financial domain actors. Assets and information can be bundled together or unbundled to disrupt existing nodes of power in an industry as financial investors look for assets to invest in and design innovative instruments to obtain partial rights to profit streams generated out of different assets. Financial intermediation unleashed novel motives. While the intermediation designed by private equity and VCs aimed at exploitation of static efficiencies and unlocking value through that process, VC intermediation sought to unleash increasing returns dynamics. This multiplicity of the governance modes is the moot point that we tried to emphasize. The emergence of a new category of institutional investors, especially Sovereign Wealth Funds and University Endowment Funds, is also highlighted.

APPENDIX 5A

SafeSave[25]

> ... *the microfinance industry has ossified! It promotes group-based micro enterprise loan products and is obstructing the development of full range of services and products that poor people want and need—flexible savings, contractual savings, loans for education and health, micro insurance and lines of credit.*
>
> —David Hulme (co-author of *Finance against Poverty*)

SafeSave, founded in 1996, is a young microfinance institute (MFI) in the slums of Dhaka, the capital of Bangladesh.[26] It began as a partnership between Stuart Rutherford, of the Institute for Development Policy and Management (IDPM), University of Manchester, and Rabeya Islam, a Dhaka housewife who ran savings clubs for slum dwellers. Rutherford earlier had started ActionAid's programme in Bangladesh and stayed on there to devise better financial services for poor people. Rutherford, with over 30 years of worldwide experience, wanted to test out his idea that the poor would welcome an MFI that offered them both savings and loans for everyday money management rather than just loans for micro businesses. His experience with existing MFIs made him sceptical of usefulness of self-help groups and of joint liability, both to the clients and to

---

[25]This case is an early summary of Kakani and Thakur (2009).

[26]Located in the South Asia region, Bangladesh ranks low on most development indicators. World Bank figures say that Bangladesh had a relatively higher poverty incidence compared with other South Asian and East Asian countries.

the institution.[27] He believed that frequency, reliability and flexibility of services mattered more.

About one-third of Dhaka's 11 million people live in slums.[28] Banks do not serve them, so they use home savings, moneylenders or find a friend willing to serve as a 'money guard'—devices that are not always reliable. SafeSave aimed to serve such people as their money-management resource. It offered both saving services and loans. It treated clients as individuals; there were neither groups nor guarantors for loans and no meetings to attend. Clients may be men, women or children, though children under 16 cannot borrow. It offered a savings account to any resident of a branch working area, up to 1 km walking distance from the branch office. Product rules were issued in writing to all. As combination money-guards/loan officers,[29] employees visit each client each day in their home or business to transact deposits, withdrawals, disbursements and repayments. Such home visits are especially important because most clients are women and because the custom of purdah severely restricts the movement of Bangladeshi women in public.

There is no mass-promotion of SafeSave's services; all clients are signed up by a collector or enrolled by the branch manager in the branch office. On the savings side, clients may deposit as little as 1 taka (= USD 0.015) when the collector calls at their house each day. Balances in its passbook savings accounts earn interest, and clients can make deposits or withdrawals at any time in any amount. Clients may withdraw up to 500 taka per day at their doorstep, or up to 5,000 taka at the branch office within a guaranteed maximum of 10 minutes. Clients may close their accounts any time they wish, provided that any past loan or fee balances have been cleared.

---

[27]Bangladesh Grameen Bank has pioneered lending to poor people. Their customers are expected to form savings groups and to guarantee other group members' borrowings. These borrowings must normally be for productive or money-earning equipment and there are rules for repayment. Clients able to undertake all this have, on the whole, been poor but not the very poor.

[28]Usually, a family consists of 6–7 members living in a one-roomed hut. They will cook on an open fire and draw water from a standpipe nearby. Each member would have around two pairs of clothes.

[29]Community-based lenders know who is creditworthy and who is not; so they do not need to demand collateral, avoiding a lot of paperwork. Another way to avoid asking for collateral is group lending. If everyone loses when one defaults, the group will deal with the defaulter. Lenders can eliminate even more paperwork if they do not have to ask what the loan is for.

Loans are not mandatory, and there is no minimum amount repayment. Like credit-card debt, loans have no fixed terms and no fixed repayment schedules. One loan may be taken per household at a time. Loan interest is high at 3 per cent per month on outstanding balances.[30] A minimum savings balance equal to one-third of the loan balance is required as collateral at all times. There are no other forms of collateral required, nor does it require personal guarantors. Each month the minimum payment is the interest due, but principal repayment is left entirely flexible. In 2007, SafeSave was serving 13,000 clients from eight branches. The average savings balance was 1,500 taka, and average loans balance was 3,400 taka.

At every branch, a manager, an assistant manager and an office helper work. Each branch has 8–11 field workers, collectors, depending on the size of the area. Employees at SafeSave work out of simple, one-room branches with minimal furniture and no vehicles. Each month, SafeSave's field workers handle more than 100,000 small transactions. SafeSave keeps salaries low by employing bank workers who themselves live in the slum and have just enough education to manage basic arithmetic (usually about eight years'). They travel on foot. From 2003 onwards, SafeSave collectors started using handheld computers. The handheld computers had been designed in such a way that a collector needs to have just basic knowledge of reading and mathematics to make use of it. Also, it is very difficult for a collector to be able to embezzle money. These devices have not only increased the internal control in the organization but also diverted staff time away from unproductive activities (such as, reconciliation of client passbook with the Management Information system [MIS] data) to productive activities (such as customer service or client mobilization).

In a survey of Dhaka slums, Calles (2005) found that the clients of SafeSave preferred it over other MFIs as they did not want to be part of the group mechanism (self-help groups). The reasons they gave included: being afraid to cover the costs of failing group members; being denied access because they were the poorest or considered risky; unwillingness to let other people know what they were using the money borrowed for; and not involving others too much in their personal decisions. The survey also found that even without deadlines, repayment levels of SafeSave loans

---

[30]Loans for the poorest and especially the very poor are usually not available. For the comparatively wealthier lot (say, the ones having micro-businesses), loans are usually available from *mahajans* (local money lender) at an interest rate starting at 6 per cent per month and they average at 10 per cent per month.

were high as clients feared losing access to financial services and they also got reminded almost every day when the collector visits him/her.

While most writers make negative remarks about informal finance, Mark Schreiner (2001) pointed a few basic virtues in them: (*a*) slashed transaction costs, (*b*) supply of not just loans but also savings and implicit insurance, (*c*) services sensitive to constraints faced by members; (*d*) substitution of confidence in character for physical collateral; (*e*) socially enforced and/or self-enforced contracts and (*f*) sequences of repeated transactions. Schreiner pointed that perhaps SafeSave seems to have done this. As the Nobel Prize-winning economist Robert Fogel has pointed out, hungry people cannot work their way out of poverty. So, first, savings must be integrated with loans to create a single financial system. Second, controls on the use of small-scale loans should be eliminated. And third, lending bodies must be community-based so that they do not waste on paperwork. That is what organizations like SafeSave have done.

The SafeSave experiment was controversial due to high interest rates and the collateral-less lending facility. However, 10 years on, we can see that the poor welcomed the services enough for SafeSave to grow and become profitable. With a pre-tax return on equity over 10 per cent, it is financially sustainable even though it took commercial borrowings in 2007. Research has confirmed that the SafeSave seems to be able to target the poorest people better than traditional MFIs through their flexible financial services. However, the question of the experiment being successful on a larger scale is yet to be answered.

Several international agencies are pursuing variants of the SafeSave approach in other areas. In fact, Rutherford himself is testing SafeSave's principles in a rural context. In 2002, Rutherford founded Shohoz Shonchoy at Hrishipara, a village in central Bangladesh. Shohoz Shonchoy develops and tests innovative approaches to money management services for poor and very poor villagers. Dwelling over SafeSave's future, Rutherford said, 'SafeSave will remain small but act as a centre for the innovation in creating products/services for effective delivery of savings, loans, and insurance products specifically for the very poor.'

In 2007, Rutherford stepped out of the day-to-day running of SafeSave, handing over to Rabeya's son, Mohammad Hossin Islam, who is trained in commerce. Rutherford invited him home from an unprofitable factory job in Malaysia. Observers keenly watching the entity had a lot of questions, such as: (*a*) Is this model sustainable in the long-run? (*b*) What are the ingredients which made SafeSave successful? (*c*) Can this model work in developed countries? (*d*) How can this organization grow and yet help the very poor?

APPENDIX 5B

NASDAQ vs NYSE—Institutional Contest and the Evolution of a Market

NASDAQ is a powerful global brand. We embraced the inevitability of globalized markets and became the first mover in the process of consolidation when we acquired a substantial position in LSE on financial terms favorable to us. I have been asked why we did not increase our offer for the LSE to a level that would have enabled us to purchase a majority of the outstanding shares. My response is that a key element in NASDAQ's recent success has been an unwavering discipline in respect of acquisitions. We have done five of them in my time and all have been successful. Every asset has a fair value and we offered fair value for the LSE, recognizing that competition is coming to European markets.

—Robert Greifeld, President and CEO, NASDAQ in 2006 Annual Report

In 2007, the bid of NASDAQ (National Association of Securities Dealers Automated Quotation) to gain control over LSE finally unravelled and NASDAQ invited bids for possible sale of its holdings in LSE. 2006–07, however, marked other significant developments that have a potential of catapulting NASDAQ again into a leading role in financial market making. NASDAQ is the industry leader with over 16 years of experience in what is called the 144A market. NASDAQ's offering in this segment through the PORTAL market enables companies to raise capital from qualified institutional investors in a manner more efficient and less costly than a public offer that includes retail investors. In 2006, the amount of equity capital raised through offerings that utilized a 144A tranche through PORTAL (USD 162 billion) exceeded the amount raised on NASDAQ, NYSE and AMEX put together (USD 154 billion).[31] Many believe that PORTAL could be a transformational act in capital markets. PORTAL is one of the latest in a long series of financial market making innovation that has epitomized NASDAQ's journey from its humble origins in the Great Depression aftermath in the 1930s to becoming a critical component of the innovation engine of our contemporary times. As financial markets around the globe sought new mechanisms of integration, riding on a wave of enabling regulatory stances, exchanges sought new linkages and alliances in a bid to create a global pool of liquidity. The NASDAQ–LSE failed deal epitomized such a move. Old boundaries seemed to be receding. Yet the PORTAL move, in contrast, demonstrates the evolution of new boundaries that are thematic in nature—network of actors, possibly dispersed across the globe, sharing a heuristic (such as a trading heuristic) that generates a unique value in a (bounded) network that is, however, not all-pervasive. It is something like a small world. NASDAQ's vision of becoming a market of markets represents its commitment to an 'ecology approach'—a market of markets would thrive by creating several markets. Evolution of regulation and the strategies of a new clutch of market makers such as NASDAQ that provide the institutional mechanism that supports the evolution of several such small worlds engaged in a complex strategic interplay seem to characterize the new century.

---

[31]144A refers to the SEC clause that covers private placements. Many companies have started feeling that the regulatory and legal costs of going public is becoming too high (specially for smaller companies) and prefers the private placement route. NASDAQ's PORTAL market is aimed at initiating secondary trading of private placements amongst institutional investors (current bar at USD 100 million and a maximum of 499 investors to qualify as 144A category for the issue)—to generate greater liquidity in the market. Goldman Sachs earlier started a similar move (GSTrUE) but competitors did not participate in it. PORTAL is the first platform from a neutral market maker, so to say. Months after PORTAL was launched, Citigroup, Lehman Brothers, Merrill Lynch, Morgan Stanley and Bank of New York Mellon (Bank of America, Credit Suisse and UBS joined the initiative) announced plans to launch another rival platform called Open Platform for Unregistered Securities, or OPUS-5. 144A represents a flight away from regulation, like many other experimental markets such as the Alternative Investment Market in London (see Appendix 5C) designed to make it easier for small companies in particular to raise finances.

Early History: Roots in the Financial Mayhem of the Great Depression

The NASDAQ of today owes its origins to the days of the Great Depression in the US. When President Franklin Roosevelt came to power with pledges to reform the financial markets, he tapped Joseph Kennedy (later to be the patriarch of one of America's leading political families) to head the newly formed SEC to regulate the financial markets. Joseph Kennedy was a strange choice, for in the early part of the century he courted some of the most notorious stock manipulators of his days.[32] Regulating the exchanges, such as the NYSE, was relatively easier for they were concentrated places of trading, although getting control over the broker/trader community was not an easy task by any means. But beyond the exchanges, which provided a central place for price discovery, there was the amorphous over-the-counter (OTC) market that was in reality a densely meshed complex network of brokers/traders who traded amongst themselves. Some of the worst manipulations, abuses and outright thievery occurred in this OTC market in the 1920s. After the recovery of the 1930s, pockets within the OTC community realized that they would have to evolve to some mode of self-regulation to generate credibility amongst the investing public, but their efforts mostly did not work since it lacked teeth. The question was what would induce/compel traders to join cooperatively to clean up their act!

The answer came in the *Maloney Act*, mooted by the Investment Bankers Conference, Inc. supported by Congressman Francis Maloney who was the Chairman of the Senate Banking Committee. The act gave industry associations the right to register with SEC and enforce a code of conduct on their members transforming them to quasi-enforcement agencies. One element of the act gave the right to members of registered securities association to trade with other registered members at wholesale prices, while they could trade with outsiders at retail prices. This regulatory stroke created a marvellous incentive—it led to the formation of the National Association of Securities Dealers (NASD) and some 1,500 of the estimated 6,700 traders joined within a year so that at least a tab could be kept on the activities of registered traders. By 1945, NASD had 25,000 members. But given the nature of the OTC markets and the

---

[32]Rumour has it that Kennedy was a leading player in the pool game, where groups of traders would form cartels (pools) that would either jointly beat a stock up or down, a very important activity during the bull-run that preceded the crash of 1929 (Smith, 2001).

state of technology, NASD could do little to help investors get uniform prices. In the absence of a central floor that could centralize pricing information, which was possible in the exchanges, the OTC markets were in reality several markets. A broker in Philadelphia might charge several dollars more per share than a trader in New York or vice versa depending on many layers of local market dynamics. The NASDAQ system of collecting quotes and displaying them via a centralized computer network for all to see would not come till 1971, when NASD became a pioneer in embracing the evolving computer technology to change the rules of operation of the OTC market, albeit with a significant push from the regulators.

OTC Markets and the Move towards the Electronic NASDAQ

The stock exchanges in the US, notably the NYSE—the most powerful and influential amongst the several national/regional exchanges—were organized as 'specialist driven' exchanges. All orders in a stock in this set-up are actually transacted by this specialist, who stands inside what is called a trading post, right on the exchange floor. The specialist organizes an auction, so to say, to discover the best price. Specialists are therefore auctioneers who have purchased floor space on the exchange. The fact that buy and sell orders almost always go through the specialist is an important attribute of the architecture of order flow in NYSE—this is crucial to the centralization of the price discovery process. This also relates to the 'discourse on transparency' associated with such centralized exchanges. In NYSE, each stock listed had only one specialist—an exclusive right. NYSE also has always restricted the number of specialists allowed—so that it is like a private club with limited seats—you can enter mostly by buying a seat from someone else. And the centralization of information on order flow in a stock makes the specialist the most knowledgeable person on that particular stock—a position that is immensely valuable. In exchange for this exclusive right, specialists are also mandated by the exchange to maintain an orderly market in the stocks that the specialist is responsible for. Specialists generally, therefore, would also keep inventories of stocks and buy and sell on their own account as well. Inventory holding, however, introduces risks for the specialist and to mitigate that the specialist traditionally had another information advantage. Only the specialist knew how many buy or sell orders were stacked up at any given point in time—a measure of depth of the market—which other market participants could not observe. This monopolistic advantage gave them the price setting capability at any point in time. This would continue to be the structure of NYSE till around 2002 when various reforms were initiated mostly as a response to other modes of organizing the trade that manifested itself in the form of NASDAQ's growth and the rise of several Electronic Communication Networks (ECNs).

But the OTC market was organized quite differently—there was no centralization and it was difficult to comprehend the dynamics of the meshed network unless you were inside it. The centre of gravity of the market shifted around as regional nodes of concentration of trading transactions rose or ebbed. After the crisis of 1930s, the OTC markets limped back to life again and by the 1950s recorded brisk trades, both in the secondary markets as well as in public offerings, taking enterprises public in the OTC circuit. For the regulator, however, the OTC market was still beyond comprehension and in early 1960s, SEC commissioned a very large study which led to a three-volume report called the *Special Study of the Securities Market*, submitted to the Congress in 1963. The report broke down the OTC into two segments—a retail segment where brokers bought and sold on behalf of customers and a wholesale segment, who acted as something like a warehouse of a stock. Small wholesalers handled just a few issues, whereas larger wholesalers handled as much as 200–300 issues. The wholesalers were market-makers and they would play more significant roles in bringing companies public as well. Some 500 broker–dealer firms existed across the country, out of which almost 3,300 dealt only with the OTC market. One reason why so many brokers focused on the OTC market was because, unlike the exchanges, OTC did not charge steep membership fees. Neither did it limit the number of members so that entry and exit into the trade was relatively easy. The OTC market also traded in stocks that were generally off-limits in NYSE or other regional exchanges—they were mainly SMEs; in those days less than a third of the stocks traded were of enterprises that had assets of more than USD 10 million.

Another important observation of the report was the fact that a bulk of the 1,200 wholesalers concentrated on micro-movements of the market—quoting prices in response to the incoming order flows. There was relatively little effort on getting information on the real performance of the underlying enterprises. One of the major recommendations of the report was the creation of a centralized computer network that could collect quotes from the dispersed trading network to aid better price discovery. The ability of traders to see each other's quote behaviour would allow them to trade with thinner spreads (by reducing uncertainties, especially during times of turmoil/volatility), reducing transaction costs and growing the market, it was argued. The report urged the NASD to lead this new role of automation, failing which leadership in the wholesale pricing market might shift to other players who would give investors alternative trading networks. (The future evolution of ECNs would bear testimony to the credibility of that threat!)

Automation of Electronic Markets: Formation of NASDAQ

The financial markets in the US collapsed again in late 1960s, badly hitting NYSE specialists and OTC market-makers. It was in that tumultuous environment that the NASDAQ—the computerized quotation system of NASD—finally debuted in February 1971. It created something like an NYSE trading floor for NASDAQ, albeit a virtual trading floor whose only physical artefact was the secret location of the server system at Trumbull, Connecticut. The NASDAQ provided three levels of service. The first level was called Level 1 service, quite similar to a quote that might be appearing in a newspaper meant to convey a representative quote. In 1980, the representative quote was replaced by the highest bid to buy and the lowest offer to sell.

Level II, the next tier, consisted of quotes of all market-makers in order of price. This level of quotes cost more (in terms of access fees) and provided subscribers with an idea of the depth of the market and hence a cue about the near-term price movement—crucial for those who would engage in large volume trade. Level II quotes provided an unprecedented amount of information to a large network of traders/investors. Although this type of information (on the depth) was also released earlier through what were called 'pink papers', it was nowhere near the real-time touch of the NASDAQ Level II screens.[33] There was another Level III, where subscribers (restricted to market-makers alone) could put in or retract quotes. This was a privileged position granted to the market-makers. The market-makers also had another privilege. At that time, the limit orders posted by customers were not visible in the quote display system; so no one, other than the market maker (or dealer) who handled a customer

---

[33]Level II type of information for NYSE was the preserve of the specialists for a long time till around 2002, when alternative information disclosure mechanisms were put in place.

limit-order, could view it. Years later, this would change due to intervention of SEC.

But selling this proposition to the NASD, which was a member controlled organization, was not easy at all. The centralization of the price discovery would standardize the market for each stock creating a uniform price. It was hoped this would reduce the spreads—and that would hurt the earnings of the dealers/traders. But what tilted the decision was the possibility of a massive increase in trading volume as new investors could be drawn into the NASDAQ circuit. There were several other developments that made this a feasible proposition. NYSE at that time was at loggerheads with a bunch of new investors—mutual funds, insurance companies—who wanted membership of the floor enabling them to trade commission-free. But NYSE steadfastly held on to its monopoly, preserving the commission-rights of the existing trader members. Taking this opportunity, several regional exchanges started offering memberships and fiercely competing for order flow of listed stocks with NYSE. Some regional exchanges also crafted mechanisms that allowed non-members to trade commission-free—in violation of the *Maloney Act*. Prodding from the SEC, however, put an end to these practices quite early. So the securities trading ecosystem was in need of institutional innovation as new sets of players sought to connect to the system in novel modes. Initial plans of NASDAQ included trading of NYSE listed shares—which was traditionally beyond the OTC markets' ambit. Small member/traders of NASDAQ in particular were elated by this possibility, but NYSE created hurdles fearing it would divert order flows from the floor as large investors and traders might start trading amongst themselves bypassing the specialist, and the NASD finally chose not to include trade of NYSE listed shares as a compromise that would ease the launch of the automated quotation platform.

NASDAQ, after all, the protagonists claimed was a complement to NYSE—its target was future firms like Intel, not the General Motors and such old manufacturing giants. And NASDAQ grew in fortune and fame to probably bypass the NYSE in terms of clout as it played host to listings of the new wave US start-ups that grew into giants, powered by new technology and innovation. And one crucial feature that allowed NASDAQ to play that role was the liquidity that it provided to the stocks of small new companies. Liquidity increased tradability, which often bolstered the prices as buyers of a liquid stock knew that exit was easy. This made listings easier in NASDAQ for such firms—and the basic NASD structure of multiple market-makers (with little entry barriers) for each stock, forcing competition in market-making, provided a crucial institutional underpinning.

In 1982, NASDAQ created the NASDAQ National Market (NNM), where information on price and volume of each trade was conveyed exactly 90 seconds after trade execution. The NNM was intended to finally put the OTC exchange at par with the NYSE in terms of price information. A higher bar in terms of financial reporting and corporate governance was set for NNM companies compared to other OTC stocks (to match the venerable NYSE blue chip)—initially just 40 of them made it, but by end of the decade there were more than 2,500 of them. In 1982, NASDAQ also created the small-order-execution-system (SOES), which allowed automatic execution of small (retail) orders at the prices broadcast by NASDAQ dealers instantaneously.

The late 1980s was marked by another financial crisis—the meltdown of 1987. The market-maker's role was again at the centre of controversies. Previously a market-maker's participation in SOES was voluntary—so, in a rapidly falling market, he could also ignore the orders through SOES—and on Black Monday, many dealers in fact refused to take SOES orders. In June 1988, SOES order (less than 1,000 shares) execution became mandatory for dealers at the prices that the dealers advertised. As often happens, an innovation designed to solve one problem creates several others, and mandatory SOES order fulfilment was exactly such a step. It created the first generation of what would be known as 'day traders'—people who earned their living by trading their own account.

Trading Wars and the Day Traders

When SOES became mandatory, a new species of traders (derogatorily called SOES bandits) quickly devised a way to use the system to their advantage. They congregated in special brokerages that offered direct access (hardwired) to NASDAQ systems. NASDAQ requirements allowed brokerages to use SOES only for their customer orders, which was a way of saying that it could not use SOES to trade on own account. Several brokerages, however, gave direct access to the brokerage access points to their customers. Market-makers priced their shares usually in tandem with one lead dealer, known as an ax, for a particular stock. When the ax raised the price, others would follow, but sometimes there were little time lags and the SOES bandit would swoop to reap the benefit of the short arbitrage window available routing the order through the automated SOES system. The market-maker would be caught unaware. By 1995, close to 80 per cent of the SOES trades were originating from the SOES bandits creating a new war of words and a new look into rules again. The SOES bandits surely argued that they were bringing liquidity and efficiency into the markets and they were right about it. On the other hand, the market-makers also had certain disadvantages—they had to enter orders manually. In some cases they had to negotiate for prices over a separate network—the *SelectNet* where dealers traded amongst themselves. NASDAQ rules forbade them from entering SOES orders on behalf of customers for stocks in which they made the market. And they could not use the SOES mandatory execution system for trades that they made on their own behalf. SOES bandits also used very sophisticated software that would search for and detect 'stale' quotes automatically.

NASD intervened and changed rules again—SOES users were disallowed order splitting, SOES orders from professional trading accounts (PTAs or accounts that demonstrated a professional trading pattern) were prohibited, limitations were placed on the size of SOES trade to 500 shares, and so on. SEC granted the rule changes, siding with the market-makers. But the PTA rule, in particular, was soon challenged in court and the SOES bandits won the case—the provision was rescinded. But this conflict marked the advent of a new group of traders whose interest often would conflict with that of the market-makers.

Allegations of Cartelization and Antitrust Enquiry

But NASDAQ would soon be gripped by another controversy—two professors of finance studying NASDAQ dealer quote patterns argued in a paper that dealers appeared to be consistently avoiding quoting in odd-eighths (one-eighth being the tick), in effect widening the bid-ask spreads. This led to an enquiry by the Justice Department, several civil lawsuits and ultimately an SEC intervention in what became famous as the 21 (a) report that indicted the NASD for failing to carry out its duties of regulation of the NASDAQ. For several years NASDAQ faced enquiries that looked into its practices and the SEC finally brought in four specific charges of failure against the dealers on different forms of collusive behaviour that resulted in increasing the spreads.

But there were others, such as the Financial Economist Roundtable, that argued that deciphering collusion was not so easy and offered several other reasons why the quoting norm existed among NASDAQ dealers.

Market-makers would want to avoid being deluged with orders especially when they knew that the other party had greater information about a stock's near-term direction. Widening spreads would protect them, while they could execute orders on the SOES, which was not visible on the Level II quote. Dealers would also want to preference, particularly market orders from uninformed retail customers, and traditionally dealers used to offer kickbacks to brokerages for such order delivery—precisely because they were safe orders. In addition, NASDAQ dealers also traded with other dealers in networks such as *SelectNet* or with savvy institutional investors (large order handlers) in networks such as *Instinet*. Traders negotiated over prices in these networks—by offering and withdrawing quotes to discover prices—and spreads were rather thin in this market.

The controversy, however, brought out the fact that markets are complex and understanding it from outside is difficult, particularly why and how different norms and institutions evolve. There are several layers of facts, so to say. It also led to changes in the order-handling system at NASDAQ. SEC mandated NASDAQ to display the size and price of customer limit orders—thus erasing the difference between the NYSE system of order driven market (where the best price is quoted by the specialist even if the best price is from a customer and not his own) and the NASDAQ system of quote driven market (where the quotes represented the market-maker quotes, creating an additional layer of information asymmetry). NASDAQ was also mandated to open up the previously exclusive electronic trading networks, *Instinet* and *SelectNet* and allow customers direct access. The separation between the execution trail of small and large orders, thus, was done away with.

Both these changes would be revolutionary; changing the face of equity trading at NASDAQ and clearing the way for the rise of the ECNs. The rule changes removed a few important layers of information asymmetries enjoyed by the market-makers and it did lead to a further narrowing of spreads at a time when dealer members had to spend large amounts in upgrading their systems to comply with the new order-handling heuristics. One particular effect was that several Wall Street firms reduced the number of stocks they handled as market-maker, reducing levels of competition. Few of them also moved away from the smaller stocks so that the concentration effect was larger for smaller stocks and an NASD sponsored study found that the lowering of spreads was more a phenomenon associated with stocks of larger enterprises that were traded more vigorously. In December 1997, when some 30 NASD securities firms settled the class-action suit by reportedly paying up

USD 910 million in damages, they had got into the largest civil antitrust settlement in history in the US till then. But the concern over spreads was becoming important for NASDAQ in other ways as well; NYSE was trying to woo away the larger NASDAQ firms—the stars (who had enough analyst attention)—with claims of lower spreads in the specialist market and NASDAQ's response was also aimed at preventing such defections. But were the changes benefiting the smaller firms—that question would remain, especially because the changes weakened the market-makers whose intervention was crucially important for the smaller firms.

The Rise of ECNs and Competition for Provision of Liquidity Services

NASDAQ, however, was soon overwhelmed by a new threat—the newly rising ECNs that took away almost a third of order flow from NASDAQ market makers. New generation ECNs proved to be a greater threat than the old NYSE. ECNs were electronic networks that automatically handled trades. Instead of dealing with a market maker, a trader wishing to buy shares would have to exactly match the price offered by a seller. ECNs were active for a long time but they were something like a private network. *SelectNet* was one such network used by dealers in NASDAQ to trade with each other. *SelectNet* deals did not get reported in the Level II displays, and hence traders could trade huge volumes without affecting the overall price quote. Trading over *SelectNet* also had complex price discovery processes where traders would post and withdraw quotes, break up orders or do several other things to find the right price. The ECN price quotes would also generally retain anonymity, unlike the NASDAQ Level II, where the market-maker identity was revealed. SEC's order handling rule of 1997 meant that the ECN quotes would now find a place in the Level II displays alongside the quotes of market-makers. The source behind any ECN order would, however, remain anonymous. Several ECNs sprang up quickly enough, growing at a rapid pace along with the bull run of the late 1990s—*IslandIsland, Archipelago, Instinet*, REDI, etc. became household names. Customers patched on to the ECNs through what were called direct-access brokerages which let customers themselves decide how they would like their orders to be routed through software that they licensed out. ECNs provided lightning speed of transaction, which was important for traders working on small movements of the market—the day traders. And they preferred the NASDAQ stocks since Level II displays of NASDAQ provided a highly granular data that made complex trading strategies possible. NYSE price data, in contrast, was still monopolized by the specialists. NASDAQ attracted a whole host of day traders, increasing liquidity and shifting the market to higher gears.

Instinet and *Island*—Two ECNs with Different Backgrounds

Instinet was designed in 1969 by a former broker named Jerome Pustilnik who wanted to create a trading venue centred on high-volume NYSE stocks as an alternative to the Big Board. It would function like networks of professional trading firms but would be automated. Using *Instinet*, any trading firm that rented a dedicated terminal could patch into a global network. But the move did not pick up well and volumes remained low. In early 1980s, the advent of programmed traders, who needed speed of execution, found *Instinet* a handy trading platform to capture the tiny per share profits. Volumes grew in *Instinet*. By 1987, *Instinet* had repositioned into the OTC market as well and Reuters had bought out the network for a reported USD 110 million. By mid-1990s, 5,000 brokers subscribed to it and volumes grew to 20 per cent of NASDAQ volumes. It had also linked to 15 other exchanges (by purchasing seats in them as a brokerage) and provided a global network to trade to its clients. It also continuously provided tweaks to its clients to help identify new and profitable trading strategies through software use. *Instinet* served the professional trader and was positioned as such.

Island, in contrast, had a different root and it targeted the day traders. Whereas *Instinet*, with its British ties, came off as an exclusive country club of traders from patrician financial firms, *Island* began as a rebel upstart, mirroring the free-wheeling day trader. It was an outgrowth of the brokerage called Datek which catered to day traders. Datek's founders had developed a trading platform similar to the one used by professional traders that allowed customers to route orders directly to the NASDAQ market. It could transmit and receive information over the internet and could operate on a PC—features that reduced its costs drastically. It launched in 1996, initially matching orders for its own customers, and the rule change in 1997 moved the *Island* quotes to the Level II display. As time passed, *Island* also made it easier for day trading firms to route orders through its systems. In 1999, *Island* launched into the lengthy process of applying for recognition as an exchange. By 2001, *Island* volumes grew larger than *Instinet* and it began providing Level II kind of information to its customers for free, unlike the subscription-based access that NASDAQ provided. *Island* set a new benchmark in information disclosure that other ECNs followed. *Island*'s Level II book, however, had one serious drawback—it showed quotes only on its own network while trade was proceeding in other ECNs and in NASDAQ. To get around this problem, several ECNs tried getting into linkages that would provide mutual access.

Archipelago, another next generation ECN, in which CNBC acquired a stake in 1999, provided a Level II display that had other ECN quotes and so its prices more closely followed the NASDAQ price. *Archipelago*'s other partners included Goldman Sachs, J.P. Morgan and American Century Investors, and their involvement shows how the financial powerhouses, who have a long-term take in NASDAQ success, hedged their position in the rapidly changing equity market environment. *Instinet* took a stake then in *Archipelago* and finally *Archipelago* acquired the Pacific Exchange in 2001, and the new Pacific Exchange started trading both NASDAQ and NYSE shares.

The rise of ECNs was a threat to both NASDAQ and NYSE; NYSE reacted by setting up its own ECN called NYSE Direct+ that allowed customers to match orders automatically. NASDAQ reacted by attempting to become the market of markets, announcing plans of creating a SuperMontage that would integrate the quote display of ECNs and market-makers. Liquidity would come from member dealer firms as well as the ECNs, if they chose to subscribe to it. The rise of ECNs represented two novel features of the evolving markets. Day traders became a very important source of turnover and liquidity competing with the traditional market-makers—the two sets depended on different trading dynamics and underlying institutional support mechanisms. ECN activity during off-trading hours and its international linkages forged through tie-ups with other exchanges created the feasibility of 24-hour trading and a global pool of liquidity. ECNs also introduced decoupling between the primary and secondary market service provision. The traditional players—NYSE and NASDAQ—had to react to this new trend. As the two giants reacted, the rise of new voices (the day traders) and the nimble moves of the privately owned ECNs meant that the traditional member-controlled governance structure would soon unravel. Two governance modes were in contest—a member-controlled mode and a private mode of supplying of enforcement rules of the market platform.

Inter-exchange competition, rooted in crafty design of markets and platforms, had come of age. Both NASDAQ and NYSE began moves to privatize themselves. NASDAQ privatized and listed in July 2002. It also began pursuing a strategy of international expansion, not only trying to list a growing number of foreign firms to provide them access to US capital formation processes, but moved to set up foreign franchisees that could potentially energize the domestic capital formation process in those countries under rules that NASDAQ market-making pioneered. In Japan, it started off NASDAQ-Japan in 2000 in collaboration with a new generation Japanese internet incubator and VC firm, Softbank, run along the lines of CMGI in the US, whose strategies reflected a stark contrast to the traditional Japanese modes of financing and governance. Within a year, 56 companies had listed and a quarter of Japanese IPO debuted on NASDAQ-Japan. Several of the top US NASDAQ companies also started trading in NASDAQ-Japan.

The 21st century, therefore, began with intense activity emanating from the new context of inter-exchange competition—for liquidity and for listings. Innovative market designing, formation of alliances and cross-linkages would dominate strategic moves of the exchanges. (Account based primarily on Ingebrestsen, 2002.)

APPENDIX 5C

Alternative Investment Market (AIM) of London Stock Exchange (LSE)

To ease listings for small companies, the AIM was created in 1995 with just 10 companies as a market attached to the Main Market of LSE. This was also the prime concern that traditionally guided the National Association of Security Dealers in creating NASDAQ. Over the past few years, it has come of age, becoming a vital link in the risk capital financing chain, that is, supporting innovation in enterprises in UK and internationally. In 2006, AIM companies raised around the same as the whole of NASDAQ and substantially more than exchanges in Frankfurt, Toronto, Tokyo and Sydney. Around 1,600 companies traded on AIM in August 2007. AIM's recent growth has been nothing short of phenomenal. Company numbers have tripled in size since the year 2000. The year 2006 was yet another record year with the amount of money raised almost double that of 2005, which was almost double that of the year before. The total value of shares traded on AIM in 2006 was GBP 58 billion, up 23.3 per cent on the comparable figure for 2005. The scope of the market has expanded too. The number of sectors represented has increased by 20 per cent in a little over a year. The number of countries represented has also almost doubled in two years and the number of international companies joining AIM has increased tenfold since the year 2000. AIM stocks have become a mainstream asset class. Since 2003, the proportion of AIM shares owned by institutions has increased from 35 per cent to 57 per cent. This underlines just how much AIM has changed from retail to a professional market in the space of just a few years.

AIM has a ready supply of knowledgeable investors with capital to invest, regulations that are flexible enough to cope with the specific needs of these companies (in what is now called balanced regulation—low initial and continuing listing costs, no norms on minimum balance sheet size, minimum number of years of existence or minimum free float criterion) and a substantial community of advisers who specialize in the SME sector. This is hugely important. The average market capitalization of an AIM company is around GBP 50 million or just under USD 100 million, and yet they can find advisers willing to help them raise capital and analysts willing to research them. Compare this to NASDAQ, a market set up originally to deal with growth companies, where now companies valued at less than USD 1 billion (average market cap at NASDAQ) are referred to as 'orphans' and find it difficult to attract the attention of analysts and to draw funds from institutional investors (in what several people refer to as structural problems in US financial markets). This has begun to attract companies from the so-called cradle of capitalism to AIM. In 2007, there were 47 Chinese listings and 20 from Israel (a traditional innovation hub), 111 from US/Canada (the largest foreign listing source) and around 1,100 from the UK. There were a few issues from India as well—real estate and entertainment being prominent among them. The early globalization of the market has been its important feature. In 2006, a quarter of the listings and a third of the capital raised went to overseas enterprises.

Table 5C.1: Comparative Direct Listing Costs at AIM and NASDAQ

DIRECT LISTING COSTS (estimates in USD)			
AIM IPO		NASDAQ IPO	
Item	*Cost*	*Item*	*Cost*
Nomad/broker fee	2,000,000	Underwriting fee	3,500,000
Corporate financial fee	500,000	Legal fees	500,000
Company Counsel	262,000	Miscellaneous expenses	145,000
Nomad counsel	300,000	Printing fee	75,000
Accounting fee	312,000	Accounting fee	65,000
AIM Fee	7,300	NASDAQ Listing fee	100,000
Registrar fee	45,000	SEC and NASD Registration fee	107,000
Total	**3,426,300**	**Total**	**4,472,000**

Source: Mendoza (2007).

Table 5C.2: Annual Costs of Listings at AIM and NASDAQ

Direct Ongoing Costs for Continued Listing (in USD Estimates)			
AIM		NASDAQ	
Item	Cost	Item	Cost
Nomad fee	90,000	Sarbanes-Oxley Compliance	2,000,000
Annual fee	7,300	Annual fee	17,500
Accountants	50,000		
Total	147,300	Total	2,017,500

Source: Mendoza (2007).

One innovative mechanism that allows AIM to design flexible regulation is the use of private advisers called Nominated Advisors (Nomads) for screening IPO and continuing to monitor and guide listed firms. AIM's regulation takes a comply-or-explain stance and is 'principle based' rather than rule based—allowing the scope to Nomads and listed firms to device unique modes of information disclosure that would balance the needs of investors against the costs of reporting. This customized approach differs substantially from the traditional mode of uniform regulatory reporting, which increases regular compliance costs. AIM also came out with a series of industry/sector/business specific disclosure formats. Because of this, the role of the Nomads is even more important—they are the most important gatekeepers to the AIM. Rules on Nomads selection are therefore very stringent and they have a responsibility to the investors, including a legal liability in case of an investor lawsuit. Nomads also pledge a very valuable *reputation capital* and Nomads with a positive reputation has a signalling effect on the investor community. Nomads also have deep specialization in the industry and that is a consideration in the choice of the Nomad while a firm seeks listing at AIM.

The AIM listing norms also differ from the regulatory strategy followed in other European new markets—such as the *Neur Market*, which emphasized heavy disclosure as a tool to generate trading interest and liquidity in shares of small high risk enterprises. The compulsory disclosure norms in AIM, however, are lower, but there is significantly higher level of voluntary disclosures by listed firms mainly because of the advice of the Nomads. For secondary trading, AIM has a mixture of what is called 'order driven' and 'quote driven' market—a hybrid model that was characteristic of the NASDAQ system of early 1990s (before the antitrust intervention)—providing an important role for the market maker for the stock. In some way, therefore, the AIM initiative seeks to bring back the market maker and the investment adviser to the centre stage as investment agents who would nurture a fledgling small enterprise, which otherwise would not enjoy a research/analysis or trading focus.

APPENDIX 5D

Emerging Institutional Investors—Sovereign Wealth Funds[34]

The last decade of the 20th century also saw the rise of an interesting class of wealth-managers—state controlled 'sovereign wealth funds'—whose investments are primarily denominated in the hard currencies of the world. According to estimates provided by Oxford Analytica, these sovereign wealth funds controlled around USD 2,200 billion around 2005, with around USD 2,100 billion with the 20 of the largest amongst them. The seven biggest would be funds belonging to Abu Dhabi (USD 625 billion), Norway (USD 322 billion), Singapore-GIC (USD 215 billion), Kuwait (USD 213 billion), China (USD 200 billion), Russia (USD 128 billion) and Singapore-Temasek (USD 108 billion).[35] Sovereign funds, in terms of cumulative size of the asset class, are larger than hedge funds (USD 1500 billion), or private equity funds (USD 100 billion), but much smaller than mature institutional investors (USD 53,000 billion) and official foreign currency reserves (USD 5600 billion).

Many observers, however, expect that sovereign funds would soon exceed official currency reserves in terms of their size. These funds exist primarily because several countries have surplus savings over investments that end up in the hands of the government—either because of

---

[34]This appendix has been taken from Wolf (2007).
[35]Temasek has been formed as an investment arm of Government of Singapore, while Singapore-GIC was mandated to manage the foreign currency reserves of Singapore.

commodity wealth (Norway and Gulf countries) or because of success of export-oriented manufacturing/service economy (such as China and Singapore). Citibank, one of the largest full service banks in the world, had at one point large ownerships by Government of Singapore Investment Corporation (GIC)(11.1 per cent), Kuwait Investment Authority (6 per cent), Abu Dhabi Investment Authority (ADIA) (4.9 per cent) and Saudi Arabia Kingdom Holding Company (4.3 per cent). Similarly, in India, the largest private bank (ICICI Bank Limited) and the largest Indian telecom firm (Bharti Airtel Limited) are owned by investment arms owing allegiance to the Government of Singapore such as GIC and Temasek.

The aim of these funds can differ—for the Russian funds it is primarily stabilization with a short term horizon and liquid investments, but for the Chinese, the creation of Chinese Investment Corporation with USD 200 billion transferred to it from China's massive foreign exchange reserve accumulation has a mandate of generating attractive returns (compared to the abysmally low returns from the official foreign exchange holdings). China Investment Corporation is being managed like a private equity, making strategic investments in asset acquisition across the globe. One such deal was the acquisition of a significant stake in Blackstone group—one of the largest private equity groups in the US. In contrast, we have Norway's fund managing its wealth through small ownership stakes in a highly transparent manner—which precludes strategic motives—unlike the Chinese and the Qatar funds that have a strategic mandate. The Singapore funds operate a transparent investment strategy but focus on limited number of large investment exposures in fewer assets (for example, telecom sector). How are investments from such funds different from private equity or public equity investments?

APPENDIX 5E

Categories of Institutional Investors: University Endowment Funds[36]

University endowment funds, as a category of institutional investors, are a significant force in the US financial system. They are large not only in terms of the assets they control, but importantly, they have been at the forefront of financial innovation generating returns for their university clients that have far exceeded the median returns of institutional investor class who operate under more conventional investment norms. The largest of the endowment funds that also generate the largest returns manage investments in a widely diversified portfolio of asset classes. Allocation amongst asset classes is recalibrated carefully to reap all arbitrage options. Newer asset classes are also explored to continuously widen the portfolio (traditional asset classes constitute less than half of the total portfolio of the top five university endowments—Harvard, Yale, Stanford, Texas and Princeton).

Amongst private equity fund sources, for instance, university endowments were very important early on when the asset category had not yet become a widely held asset. Such early investments also gave the funds grandfather rights to get favourable allocations in later rounds when the asset class had started generating greater following. As a result, university endowment's return from private equity asset class has outstripped other investor categories quite consistently. In fact, the innovative investment strategies of the top university endowments are tracked in the US by investment advisors and several retail investors in order to build their

---

[36] This appendix has been taken from Harvard University website.

own portfolios. Embracing of newer asset classes by these funds are seen as strong signals about the emergence of those asset categories.

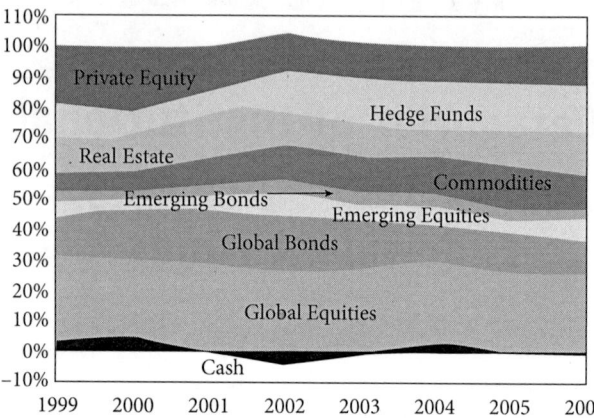

Figure 5E.1: Super Endowment Funds Asset Allocation over Time

(*Fund size greater than USD 10 billion*)

Source: Frontier Capital Management Llc., available at http://www.frontiercm.com/downloads/knowledge_bank/Harvard%20and%20Yale.pdf (accessed on 10 December 2008).

Harvard University's endowment fund (the largest university endowment fund in USA), that is a corpus generated from almost 11,000 individual funds (each with a different support purpose), returned a yield of 23 per cent in 2006–07. It is managed by the Harvard Management Company, formed in 1974 as an independent subsidiary to manage the corpus of the university at a cost that is lower than the costs of subcontracting. At 2007 fiscal end, the fund stood at around USD 35 billion. The return generated by the fund compares favourably to that recorded by other large investment management institutions. Specifically, the endowment's return of 23 per cent outperformed the median for the 151 large institutional funds as measured by the Trust Universe Comparison Service (17.7 per cent), as well as the 20.9 per cent that marks the top five percentile. The 23 per cent return for the last fiscal year brings the endowment's annualized 10-year performance to 15 per cent and the five-year annualized return to 18.4 per cent. Since its inception, Harvard Management Company (HMC) has averaged an annualized rate of return of 13.3 per cent—significantly large compared to returns in mature US financial markets. The annual payouts from the fund (roughly around 5 per cent) is an important source of the operating budget of the university—financing close to a third of the total budget in the last few years.

Epilogue

This book attempted to capture the notion of strategic thinking—strategy as thought and acted upon. Strategy needs as much to be felt as analysed and understood in logical terms. Ambition and power inheres and remains intertwined inextricably to any narration or thoughts of strategy as does the need for generating sustainable revenue streams. A search induced by an ambition or the deep sense of individuality that seeks a mark of differentiation makes possible the cognition of threats or node(s) of power to be overcome. So, articulation of incompleteness or weaknesses of current champions (winner nodes) deserve special attention. Is not it difficult to even believe that the current leader is fallible? And to work towards that end right when his/her glory is at a peak should not be easier either.

A strategist, as we narrated, seeks to topple the applecart of current governance in order to set up the altered mode of governance. A win is thus achieved. Contrarily, a current winner seeks a preservation of the current governance. It is in this melting pot of action that strategy appears as an integrated discipline; it promises a specific dessert—the win in a conflict. Conflicts require boundaries to be evoked, battlelines to be drawn. Discourse of strategy usually invoked descriptions of integration of various management functions as what strategy as a discipline should achieve but did not specify clearly how that integration would be achieved or what would be its moorings. Zeroing in more clearly on the notion of power provides a mooring. Governance and tweaks in such modes of governance was the theme around which the narration in the book evolved and sought a multidisciplinary integration.

We do not agree that strategy is a top management activity alone. Strategic thinking is a mode of thinking; it is a skill that cannot only help someone lead a pragmatic life with success. It helps an individual navigate through conflicts and one aspect of pragmatic life deals with conflicts of myriad kinds. Pragmatic life is textured in multiple dimensions that defy a capture in certain singular dimension such as money. In this book, however, we explored only the business dimension, mostly within a context of senior power-holders who would take major decisions regarding organizations. But a strategy story is important for the plebeians as well. Only the specific manifestation of the exercise of power or the reading of the threat would change in that case. But a capability to read it and act on it is essential in successful conduct of pragmatic life. It is a strategic understanding of a plebeian that would induce cooperation with senior power-holders as a practical mode of engaging with a larger threat.

This book has two foundational departures; first, it roots the strategy account in an 'individual', exorcized in the mainstream literature except in the form of the dramatic leader, and second, it in no uncertain terms root the strategy discourse in a pursuit of power. That raises the most important question: what is the purpose behind seeking power? Can seeking power have a greater purpose than the individual's own dessert? These are important questions we did not engage in. We would end by leaving the reader with a thought. During the early years of the rise of India's nationalist political ambitions that sought to achieve self-rule, Mahatma Gandhi had articulated a notion of power-holder as trustee. Notion of welfare was its essential hallmark. Preservation and enhancement of assets was the purpose of the trustee leader. Are not we all trustees, in a deep sense? We manage this world and its resources only to leave it to the next generation? Is not that like holding the asset in trust? But what can be the pragmatic institutional design of such trustee based business? Most contemporary organization designs, we feel, fail on this count; it does not serve an abiding good, a common good, so to say. Organization as benefiting shareholders can only get plebeian support through violent coercive acts that organizational life reveals in plenty. We remain confused. But a hope shines!

References

Arthur, Brian. 1994. *Increasing Returns and Path Dependence in the Economy*. Ann Arbor: University of Michigan Press.
ASSOCHAM. 2009. Press Releases. 2009, November. 'Faced with Fierce Price-war, Telecom Sector Added a Meager 16 Paise in Revenue per New User in Q2 FY'10: ASSOCHAM'. Available online at http://www.assocham.org/prels/shownews.php?id=2239 (accessed on 21 April 2010).
Axelrod, R. 1984. *The Evolution of Cooperation*. New York: Basic Books.
Baker, George and George David Smith. 1998. *The New Financial Capitalists: Kohlberg Kravis Roberts and the Creation of Corporate Value*. Cambridge University Press.
Banerjee, Parthasarathi. 2005. 'Bridging the Digital Divide: A Case of Joint Production of Information through Kiosks', *Comparative Technology Transfer and Society*, 3(3): 230–63.
———. 2007. *Biomedical Innovation in India—With a Comparison to China and Others*. New Delhi: Har-Anand Publications Pvt. Ltd.
Baron, David P. and David Besanko. 2001. 'Strategy, Organization and Incentives: Global Corporate Banking at Citibank', *Industrial and Corporate Change*, 10(1):1–36.
Bello, H. M., M. Sepiriti, and E. M. Letete. 2009. 'Competition, Market Structure and Market Power in the Insurance Industry in Lesotho', *ICFAI Journal of Financial Economics*, 7(1):7–15.
Benkler, Yochai. 2002. 'Some Economics of Wireless Communications', *Harvard Journal of Law & Technology*, 16(1) (Fall). Available online at http://jolt.law.harvard.edu/articles/pdf/v16/16HarvJLTech025.pdf (accessed on 6 June 2011).
Bruck, Connie. 1988. *The Predators' Ball*. New York: Simon & Schuster.
Calles, Erika. 2005. 'Microfinance according to SafeSave—A Better Way to Target the Poorest? A Minor Field Study from Bangladesh', D-level thesis, Sweden: Uppsala University.
Chandler, Alfred D., Jr. 1962. *Strategy and Structure: Chapters in the History of the American Industrial Enterprise*. Cambridge, MA: MIT Press.
Cusumano, Michael. 1985. *The Japanese Automobile Industry, Technology & Management at Nissan & Toyota*. Harvard East Asian Monographs. (Reprinted as

The Japanese Automobile Industry, Technology and Management at Nissan and Toyota in 1991).

Ferrary, Michel. 2003. 'The Gift Exchange in the Social Networks of Silicon Valley', *California Management Review*, 45(4):120–38.

Foucault, T. and C. Parlour. 1999. 'Competition for Listings', CEPR Discussion Paper No. 2222. Available online at http://www.cepr.org/pubs/new-dps/dplist.asp?dpno=2222 (accessed on 6 June 2011).

Fruin, W. Mark. 1992. *The Japanese Enterprise System: Competitive Strategies and Cooperative Structures*. Oxford: Clarendon Press.

Government of India. 2007. 'Report on Financing of Enterprises in the Unorganized Sector', National Commission for Enterprises in the Unorganised Sector. Available online at http://nceuis.nic.in/Report_on_NCEUS_NAFUS.pdf (accessed on 6 June 2011).

Granovetter, Mark and Patrick McGuire. 1998. 'The Making of an Industry: Electricity in the United States', in Michel Callon (ed.), *The Laws of the Markets*, pp. 147–73. London: Blackwell Publishers. *The Sociological Review*, 49(June): 323–34.

Hindu. 2001. 'An Interview with Ms Leena Christi—HR Head, Bangalore Labs, Bangalore', *The Hindu Opportunities: A Guide to Better Positions and Better Performance*, 12 September. Available online at http://www.hinduonnet.com/jobs/0109/05120012.htm (accessed on 29 May 2011).

Hippel, Eric von. 1998. 'Economics of Product Development by Users: The Impact of "Sticky" Local Information', *Management Science*, 44(5): 629–44.

Indian Express. 2007. 'Exodus at Escorts Hospital Continues', *Indian Express*, 1 June.

Indo-Asian News Service. 2007. 'Naresh Trehan Back on Duty at Escorts Hospital', *Hindustan Times*, 20 May.

Ingebretsen, Mark. 2002. *NASDAQ: A History of the Market that Changed the World*. USA: Forum.

Kakani, Ram Kumar and Tejas Joshi. 2006. 'Cross Holding Strategy to Increase Control: Case of the Tata group', XLRI Jamshedpur Working Paper No. 06-03: http://ssrn.com/abstract=889394 (accessed on 6 June 2011).

Kakani, Ram Kumar and Munish Thakur. 2009. 'Barings Private Equity Partners Limited: Banking Services for the Poor in Bangladesh', Richard Ivey School of Business: Ivey Publishing Case 9B09MB092. Available online at http://cases.ivey.uwo.ca/Cases/Pages/home.aspx?Mode=showproduct&prod=9B09M052 (accessed on 28 June 2011).

Kao, John. HBS Case No. 9-395-144.

Khosrow-Pour, Mehdi. 2002. *Annals of Cases on Information Technology*. PA, USA: Idea Group Inc (IGI).

Knight, Frank. 1921. *Risk, Uncertainty and Profit*. Boston: Houghton Mifflin Co. Available online at http://www.econlib.org/library/Knight/KnRUPCover.html (accessed on 27 June 2011).

Kodama, Mitsuru. 2003. 'Case study of NTT DoCoMo', *Journal of High Technology Management Research*, 14(2): 307–30.

Kumar, Jayesh. 2005. 'Capital Structure and Corporate Governance', presented at Winter Research Conference, 19 December 2004, Centre for Analytical Finance, Indian School of Business Hyderabad. Available online at http://www.isb.edu/caf/htmls/JayeshKumar_CapitalStructure_andCorporate Governance.pdf (accessed on 6 June 2011).

Lala, R. M. 1981. *The Creation of Wealth: A Tata Story*. Bombay: IBH Publishing Company.

———. 2004. *The Creation of Wealth: The Tatas from the 19th to the 21st Century*. New Delhi: Penguin Viking Publishers.

Landler, Mark. 2001. 'Hi, I Am in Bangalore (but I Dare Not Tell)', *New York Times*, 21 March. Available online at http://www.nytimes.com/2001/03/21/technology/21CALL.html?ex=1194843600&en=9d23c804e918bbfe&ei=5070 (accessed on 29 May 2011).

Langlois, Richard. 1996. 'Schumpeter and Personal Capitalism', University of Connecticut, Department of Economics, Working Paper No. 1996–05, March.

Langlois, Richard. N. and Paul L. Robertson. 1995. *Firms, Markets and Economic Change: A Dynamic Theory of Business Institutions*. London: Routledge.

Macey, J. and M. O'Hara. 1999. 'Regulating Exchanges and Alternative Trading Systems: A Law and Economics Perspective', *Journal of Legal Studies*, 28 (January): 17–54.

———. 2002. 'The Economics of Stock Exchange Listing Fees and Listing Requirements', *Journal of Financial Intermediation*, 11(3): 297–319.

Mahoney, P. 1997. 'The Exchange as Regulator', *Virginia Law Review*, 83(7), 1453–500.

Mendoza, Jose M. 2007. 'Securities Regulation in Low-tier Listing Venues: The Rise of the Alternative Investment Market'. Available online at http://works.bepress.com/jose_mendoza/1 (accessed on 10 December 2008).

Mintzberg, Henry. 1987. 'Crafting Strategy', *HBR*, July–August: 66–75.

Mintzberg, Henry and James A. Waters. 1985. 'Of Strategies, Deliberate and Emergent', *Strategic Management Journal*, 6(3) (July–September): 257–72.

Mito, Yuko. 'Corporate Culture as Strong Diving Force for Punctuality—Another "Just in Time"'. Available online at http://www.hitachi-rail.com/rail_now/column/just_in_time/index.html.

Miwa, Yoshiro and J. Mark Ramsayer. 2002. 'Apparel Distribution: Inter-firm Contracting and Intra-firm Organization', in Yoshiro Miwa, K. G. Nishimura, J. M. Ramsayer (eds), *Distribution in Japan*, New York: OUP.

Miwa, Yoshiro, K. G. Nishimura and J. M. Ramsayer (eds). 2002. *Distribution in Japan*. New York: OUP.

Miwa, Yoshiro and M. J. Ramseyer. 2001. 'Apparel Distribution: Intra-firm Contracting and Inter-firm Organization', CIRJE Paper F-103.

Nelson, Richard and Sydney Winter. 1982. *An Evolutionary Theory of Economic Change*. Cambridge, Massachusetts and London: Belknap Press.

Network Magazine India. 2001. 'Bangalore Labs Bags 10 New Accounts, Expands Presence', *Network Magazine India*, October 2001. Available online at http://www.networkmagazineindia.com/200108/news1.htm (accessed on 6 June 2011).

News, Net ProActive Services. Available online at http://www.netproactiveservices.com/content/blinnews.htm (accessed in December 2008).

Pagano, M. 1998. 'Changing microstructure of European equity markets', in G. Ferrarini (ed.), *European Securities Markets: The Investment Services Directive and Beyond*. Kluwer Law International.

Pilling, David. 2007. 'Running Like Clockwork', *Financial Times*, 6 July 2007.

Pine, J. B. 1993. *Mass Customization: The New Frontier in Business Competition*. Cambridge, MA: Harvard Business School Press.

Rao, Prashant L. 2002. 'Bangalore Labs: India's First MSP', *Express Computer*, 24 June. Available online at http://www.expresscomputeronline.com/20020624/company1.shtml (accessed on 29 May 2011).

Roeser, Allison. 2004. 'Respect', *Tufts Daily*, 4 October, p. 3–4. Available online at http://repository01.lib.tufts.edu:8080/fedora/get/tufts:UP029.025.048.00019/bdef:TuftsPDF/getPDF (accessed on 6 June 2011).

Saha, B. '2004. 'State Support for Industrial R&D in Developing Economies: Telecom Equipment Industry in India and China', *Economic and Political Weekly*, 39(35): 3915–925.

Schatzki, Theodore, K. Knorr-Cetina and Eike von Savigny. 2001. *The Practice Turn in Contemporary Theory*. London and New York: Routledge.

Schreiner, Mark. 2001. 'Informal Finance and the Design of Microfinance', *Development in Practice*, 11(5): 637–40.

Sivaraman, Vasant and Adithya Anand. 2008. 'Tata Steel Limited: Convertible Alternative Reference Securities', HBS Case No. 908N01.

Smith, Mark B. 2001. *Towards Rational Exuberance*. New York: Farrar, Strauss & Giroux.

Sosnoski, Daniel. 1996. *Introduction to Japanese Culture*. Boston, Rutland, Vermont and Tokyo: Tuttle Publishing.

Sreeraman. 2007. 'Naresh Trehan Removed from Escorts Hospital', MedIndia.com Online News, 19 May 2007.

Stocking, G. W. and Myron Watkins. 1946. 'The Aluminum Alliance', in *Cartels in Action: Case Studies in International Business Diplomacy*, pp.216–273. New York: William S. Hein & Co., Inc.

Subramanian, Nithya. 2007. 'Fortis Hopes to Partner Naresh Trehan in Medicity Project', *Hindu*, 29 September.

Swaminathan, A. 2001. 'Resource Partitioning and the Evolution of Specialist Organizations: The Role of Location and Identity in the U.S. Wine Industry', *Academy of Management Journal*, 44(6): 1169–185.

Takeishi, Akira and Takahiro Fujimoto. 2001. 'Modularization in the auto industry: Inter-linked Multiple Hierarchies of Product, Production and Supplier Systems', CIRJE Working Paper No. 107. Available online at http://

www.cirje.e.u-tokyo.ac.jp/research/dp/2001/2001cf107.pdf (accessed on 6 June 2011).

Times of India. 2001. 'Bangalore Labs Acquires a New Asian Face', *Times of India*, 5 November 2001. Available online at http://timesofindia.indiatimes.com/cms.dll/articleshow?art_ID=1359277082 (accessed in December 2008).

Updegrove, Andrew. 2007. 'FTC Caps Rambus Royalties', *Consortium Standards Bulletin*, 4(2). Available online at http://www.consortiuminfo.org/bulletins/pdf/feb07/update.pdf (accessed on 10 December 2009).

Varadarajan, Tunku. 1999. 'A Patel Motel Cartel?', *New York Times*, 4 July, editorial.

Weber, Max. 1921/1968. *Economy and Society*. Totowa, NJ: Bedminster Press.

Wolf, Martin. 2007. 'State Capitalism: The Rise of Sovereign Wealth Funds', *Financial Times*, 15 October.

Womack, James P., Daniel T. Jones and Daniel Ross. 1990. *The Machine That Changed the World*. Rawson Associates, New York: Simon & Schuster.

Yakubovich, Valery, Mark Granovetter and Patrick McGuire. 2005. 'Electric Charges: The Social Construction of Rate Systems', *Theory and Society*, 34(5–6): 579–612.

Young, Allyn. 1928. 'Increasing Returns and Economic Progress', *The Economic Journal*, 38(152): 527–42.

Zuckerman, Ezra W. 2000. 'Focusing the Corporate Product: Securities Analysts and De-Diversification', *Administrative Science Quarterly*, 45(3): 591–619.

Index

ASICs 50, 51, 52, 55, 100, 155
Abuse of Dominance 231, 266, 269
Access to asset 74, 75, 244
Actor 4, 5, 9, 10, 13, 15, 17, 18, 20, 23, 29, 31, 39, 53, 84, 104
Adjacent Assets 64, 68, 117
Administrative fiat 17, 72, 254
Agriculture Produce Marketing Committee 247
Alcoa 231, 232, 233, 234, 235,
Alibaba.com. 252
Alliance 23, 25, 129, 188, 235, 326
Alternative Investment Market (AIM) 306, 327
AMD-Intel conflict 227
American Depository Receipts (ADRs) 279
Amazon.com 292
Anglo-Saxon Common Law Tradition 217
Application Programming Interfaces (APIs) 302
Application Specific Integrated Circuits (ASICs) 50,
Arthur, Brian 54, 55
Assets 72, 74, 81
  Asset or Resources 70
  Asset Bundling 50
  Asset Ecosystem 79
  Asset Holder 79, 80, 81
  Asset severalty 33
Association of Edison Illuminating Companies (AEIC) 16

Automotive Industry Action Group (AIAG) 233
Autonomy 55, 85, 130, 274

Balance of Power 57, 64, 149, 166
Balaji Films 8
National Bank for Agriculture and Rural Development (NABARD) 270
Barstow System 6, 7, 15
Belief 1, 12, 98, 99, 105, 106, 113, 240, 274
Blocking Patents 116
Blu-Ray 44, 45
Board of Control for Cricket in India (BCCI) 74, 78, 80,82
Bollywood 63, 109, 111, 112, 238, 239
Board for Industrial and Financial Reconstruction (BIFR) 277
Boundary 4, 15, 23, 82, 97, 100, 117, 146, 155, 245, 254, 260, 268, 292
BPR 14, 145, 169, 170
  Broken Assets 99
Bundled 98, 151, 244, 308
Bundling 45, 50, 57, 73, 98, 151, 229, 303
Bungee Studios 24
Bureau of Indian Standards (BIS) 242
Business Groups 161, 220
Business Process Reengineering (BPR) 14, 94

Capital 82, 94, 282
Capital Equipment Structure 62
Cartel 37
Cash Flow Rights 278
Chandler/Chandlerian 145, 166, 188, 185, 192, 285
Channel Nine 74, 75, 77
Change Management 175, 176
Cisco Systems 34, 47
Civil Law Tradition 217
Civil Society Groups 165
Club 121
Coalition 3, 17, 148, 150, 182,
Cohort 13, 14, 61
Commoditization 59, 61, 63, 105, 131, 225, 226, 250
Commodities Exchange (COMEX) 103
Commodity 101, 144, 147, 225, 231, 269, 270
Common Assets 123, 128
Common Law tradition 217
Common Pool 119, 120, 121
Common Pool Assets 64, 113
Companies Act 14
Compulsory Stack 116
Computer Numerical Control (CNC) 86
Computed Tomography (CT) scanners 127
Contemporary Accounts 38, 92, 178
Contest 127, 149, 165
Contextual Specificity 24
Contract 32, 254, 255, 257
Control Over Pricing 148
Control Rights 278
Convertible Alternate Reference Securities (CARS) 279
Coordination 54, 77, 85, 92, 127, 128, 136, 153, 167, 178, 183, 191, 214, 221, 246, 249, 250, 253
Corporatist denial 100
Corporate Governance 263, 304, 320
Cost Leadership Strategy 85, 132

Countervail/Countervailing 39, 80
Cross-shareholdings 279

Danone 26
Deal-making 192
Decreasing Return 11, 54, 57, 58, 59, 85, 100, 105, 134, 146, 192, 215, 222, 226, 253, 281, 288
Decree 125, 227, 232
Deterrence 48, 58, 61, 71, 138, 215, 222, 226, 230, 245, 267, 288
Differentiation 23, 59, 61, 153, 221, 266, 268, 269
Disclosure of information 120, 288
Deskilled 85
DoComo 182, 187, 286
Dosa king 276, 277
Dual Class Equity 278
Dynamic Coordination 215, 226, 249, 250
Dynamic Transaction cost 92

e-Choupal 101, 102
Economies of Scale 38, 39, 62
Ecosystem 68, 79, 81, 249, 251, 297
Electronic Data Processing (EDP) 260
Electricity Industry 5, 15
Embeddedness 5, 7
Employee Stock Ownership Plan (ESOP) 206
Equity Market Design 291, 304
Essential Patents 116
Exclusionary Power 115
Executive Authority 216
Executive Power 157, 161, 186
Extra-organizational power 147, 182

Facherbaiter 86, 87
Factor Markets 220
Factory 84, 98, 167, 168,
Fast Moving Consumer Goods (FMCG) 8
Federal Communication Commission (FCC) 35

Federal Trade Commission (FTC) 124
Federation of Indian Exporters (FIE) 277
Forward Contracts 269
Forward Markets Commission (FMC) 269
Fiduciary 76, 77, 78
Film 107
Financial Intermediation 275, 277, 280, 292, 308
Financial Technologies Limited (FT) 270
Fixed Assets 82, 83, 94
Foreign Currency Convertible Bonds (FCCBs) 279
Free Market 213, 217, 262
Fujitsu 52, 56, 57, 175, 182
Full-custom Method 51
Future Asset 125, 240

Gate Array 61, 134
Generic Strategies 51, 93
Global Depository Receipts (GDRs) 279
Gross Domestic Product (GDP) 63
Godrej 8
Goldman Sachs 73, 314, 325
Google 35, 36, 114, 278
Governance 10, 19, 79, 88, 123, 131
Governance Assets 132
Granovetter, M. 7, 17
Garware Marine Industries Limited 272

High Definition (HD) Video 44, 45
Homunculus 17, 64, 98, 100, 112, 150, 156
Human Resources 84

ICICI Bank Limited 270, 332
i-Mode 157, 182, 187, 188, 253
Incentive System 158, 172, 174
Increasing Returns 11, 48, 54, 55, 57, 59, 61, 93, 100, 101, 110, 115, 134, 168, 185, 189, 215, 226, 242, 245, 249, 250, 268, 269, 281, 290
Increasing Return Dynamics 55, 187, 247
Index 9, 96, 289, 290
Indian Food Fermentations Limited (IFFL) 276
Indian Tobacco Company (ITC) 8, 101, 102
Industrial Disputes Act 263
Industrial District 114
Information Encapsulation 49, 151
Institution 18, 27, 28
Institutional Contest 41, 126, 275, 313
Institutional Gatekeepers 39
Institutional Moorings of Finance 282, 284
Institutions of Practice 31, 39, 69
Intellectual Property (IP) 32, 124
Integrated Circuits (ICs) 51
International Business Machines (IBM) 34
IP Asset 32, 47
Inter-category Contest 267
Inter-firm 14, 31, 39, 61, 63, 137, 221, 235
Inter-firm Interstices 13
Inter-exchange Competition 304, 307, 326
Inter-Organizational Common Pool 120
Intermediation 102, 122, 146, 275, 308
International Cricket Council (ICC) 78
Intra-organizational Coordination 154, 247

J.P. Morgan 38
Japanese distribution system 261, 262
Joint Assets 101, 123
Joint Venture (JV) 78
Joint Electron Devices Engineering Council (JEDEC) 124

Index

Junk Bond 297
Jurisdiction 218, 219

Kashtakkoottu 59
Key Performance Appraisals (KPA) 93
Knight, Frank 9, 110
Knightian 110
Kohlberg Kravis and Roberts (KKR) 294, 295

Language 4, 8, 9
Legal Artefact 14, 97
Leveraged Buyout (LBO) 283
Licensee's 236
Licensors 236
Life Insurance Corporation of India (LIC) 270
Linux 12
Litigation 34, 91, 119, 227, 232
London Interbank Offered Rate (LIBOR) 96
London Stock Exchange (LSE) 307, 327
LSI Logic Path 52
Lumpy Fixed Asset 45, 50, 221

Managerial Capitalism 284, 293
Managerial Hubris 287
Mandi 248, 254
Market 212, 213, 214
  Market-makers 305, 317, 318
Market Power 108, 221, 235
Marshal, Alfred 121
Marshalian Agglomeration 120
M-form 99, 131, 132, 163
Milieu 10, 20, 19
Microfinance Institute (MFI) 309
Microsoft 24, 54, 101, 128, 219, 223, 229, 267
Modular Assets 73, 129, 132
Modularization 130, 131, 132, 133, 134, 135, 302
Module 129, 130, 131, 136, 302

Module Integrator 131
Moore's Law 212
Morgan Stanley Capital International (MSCI) 289
Motives 12, 57, 38, 63, 244, 332
Multi Commodity Exchange (MCX) 103, 250, 270

Naming 2, 4
NASDAQ 286
National Commodity and Derivative Exchange (NCDEX) 103, 270
National Electric Light Association (NELA) 16
National Multi Commodity Exchange (NMCE) 270
National Stock Exchange (NSE) 270
Negotiation 152
Nestlé India Ltd 276
News Corporation 76
Network 121, 127, 131, 243, 246, 250, 251, 258, 265
New York Stock Exchange (NYSE) 49, 305
Nodal Power 49, 80, 151, 153, 155, 159, 178, 182, 185
Nodes 10, 37, 39, 40, 44, 45, 50, 67, 151
Non-standard goods 237
North, Douglass 28, 29
Nokia 186
Notion of Assets 11, 64
Nouveau Marché 306
Novel Profit 11, 100

Off-organization Control 100
Oligopoly 46, 179, 222
Open Market 233
Open Source Software 118, 119
Open Spectrum 40, 41, 43
Operating Procedures 88, 90
Opportunism 90, 91, 92, 155, 241, 248, 254
Organization Boundaries 148

Organization Design 167, 186
Organizational Fiat 185
Organizational Restructuring 182
Organizations 11, 29, 41
Original Equipment Manufacturers (OEMs) 32, 227
Over the Counter (OTC) 96, 315

Patent Pool 115, 116
Patents 34, 116, 119
Platform 102, 109, 135, 242, 251, 271, 304
Pool 117, 118
Porter, Michael 61, 85
Power 18, 28, 37
Practice 28, 29, 30
Practice turn 5
Price-based Markets 253
Price Clearing Market 29, 147, 247
Price Mechanism 171, 247
Price System 6
Priceline.com 122, 123
Pricing Norm 5, 7, 15, 252
Primary Market 304
Principal–agent Problem 287
Private Equity 294
Privatization 217, 219, 307
Privatization of Exchanges 304, 307
Processing Gain 42
Product 135, 136, 137
Profit 58, 110
Property Right 35, 41, 47, 55, 59, 68, 80, 91, 110, 246
Public-private Partnership 255
Pyramidal Holdings 278

Radio Corporation of America (RCA) 116
Rambus 124, 125
Random Control Trial 28, 127
Real Estate Investment Trust (REIT) 255
Red Chillies Entertainment 8
Regulation 215, 216, 261

Relevant Market 267
Reliance Group 108, 201, 202
Rent 58
Rent like Return 222, 278
Resale Price Maintenance 31, 261, 262
Residual Rights 287
Resource based view 70, 71, 137
Resource Market 72, 137
Resources 70, 71, 72
Restructuring 64, 65, 79, 297
Right to Return Unsold Goods 30, 261, 262
Risk 9, 108, 89, 90
Risk Aversion 106, 107
Risk Market 95, 99, 100
Risk-Taking 106, 109
Routines 153, 154
Rule 155, 166
Rule-following 155

SAP 259
Sarbanes-Oxley Legislation 293
SafeSave 280, 281, 309, 310, 311, 312
Scarcity 58, 71, 109, 168
Secondary Market 304, 317, 325
Sovereign Wealth Funds 331
Securities and Exchange Commission (SEC) 286
Serial Entrepreneurship 294, 299
Shannon's Information Theory 41
Simple Original Equipment Manufactures (OEMs) 32
Small Scale Industries 264
Softbank 250
Spillover 115, 121, 183, 185
Stakeholder 74, 159, 161, 174
Stallman, Richard 12
Standalone Product 243
Standard 76, 90, 128, 130
Standardization 62, 89, 105, 266
Standard Operating Procedures (SOPs) 154
Star 8, 117, 292
Star Assets 64, 104

Static Transaction Cost 92
Stevens, Andrew 139
Sticky information 133, 181, 224
Stock Exchange 304, 307, 316
Stock Keeping Units (SKUs) 30
Straight-through processing 225
Strategic Actor 10, 15, 20
Strategic Commitment 82
Strategic Investments 332
Strategic Acts 9, 10, 15, 21, 22, 39, 66, 69, 214
Strategic Move 284, 299, 326
Strategist 1, 2, 8, 10, 14, 19, 20, 53, 57, 219, 272, 279
Strategy 10, 11, 20
Strategy Languages 8
Sunk 40, 43, 48, 79
Synchronous Dynamic Random Access Memory (SDRAM) 124, 125
Systemic 242, 243 245

Tacit Knowledge 154, 157
Tamil Nadu Industrial Development Corporation (TIDCO) 277
Tata Group 164, 165, 166, 193
Taylorist System 87
Torvalds, Linus 12
Technology Development Investment Corporation of India (TDICI) 277
Toyota 63, 87, 88, 90, 167
Temporal 168, 180, 182, 216
Thick Network Market 65, 214, 237
Three-tier System 259
Threat 116, 119, 147, 150
Trade Union Act 263

Traditional Assets 253
Transaction Cost 90, 254, 255, 256

Unbundling 51, 59, 95, 98, 163, 288, 293, 296
Uncertainty 9, 108, 109
Unfolding 24, 25, 103
Unions 165
Unit of analysis 13, 14, 61, 272
Universal Product Code (UPC) 30
University Endowment Funds 308, 333
US wine regulations 268

Valorization 68
    Devalorization 8, 68, 289
Valuation 15, 33, 43, 64, 86, 112, 127, 128
VC Financing 286, 303
Venture Capital (VC) 60, 192, 300, 301
Vodafone 252
Voice 4, 37, 39, 55, 282
Volumetric Production Payment (VPP) 95
Vote/Voting 37, 39, 40, 44, 105

Wahaha 25, 26, 123, 124, 265
Walrasian Market 29, 37, 65, 236, 237
Weber, Max 6
White Revolution 275
Wholesaling 30, 35
Win 11, 12, 19, 31, 34, 66
Wiring 133, 134
Wittgenstein 1, 5
Wright System 6, 7

Young, Allyn 54, 55

About the Authors

Biswatosh Saha has been involved in research on innovation, strategy and studies of power, especially in the area of knowledge generation and pedagogy. He has been working with Indian Institute of Management Calcutta, Kolkata, India, for the last four years. He has published several papers in international journals.

Parthasarathi Banerjee has been involved in research on business policy, innovation, and science and technology policy and related areas for the last two and a half decades, and has been working with National Institute of Science, Technology and Development Studies (Council of Scientific and Industrial Research), New Delhi, where he is currently the Director. He has published eight books and several journal/book papers; his latest book was on biomedical innovation.

Ram Kumar Kakani has a Doctorate in Management and is a Fellow at Indian Institute of Management Calcutta, Kolkata, India, 2002. He was a visiting scholar at Copenhagen Business School in Denmark. His areas of interest include business analysis, corporate finance, corporate strategy and study of business groups.